The Empire of Disgust

The Empire of Disgust

Prejudice, Discrimination, and Policy
in India and the US

edited by
Zoya Hasan
Aziz Z. Huq
Martha C. Nussbaum
Vidhu Verma

OXFORD
UNIVERSITY PRESS

OXFORD
UNIVERSITY PRESS

Oxford University Press is a department of the University of Oxford.
It furthers the University's objective of excellence in research, scholarship,
and education by publishing worldwide. Oxford is a registered trademark of
Oxford University Press in the UK and in certain other countries.

Published in India by
Oxford University Press
2/11 Ground Floor, Ansari Road, Daryaganj, New Delhi 110 002, India

First Edition published in 2018
Second impression 2018

ISBN-13 (print edition): 978-0-19-948783-7
ISBN-10 (print edition): 0-19-948783-9

ISBN-13 (eBook): 978-0-19-909376-2
ISBN-10 (eBook): 0-19-909376-8

Typeset in Adobe Garamond Pro 10.5/12.5
by The Graphics Solution, New Delhi 110 092
Printed in India by Nutech Print Services India

'To a happier year'

Contents

Acknowledgements

The editors wish to thank the University of Chicago's Delhi Center for generously funding the conference at which these papers were originally presented and for creating a marvellous space for intellectual exchange. We express particular gratitude to Aditi Mody for her tremendous efficiency and helpfulness. Beyond this, those of us from Chicago also owe a large debt of thanks to the University of Chicago Law School and to our dean, Thomas Miles, for encouraging and assisting our efforts. Emily Dupree was the research assistant for the conference, and the volume, and she has been amazing throughout the process, helpful, prompt, and with a high level of intellectual understanding of the topic.

Introduction

Come you Outcaste, dispelled be the burden of all insults,...
With holy water made sacred by the touch of everybody
On the short of this Bharat's ocean of the great Humanity.
　　　　　—Rabindranath Tagore, song composed in June 1910[1]

All known societies exclude and stigmatize one or more minority groups. Frequently, these exclusions are underwritten with a rhetoric of disgust. People of a certain group, it is alleged, are filthy, hyper-animal, not fit to share such facilities as drinking water, food, and public swimming pools with the 'clean' 'fully human' majority. But exclusions vary in their scope and also in the specific disgust ideologies underlying them. Legal and social remedies need to be cognizant of these variations and to craft policies aptly targeted at the particularities of the bad behaviour addressed. Therefore, legal and social remedies need to engage in a comparative study of stigma and prejudice, learning from history and the experience of other societies, and choosing social, legal, and institutional policies in the light of that learning.

Stigma has been a central category in social theory, at least since sociologist Erving Goffman's pathbreaking work of that title.[2] Psychologists have made considerable progress over the past few decades in understanding and charting the mechanisms by which societies marginalize and discriminate. In particular, Paul Rozin's pathbreaking work on disgust, with a team of researchers who continue to make new discoveries, has

[1] English translation by Kalpana Bardhan, *Songs of Love, Nature and Devotion: Selected Songs of Rabindranath Tagore* (New Delhi: Oxford University Press, 2008).
[2] Erving Goffman, *Stigma: Notes on the Management of Spoiled Identity* (Englewood Cliffs, N.J.: Prentice-Hall, 1963).

revolutionized our understanding of our fraught relationship with our own animality, which leads so often to evasive stratagems that impute animality (only) to other groups, not one's own, and then targets that group or groups for exclusions of various types.[3] That work has been used by legal theorists such as William Ian Miller, in *The Anatomy of Disgust*,[4] and by Nussbaum, in *Hiding from Humanity: Disgust, Shame, and the Law*.[5] Conservative theorists, meanwhile (for example, Lord Devlin in Britain, and Leon Kass, chair of the President's Council for Bioethics in the Bush administration in the United States[6]) continue to appeal to popular disgust as a legitimate motive to make certain consensual acts illegal, and to engage in other exclusionary behaviour.

We note at the outset that one of the most astute theorists of disgust and exclusion, the great B.R. Ambedkar, attempted to translate his understanding of majority tyranny and exclusionary behaviour into constitutional law, with considerable, though not complete, success.[7]

---

[3] Paul Rozin, Jonathan Haidt, and Clark McCauley, 'Disgust: The Body and Soul Emotion', in *Handbook of Cognition and Emotion*, eds T. Dalgleish and M. Power (Chichester: John Wiley, 1999), 429–45, for an overview of Rozin's work; for other references, see Martha C. Nussbaum, *Hiding from Humanity: Disgust, Shame, and the Law* (Princeton: Princeton University Press, 2004), and for subsequent work, see references in Martha C. Nussbaum, *From Disgust to Humanity: Sexual Orientation and Constitutional Law* (New York: Oxford University Press, 2010).

[4] William Ian Miller, *The Anatomy of Disgust* (Cambridge, MA: Harvard University Press, 1997).

[5] Nussbaum, *Hiding from Humanity*.

[6] Patrick Devlin, *The Enforcement of Morals* (London: Oxford University Press, 1965); Leon Kass, 'The Wisdom of Repugnance', *The New Republic* 22 (1997): 17–26, and later published as a pamphlet. Devlin focused on the Wolfenden report's proposal to decriminalize consensual homosexual relations, a proposal that he used the appeal to disgust to oppose. Kass wrote his article while chair of the President's Council for Bioethics in the Bush administration. Ostensibly directed at proposals to legalize human cloning, his argument had implications for many other controversies. In *From Disgust to Humanity*, Nussbaum cites from a recent pamphlet literature from segments of the Christian Right attempting to arouse disgust at consensual homosexual acts.

[7] Martha C. Nussbaum, 'Ambedkar's Constitution: Promoting Inclusion, Opposing Majority Tyranny', in *Assessing Constitutional Performance*, eds Tom Ginsburg and Aziz Z. Huq (New York: Cambridge University Press, 2016); and also Martha C. Nussbaum, review of *Annihilation of Caste*, by B.R. Ambedkar, ed. S. Anand, *The New Rambler Review*, online.

Ambedkar, well aware of human malice through his experience as a Dalit, commented in 1948, when he proposed the new draft constitution before the Constituent Assembly, 'If things go wrong under the new Constitution, the reason will not be that we had a bad Constitution. What we will have to say is, that Man was vile.'[8] The vileness of which he spoke, manifold and tenacious, continues to undermine the implementation of Constitutional ideals—just as related bad behaviour undermines legal and constitutional norms in the United States. Because of the salience of untouchability in the Indian founding, India has, on the whole, been more explicitly aware than the United States of the dangers inherent in the appeal to disgust, an appeal that was sternly repudiated by the Delhi High Court when it invalidated the sodomy laws (subsequently reinstated by the Supreme Court).[9]

Still, so far, we lack a detailed comparative study of the varieties of prejudice and stigma that would help both law and society do better in the struggle against stigma and exclusion. It is easy to see (and emphasized in the psychological literature) that common tropes turn up in many different types of discrimination. But the different forms of prejudice are not the same. And the legal and social remedies are also not the same. So there is a job to do, and there are reasons to believe that this job, well done, will offer a good deal to politics and law.

We are not planning to be reductionistic in this focus on disgust and stigma. Prejudice and discrimination are not exhaustively traceable to disgust. Other psychological factors, such as fear of imagined violence or guile and competitive envy, also need exploration, and recent studies have shown clear evidence of unconscious group bias that is not clearly ascribable to any determinate emotional origin. Furthermore, discrimination has an important institutional aspect that is not reducible to bad intent: policies may be objectionably discriminatory even if they are not enacted with malign intent, and these factors also require close comparative study. Theorists need to examine the many ways in which discrimination is sustained by structures, as well as by popular sentiment and discourse.

---

[8] B.R. Ambedkar, Speech, 4 November 1948; Keer, Dhananjay, *Dr. Ambedkar: Life and Mission* (Bombay: Popular Prakashan Private Limited, 1990), 410.

[9] *Naz Foundation v. Govt of NCT of Delhi*, 160 Delhi Law Times 277 (Delhi High Court 2009). This case and the subsequent reinstatement are analysed, with a focus on disgust, in Nussbaum's paper 'Disgust or Equality?' in the present volume.

Therefore, while considering ideas of stigma and disgust as a kind of philosophical/psychological hub from which various aspects of the project radiate outwards, giving it unity, we also devote sustained and independent attention to data about discrimination and to discrimination's institutional side, in housing, education, employment, and political representation. While we develop a theory in this introduction that unifies many of the chapters, we are theoretically pluralistic. On the side of remedies, we examine group resistance to subordination, as well as institutional, legal, public choice, and educational remedies. We also consider the emotional structures inherent in public culture. In a modern democracy, it is not acceptable to manipulate the psyches of individuals through coercive intervention into the development of young children in the family, where many baneful emotions are formed. However, a public culture that combats stigma has many aspects, of which laws and official policies are only a part; the use of public rhetoric, public art, and public ceremonies can also have an anti-stigma role.[10]

The present volume derives from a conference held in December 2016 at the University of Chicago Delhi Center. We were fortunate to have assembled a very distinguished group of speakers, drawn primarily from India and from our own university. Exchanges among the authors and with a very thoughtful audience during the conference shaped further work on the chapters. A tradition of our law school has been to include student papers. We follow that custom here, with three papers by advanced postgraduate students from the United States and India, which fully hold their own with the other papers.

Disgust: The Theoretical Background

Let us now describe the issues in more detail, using as a template the theory of disgust and stigma that Nussbaum has proposed, drawing on Rozin's research—not because the project as a whole is in all respects based on it, but because it makes the relevant questions clear, and shows the need for our comparative project.

All humans appear to share an acute discomfort when confronted by their own bodily fluids, excretions, and smells, and by the decay of the corpse. Nussbaum uses the term 'primary disgust' for a shrinking

---

[10] See Martha C. Nussbaum, *Political Emotions* (Cambridge, MA: Harvard University Press, 2013), comparing Indian and US examples.

from contamination by such objects and by other objects that closely resemble them in smell or feel (such as insects and animals that are slimy, smelly, and the like). Primary disgust, though not present at birth, is culturally universal, and is probably grounded in inherited tendencies. Although this aversive reaction may in some cases protect people from real danger (and perhaps that was its evolutionary origin), Rozin shows that its cognitive content is quite different from that of fear: it is about contamination, not danger; it is a reaction to the animality and decay of the human body; and it is both under-inclusive and over-inclusive for real danger. (Many dangerous things are not disgusting, and people feel disgust even when they are rationally convinced that danger is absent.) Rozin concludes that, in disgust, we are rejecting something about our own animality.

All that might be harmless enough, although one could argue that it is always problematic to encourage this sort of self-loathing. In all known societies, however, people do not stop there, and now we arrive at what Nussbaum calls 'projective disgust'. People seek to create a buffer zone between themselves and their own animality, by identifying a group (often a powerless minority) who can be targeted as the quasi-animals, and projecting onto that group various animal characteristics, which they have to no greater degree than the ones doing the projecting: bad smell, animal sexuality, and so on. The so-called thinking seems to be, if those quasi-animal humans stand between us and our own animal stench and decay, we are that much further from being animal and mortal ourselves. There is no society in which we do not find subgroups, to whom, irrationally, properties of smelliness, hyper-sexuality, and, in general, hyper-animality are imputed.

There are many varieties of disgust stigma. In European anti-Semitism, Jews were depicted as hyper-bodily, smelly, and hyper-sexual, but also as crafty and intelligent.[11] African Americans, by contrast, were and, unfortunately at times, still are imagined as hyper-sexual, hyper-bodily, and also smelly, bestial, and stupid. Again, African Americans were imagined as physically powerful and both physically and sexually aggressive. To upper Hindu castes who observed untouchability, untouchables were seen not only as foul, but also as weak and not particularly aggressive. People with severe mental and physical disabilities are often found physically disgusting, and contact with them is avoided, but they are

---

[11] See references to the historical literature in Nussbaum, *Hiding from Humanity*.

seen as weak and subhuman, and not feared. Much the same is true of people who are ageing. These differences are important, and yet a common set of threads runs through all.

What about conservative propaganda that links disgust with same-sex acts? The US pamphlet literature attempts to whip up animosity towards gays and lesbians (though above all, gay men), by prominent use of the tropes of projective disgust. The standard way of doing this is to focus obsessively on anal sex and to describe it in terms apt to elicit revulsion. All sorts of abstract claims are made, such as that gays eat faeces and drink raw blood. A related trope is the idea that gays travel a lot and thence bring germs into America—fascinatingly reminiscent of Nazi propaganda linking Jews to a variety of diseases.[12] In India, we find related phenomena, and Indian law has made the role of disgust and stigma clear.

Projective disgust always leads to some type of avoidance of bodily contact. Again, the type and extent vary. African Americans were forbidden to use white people's drinking fountains, swimming pools, lunch counters, hotel beds—and, of course, sexual contact was strictly forbidden, and a felony in many states (widely though, white men always had sexual relationships with and sexually abused black women). And yet, an African American might prepare and serve food for a white family, and the family did not mind this at all. An Indian Dalit, by contrast, could never serve food in an upper-caste family, and Dalits also could not share lodging or drinking taps (as Ambedkar relates, describing his childhood in Madhya Pradesh). The crazy irrationalities of these ideas are manifold. One role for a comparative project such as ours is to reveal such capricious irrationalities, along with the pain and exclusion they inflict.

People with disabilities remind so-called normal people vividly of the limits and frailties of the human body, and they are often removed from the public gaze on grounds that people do not like to look at them or associate with them. For a long time in the United States, people with both mental and physical disabilities were excluded from public education on the grounds that 'normal' children found it upsetting to associate with them. An important US Supreme Court case, *City of Cleburne v. Cleburne Living Center, Inc.*[13] dealt with an attempt by a Texas city

[12]   Robert N. Procter, *The Nazi War on Cancer* (1997; Princeton: Princeton University Press, 2000). Extensive references to the pamphlet literature are given in Nussbaum, *From Disgust to Humanity*.
[13]   473 U. S. 432 (1985).

to zone out a home for people with mental retardation. The zoning law was declared unconstitutional on the ground that it was motivated by 'animus' towards people with disabilities. There is much more to be said about this sort of animus, and about the ways in which educational and social policy may combat it.

One of the most tenacious types of prejudice is prejudice against people who are ageing. They are stigmatized in popular culture and discourse, and very often law gives sanction to those forms of stigma. The bodies of ageing people remind younger people of their own frailty and mortality, and popular discourse portrays those bodies as incompetent, unattractive, even revolting. Moreover, even ageing people themselves often come to feel disgust with their own bodies, as new research is proposing. This may well be the new issue for our time, since discrimination on the basis of age deprives all societies of valuable human capital. Saul Levmore and Nussbaum have written on this group of issues, which seem to have been little debated in India, and we want to inspire a lively debate.[14]

One case that cuts across all the others is class. Legal theorist William Ian Miller argues (following George Orwell) that class subordination is driven by the dynamic of bodily disgust and is therefore very difficult to remedy, even in a democracy. But many theories of class hierarchy do not make stigma and disgust central features. One of our chapters takes on this difficult question.

Prejudice against Muslims is multiform in today's world, and our project permits us to describe some of its types and nuances. In India, prejudice against Muslims is ubiquitous, and often sustained by a rhetoric of disgust: Muslims have been portrayed as hyper-fertile and hyper-animal.[15] In the United States, by contrast, the dominant axis of prejudice is fear rather than disgust, but Muslims, it appears, are at the same time regarded as an ethno-racial as well as a religious group.

Now to remedies. The project's accent is on understanding prejudice and discrimination, not on crafting specific remedial interventions, but understanding is a necessary prelude to successful remediation, and it does suggest directions for legal and social change. We hope to give at

[14] Saul Levmore and Martha C. Nussbaum, *Aging Thoughtfully: Conversations on Retirement, Romance, Wrinkles, and Regret* (Oxford University Press, 2017).

[15] See Martha C. Nussbaum, *The Clash Within: Democracy, Religious Violence, and India's Future* (Cambridge, MA: Harvard University Press, 2007), on the use of disgust propaganda in the Gujarat pogrom of 2002.

least a flavour of what directions might be valuable. Nussbaum's general normative conclusion in 2004 was that close study of the operations of disgust should give us reasons not to base laws upon it. But simply not making law in response to the signal of popular disgust is not enough to uproot discrimination. Institutional structures built on prejudice often need to be altered, and steps need to be taken to replace the damaging public discourse with a different discourse, the old exclusionary social structures with different structures. An example will help. Children with mental and physical disabilities in the United States used to be excluded from public education by law, as mentioned earlier. In the 1970s, courts declared that this exclusion was unconstitutional, and that schools might not behave that way. However, since the whole system of education as well as the physical environment had been built for the 'normal' child, much more needed to be done. The wide range of laws and policies that by now have supported the public education of children with disabilities are but a part of what needs to be done. Still, this is a pretty successful case of work against stigma through institutional, environmental, and social change, and it can be examined for clues as to strategies that might bear fruit in other cases.

Remedies need to combine legal change with attention to social attitudes and to workplace arrangements. They must therefore be, to some extent, culture-specific, but at the same time, a comparative study of legal and social arrangements in India and the United States can yield ideas that may work across large national and cultural differences, suitably modified.

Our project is thus comparative in two distinct senses: we compare the different areas of prejudice and stigma, and we also compare both prejudices and remedies in the two nations that are our focus. It is comparative, as it emerged, in a further sense as well, in that it is the multidisciplinary intersection of law, philosophy, sociology, psychology, and political science.

Chapter Summaries

Our first two chapters adopt distinct methodological approaches to illuminate the unique dynamics of the Indian caste system today. Dipesh Chakrabarty's chapter on caste begins with the tragic recent case of a Dalit doctoral student at the University of Hyderabad who took his own life in 2016 in the wake of being punished by the university for participating in student activism on behalf of Dalit students. The chapter explores the pervasiveness of psychological reactions of disgust and stigmatization in response to Dalits, even among relatively progressive Indians, drawing on both autobiographical and social science perspectives. It further grapples with the failure of Indian scholars, including those within the subaltern studies tradition, to grapple effectually with the status of Dalits. Drawing instead on the conceptual frameworks of Frantz Fanon and Louis Dumont, Chakrabarty argues that untouchability is worthy of attention not only because it is constitutive of Brahminic purity, and hence of some of the key hierarchies in Indian society, but also because the physical body of the Dalit can function as a timely reminder of human dependence on the non-human for survival. In the age of the Anthroprocene, as climate change reaches catastrophic levels, Chakrabarty argues this reminder is all too needful.

Working in a different register, Ashwini Deshpande uses econometric tools to examine the efficacy of affirmative action, in the form of reserved places for Scheduled Castes and Scheduled Tribes at government-run educational institutions. Common arguments against affirmative action in these contexts hinge primarily on the stigma of receiving a reservation, which is said to dissuade and then demoralize eligible applicants. By examining data from a sample of persons eligible for reservations, but who vary in accepting or rejecting the resulting placement, Deshpande is able to explore the reasons for declining an affirmative-action slot. Rather than stigma, she finds that bureaucratic obstacles, as well as a lack of knowledge about that option, explained far more of the non-uptake than stigma. Consistent with this finding, Deshpande uses qualitative surveying of a non-representative pool of quota beneficiaries to better understand their experiences. She finds a wide range of obstacles to social and educational progress, but concludes that those who receive a reservation generally support the policy and believe they could not have achieved what they, in fact, managed to do without the aid of some kind of affirmative action.

In the US context, caste has no obvious role. Race, however, has operated to similar effect in different ways at historical junctures. The following two chapters directly address pivotal questions of race's effects in the American context. In his chapter, Justin Driver develops the connection between fears about interracial sex and the prolonged battle over school segregation in the last half of the twentieth century. The fear of miscegenation, and more precisely the fear of black male sexuality, Driver

explains, played a large role in the private psychology and public justifications of mid-century segregationists. He more specifically explores the
relation of school desegregation, miscegenation-related fears, and private
violence against African Americans, for instance, in the case of Emmett
Till, a 13-year-old boy notoriously lynched in August 1955. So powerful
was miscegenation-related anxiety, Driver recounts, that it shaped the
legal reform strategies of groups such as the National Association for
the Advancement of Colored People (or NAACP), which deliberately
sought out litigants who were either old enough to seem desexualized, or
who were female. It also led the federal courts to defer and delay ruling
on challenges to anti-miscegenation statutes that existed at the state level
through to the 1950s. The chapter concludes by tracing the invalidation
of anti-miscegenation measures by the US Supreme Court in 1964 and
the consequent efforts to preserve racial segregation by resorting to sex
segregation within schools.

In the United States, explicit embraces of racial hierarchies have
played a diminished role in public discourse at least until the 2016 election cycle. Emilio Comay del Junco argues that four different forms
of racism have persisted, notwithstanding the reduction in overt racial
rhetoric. First, there is the explicit denial of the equal humanity of a
racial group. As Comay del Junco notes, this was the case with respect to
African Americans through much of US history. Second, he identifies a
failure to evince the same level of concern for the well-being of a racial
minority as would be shown for a cognate group. He argues that the
stigmatization of poverty and welfare in the US context is well explained
by malign neglect of this precise sort. Finally, Comay del Junco identifies two categories wherein people violate their own principles of racial
equality: first, implicitly biased actions of which an agent is entirely
unconscious, and second, racially akratic action—or action knowingly
taken against one's best, all-things-considered judgement. Into these
final two categories, Comay del Junco places such phenomena as micro-
aggressions that sum over time to durable forms of social stratification.
As he explains, this typology of causal mechanisms suggests that racism cannot be addressed by individually focused means alone, but also
requires structural solutions.

The following two chapters take on gender inequalities from a global
perspective. Emily Dupree challenges the widely held view that gender
is a natural or biological kind. Instead, she argues that it is best understood as a dominant or subordinate status created by an interconnected
network of beliefs, behaviours, customs, and institutions. Drawing upon

and seeking to advance the work of gender theorists in the recent trans feminist literature, as well as more established gender theorists such as Judith Butler, Dupree identifies three components of gender stereotypes that persist across a wide range of national cultural contexts, including the United States and India.

First, the family is conceived as a private sphere in which men and women have distinct role specializations that conduce to inequality and injustice. Second, women are assimilated into a heteronormative hierarchy in which marriage plays a defining organizing role. Third, women are expected to provide a lion's share of care and emotional work, both inside the home and in the workplace. Across these three architectonic features of gender stereotypes, Dupree argues, stereotypical views, rather than biological facts, provide a necessary foundation. Against this gender hierarchy, Dupree argues for gender abolition as a necessary step beyond liberal notions of equality.

The second chapter takes an Indian perspective. Why, Vidhu Verma asks in her chapter on gender inequality in India, has the promise of formal equality contained in the constitution not yielded a system in which women and men are full and equal individuals under the law? She identifies gaps in the law, the limits of law as a catalyst of equality, and the persisting presence of both ideological and structural constraints. The Indian Constitution of 1950, Verma explains, did not address equality in the workplace. The ensuing constitutional jurisprudence has had a consistently conservative tilt, which is especially apparent in cases concerning rape and sexual violence. The sub-constitutional criminal law of rape, moreover, was organized around the idea of women's 'modesty', limiting its remedial efficacy. Finally, from within India, forces of religious conservatism have resisted change, while the external forces of economic globalization have made carceral regulatory strategies more perilous.

Ageing and the aged are the focus in the next two chapters. In his contribution, Saul Levmore focuses on two seemingly disparate practices—the American legal prohibition on mandatory retirement provisions in employment contracts, and patterns of anti-ageing cosmetic surgery in the United States (a practice now largely outside law's concern). Levmore proposes that the law's decision to intervene on the first question, and to leave the second unregulated, has matters backward. Prohibitions on mandatory retirement clauses have perverse and unanticipated consequences, he argues, harming employers, potential workers in their 50s, and older employees who would benefit from the existence of a critical mass of retirees in their age cohort. In contrast to these perverse effects from the law, Levmore expresses concern about the growing popularity of unregulated anti-ageing interventions. These, he argues, reflect and reinforce the stigma and negative profiling attached to age. They may also have some regressive effects because the wealthy are more able to hide their age than the less financially secure. In the cosmetic surgery context, he therefore suggests, a change in social norms, or even a legal intervention, might be beneficial for all.

In her chapter on ageing, Martha C. Nussbaum identifies Cicero's dialogue *De Senectute* as the first philosophical treatment in the Western tradition of the social discrimination and stigma attached to ageing. Building on Cicero's arguments, Nussbaum argues that ageing and its signs are associated with death, and therefore regarded with a particular fear and a particular disgust closely linked to that fear. As a result, the aged are stigmatized in popular culture and discourse, and the law often gives sanction to these stigmatic harms. Nussbaum points to research that shows that even ageing people themselves come to experience disgust with their own bodies. Beyond the unhappiness that this causes, she argues that stigma leads to discrimination against ageing people in employment and in informal social settings. We have not on this score, she concludes ruefully, come all that far beyond the time of Cicero. By way of redress, she suggests ageing people need a political movement akin to the disability movement, and zeroes in on compulsory retirement rules as especially pernicious.

Three chapters address sexual orientation and transgender rights. Martha C. Nussbaum's chapter on sexual orientation in Indian constitutional law begins by setting her theory of disgust, which builds on the research of US experimental psychologist Paul Rozin and his colleagues. In this theory, Nussbaum distinguishes between *primary disgust*, a shrinking from contamination by bodily fluids, excrement, and the like, and *projective disgust*, whereby people seek to create a buffer zone between themselves and their own animality by targeting another group as quasi-animals and projecting onto that group various animal characteristics. As she shows, it was Victorian-era colonial legal reforms, rather than long-standing Hindu traditions, that introduced and justified sanctions of homosexuality based on projective disgust. The resulting section 377 of the Indian Penal Code (IPC), she explains, was struck down by the Delhi High Court in 2009, but its judgment was subsequently reversed by the Indian Supreme Court in a thinly reasoned opinion. Nussbaum shows how her theory of disgust both supports the Delhi

High Court's ruling, and provides grounds for condemning the Supreme Court's contrary judgment.

The two other chapters on this topic focus on a recent decision of the Indian Supreme Court concerning transgender rights entitled *National Legal Services Authority v. Union of India*. Although *National Legal Services Authority* advanced transgender rights, both chapters are alert to its shortcomings and limitations. Jeffrey A. Redding observes that the decision in *National Legal Services Authority* does not rest upon a generalized right to choose one's gender identity, but assumes instead the existence of a demarcated group named 'transgender people'. As Redding explains, this taxonomy, in turn, depends upon an appeal to Indian (and in particular, Hindu) history. The distinction, Redding argues, not only separates questions of transgender rights from questions of women's rights and cisgender individuals' struggles for recognition and rights, it also conduces to new forms of separation. The court's opinion hence mandates separate bathroom facilities—a remedy that in other jurisdictions has been challenged as legally and morally objectionable. Finally, Redding draws out subtle ways in which disgust continues to inform the taxonomical assumptions of *National Legal Services Authority*, drawing on Nussbaum's scholarship in addition to work by James Scott and Sara Ahmed.

H.R. Vasujith Ram, in contrast, situates the decision in *National Legal Services Authority* in its jurisprudential context by cataloguing ambiguities within the decision and subsequent legislative and judicial developments. Like Redding, Ram identifies and critiques the fixed and restrictive definition of transgender identity that animates the decision. He further explains how this taxonomical innovation is likely to have unanticipated consequences for transgender individuals under other statutes, including Indian election and inheritance laws. The decision, in Ram's view, also fails to analyse the complex interaction of transgender and caste identity. Ram goes on to explore various legislative responses to *National Legal Services Authority*. These include a December 2014 private member's bill and government statutory proposals introduced in 2015 and 2016. He demonstrates how these efforts, paradoxically, recapitulate many obsolete understandings of transgender identity drawn from ill-informed stereotypes and lurid popular culture tropes.

Two chapters next address the question of disability in India. Anita Ghai in her chapter draws on a range of autobiographical and biographical experiences to explore the absence of disability as an object of inquiry or solicitude in progressive social movements. In the feminist movement in India, just as in the broader social context, Ghai explains that disabled women are rarely recognized as persons, and their distinctive challenges and concerns are not articulated as politically pressing. By way of contrast to this pervasive political silencing, Ghai points to the striking statue of Alison Lapper, an English artist born with phocomelia, in Trafalgar Square as a validating recognition and portrait of resistance. Rejecting a subordinate role for the disabled in progressive social movements, Ghai underscores the importance of recognizing the sexual desires and identities of disabled women by resisting their desexualization and by disseminating accurate education to parents.

Nandini Ghosh focuses upon the cultural context in which discrimination against those with disabilities occurs in India. She identifies a central, organizing norm of 'ableism' that comprises a network of beliefs, processes, and practices that produce and reproduce conceptions of the norm and the deviant in terms of bodily and mental performance. Ghosh explores how ableism shares a paternalistic welfare system and leads the state to legitimate disgust for bodies perceived as unproductive. By mining direct testimony from disabled persons, their families, and others, Ghosh demonstrates how ideological frames shape self-evaluation, self-esteem, and intra-familial judgements of worth and dignity. Disgust slips easily, in Ghosh's account, into physical abuse and public shaming. In response, legislation in India has been sporadic and incomplete. Ghosh concludes by exploring the Rights of Persons with Disabilities Act of 2016, demonstrating its many weaknesses and continuities with historical and cultural patterns of exclusion and suppression.

Chapters by Aziz Huq and Zoya Hasan then take up the treatment of Muslims in the United States and India, respectively. Huq first documents the pervasiveness of anti-Muslim views in both the United States and Europe. Those adverse views are closely related to adverse views of migrants more generally, and appear correlated with experiences of economic adversity and perceptions of cultural besiegement. Huq then considers potential legal responses to increasing anti-Muslim prejudice. Observing that both theorists and judges in America and Europe have alternated between treating anti-Muslim bias as a variant of racism or a species of religious discrimination, Huq argues that the former is likely to provide a more effectual framework for responding to discrimination. A race-discrimination focus under current doctrinal approaches, he contends, places the emphasis on the discriminator's beliefs (rather than the victim's self-conception), and points towards anti-disparate-impact rules, rather than accommodation, as a solution for animus against Muslims.

In her chapter on India, Zoya Hasan charts the way in which policy-making on social discrimination in India has failed to grapple with extensive discrimination against Muslims. Until the 2006 *Sachar Commission Report*, reform efforts were stymied by the absence of evidence. But after the report's damning account of extensive socio-economic discrimination and disparity, no major change has occurred. In light of this failure, Hassan charts the ways in which state and policy institutions have perpetuated, rather than mitigated, inequalities. These include, for instance, the partial reach of reservations in educational and political institutions. Compounding these forces, Hassan explains, is the increasing spread of prejudice and fear of Muslims, which, in part, exploits stereotypes about Muslim gender relations and, in part, flows from institutional biases.

From religious classification, the volume turns to class. Laura Weinrib's chapter investigates class issues in the US context, including the different ways in which disgust can channel responses to poverty and class-based inequality. Rather than suggesting a singular relationship, Weinrib points out that disgust can conduce to a reformist impulse (in the case of George Orwell's *The Road to Wigan Pier*) or to the enactment of vagrancy and other exclusionary measures designed to exclude the poor from view. Further complicating matters, reactions to class are often intertwined with racial sentiments. Indeed, a common liberal worry about class-based remedial efforts is that they will distract from race-based remedial efforts. In the constitutional context, judicial review of wealth classification seemed conceivable in the late 1950s and early 1960s, but was rejected by the Supreme Court in the early 1970s. Advocates for the poor then turned to legislatures, with limited success. Weinrib closes by expressing scepticism about the potential for disgust to play a central role in future reformist efforts. Rather than the element of disgust, she suggests, it is the policing of class boundaries and privileges that is most troubling.

The volume closes with two chapters about the general theory of discrimination. Drawing on his important monograph *A Theory of Discrimination Law*, Tarunabh Khaitan formulates a new theoretical account of the primary purpose of discrimination law. This account posits that all persons require secure access to a set of four basic goods. Membership in certain types of groups, which depends on either an immutable trait or a choice that is valuable and fundamental, can imperil the secure access to at least three of those goods when that group suffers substantial, pervasive, and abiding relative disadvantage compared with cognate groups. This relative disadvantage comprises in practice, among other things, a greater exposure to the potential loss of negative liberties, a narrower range of valuable life opportunities, and an enduring loss of self-respect. The function of discrimination law, on Khaitan's account, is to rupture the linkage between group disadvantage and relative disadvantage. Its central aim, correspondingly, is to reduce and ultimately remove significant advantage gaps between the protected group and a cognate group. By eliminating the disadvantage attendant on membership in a protected class, Khaitan concludes, it is more possible that such belonging will contribute to a good life.

Richard McAdams's chapter canvasses the three dominant economic theories of discrimination with the aim of determining which is most persuasive as an account of observed discrimination, and as a justification for existing discrimination law. The first theory, associated with Gary Becker, posits that discrimination reflects a preference for not associating with members of a racial group. As McAdams notes, this theory is ill matched to the observed racial realities of twentieth-century America, in which close racial contact was quite common, albeit limited to hierarchical situations. The second theory, associated with Kenneth Arrow, posits that discrimination is a function of statistical inference on the basis of race about unobservable qualities. McAdams observes that such inferences might be based on either justified or irrational generalizations. Finally, the 'status production' theory of discrimination explains various forms of racist behaviour in terms of the creation and maintenance of status based on a racial identity. McAdams argues that the latter provides more explanatory power than other models. He suggests that recognition of the force of status production theories of discrimination has implications for the specific form of discrimination law, and, in particular, the question whether anti-discrimination norms must be symmetrical in protecting all groups equally.

Our dedication is taken from E.M. Forster. He allowed *Maurice*, his novel about same-sex love, written in 1913–14, to be published only after his death (it appeared in 1971), because he judged that Britain was not ready for a novel in which two gay men fall in love and ultimately live happily. He dedicated it 'To a happier year', and we borrow that for our own volume. Some of the types of prejudice and stigma we investigate have diminished somewhat, in some places, but all remain large problems for our two countries, since majoritarian democracy (as Ambedkar knew) is rarely respectful of minority lives. We offer this volume in the hope that it will provide suggestions for legal and social change, preparing the 'happier year' of the future.

1

The Dalit Body

A Reading for the Anthropocene

Dipesh Chakrabarty

Situating the Dalit body

Rohith Vemula, son of a Dalit mother and a low-caste father and himself a doctoral student at the University of Hyderabad, took his own life on 17 January 2016. This is how he protested against the university authorities for penalizing him for taking part in Dalit student activism. Vemula did not stop at making a statement with his body; he also left some thoughts about the low-caste/Dalit body itself in a suicide note explaining his decision to bring his short life to a tragic end. The 'value of a man' in the society he had lived in, observed Vemula in his parting note, had always been 'reduced to his immediate identity and nearest possibility': 'To a vote … [or] to a number. To a thing. Never was a man treated as a mind. As a glorious thing made up of stardust. In very field [*sic*], in studies, in streets, in politics, and in dying and living.'[1]

---

[1] Vemula's suicide note as reproduced in *Times of India*, 19 January 2016.

Vemula's note leaves us with some thoughts about two ways one could transcend the 'untouchable', stigmatized Dalit body: by treating every human being as a 'mind' without reference to his or her socially marked body; the other way was to look beyond the 'individual' body of the Dalit person and think of the material that connects all bodies to the matter that makes up our universe—ancient atomic and sub-atomic particles, the 'stardust' of Vemula's description that circulates through our and other bodies in the cosmos all the time. This second perspective was no idle imagination on Vemula's part. He was a student of science and an avid reader of Carl Sagan and even quoted Sagan in one of his Facebook posts as saying, 'Our species needs, and deserves, a citizenry with minds wide awake and a basic understanding of how the world works.'[2]

In this chapter, which I see as a tribute to Vemula's memory, I reconsider the question of the Dalit body in light of the quotation from Carl Sagan that Vemula ponders: 'Our species needs and deserves a citizenry with a … basic understanding of how the world works.' The problem of global warming—or what is often called anthropogenic climate change—has underlined the need to understand the human story afresh. Sagan's reference to the 'species' gestures towards a very long-term and collective history of *Homo sapiens* and their journey through time, while his phrase 'how the world works' points us towards questions about where humans fit into the story of how the planet functions as a quasi-systemic entity, linking up the human with the non-human and the living with the non-living.

However, if Vemula's interest in Sagan's thoughts provides one of the starting points of this essay, my other point of departure comes from Martha Nussbaum's stimulating and generative reflections on stigmatization—and, in particular, the emotion of disgust—as they feature in the philosophy of modern, mainly American, law.[3] It is not the specifics of her arguments that concern me here—though some of her conclusions such as that we should be sceptical about 'relying on [disgust] as a basis for law' since 'disgust has been used throughout history to exclude and marginalize groups' may well apply to India—but points where her thoughts touch on the evolutionary psychology of humans.

---

[2] Rohith Vemula, Facebook, 10 November 2016. Full Facebook feed available at https://www.facebook.com/rohith352?ref=br_rs.

[3] Martha C. Nussbaum, *Hiding from Humanity: Disgust, Shame, and the Law* (Princeton and Oxford: Princeton University Press, 2004).

Of course, Nussbaum does not elaborate on these points even when she broaches them, as they are often points she needs to both recognize and bracket in order to proceed with her own exposition. But it is what she brackets that interests me in this essay. So it would probably be more accurate to say that my argument forms itself, as it were, on the margins of Nussbaum's text, by following up on what she acknowledges but does not feel obliged to pursue.

Nussbaum acknowledges, for instance, that the emotion of 'disgust' probably entails elements that belong to a deep history of the human species, including 'magical ideas of contamination, and impossible aspirations to purity, immortality, and non-animality, that are just not in line with human life as we know it'. Disgust may have played, she suggests, a 'valuable role in our evolution', and it is not just possible but indeed 'very likely' that it plays 'a useful function in our current daily lives'. Perhaps its function of 'hiding from us problematic aspects of our humanity is useful: perhaps we cannot easily live with too much vivid awareness of the fact that we are made of sticky and oozy substances that will all too soon decay'.[4] 'Some self-deception', she writes, 'may be essential in getting us through a life in which we are soon bound for death, and in which the most essential matters are beyond our control.' Nussbaum leaves it there, as her main purpose in the book is to call for 'a society where such self-deceptive fictions do not rule in law and in which—at least in crafting the institutions that shape our common life together—we admit that we are all children [that is, equals without a father figure] and that in many ways we don't control the world'.[5]

Nussbaum also leaves aside—logically, from her perspective—questions of emotions that may be shared between humans and other animals: 'I have said that emotions are "human experiences", and of course they are that; but most contemporary researchers, and many in the ancient world, also hold that some non-human animals have emotions, at least of certain types … I shall leave that issue to one side for now, however, focusing on the human emotions that are the standard material of law.'[6] Nussbaum's thoughts are focused on the human alone, and as with many other liberal thinkers, she thinks of principles that could potentially be applicable to every individual human being, irrespective of the total

---

[4] Nussbaum, *Hiding from Humanity*, 14, 72, 83, 89, 91–3, 94–5, 116.
[5] Nussbaum, *Hiding from Humanity*, 17
[6] Nussbaum, *Hiding from Humanity*, 23–4, 50.

number of humans on the planet. Nussbaum proceeds—rightly, again, from her perspective—from the assumption of 'equal worth of persons, and their liberty' as she elaborates some 'core' legal principles that she considers essential for the flourishing of all individual humans whose lives are governed by institutions that subscribe to liberal principles.[7] Nussbaum's thoughts are anthropocentric by choice.

The 'Dalit question' in India, or the persistence in modern Indian institutions of the old problem of 'untouchability' in new forms, illustrates at once why both Nussbaum's critique and rejection of disgust as a basis for social management and Carl Sagan's view of the human body as 'stardust' (as Vemula summarized it) are *both* relevant concerns today. They are relevant, but they are also somewhat at odds with each other. In the Brahmanical scheme of things, the body of the 'untouchable' person was considered untouchable precisely because it was invested with a certain degree of disgust-arousing significance. This disgust was the emotional source of the marginalization and oppression of the Dalit. From Nussbaum's position, rejecting such a degrading construction of the human body in favour of the individualized body that underwrites the 'equal worth of persons' principle is one way to overcome the Dalit's body. And it perhaps speaks to Vemula's complaint that the Dalit could never be seen as someone who had overcome his/her body, and therefore, as he put it, 'as a mind'. The body as 'a glorious thing made up of stardust', however, is a construction that sees the human/Dalit body as connected to everything else in the cosmos, to its ancient past, and its present. The view here is neither anthropocentric, nor one that individuates the human body. While, in Nussbaum's view, human flourishing refers to conditions under which all individual humans can potentially flourish, the body as 'stardust' dissolves the individual body into some connected view of the physical universe and goes beyond the question of human flourishing. The use of the adjective 'glorious' by Vemula in describing this view of the body perhaps signifies the majesty and miraculous nature of the body as it seemed to have appeared to Vemula's scientific eyes. He clearly saw this as another powerful way to escape in imagination the limits violently imposed on his 'low-caste', Dalit-identified body.

In this chapter, I propose a reading of 'the Dalit body'—admittedly an abstract construction about which I will have more to say shortly—by

---

[7] Nussbaum, *Hiding*, 61

placing such a body at the intersection of the two different traditions of thought that I have collected under the signs of Nussbaum and Sagan. My recent work on climate change convinces me of a complexity that marks the present moment in human history. It is this: while we cannot *not* think of human flourishing and questions of justice between humans as we move deeper into the present century, pursuing these questions with no reference to how even individual human bodies are connected to non-human elements on the planet—both living and non-living— can in the end imperil human flourishing. The overlaps between the literature on climate change and Earth system science convince me that, with the number of humans on the planet today, we need to be increasingly aware of these connections in the interest of our own flourishing. That we are made up of 'sticky and oozy substances that will all too soon decay' may have to become a part of our everyday awareness. Not only that. The point that not humans but microbial and other small forms of life constitute both by weight and numbers the bulk of life on the planet and are central to the drama of life—from the production of soil to the internal workings of the human body, not to speak of the maintenance of the share of oxygen in the atmosphere—may have to be assigned, as the climate crisis unfolds, the status of a salutary fact that humans will need to keep in mind in thinking about planetary conditions that make our existence and flourishing possible.[8]

The Dalit body, as imagined in the oppressive Brahmanical schema, is marginalized because of its forced contact with death and waste matter; however, it is also one example—bracketing for the moment the relations of oppression that upper castes have built around it—of the human body imagined as intrinsically connected to the non-human and the non-living. We could find similar, and probably a lot more benign, examples in the older religious myths of Native Americans, American Indians, tribes in India and Africa, and of the Australian aboriginals with the crucial difference, of course, that in the context of caste, Dalits were marginalized and oppressed precisely because of such perceived connections.[9] What I do here is to think about ways in which the traditionally castigated Dalit body could be reconstructed to act as an ethical horizon

---

[8] Dipesh Chakrabarty, 'Humanities in the Anthropocene: The Crisis of an Enduring Kantian Fable', *New Literary Review* 47, nos 2–3 (2016): 377–97.

[9] See, for instance, Déborah Danowski and Eduardo Viveiros de Castro, *The Ends of the World* (London: Polity, 2016) on these questions.

for the present (without ignoring or condoning any of the deprivations that actual Dalit bodies suffer).

The Invisibility of the Dalit Body

The phenomenology of the Dalit body, as Sundar Sarukkai has argued, clearly lies in the Dalit—and the Brahman, too, in a perverse manner—being severely deprived of something profoundly important to human beings, the touch of other humans.[10] Matters of bodily comportment and performance thus play a crucial role in the history of 'untouchability' in South Asia. One cannot theorize 'untouchability' without theorizing the body and its cultural location in the long and varied histories of oppression of Dalits in the subcontinent.

Yet there is a certain kind of forgetfulness about this body that marks the vast and otherwise learned literature on caste and untouchability in India. Symptomatic of this, I now think, was the invisibility of the 'Dalit question', even in as self-consciously radical a project as subaltern studies. Most, if not all, of Ranajit Guha's examples of acts of physical domination and subordination in everyday life in nineteenth-century rural India in his classic book, *Elementary Aspects of Peasant Insurgency in Colonial India* (1983), came from the literature on caste,[11] but caste was almost an absent category in our shared analytical framework. It was not as though we did not know about caste and its terrible inequities, but caste was sublimated into the categories 'peasant' and 'class' in the interest of a historiography that was meant to advance a politics of revolutionary transformation of Indian society, a transformation we understood through the prism of a Marxist outlook, however dissident and democratic its spirit may have been. The subject of humiliation in everyday life was an embodied subject—a low-caste or Dalit person sporting a moustache, carrying an umbrella, wearing shoes or breast cloth gave affront to members of dominant groups in particular societies and elicited violent responses of abuse and torture. The humiliated body was marked by caste and its rules of exclusion, yet caste was what we

[10] Sundar Sarukkai, 'Phenomenology of Untouchability', in *The Cracked Mirror: An Indian Debate on Experience and Theory*, eds Gopal Guru and Sundar Sarukkai (New Delhi: Oxford University Press, 2014; 2012),157–99.
[11] Ranajit Guha, *Elementary Aspects of Peasant Insurgency in Colonial India* (New Delhi: Oxford University Press, 1983).

did not discuss in subaltern studies for a very long time until criticisms from the likes of Kancha Ilaiah made us aware of this serious gap in our intellectual endeavour.[12]

True, traditional Marxist categories are often blind to 'caste' and tend to fold it into the category 'class', but that problem had already been recognized as such. So why did we, academics working on South Asia with most of us having grown up and experienced caste in its multiple manifestations in different parts of the subcontinent, not recognize caste oppression for what it was—a form of oppression whose logic of humiliation and exclusion expressed itself through the materiality of embodied practices? There are, of course, many factors that have contributed to this elision of the centrality of the Dalit body in narratives of Dalit suffering. One could point to the plethora of caste studies in the 1960s and the 1970s that aimed at highlighting facts about social mobility within the caste 'system' in order to dispute the European canard that the so-called caste-system was a straitjacket that held people inevitably confined to the caste (jati) they were born into.[13] The category 'caste' belonged here to an emerging discipline of Indian sociology. Dalits and the question of untouchability were folded into the problem of caste, and caste—like race (though many argued caste was not race, and there was a whole CIBA foundation volume dedicated to this question alone)—was seen as a form of inequality that democracy, socialism, or sheer market or developmental logic were meant to take care of in the end.[14]

There was also an idealistic strain in criticisms of caste-related oppression that portrayed a 'spiritual' history of India or Hinduism by emphasizing the emancipatory potential of the Bhakti movement— a devotional form of religion that borrowed anti-hierarchical elements

[12] Guha, *Elementary Aspects of Peasant Insurgency in Colonial India*, Chapter 2. See also Kancha Ilaih, 'Productive Labour, Consciousness and History: The Dalitbahujan Alternative', in *Subaltern Studies: Writings on South Asian History and Society*, eds Shahid Amin and Dipesh Chakrabarty (New Delhi: Oxford University Press, 1996), 165–200. Ilaih began by saying, 'Mainstream historiography has done nothing to incorporate the Dalitbahujan perspective in the writing of Indian history: *Subaltern Studies* is no exception to this.'

[13] The late Professor M.N. Srinivas acted as a pioneer in providing some of the basic conceptual tools—such as 'Sanskritization'—deployed in this literature. André Béteille is, of course, another intellectual stalwart of this period.

[14] Anthony de Ruecke and Julie Knight (eds), *Caste and Race: Comparative Approaches, A Ciba Foundation Volume* (London: J. & A. Churchill, 1967).

from both Hindu and Islamic sources—in a gesture to give the egalitarianism of Indian democracy a deep historical genealogy. In modern discussions of this literature, the problem of the body (of the Dalit) was often converted into a problem of spirit, a matter of consciously or unconsciously held attitudes that could be spelt out and questioned in religious texts. This was a civilizational narrative of India in which certain Indic texts are seen as having prefigured solutions to problems that the nascent Indian democracy born after 1947 would have to face. One good example are the Patel lectures the famous Sanskrit scholar Dr V. Raghavan delivered in Delhi in 1964 at the invitation of Indira Gandhi who was then the minister of information and broadcasting. In these lectures, Raghavan took his audience through an enlightening tour of the various phases of the Bhakti movement from the sixth to the seventeenth centuries in India to paint, as John Stratton Hawley puts it, 'a sweeping panorama of India's democratic instincts as they existed before the word "democracy" was coined'.[15]

The blindness to the problem of the body was not just a question of how—that is, through what methods—we discussed caste. There was more to it. I left India when I was 27. In those 27 years of growing up in India, I never heard a single argument—either in school or at home or in social conversations—defending the practice of 'untouchability', and yet it remained in everyday life in various forms, some more subtle than others. Of course, knowledge mattered. Knowing about a problem usually leads to action or policy calculated to address it. Hence, the various measures India has taken so far to address the problem of untouchability, beginning of course with the remarkable step of pronouncing it illegal in independent India. Yet discrimination—and practices based on age-old assumptions about the body of the Dalit—never really ceases. Why?

Here we need to make a distinction, it seems to me, between, say, particular practices of discrimination and something we may call 'prejudice'. We become cognitively aware of discriminatory practices and seek to explain them with the various knowledge systems at hand. This is how the various disciplines of history, anthropology, or law would create out of the changing realities of caste their particular object of research and investigation. These knowledge systems, at the same time, also suggest steps for remedial action that may lie in the realms of legislation, economy, politics, or even in consciously held attitudes. Prejudice is

---

[15] John Stratton Hawley, *A Storm of Songs: India and the Idea of the Bhakti Movement* (Cambridge, Mass.: Harvard University Press, 2015), 24.

something different. It refers to the judgement you make of someone before you consciously judge them—it is in that sense, *pre*-judice, as Gadamer explains in *Truth and Method*.[16] These we imbibe from the earliest phase of our childhood, as we come into the symbolic order and as grown-ups explain the world to us and guide us into it, as they necessarily have to. Prejudice becomes part of our habitus (to switch from Gadamer to Bourdieu). Often, you see the knowledge/prejudice split in the same person, or, if my logic is right, probably in all of us.

In the interest of time and space, let me illustrate this point with the help of an autobiographical anecdote. I apologize for making autobiography stand in for ethnographic research but then 27 continuous years in one place is much longer than the time an anthropologist would typically spend in the field over his/her entire life. So perhaps I can claim a certain right to speak as a native-turned-ethnographer. When I was growing up in Calcutta in the 1950s, there was a very famous Bengali poem on the figure of the sweeper that was included in my school text. It was a stridently anti-untouchability poem beginning with lines that Bengalis of my generation can still recite from memory: '*ke bole tomare, bondhu, asprishya ashuchi?*' (Who dares to call you untouchable and impure, my friend?). Satyendranath Datta, the grandson of the famous nineteenth-century rationalist Akshaykumar Datta, wrote it. Datta died young at the age of 39 in 1922. He was an ardent admirer of Gandhi, so the poem probably was composed in the years after Gandhi came back to India permanently in 1915. The poem clearly had a long life and turned up in my school text some 40 years later. My mother, who was a teacher of Bengali literature in a high school, would teach me the poem, explaining with much sincerity and fervour the injustice of untouchability and how its every precept violated all fundamental principles of human equality and justice. Yet every morning, Lakshman, a Bihari Dalit man appointed by the city corporation to sweep our neighbourhood clean, would moonlight by cleaning the lavatories of the houses of our street (both of these were standard practices then: the city authorities would invariably get Dalits to do scavenging work, probably a practice even today, and the sweepers, in turn, would make additional money by taking up private employment during their official working hours). My parents had a good relationship with Lakshman—he would leave

---

[16] Hans-Georg Gadamer, *Truth and Method*, (London: Sheed and Ward, 1979), 239–40.

with them his money and other valuables whenever he went home on leave—and never treated him as an untouchable person during these social visits. But every morning, when he came into our house as a sweeper wielding a large, wet, and dripping *jhadu* (broomstick) with which he cleaned our lavatory, my mother would scramble to ensure that nothing—no draperies or pieces of furniture—was touched by him or the jhadu, producing in the process quite a panicky commotion in the household. Lakshman himself would also walk around assuming a stiff and awkward bodily posture at these moments, taking care to maintain a 'proper' distance between his body-with-the-jhadu and the furniture and the people of the household, so that upper-caste sensitivities about waste matter and pollution were not in any way offended. Richer households would actually build a separate entrance, sometimes even a separate spiralling staircase, for the use of the sweeper.

Growing into my high-school years, I came to think of this every-day event as expressive of some kind of hypocrisy on my mother's part. Perhaps she really did not believe in what Datta's poem said, the message of which she would explain to me by way of teaching me the right values of India's egalitarian democracy. I realized later that I was perhaps wrong. My mother was sincere in explaining to me the injustice of untouchability. What was in evidence on Lakshman's entering our house was prejudice in the Gadamerian sense: my mother's deeply Brahmanical sense of her own body was perhaps revolted by the thought that Lakshman and his jhadu dripping with water that may been used to clean faecal matter—an extended untouchable body, really—might come into contact with anything in our household. The point was not about hygiene. It was about the body of the Dalit qua Dalit. Formal knowledge of the oppression of Dalits historicizes or sociologizes the figure of the Dalit. Once you know the historical context that aids the exploitation of Dalits, you evolve policies aimed at changing the context of Dalit lives. But prejudice—the judgment you have before you deliberately judge—reproduces a structure where time constitutes a very long and stable present.

The Dalit Body As Inscription and Abstraction

The 'Dalit body' I mention here is, as I have already said, an abstraction. Since this abstract figure may be mistaken for an essentialist, Orientalist, or static view of the body of the Dalit on my part—as a denial of history, that is—let me begin with full acknowledgement of the empirical fact that, on the ground, there is perhaps no one who can correspond to 'the Dalit' of my description. On the ground, there are only the bodies of the members of so many different jatis that were traditionally considered 'untouchable'. As the Australian scholars Oliver Mendelsohn and Marika Vicziany once observed, 'The Untouchables are organized into jatis just as other Hindus are'—'Chamar, Bhangi, Dhobi, Pulaya, Paswan, Madagi are some of the many hundreds of Untouchable jatis scattered through every region of India.' And they added, 'At the local level everyone knows that there are particular Untouchable castes, rather than Untouchables in general.'[17] Dalit intellectuals have themselves related sometimes the degree to which being treated as an 'untouchable' was a function of time and place, that is, dependent on the opportunism and selfish interests of the higher castes. A. Shukra (a pseudonym), born in Pune to Punjabi parents belonging to the Ravidasi (worshippers of Ravidas) caste of Chamars, mentions in an autobiographical essay how the treatment his family received at the hands of their social superiors varied from their time in the village when they were not allowed to use the water-pots of upper castes, to the time when he had acquired education and his services were needed by the same social superiors. The 'rules of untouchability', he found out, 'were complex and hypocritical'.[18]

This empirical diversity and the various historical changes are not denied by the conceptual exercise I undertake here. My treatment of the Dalit body is somewhat like Frantz Fanon's treatment of the 'black body' in his *Black Skin, White Mask*. The 'black man' has no corporeal schema, suggested Fanon, using Hegel and Merleau-Ponty, meaning that the 'black man' could never forget his blackness; he could not ever forget the colour of his limbs or backside, like 'normal' persons do when in their everyday being or when they are asleep, say. The black man's sense of his own body, said Fanon, was always refracted through a third-person consciousness: 'In the white world the man of

[17] Oliver Mendelsohn and Marika Vicziany, *The Untouchables: Subordination, Poverty and the State in Modern India* (Cambridge: Cambridge University Press, 1998), 6.

[18] A. Shukra, 'Caste—A Personal Perspective', in *Contextualising Caste: Post-Dumontian Approaches*, eds Mary Searle-Chatterjee and Ursula Sharma (Oxford: Blackwell, 1994), 171.

color encounters difficulties in the development of his bodily schema. Consciousness of the body is solely a negating activity. It is a third-person consciousness.'[19]

This body of the 'black man' that Fanon discussed may have been empirically unavailable for the purpose of verifying his proposition. It is possible that the 'black men' Fanon knew, including himself, were entirely capable of losing all consciousness of the colour of their skin while asleep. But that was not Fanon's point. His abstraction, the 'black body', was central to a certain structure of racist oppression he wanted to make visible. The 'Dalit body' as employed here is a similar construction. I use it to make a point about how we might think about the human body and its relationship to the environment. The empirical variations in the history of the different groups of Dalits who now constitute India's Scheduled Castes do not concern me here. For whatever the elements of plurality and variation in the history of untouchability in Indian social history, the body would have to be central to the phenomenon itself. The practices that tend to make a human being 'untouch-able' focus on the body of the person concerned: it is their touch, shadow, their bodily signs and excretions, their food, and the like, that were and are seen as polluting.

Louis Dumont's classic study of caste, *Homo Hierarchicus*, is helpful here. 'It is clear', wrote Dumont, 'that the impurity of the Untouchable is conceptually inseparable from the purity of the Brahman ... In particular, untouchability will not truly disappear until the purity of the Brahman is itself radically devalued; this is not always noticed.' Dumont continues to comment on the centrality of the association between the cow and death in the constitution of the defiling nature of the untouchable person:

> It is remarkable that the essential development of the opposition between the pure and the impure in this connection bears on the cow.... The murder of a cow is assimilated to that of a Brahman, and we have seen that its products are powerful purificatory agents. Symmetrically, untouchables have the job of disposing of the dead cattle, of treating and working

[19] Frantz Fanon, *Black Skin, White Mask*, trans. Charles Lam Markmann (New York: Grove Press, 1967; 1952), 110. See also the discussion in David Macey, 'Adieu Foulard, Adieu Madras', in *Frantz Fanon's Black Skin, White Mask: New Interdisciplinary Essays*, ed. Max Silverman (Manchester and New York: Manchester University Press, 2005), 22.

their skins, and this unquestionably [is] one of the main features of untouchability.[20]

Dumont's powerful study has been much criticized in the literature on caste and we do not have to debate either his propositions or his methods. But a sharp memory of the body he describes—mediated sometimes by the reminiscences of a person no less than the great Ambedkar himself—animates Gopal Guru's powerful efforts to conceptualize the experience of being Dalit. 'During the Peshwa rule in nineteenth-century Pune', recalls Guru, 'the Brahmins forced the untouchables to tie an earthen pot around their neck and a broom around their waist. The pot was to spit in and the broom to erase their footprints that were also considered polluting.' Mahars, the untouchable caste that Ambedkar belonged to, were expected to carry sticks with bells attached to them so that the 'noise of the bell would communicate the undesirable arrival of untouchables in the main village'. This past is not quite dead for Guru. 'Thus,' he remarks, 'the Peshwa rule seems to have developed the prototype of today's biometric techniques', rendering Dalit bodies into inscribed surfaces.[21]

A Reading for the Anthropocene

Let me thus return to the Dalit body that is marked by its involvement with both faecal matter and the skin of dead animals or with death itself (as in the case of the *Dom* or the *Chandala* of the famous Raja Harishchandra legend that occurs in several puranas and influenced Gandhi's thinking).[22] Recall Gyan Prakash's description of 'untouchable' bonded labourers in Bihar—the landlords would always ask them to do the first ploughing of the land every cultivating season for the upper castes did not want to risk their bodies by facing the

---

[20] Louis Dumont, *Homo Hierarchicus: The Caste System and Its Implications*, trans. Mark Sainsbury, Louis Dumont, and Basia Gulati, complete revised English edition (Chicago: The University of Chicago Press, 1980; first published in French, 1966), 54

[21] Gopal Guru, 'Experience, Space, and Justice', in eds Guru and Sarukkai, *The Cracked Mirror*, 84–7.

[22] The Sanskrit word 'Chandala' designates someone who deals with corpses. The Doms are a particular variety of 'Chandalas'.

death-dealing matter the earth was meant to give off at the touch of the first plough.[23] The Dalit's body was thus the buffer between life and death. It absorbed all that could spell death to humans. The prejudice against that body was and is part of the habitus of upper-caste embodied selves.

I do not wish to enter policy or legal debates here—firstly, because I am not competent to do that, and, secondly, because the prejudice against the Dalit body has survived legal and policy initiatives (which is not to devalue these initiatives—we need them). Subaltern studies failed to account for the Dalit because it had no material theory of the body, its 'subaltern' was a representative of an 'insurgent consciousness'. But that is not where I want to return. I want to suggest to you that once you grant me the structure of exclusion—the reaction of disgust it produces in the bodies of 'cleaner' castes—we can think of the Dalit body as precisely the body that helps us to think of the planet in this age of environmental crisis that passes by the name of 'global warming'. To do so, however, we need to get beyond the moves in political philosophy that privilege the abstract, unmarked individual body either as the carrier of rights or as the ground on which to situate that Marxist category of 'abstract labour', so necessary to Marx's critique of capital. Our thoughts on human flourishing perhaps cannot be grounded any more in frameworks that focus on the individual human, irrespective of the total number of humans on the planet, and that thus bracket all questions of connections between human and other forms of life and their profound relationship to the Earth-system processes.

Fanon said, as I have mentioned before, the black person had no 'corporeal schema'. It is possible for a non-black person to forget, for instance, what his or her own particular body looks like and be aware in everyday consciousness of just a bodily schema, such as having a vague awareness that he or she has two hands without necessarily remembering or visualizing the colour or the shape or the age of the hands. The racialized and oppressed black person, according to Fanon, could not do that, for he or she could never forget—even in their sleep—that he or she was black, so deep was the mark that race left on their own embodied sense of themselves. One might be tempted to think likewise

---

[23] Gyan Prakash, *Bonded Histories: Genealogies of Labor Servitude in Colonial India* (Cambridge: Cambridge University Press, 2003).

of the Dalit body. One could argue that the Dalit person, his or her body always already marked by its proximity to and contact with faeces and animals under conditions where the Brahmanical schema of the body dominates, can never experience a general schema of the human body. The Brahman's disgust, as Dumont argues, is inseparable from the stigma the Dalit body bears.

I would, however, resist surrendering completely to such a line of thinking. To put the Brahmin's disgust and the Dalit's closeness to faeces and dead animals into an inseparable binary opposition is to remain locked in a kind of humanism that overlooks the live matter in faeces and animals, dead or alive—in short, the question of microbes. Since this fact is often forgotten in ontological thinking about the human, where the human stands all alone and in abstraction from other life forms in the world, we could look upon the Dalit's body as both an acknowledgment and a reminder of all the other living bodies we need in order to keep our human bodies alive. If we could get out—even in pro-Dalit thought that only focuses on injustice between humans—of anthropocentric thinking, then we could see the Dalit's body as the body that makes us aware of all the networks of connections between different life forms that enables humans, as a form of creaturely life, to survive. The Dalit's body is itself constructed non-anthropocentrically—it is always human *with* animals, live or dead, and embedded in the world of microbes (with its relationship to waste). In that sense, the Dalit's is what I might call the planetary body. In saying this, I do not at all mean to romanticize the vulnerability of the bodies of the poor, be they Dalit or not. The thoughts I present here do not, for instance, in any way undermine the demand for more health-care services for the Dalit poor. Nor should my argument suggest that we make ourselves vulnerable to diseases and death. My point is about a different question: How do we (re-)imagine the human body today when global warming accompanies globalization, threatening planetary life with grave dangers? Do we continue to see the human body as something to be groomed in separation from all the connections we have with other forms of life or something that is a site where various forms of life, including the human one, converge (as in the case of any other animal body)? The Dalit body gives me a vantage point from which to think about such an imagination of the body—for this imagination is embedded in the very construction of this body. But that is not *as such* an argument against human flourishing, nor for justifying the deprivations and humiliations inflicted on the poor and the underprivileged.

Let me once again take a step back and explain.[24] It is becoming increasingly clear that the present scale of human activities is causing very serious disturbances, not only to the Earth system but also to the distribution of natural reproductive life on the planet. 2015 was the first year when the average surface temperature of the world rose by one degree Celsius above the pre-industrial average, thus taking us closer to the threshold of a two-degree rise, a Rubicon we are told we must not cross if we are to avoid what the United Nations Framework Convention on Climate Change (UNFCC) of 1992 described as 'dangerous anthropogenic interference with the climate system'.[25] 2016, as one meteorologist put it, was considered to be 'off the charts' as far as global warming is concerned.[26] Scholars conducting research on human-induced species' extinction in the context of anthropogenic climate change have long recognized the 'overreach' that humans have achieved, often to their own detriment, in the various ecosystems they inhabit.[27] In addition, well-known arguments about 'the great acceleration' and 'planetary boundaries' that some Earth scientists and other scholars have put forward are statements,

[24] This paragraph draws on my essay 'Humanities in the Anthropocene.'

[25] Tim Lenton, '2^0C or not 2^0C? That is the Question', *Nature* 473 (5 May 2011):7, http://www.nature.com/news/2011/110504/pdf/473007a.pdf, accessed on 11 February 2016. For the exact wording of the phrase, see *United Nations Framework Convention on Climate Change* (New York: United Nations, 1992), Article 2, 4, https://unfccc.int/resource/docs/convkp/conveng.pdf, accessed on 11 February 2016.

[26] Eric Holtaus, 'When Will The World Really Be 2 Degrees Hotter Than It Used To Be?', *FiveThirtyEight*, 23 March 2016, http://fivethirtyeight.com/features/when-will-the-world-really-be-2-degrees-hotter-than-it-used-to-be/, accessed on 25 March 2016. I am grateful to my colleague James Chandler for drawing my attention to this article.

[27] Jessica C. Stanton, K.T. Shoemaker, R.G. Pearson, and H.R. Akçakaya, 'Warning Times for Species Extinction due to Climate Change', *Global Change Biology* 21 (2015): 1066–77; Rodolfo Dirzo, Hillary S. Young, Mauro Galetti, Gerardo Ceballos, Nick J.B. Isaac, and Ben Collen, 'Defaunation in the Anthropocene',, *Science* 345, no. 6195 (2014): 401–6; Celine Bellard, Cleo Bertelsmeier, Paul Leadley, Wilfried Thuiller, and Franck Courchamp, 'Impacts of Climate Change on the Future of Biodiversity', *Eco. Lett.* 15, no. 4 (April 2012): 365–77; Gerardo Ceballos, Paul R. Ehrlich, Anthony D. Barnosky, Andres Garcia, Robert M. Pringle, and Todd M. Palmer, 'Accelerated Modern Human-Induced Species Losses: Entering the Sixth Mass Extinction', *Science Advances* 1, no. 5 (19 June 2015): 1–5.

precisely, about ecological overshoot on the part of humans. As one of the authors of the 'great acceleration' thesis put it, 'the term "Great Acceleration" aims to capture the holistic, comprehensive and interlinked nature of the post-1950 changes simultaneously sweeping across the socio-economic and biophysical spheres of the Earth System, encompassing far more than climate change.'[28] Their data document exponential rise in human population, real GDP, urban population, primary energy use, fertilizer consumption, paper production, water use, transportation, and so on—all happening after the 1950s. And there is corresponding rise in 'Earth systems trends' to do with the emission of carbon dioxide, methane, nitrous oxide, ocean acidification, loss of stratospheric ozone, marine fish culture, shrimp aquaculture, tropical forest loss, terrestrial biosphere degradation, and so on.[29] Similarly, the idea of nine 'planetary boundaries' that humans should avoid crossing that was put forward in 2009 by Johan Rockström and his colleagues at the Stockholm Resilience Centre was also an exercise in measuring human ecological overshoot.[30] Some Earth system scientists recently observed that 'the present anthropogenic carbon release rate [around 10 Petagram C year; 1 Pg = 10^{15} grams] is unprecedented during the [entire] Cenozoic (past 66 Myr)'. Further, they said, 'the present/future rate of climate change and ocean acidification is too fast for many species to adapt' and will likely result in 'widespread future extinctions in marine and terrestrial environments'. We are, effectively, in 'an era of no-analogue state, which represents a fundamental challenge to constraining future climate projections'.[31]

[28] Will Steffen, Wendy Broadgate, Lisa Deutsch, Owen Gaffney, and Cornelia Ludwig, 'The Trajectory of the Anthropocene: The Great Acceleration', *The Anthropocene Review* 2, no. 1 (2015): 1–18.

[29] Steffen et al., 'The Trajectory of the Anthropocene.'

[30] J. Rockström, W. Steffen, K. Noone, A. Persson, F.S. Chapin, III, E. Lambin, T.M. Lenton, M. Scheffer, C. Folke, H. Schellnhuber, B. Nykvist, C.A. De Wit, T. Hughes, S. van der Leeuw, H. Rodhe, S. Sörlin, P.K. Snyder, R. Costanza, U. Svedin, M. Falkenmark, L. Karlberg, R.W. Corell, V.J. Fabry, J. Hansen, B. Walker, D. Liverman, K. Richardson, P. Crutzen, and J. Foley, 'Planetary Boundaries: Exploring the Safe Operating Space for Humanity', *Ecology and Society* 14, no. 2 (2009): 32, http://www.ecologyandsociety.org/vol14/iss2/art32/, accessed on 20 February 2016.

[31] Richard E. Zeebe, Andy Ridgwell, and James C. Zachos, 'Anthropogenic Carbon Release Rate Unprecedented during the Past 66 Million Years', *Nature geoscience*, published online 21 March 2016, http://www.nature.com/ngeo/index.html, accessed on 24 March 2016.

Not only have marine creatures and many other terrestrial species not had the evolutionary time needed to adjust to our increasing capacity to hunt or squeeze them out of existence, but our greenhouse gas emissions also threaten the biodiversity of the great seas, and thus endanger the very same food web that feeds us. Jan Zalasiewicz and his colleagues on the sub-committee of the International Stratigraphy Commission charged with documenting the Anthropocene—the name Earth system scientists propose for our present geological period, indicating the end of the most recent geological period, the Holocene that began about 11,700 B.P.—point out that it is the human footprint left in the rocks of this planet as fossils and other forms of evidence, such as terraforming of the ocean beds, that will constitute the long-term record of the Anthropocene, perhaps more so than the excess greenhouse gases in the atmosphere. If human-driven extinction of other species results—say, in the next few centuries—in a Great Extinction event, then (my geologist friends tell me) even the epoch-level name of the Anthropocene may be too low in the hierarchy of geological periods.[32]

While many scholars in animal studies used to argue in the 1970s and the 1980s—and many still do—that humans could take charge of the planet or 'nature' by extending the human moral domain all over it, the knowledge that the bulk of life is microbial in form upsets that thinking. As Martin J. Blaser observes, microbes not only 'outnumber all the mice, whales, humans, birds, insects, worms, and trees combined—indeed all the visible life-forms we are familiar with on Earth—they … outweigh them as well'.[33] Could we ever be in a position to value the existence of viruses and bacteria hostile to us, except in so far as they influence—negatively or positively—our lives? Here again, the question is complicated by the fact that ecology and pathology often give us changing and contrary perspectives. Bacteria and viruses have played critical and, often, positive roles in human evolution, such as the ancient stomach bacteria *H. (Helicobacter) Pylori*. But since the rise of antibiotics and the consequent changes in the biotic environments of our stomach,

[32] 'If global warming and a sixth extinction take place in the next couple of centuries, then an epoch will seem too low a category in the hierarchy [of the geological timetable].' Professor Jan Zalasiewicz, personal communication with author, 30 September 2015.

[33] Martin J. Blaser, *Missing Microbes: How the Overuse of Antibiotics is Fueling Our Modern Plagues* (New York: Picador, 2014), 13–14, 15, 16.

however, *H. Pylori* has come to be seen as a pathogen.[34] We cannot be responsible stewards for these life forms even when we cognitively know about the critical role they have played—and will continue to play—in the natural history of life, including that of human life itself.[35] This much, however, is increasingly becoming clear: that human life and the question of its continuation on the planet is deeply tied to the fact that multiple other life forms have to flourish in order for us to enjoy the food web in which we are embedded even if we are situated at a critical nodal point of the web.

This raises new questions about our given political categories that are usually imagined in profoundly anthropocentric ways. Take the human–animal conflict that is ubiquitous in South Asia today. The so-called 'monkey menace' in Delhi, caused by habitat loss for monkeys, is a matter of everyday experience. Almost every week, for example, the media carries reports about human–leopard or human–elephant conflicts (as a simple Google search will confirm). The question is: Contra Hannah Arendt, can the figure of the refugee remain only human anymore? Should we not think of wild animals such as leopards, monkeys, and elephants that turn up as unwelcome guests in South Asian cities as refugees too? And we have not even begun to think about our relationship to microbial life though biologists have some definite knowledge of their role in our pasts and futures (viral responsibility for human differences of phenotypes, for instance). However, to find a beginning to such thinking, we need to imagine the human not in isolation from other forms of life, in the blinding light of humanism, as it were, but as a form of life connected to other forms of life that are all connected to the geobiology of the planet and are dependent on these connections for their own welfare.

I call this new imagination of the human, the planetary body or the body we need to imagine as part of a new planetary consciousness. This is indeed the meaning that I suggest Rohith Vemula intended when, in his suicide note, he celebrated 'man as a glorious thing made up of stardust'. This statement was not a piece of empty rhetorical flourish, nor a figment of romantic imagination but actually a scientific idea on which

---

[34] Blaser, *Missing Microbes,* Chapter. 9.

[35] Luis P. Villarreal, 'Can Viruses Make Us Human?' *Proceedings of the American Philosophical Society* 148, no. 3 (September 2004): 296–323; Linda M. van Blerkom, 'Role of Viruses in Human Evolution', *Yearbook of Physical Anthropology* 46 (2003) 14–46.

my Chicago colleague Neil Shubin has written illuminatingly: 'Each galaxy, star, or person is the temporary owner of particles that have passed through the births and deaths of entities across vast reaches of time and space.'[36] Vemula's thoughts—his protest against the oppressions of caste and against what is in India called 'vote-bank politics'—shuttled between two perspectives: a humanist one ('never was a man treated as a mind') and a non-anthropocentric perspective derived from science, of man seen as 'a glorious thing made up of stardust'. The Dalit body, with its inseparability from waste/microbes, animals, and life and death processes, remains—precisely because of the Brahmanical disgust—a site of simultaneous avowal and disavowal of humans as we urgently need to imagine them. All we need to do, to make a small beginning, is to convert the negative sign under which the Brahman classifies the Dalit body into a positive one, and to supplement with non-anthropocentric perspective the exclusive anthropocentrism that sometimes limits even informed, thoughtful, and insurgent Dalit critiques of the Brahmanical schema of oppression.

[36] Neil Shubin, *The Universe Within: The Deep History of the Human Body* (New York: Vintage Books, 2013), 33.

2

Stigma or Red Tape? Roadblocks in the Use of Affirmative Action

*Ashwini Deshpande**

Critics of affirmative action (AA) have for long argued that the policy is unfair to non-beneficiaries because it denies entry to eligible and

* Acknowledgement: Department of Economics, Delhi School of Economics, University of Delhi, Delhi. The 'Education and Social Mobility Survey, 2014-15' used for some of the results reported in this chapter has received funding from the European Union Seventh Framework Programme (*FP7/2007-2013*) under *grant agreement* n° 290752. This survey would not have been possible without my PhD student Apoorva Gupta's initiative and efforts, and her excellent leadership and management of the survey. I would like to thank her and the entire team of research assistants for their sterling fieldwork. Thanks are also due to Yatish Arya, Mrinalini Jha, and S. Prasham for their help with the qualitative interviews and to Lakshita Jain for her help with transcribing interviews and organizing the background data for the qualitative section. Abhinash Bora, Rajesh Ramachandran, and participants at the conference on 'Prejudice, Stigma and Discrimination: Combatting Exclusions Through Policy and Law,' University of Chicago, Delhi Centre, gave extremely useful comments. I take responsibility for all remaining errors and omissions. The full version of the paper can be found at http://www.cdedse.org/pdf/work280.pdf.

meritorious candidates for prized positions.[1] This is now complemented by a view that AA is harmful to the beneficiaries because of two reasons. One, it sets beneficiaries up for failure due to potential 'mismatch' because they are granted entry into programmes that they might not be equipped to handle. Two, it doubly stigmatizes them: in addition to the stigma on account of their identity, it stamps them with a stigma of incompetence. Thus, the argument goes, AA ends up doing more harm than good.

The question of the added stigma of AA is hard to gauge as low-ranked groups are often negatively stereotyped for a multiplicity of reasons, including being considered incompetent. Thus, if they are stigmatized in institutional contexts where they have gained entry through AA, it is not immediately apparent to what extent AA might be responsible for the incremental increase in stigma, over and above what they would have experienced on account of their 'stigmatized ethnic identity'.[2] Typically, because AA is seen as a policy that grants entry to presumably less 'meritorious'[3] individuals from low-ranked groups in place of more 'meritorious' individuals from high-ranked groups, it is widely resented, both by those who are denied entry, as well as the general public who might not be personally directly affected by AA. Thus, AA beneficiaries might often face hostility and discrimination inside institutions where they gain access. However, would they be less stigmatized had they not availed of AA to gain entry into a given institution, and had instead chosen another trajectory of study or work? This is a counterfactual question, and thus is not easy to estimate precisely.

There are three important dimensions of stigma of AA that can be explored more directly. First, do beneficiaries internalize the stigma they

---

[1] L.M. Leslie, D.M. Mayer, and D.A. Kravitz, 'The Stigma of Affirmative Action: A Stereotyping-Based Theory and Meta-Analytic Test of the Consequences for Performance', *Academic of Management Journal* 57, no. 4 (2014): 964–89.

[2] Gerald D. Berreman, 'Self, Situation and Escape from Stigmatised Ethnic Identity' (paper, 70th Annual Meeting of the American Anthropological Association), http://eric.ed.gov/?id=ED058344, accessed on November 2016.

[3] A. Deshpande, *Affirmative Action in India*, Oxford India Short Introduction Series (New Delhi: Oxford University Press, 2013). The notion of using examination scores as an indicator of merit is problematic. However, examination scores are widely viewed as indicators of merit, and given that AA beneficiaries enter with lower scores, they are commonly viewed as less meritorious.

encounter in institutional settings where they have gained entry through AA? Second, more importantly from a policy perspective, does the fear of stigmatization affect the uptake of AA? Third, what is the experience of assimilation and integration of those who have availed of AA or reservations to gain entry? This latter dimension should be explored for all AA beneficiaries regardless of the degree of success they achieve in the programme, but given the focus on mismatch and anecdotal accounts of beneficiaries dropping out, it is especially important to record the experiences of those beneficiaries who successfully graduate.

The analytical apparatus of social psychology is particularly useful to probe the first question of internalization and its possible effect on beneficiary performance. In a companion paper,[4] I have attempted to explore the issue of 'externalization'—beneficiaries are stigmatized by their peers as incompetent, that is, stigma exists, versus 'internalization'—beneficiaries internalize the low valuation that their peers place upon them, lowering their own self-worth, that is, existence of stigma leads to a lowering of self-worth. While earlier literature treated the existence of stigma as synonymous with its internationalization by the stigmatized individuals, the more recent literature, particularly the Stereotype Content Model[5] questions the almost automatic presumption of internalization, and emphasizes the distinction between the existence of stigma (externalization) and its internalization.

In this chapter, my attempt is to investigate the second and third questions: Do individuals who are eligible for affirmative action lower their uptake because of fear of added stigmatization? Also, what were the actual experiences of individuals as they entered institutions, marked as AA beneficiaries? Given the multifaceted nature of these questions, I believe that a mixed-methods research methodology is most useful to get a glimpse into the nuances that shape these somewhat intractable issues. The assessment of uptake is hampered by lack of suitable data, as existing data sets do not allow us to estimate how uptake is affected by other factors, of which fear of stigmatization might be one. More broadly, data on the use of reservations are very hard to come by, even simply the

---

[4] A. Deshpande, 'Double Jeopardy? Caste, Affirmative Action and Stigma' (working paper, UNU-WIDER, Helsinki, 2016/71).

[5] S.T. Fiske, A.J. Cuddy, P. Glick, and J. Xu, 'A Model of (Often Mixed) Stereotype Content: Competence and Warmth Respectively Follow from Perceived Status and Competition', *Journal of Personality and Social Psychology* 82, no. 6 (2002): 878–902.

numbers of people using reservations.[6] I conducted a primary survey on a larger question of 'education and social mobility' in Delhi during 2014–15. Since I was curious about the role of stigma in the uptake of AA, I included a module in the survey in order to assess precisely the uptake of quotas by those who are eligible, and what factors account for non-use of AA. The main result from these data is that the bulk of non-use of quotas is not due to fear of added stigmatization. The overwhelming reasons for non-use are bureaucratic hurdles and red tape, which can be interpreted as institutional apathy or roadblocks preventing the successful implementation of the policy. Comparing individuals from the Scheduled Castes (SCs) or Dalits to those from Other Backward Classes (OBCs), I find that non-use of quotas due to possible additional stigmatization is a smaller factor for SCs, who belong to castes that are already highly stigmatized, than for OBCs, who belong to castes and communities that might be low-ranked, but not necessarily stigmatized.

Additionally, with a team of students, in a separate small survey, we identified 'reserved category' individuals who had successfully graduated. We conducted semi-structured interviews that collected basic background information from everyone, but also included a qualitative component for personal narratives. The idea was to hear voices from the ground, especially from those who had successfully graduated. The section on 'Experiences of Successful Quota Students' contains a summary of the interviews. Needless to add, this component is exploratory and preliminary, and the idea is to pave the way for further research along this direction.

The rest of the chapter is organized as follows. The next section briefly describes the basic features of AA in India along with a brief review of the literature. After that, the results of the quantitative estimation based on data from the 'Education and Social Mobility' survey are presented. Then, a preliminary analysis of the qualitative interviews is given. The last section contains a discussion of the results, along with concluding comments.

Review of Related Literature

The affirmative action policy in India is primarily caste-based,[7] and consists of reserved seats or quotas in government-run educational

---

[6] I am engaged in a project, along with Marc Galanter, to collect data on the use of quotas.

[7] Additionally, 33 per cent seats are reserved for women in elected positions in rural and urban local bodies.

institutions, government jobs, and at all levels of government. 22.5 per cent seats are reserved for SCs and Scheduled Tribes (STs)—administrative umbrella categories that list the designated castes (jatis) and tribes. This is a modified version of a policy of reserving seats for untouchable castes[8] that started in the second decade of the twentieth century in certain parts of British India and the princely states.[9] Additionally, 27 per cent seats are reserved for OBCs[10] at the central level, in jobs since 1993, and in educational institutions since 2008. While SC and ST are administrative categories, I would also use Dalit (meaning the oppressed, a term of pride used for self-identification for castes that were considered untouchable such that any contact with them was considered polluting) and Adivasi (meaning literally, the original inhabitants) for the caste and tribal categories, respectively.

There is a small body of literature on the 'mismatch hypothesis' in the Indian context, which finds little or no evidence of mismatch.[11] There is now growing literature on the question of the added stigma of affirmative action in the context of the United States[12]. In India, this literature is in its infancy, and there are only a handful of works on this

---

[8] These were castes so low in the hierarchy that they were not even fit to be assigned a varna status (the *avarna*s, or the one without a varna).

[9] I have discussed the policy in detail elsewhere. See Deshpande, *Affirmative Action in India*.

[10] For details on the OBC category, as well as their relative placement in the caste hierarchy, see Deshpande and Ramachandran, 'The Changing Contours Of Intergroup Disparities And The Role Of Preferential Policies In A Globalizing World: Evidence From India', Centre for Development Economics Working Paper No. 267, December 2016. It should be noted that while OBC reservation at the central level is 27 per cent, states have had different quotas for certain non-SC–ST castes and communities since Independence.

[11] M. Bertrand, R. Hanna, and S. Mullainathan, 'Affirmative Action in Education: Evidence from Engineering College Admissions in India', *Journal of Public Economics* 94, no. 1–2 (2010): 16–29. See also S. Bagde, D. Epple, and L. Taylor, 'Does Affirmative Action Work? Caste, Gender, College Quality, and Academic Success in India', *American Economic Review* 106, no. 6 (2016): 1495–521.

[12] Leslie, Mayer, and Kravitz, 'The Stigma of Affirmative Action'; Krishmurthy and Edlin, 'Affirmative Action and Stereotypes in Higher Education Admissions", "Prasad Krishnamurthy and Aaron Edlin', National Bureau of Economic Research Working Paper Series, number 20629", October 2014, doi {10.3386/w20629}, available at http://www.nber.org/papers/w20629.

subject. Gudavarthy[13] and Gille[14] examine this explicitly, and various papers in Guru[15] discuss stigma related to reservations as parts of larger arguments. Gudavarthy focuses on the OBC 'politics of recognition', related to their demand for reservations, and how this might alter the terms of the discussion around 'democracy, equality and dignity' which is dominated by 'received ... dominant ... upper caste discourse'.[16] The argument is that the recent demand for quotas by higher-ranked OBCs might help de-stigmatize reservations, as it would no longer be the preserve of the traditionally stigmatized castes, who are low-ranked and considered incompetent. Gille investigates the use of quotas and finds that OBCs with greater land ownership (richer, higher status) tend not to use reservations, but that the use of reservations by SCs is not related to their economic status.[17]

In a companion paper,[18] based on concepts and theories from social psychology, I investigate, through a primary survey in colleges and departments of the University of Delhi, whether Dalit and Adivasi students internalize the stigma of incompetence that their peers mark them with. I find that the stigma is real, that is, upper-caste peers believe that 'quota students' are incompetent and do not deserve to be in the institution. This does lead to an increase in pressure due to greater 'academic performance burden' for beneficiaries, but they do not internalize the stigma, that is, they do not consider themselves less capable than their peers. However, the question of internalization is not easy to settle; Hoff and Pandey's analysis suggests that stereotype threat, or invoking a stigmatized identity, might shift the performance of stigmatized individuals in the direction of the stereotype (that is, downwards).[19] Whether this happens due to deep-seated internalization or not is difficult to gauge.

[13] A. Gudavarthy, 'Can We De-Stigmatise Reservations in India?', *Economic and Political Weekly* 47, no. 6 (2012): 55–62.

[14] V. Gille, 'Stigma in Affirmative Action Application? Evidence from Quotas in India' (mimeo, 2013).

[15] G. Guru, ed., *Humiliation: Claims and Context*, Oxford India Paperbacks Series (New Delhi: Oxford University Press, 2009).

[16] Gudavarthy, 'Can We De-Stigmatise Reservations in India?', 55, 62.

[17] Gille, 'Stigma in Affirmative Action Application?'.

[18] Deshpande, 'Double Jeopardy?'.

[19] Hoff, Karla, and Priyanka Pandey. 2006. 'Discrimination, Social Identity, and Durable Inequalities', *American Economic Review*, 96 (2): 206–11.

While the body of literature on the particular stigma of affirmative action is small, there is a very large and rich volume of historical and sociological research on the caste system, pioneered by seminal analyses of thinkers such as Jyotirao Phule, B.R. Ambedkar, and Periyar E.V. Ramasamy who have articulated insightful and searing critiques of the caste hierarchy and convincingly demonstrated how it is discrimina-tory, exploitative, and oppressive towards historically untouchable jatis associated with menial, polluting, and, hence, stigmatizing tasks. While untouchability is legally abolished in independent India, and is punish-able by law, overt and covert instances of untouchability continue.[20] Dalits, thus, battle a 'stigmatized ethnic identity' regardless of whether they use reservations. Use of reservations could add an extra dimension to the stigma, or simply confirm upper-caste prejudice that Dalits can-not make it without the crutch of affirmative action.

Does Fear of Stigmatization Affect Uptake of Quotas?

This section examines the central question of this chapter, whether there are any differences in the use of quotas between SC–STs (already highly stigmatized) and OBCs (lower ranked, but not necessarily stigmatized) that could be associated with the perception of stigma. No data set in the public domain explores this issue. Gille uses the Additional Rural Income Survey and Rural Economic and Demographic Survey (ARIS-REDS) data which ask respondents the following question: 'Have you or any member of your family taken advantage of provisions under reservations to seek admission in educational institution in 2005–06?'[21] However, this data set does not have information on whether any indi-vidual actually went to a higher educational institution, where they might have needed to use reservations. Thus, the data are highly inad-equate to investigate the issue of stigma, which could potentially arise

[20] Ghanshyam Shah, Harsh Mandar, Sukhadeo Thorat, Satish Deshpande, and Amita Baviskar, *Untouchability in Rural India* (New Delhi: SAGE Publications, 2006); Navsarjan Trust, *Understanding Untouchability: A Comprehensive Study of Practices and Conditions in 1589 Villages* (Ahmedabad: Robert F. Kennedy Centre for Justice and Human Rights and Navsarjan Trust, 2010); A. Thorat and O. Joshi, 'The Continuing Practice of Untouchability in India: Patterns and Mitigating Influences' (working paper 3, India Human Development Study, 2015).

[21] Gille, 'Stigma in Affirmative Action Application?'.

when eligible individuals, who could have used reservations, chose not to do so. Gille interprets the entire non-use of quotas as arising because of stigma, because of not being able to distinguish between those who did not use it out of choice (that is, did not use it when they could have), and those who did not pursue higher education, and therefore, the question of using or not using quotas never arose for them.[22] Also, for those who could have used reservations but did not, there could be other reasons for not using reservations, and the ARIS-REDS data do not allow the investigation of any of those reasons. Finally, inadequate as it is, in the ARIS-REDS survey, this question is asked only about the use of reservations in education, not employment. Thus, even if the question were properly framed, it would capture only one dimension of quota use. Note that this is a survey conducted only in rural areas where the proportion of quota users is lower as opportunities for higher education and government jobs (where quotas are applicable) are far lower than in urban areas. Thus, overall, this data set is not suitable to capture either the use of quotas, or the reasons behind (non-)use.

Data: Education and Social Mobility Survey, 2014–15

Results in this section are based on one module of a retrospective primary survey that I conducted for another project on 'Education and Social Mobility'. As a part of the research design, 1,049 young men who finished high school in 2003 from government schools in the city of Delhi were sampled in 2014–15. Thus, these men had already been out of high school for 11–12 years, and the survey gathered detailed information about their educational and occupational trajectories during that period. The sample consisted of one gender and was drawn from the same academic cohort from state-run high schools of relatively similar quality. Thus, the starting position of these men as they embarked on their post-high-school lives was expected to be relatively homogeneous.

I designed one module in this survey to gather information about the use of reservations—who used it and who did not, despite belonging to caste groups that were eligible for quotas—and if they did not use reservations, what reasons might account for the non-use. To the best of my knowledge, this is the only large-scale quantitative data set that enables a precise assessment of reasons for non-use of quotas by those who are eligible. In addition to data on the respondents' educational

---

[22]   Gille, 'Stigma in Affirmative Action Application?'.

and occupational trajectories, the data set has detailed information on the socio-economic characteristics of their families—parents, siblings, and close relatives as well as friends. Among other variables, I also have information on the ownership of 14 consumer durables per household. I have combined this data into an 'asset index', using the methodology of 'principal components analysis' and, based on the values of the index, divided the sample into bottom 40 per cent (asset class 1), middle 40 per cent (asset class 2), and top 20 per cent (asset class 3). This is a rough, and somewhat arbitrary, division of the respondents into 'poor', 'middle class', and 'rich'. Note that since the sample was drawn from those who studied in government-run schools, it excluded the actual rich section of the population that sends their children to private schools.[23]

Use of Reservations

Out of the total sample of 1,049 men, 396 individuals (38 per cent) were eligible for AA: 228 from the SC–ST category[24] and 168 from the OBC category. Eligibility is defined in the following way: these men belonged to beneficiary groups and had the minimum qualifications needed to take advantage of job or education quotas, or both (Class X for jobs, Class XII for higher education). Of these, 114 (27 per cent of the eligible men) used reservations in education or jobs, or both.

Table 2.1 (Part A) shows that a greater proportion of SC-STs (44 per cent), compared with OBCs (around 8 per cent), used reservation at least once in their lives. Of those who used reservations, 89 per cent were SC–STs, and 11 per cent were OBCs. Part B of Table 2.1 shows that of those who used reservation in education, the overwhelming proportion (92 per cent) consisted of SC–STs. The lower use of educational quotas by OBCs needs to be understood in the specific context of these respondents. These respondents were in undergraduate programmes during years when education quotas had not been extended to OBCs. In their verbal responses, several OBC respondents said that they would have used reservations if they had the opportunity to do so.

---

[23] The full paper with empirical details is available at Ashwini Deshpande, 'Stigma or Red Tape: Roadblocks in the Use of Affirmative Action' (working paper no. 280, Centre for Development Economics, Delhi School of Economics, New Delhi, October 2017), http://www.cdedse.org/pdf/work280.pdf.

[24] There were only two ST individuals in this survey, so they have been clubbed with the SCs.

Table 2.1   Use of Quotas by Eligible Individuals

Part A: Quota Use			
	SCST	OBC	Total
Used quota	44.3	7.74	28.79
Did not use	55.7	92.26	71.21
Total	**100**	**100**	**100**
Part B: Edu or Jobs			
	SCST	OBC	Total
Eduquota	92.31	7.69	**100**
Jobquota	79.31	20.69	**100**
Any quota	88.6	11.4	**100**

Source: Author's calculations.

Prior to assessing how many opted to use quotas for jobs, we first need to see how many worked in government jobs, where quotas are applicable. Only 13 per cent of those eligible for quotas worked in government jobs (15 per cent of SC–STs and 10.5 per cent of OBCs). Thus, the overwhelming majority of the young men in the sample were working in the private sector where quotas are not applicable. Of those who were working in government jobs, 37 per cent used job quotas, with 43 per cent of SC–STs and 22 per cent of OBCs using job quotas.

Users versus Non-Users

Let us call those who have used AA at least once 'users' and those who have never used AA 'non-users'. The stream chosen by respondents in their higher secondary years is significantly correlated with the use of quotas. Of those who are users, 52 per cent are those who opted for arts/humanities in Class XII, 20 per cent studied commerce, 12 per cent are those who opted for science without biology (the engineering stream), and 16 per cent are those who opted for science with biology.

Overall, 56 per cent users were first-generation beneficiaries; that is, no one in their families from earlier generations had used quotas. Here, the difference between SC–STs and OBCs is stark, reflecting the longer period for which SC-ST quotas have been in application. Of the SC–STs who used quotas, 54 per cent were first-generation beneficiaries, with the corresponding proportion for OBCs being 80. What is note-worthy is that despite such a long history, over half the SC–ST users are first-generation beneficiaries.

Testing for differences in various socio-economic characteristics of users and non-users, we find that on most background characteristics, users have higher socio-economic characteristics than non-users. The average years of education of fathers of users are higher than that for non-users.

The two statistically significant differences are in Class XII scores and years of education. These are users having a higher average score (57 per cent) than non-users (54 per cent) and higher average years of educa-tion (16 years, compared to non-users' 15 years). This is to be expected because those with higher scores are more likely to study further and/or apply for government jobs where they might need to use reservations. This could be either due to the fact that those who score higher marks are more motivated, and/or that their probability of getting admission into college is higher. Additionally, we should note that the more 'meri-torious', judged by the narrow criterion of Class XII scores, are the ones who actually use quotas.

Those who do not study further, if interested in government jobs, would tend to apply for jobs that are at the bottom of the hierarchy. Several of these jobs, for instance, especially positions of cleaners, have an over-representation of SC–STs such that their proportion is much higher than the mandated quotas. Thus, access to such jobs is not facili-tated through quotas. This is because, in India, cleaning is the traditional occupation of a highly stigmatized caste that is considered untouchable. If stigma were to be a reason to discourage the uptake of AA, then it should matter more to the better-off families; however, prima facie, that does not seem to be the case in our data.[25]

What Factors Explain the Use of Quotas?

The estimates reveal that OBCs in this sample are significantly less likely to use reservations compared to SC–STs for every level of Class XII scores at average levels of father's education. For SC–STs, the prob-ability of quota use increases monotonically with an increase in Class

[25] For a discussion on this issue, see A. Deshpande and T.E. Weisskopf, 'Does Affirmative Action Reduce Productivity? A Case Study of the Indian Railways', *World Development* 64 (December 2014): 169–80.

XII scores. However, for OBCs, an increase in scores beyond 76 per cent reduces the probability of using quotas to close to zero. Recall that in this particular sample, OBC men were not entitled to education quotas when they were students. This could be one reason explaining the lower use of quotas.

Examining probability of use separately for the three asset classes reveals nuances in the process. The poorest SC–STs are most likely to use quotas, and the richest OBCs least likely. This result is consistent with Gille's result that richer OBCs are least likely to use quotas, maybe because they do not need to use them.[26] Given the objective of affirmative action, that is, to enable entry for those who are not likely to make it on their own, this pattern suggests that those who need it the most are indeed the most likely to use it.

Reasons for Not Using AA

Those who did not use reservations even once were asked about the reasons behind their decision and were given six options to choose from: (a) not eligible (those who did not have the minimum marks for applying, even with the lower eligibility for reserved category candidates, or OBCs who were not eligible at the time as they were students at a time when there were no quotas for OBCs); (b) to show one could do without government help; (c) did not want added stigma of reservation (that is, of being in the 'reserved category'); (d) did not know about the scheme (information constraints); (e) no occasion to use it (for example, if the respondent went to a private institution after class XII, or was in private employment); and (f) bureaucratic difficulties. Of these, (c) is a direct indicator of 'additional stigma of reservations'. Reason (b) is more an indicator of self-confidence or high self-esteem, reflecting a positive attitude, but it could also indicate the desire to not be stigmatized as quota beneficiaries. Those who chose option (f) were further asked to verbalize the kinds of difficulties they faced. The reasons given were illuminating and offer insights into the administrative difficulties in accessing reservations. These include factors such as 'the process is complicated' and/or 'the documentation required is tough'; caste certificates from the village/ district centre were not accepted in Delhi, and individuals were asked to make fresh certificates in the city; corruption (several reported that they were asked to give bribes); and explanations such as 'tried to use

---

[26] Gille, 'Stigma in Affirmative Action Application?'.

reservations on an earlier occasion, did not make it, hence did not try to use them again'.

About 9 per cent of non-users cite additional stigma (reason [b]) as the reason for them not using reservations, and 16 per cent if both reasons (b) and (c) are included as 'stigma'. For SC–ST, this proportion citing reason (b) is roughly 2 per cent, and for OBCs, it is roughly 7. Thus, for individuals who are from groups that are already highly stigmatized, the additional stigma of reservations is not a very important concern. For OBCs, the single largest reason is bureaucratic difficulties. The proportion of non-users claiming they did not know about it is consistent with the figures on first-time use of reservations, and surprising given the long history of reservations.

To understand the socio-economic factors underlying reasons for not using reservations, we estimate multinomial logit regressions, with controls for asset class and caste group. For SC–STs, the probability of stigma as the reason for non-use is positive but small for the poorest asset class, but reduces to zero for middle and rich asset classes. However, the positive sentiment of 'don't need government help' sharply rises with asset class. For OBCs, 'not eligible', 'didn't know', and 'red tape' are more likely reasons than stigma. The probability of using stigma as a reason increases sharply across asset class for OBCs. It is useful to remind ourselves that OBCs do not face stigma similar to Dalits, and thus, it is not surprising to see that the richer OBCs are more likely to cite stigma as a reason, as these are individuals who would not otherwise be stigmatized.

Thus, there are other important reasons that contribute to non-use, and focusing on stigma would not only be a misreading of the causes, but would also take attention away from important administrative/bureaucratic reasons that hamper eligible candidates from using AA. The basic result from the present study is that stigma is not the primary reason for the non-use of quotas. Or to put it differently, the perceived costs associated with stigmatization are not as high as the perceived benefits from using affirmative action.

Experiences of Successful Quota Students

What about the experiences of those who actually enter institutions using affirmative action? To what extent is stigma a factor in their college years? This is very difficult to estimate quantitatively. In order to understand experiences of assimilation (or otherwise) of those who got into colleges on quota and successfully completed their degrees, I decided to conduct qualitative interviews with successful reservation beneficiaries.[27]

In a separate survey, 61 individuals were interviewed over a period of three months in 2015. These were mostly personal contacts of my students. The sample is not representative, and not amenable to rigorous statistical analysis, but because the respondents were known to my students, who themselves are upper middle class and therefore relatively advantaged, the experiences reported here are likely to be from the better-off among beneficiaries. If they faced actual discrimination or even battled with the perception of discrimination, then it is reasonable to conclude that those who deal with multiple disadvantages, that is, class along with a caste stigma, would face more serious issues related to assimilation. In any case, the idea was to listen to some voices in order to get greater insight into the experiences of quota beneficiaries, after they enter the institution, that is, after the formal completion of the policy: Do beneficiaries experience assimilation or rejection? As we will see in what follows, this short selection of stories contains multiple layers, in the sense that there are multiple reasons why individuals might feel marginalized, and does not reveal a straightforward narrative confirming the double stigma of affirmative action.

The Multiple Layers of Stigma

Several of the respondents reported not facing any discrimination on account of their quota status. M10, who got a PhD and now works as an assistant professor, belongs to one of the most stigmatized jatis, Chamar. His father was a government employee; thus, he is a second-generation beneficiary. His experience of being a student and employee is marked by his stigmatized ethnic identity, and he wishes he were born into another caste, as his life would have been much better. However, the stigma seems to emanate from his caste identity, rather than the fact that he used reservations. He believes 'upper castes retaliate, with violence if necessary, if Dalits dress better than them or get more marks'. M16, who is from the same caste, did not feel particularly stigmatized.

---

[27] After the data for this chapter had been collected and the first draft completed, the tragic suicide, in January 2016, of Rohith Vemula, a Dalit PhD scholar at the University of Hyderabad, brought issues of stigmatization, assimilation, discrimination, and harassment sharply to the fore in the public discourse. I have dealt with some of those issues in Deshpande, 'Double Jeopardy?'..

He had several upper-caste friends in university and found his teachers 'very helpful'. Similarly, Y61 did not feel discriminated against while he was a student, and supports reservations, but feels that we need to move to a situation where reservations become unnecessary. M4, from the Julaha caste, felt stigmatized due to his caste, not necessarily due to his quota status.

P11 felt discriminated against, and was not able to assimilate because of his shy nature. He feels reservations should be based on an income criterion, not caste, as that reinforces the feeling that lower-caste students are 'inferior'. P5 reported that lower-caste students tended to mingle with each other and did not easily mix with others. P10 reported that one of his teachers would 'distribute marks' through a list that had the reserved category status written against the names of beneficiary students, and he felt that this was discriminatory.

P6, from the Jatav caste, did not use a quota despite being eligible as he felt he could make it on his own. However, when he was on the job market, he felt that he was not equipped to compete as his 'skill set' was not sufficient. He felt university education did not provide students with the capital needed to compete well in the employment world. It is not clear to what extent he holds his background responsible for his inadequacy in meeting the demands of the job market.

M9 claims that he did not face any stigma in college, despite joining through quota, but does feel stigmatized in his workplace, as his colleagues know that he is a quota employee. M7 and M9 stressed the importance of networks for reserved category students.

Intersecting Identities

M13, who is a tribal from the North-east, felt that he was at the receiving end of racial discrimination. He also added that he might have been spared serious discrimination, as he is from a relatively better-off family. Y3 also faced taunts on account of his North-eastern identity.

M15 is visually impaired, as well as OBC. He felt stigmatized due to the 'excessive sympathy' that he received. His testimony brings to the fore the urgent need towards sensitization of peers regarding the appropriate behaviour towards people with disabilities.

M1 and M11, who are Muslim, used quotas only for admission to MA, not for prior education. They didn't feel the need to use it earlier. Their overall experience is positive and they felt that reservation helped them get that additional degree. M12, also a Muslim, did feel discriminated against on account of his religion and cited a situation where his teacher made him 'uncomfortable in the classroom by asking questions about his religion'.

M10 came to Delhi from a small town. He did not feel any bias in Delhi but did feel stigmatized on account of his caste in his hometown. He feels that these distinctions might be weaker in the metropolitan cities compared to small towns.

Accumulated Handicaps

Several students, like Y47, Y43, Y51, and P11, felt that lack of fluency in English was a handicap that most reserved category students had to battle with. M14, who has not yet started to work, felt that linguistic barriers kept him from integrating fully into the mainstream. He did not feel any overt caste-based discrimination or any additional stigma of being a reserved category student. Y43 felt severely disadvantaged due to the type of schooling he received, which after coming to university, he realized was markedly inferior to that of his upper-caste peers. Y42 echoes the weak schooling argument. P5 was a first-generation 'learner', and felt handicapped due to the fact that he had a lot to catch up with. M18 felt that the lack of fluency in English was a major obstacle for reserved category students. He felt that this 'bias is inherent in the attitudes of teachers as well. They treat them [reserved category students] condescendingly if they could not speak/write correct English ... quota students work very hard but end up scoring less than general category students'.

Y60, a Jatav, had two contrasting experiences in his undergraduate and postgraduate institutions. In the former, he faced ragging and bullying. He points out that 'category students' were demarcated and often upper-caste students refused to share rooms with them to avoid being polluted. He pointed out that the admission forms for the hostel were in a different colour for the 'category students', and this might have heightened caste consciousness. He did not face any such segregation in his master's classes.

The Time and Class Dimension

Y45 felt that discussions about quota are especially agitated in the first couple of months after university opens, but then students get on with the curriculum and admission-related issues take a back seat. Y38 felt alienated in the first year, but settled down in the second year and felt more assimilated in the second year. Both accounts seem to suggest that discrimination lessens with time spent in college.

One respondent brought out the issue of class within caste, or the 'creamy layer'. M2 felt that 'upper'[-class] Dalits discriminated against 'lower' [-class] Dalits and first-generation beneficiaries. He felt that this differentiation within reserved category students was important and some Dalits would act patronizingly towards other Dalits.

Female Voices

Most of the individuals who were interviewed were male, which reflects the unfortunate reality that beneficiaries of reservation tend to be disproportionately male. However, we were able to interview some women: 10 of the 61 respondents were female. Y57 felt stigmatized even though she was OBC (and not Dalit). She feels that stigmatizing attitudes are very common and that peers need to be sensitized towards reservations. She supports reservations wholeheartedly and asks 'inequality is going up and general category students are rising, so why should the backward students not be a given a chance to rise?'. Y56, from the Kushwaha caste,[28] felt severely disadvantaged, as her mother is illiterate, and even though she was motivated, there was nobody in her house who could help her study. She feels that it is difficult for reserved category students to adjust to the competitive life in the university. She is from Rajasthan, where everyone would ask her about what her father did and she felt that was to identify her caste. P2 did not feel any discrimination inside institutions but did not want to reveal her caste to anyone and did not want anyone to find out. She also pointed out that her teachers were all 'elite', and wondered if there had been nepotism in hiring them.

Stigmatizing Attitudes of Employees and Others

Y21 started out his college life very defensive about his caste identity and, more importantly, his reservation status. He avoided conversations with peers because inevitably those would start with a discussion about his marks, and he was afraid that by revealing his low marks, he would out himself as a reserved category student. However, as time passed, his

---

[28] This is classified as an OBC caste.

fears eased and he found himself assimilating into college life by making new friends. His overall experience was positive, but he feels that 'general category students don't understand the situation of "category" students'.

Y57, from the Sonar caste, got a prestigious scholarship after his entry into the college, for which he was chosen through open competition, being interviewed along with his peers. However, when he went to collect it, the administrative employee taunted him by suggesting that he got the scholarship because of a quota. He felt that such attitudes are very common. He feels his life would have turned out much better had he belonged to another (higher) caste. Y52, from the Chamar caste, himself never had any adverse experience in the university, but still feels that life might have been much better had he been born into another (higher) caste. Y49 also reported facing taunts from the office staff in her department who referred to her 'quota status'.

Y56 reports a story about her brother who was studying hard to prepare for university entrance exams but used to be repeatedly told that he need not bother; he would get in anyway due to quota. M17, from the Jatav caste (who declared himself to be an atheist), did not feel discrimination in college (where he had been admitted through quota), but did feel it in school. He claimed that his name had been left out from the hall of fame in his school because of his caste, despite the fact that he was a topper. Once his teacher refused to sign his scholarship letter, and he was often told that he should just sit for civil services where he will get in easily because of his quota status.

***

The reservation policy in India is a system of compensatory discrimination towards castes and communities that have been stigmatized and oppressed for centuries. The system is designed to counter exclusion that would come on account of prejudice, and allow entry to disadvantaged individuals to level the playing field in some spheres. However, due to Dalits' 'stigmatized ethnic identity', the policy of affirmative action is seen as unjust and anti-merit, as one of the dimensions of stigmatization is the assumption of incompetence.

This chapter investigates the issue of additional stigma of reservations through a mixed-methods research design. The quantitative estimates based on a primary survey in the city of Delhi indicate that use of reservation is not adversely affected due to fear of stigmatization. Red tape and bureaucratic hurdles, indicative of administrative apathy towards the policy, are far bigger constraints in the use of reservations than the fear of stigma. Overall, while stigma is one of the reasons underlying the non-use of reservations, it is not the primary reason. Also, for the already stigmatized Dalit and Adivasi individuals, it is a very small reason. It is a greater factor for the relatively rich students within the sample, than the poorer, and also a greater factor for OBCs, who do not suffer the stigma of untouchability, compared to the already stigmatized Dalits.

Instituting quotas is a way of ensuring access to higher education and good jobs. However, that is only the starting point—the test of the success of affirmative action lies in how well beneficiaries are able to integrate within institutions into which they gain entry. Rohith Vemula's tragic suicide in early 2016 has brought the issue of assimilation, alienation, and discrimination to the fore. Experiences of discrimination are unpleasant, and possibly traumatic and painful. It is likely that short interviews, such as the ones reported in this chapter, might not be able to capture the whole experience or get respondents to fully open up. Also, these are students who successfully completed their degree, which means that the combination of circumstances—their university experience, their own ability, internal motivation, and effort—worked to enable their success. This combination would be much more adverse for those who drop out.

Nevertheless, these interviews are useful and reveal, one, that even for the successful reserved category students, integration into colleges and university departments is not without challenges, but two, that success is possible; thus, affirmative action is not a lost cause. Most of the interviewees were supportive of reservations, and felt that they would not have been able to achieve what they did without it. This resonates with the findings of Bowen and Bok's seminal study of the long-term consequences of affirmative action in the United States.[29] Some, like P32 and P2, wanted reservations to be extended to the private sector. However, there were dissenting voices, who either advocated an income criterion or no reservation at all, despite themselves being beneficiaries of caste-based reservations.

The running thread in the interviews is the repeated reference to their caste, which indicates that even in contexts where affirmative action is not applicable, there is likely to be stigma arising on account of caste.

---

[29] William G. Bowen and Derek Bok, *The Shape of the River: Long-Term Consequences of Considering Race in College and University Admissions* (Princeton: Princeton University Press, paperback 2000.

Several respondents highlighted the disadvantages due to their relatively weaker pre-college background in terms of quality schooling, lack of fluency in English, lack of adequate academic support at home, and so forth. Accounts also pointed out discrimination in schools, and drew attention to a troubling tendency on the part of teachers and peers to actively thwart aspirations by discouraging lower-caste students from aiming high or pursuing their dreams. Several were told to just try for government jobs where they would get in easily on a quota, which the respondents found hurtful and insulting.

Access to quotas altered the respondents' life chances for the better. In the long run, I believe that these success stories will help weaken the stigmatizing association between low-caste status and incompetence. However, the multiplicity of challenges that beneficiaries faced indicates that affirmative action in the form of quotas is not a magic wand solution to the multifaceted problem of discrimination, and can only be one, albeit extremely crucial, link in a chain of policies that need to be designed to battle caste disadvantage.

3

Of Big Black Bucks and Golden-Haired Little Girls

How Fear of Interracial Sex Informed *Brown v. Board of Education* and Its Resistance

*Justin Driver**

In the spring of 1954, President Dwight Eisenhower invited Chief Justice Earl Warren to a small dinner party at the White House. The newly-confirmed chief justice of the United States was consumed with

* Justin Driver is the Harry N. Wyatt Professor of Law at the University of Chicago and the author of *The Schoolhouse Gate: Public Education, the Supreme Court, and the Battle for The American Mind* (Pantheon, 2018). Some selected portions of his contribution to this volume are drawn from that monograph. In addition, this chapter intermittently draws upon Justin Driver, 'Supremacies and the Southern Manifesto', *Texas Law Review* 92, no. 1053 (2014). Laura Ferry, Aziz Z. Huq, and Martha Nussbaum provided extremely helpful feedback on a previous draft of this chapter. Claire Bonelli and Samuel Fuller provided valuable research assistance. This chapter is dedicated to Morton Horwitz with whom I first had an opportunity to explore these ideas more than 15 years ago.

achieving unanimity in the upcoming *Brown v. Board of Education* decision, but Warren nonetheless made time to dine with the president.[1]
Upon arriving at the White House, Warren was surprised to learn that
one of his dining companions was John W. Davis, counsel for the South
Carolina school district in the pending school desegregation cases.
Eisenhower—despite realizing that the court had *Brown* under review—
not only sat Davis close to Warren, but also went to elaborate lengths
to tell Warren that Davis was a 'great man'.[2] Following dinner, as the
guests retired to another room for coffee, Eisenhower took Warren by
the arm and implored the chief justice to view the *Brown* case in a way
that went to the heart of fears concerning potential desegregation of
the public schools. 'These are not bad people,' Eisenhower said of white
Southerners. 'All they are concerned about is to see that their sweet little
girls are not required to sit in school alongside some big black bucks.'[3]

Eisenhower's language, while detestable, accurately identified the crux
of white opposition to school desegregation: an overwhelming dread
that racially integrated classrooms would lead to racially integrated bed-
rooms. Indeed, an all-consuming fear of miscegenation played a crucial,
underappreciated role in the *Brown* controversy. While prominent segregationists frequently identified miscegenation as the foremost reason
for opposing *Brown* and even proponents of desegregation took account
of that concern, such reasoning no longer occupies a central place in
the cultural imagination of the judiciary's effort to desegregate public
schools. Consequently, the standard scholarly account of *Brown*—the
most thoroughly scrutinized judicial decision of the twentieth century—
is deficient because it does not accord anxieties regarding interracial sex
the critical role that any coherent narrative of that case should include.
The *Brown* litigation—and the public's reaction to it—cannot be fully
understood, that is, until fears of miscegenation assume centre stage.
Recovering the case's sexual dimensions is nothing less than a vital task
if that dominant case is to be grasped in all of its complexity. Neither a
reflexive squeamishness about discussing sexual matters nor reluctance
to address stereotypes of black male hyper-sexuality should be permitted
to prevent engaging with this significant aspect of the *Brown* era.

---

[1] *Brown v. Board of Education*, 347 U.S. 483 (1954); Earl Warren, *The
Memoirs of Earl Warren* (1977), 292, New York: Doubleday & Co.

[2] Warren, *The Memoirs of Earl Warren,* 291.

[3] Bernard Schwartz, *Super Chief: Earl Warren and His Supreme Court—A
Judicial Biography* (1983), 113, New York: New York University Press.

It is, I contend in the pages that follow, simply impossible to understand the battle surrounding school desegregation without understanding the role that fear of miscegenation played in that struggle. Ten years before *Brown*, one of the pre-eminent chroniclers of racial conditions within the United States identified anti-miscegenation sentiment as forming the very backbone of Jim Crow. At every stage of the civil rights litigation involving education—from targeting graduate schools (rather than grade schools) for desegregation initially, to selecting lead plaintiffs who were difficult to caricature as sexual predators—attorneys sought to avoid inflaming such fears. The Supreme Court also demonstrated great awareness of the concerns regarding miscegenation—in its internal discussions about desegregation cases pre-*Brown*, in the way that Chief Justice Warren formulated *Brown* itself, and in its avoidance of interracial marriage and interracial cohabitation statutes post-*Brown*. The reaction to *Brown* among segregationists, moreover, often fixated upon the decision's implications for sexual intimacy between whites and blacks. Finally, after it became apparent that outright defiance of racial desegregation orders would no longer be permitted, many school districts introduced pupil assignment plans that segregated schools along gender lines. If black boys did not attend school with white girls, the thinking ran, it would be more difficult for the most reviled form of miscegenation to transpire. Although the material that follows recounts some deeply objectionable racial rhetoric and racist ideologies, it is necessary to recover those tropes of yesteryear if we are now to see clearly one of the Supreme Court's most important, venerated judicial opinions.[4]

[4] Some important modern scholarship about *Brown* has certainly referred to aspects of anti-miscegenation thought. But that prior scholarship has not pursued this trend in a systematic manner, and the sexual thread is thus left but one part of a much larger tapestry. For important modern scholarship about *Brown*, see Derrick Bell, *Silent Covenants*: Brown v. Board of Education *and the Unfulfilled Hopes for Racial Reform* (2004), New York: Oxford University Press; Michael J. Klarman, *From Jim Crow to Civil Rights: The Supreme Court and the Struggle for Racial Equality* (2004), New York: Oxford University Press; Richard Kluger, *Simple Justice: The History of* Brown v. Board of Education *and Black America's Struggle for Equality* (1975), New York: Knopf; Martha Minow, *In* Brown's *Wake: Legacies of America's Educational Landmark* (2010), New York: Oxford University Press; and James T. Patterson, Brown v. Board of Education: *A Civil Rights Milestone and Its Troubled Legacy* (2001), New York: Oxford University Press. Conversely, while other significant works of scholarship focused on interracial sex and interracial marriage mention *Brown*, they have

I

In the period preceding *Brown*, many white Americans viewed inter-racial sex and interracial marriage with open, unvarnished contempt. Perhaps the most prominent assessment of racial attitudes in the United States during this period is *An American Dilemma*, the landmark study published by Swedish sociologist Gunnar Myrdal in 1944. Myrdal argued that the nation's founding document—and, indeed, its underlying ethos—professes egalitarian aspirations, but that those aspirations have consistently been compromised by the country's debased treatment of blacks. For Myrdal, reconciling the nation's high-minded rhetoric with its actual treatment of the black race as inferior was the fundamental challenge facing the United States. The American citizen, Myrdal argued, was forced to 'frame his laws in terms of equality and to defend them before the Supreme Court—and before his own better conscience, which is tied to the American Creed—while knowing all the time that in reality his laws do not give equality to Negroes, and that he does not want them to do so'.[5]

It is impossible to overstate the significance of anti-miscegenation thought to Myrdal's understanding of race in the United States. Fear of interracial sex, Myrdal noted, is 'the principle around which the whole

---

not focused on that case in a sustained way. See Randall Kennedy, *Interracial Intimacies: Sex, Marriage, Identity, and Adoption* (2003), New York: Pantheon Books; Rachel F. Moran, *Interracial Intimacy: The Regulation of Race and Romance* (2001), Chicago: The University of Chicago Press; and Peggy Pascoe, *What Comes Naturally: Miscegenation Law and the Making of Race in America* (2010), New York: Oxford University Press. My hope is that this chapter will enable readers to appreciate that anti-miscegenation sentiment was nothing less than a pervasive force in *Brown v. Board of Education*.

Professor Randall Kennedy defines and offers context for the term miscegenation: 'The very term "miscegenation"—combining the Latin words *miscere* ("to mix") and *genus* ("race")—was coined during the presidential campaign of 1864, while the Civil War was still raging.' Kennedy, *Interracial Intimacies*, 20. Although the word 'miscegenation' was surely coined as a pejorative term, the appellation intermittently appears throughout this paper in a neutral manner as a synonym for the more cumbersome terms 'interracial sex' and/or 'interracial marriage'.

[5] Gunnar Myrdal, *An American Dilemma: The Negro Problem and Modern Democracy* (1944), 581, New York: Harper.

structure of segregation of the Negroes—down to disenfranchisement and denial of equal opportunities on the labor market—is organized'.[6] If white Americans were to bestow true equality upon blacks, the thinking ran, it would be impossible to prevent blacks from eventually having sex and intermarrying with whites. Myrdal observed that many segregationists defended their anti-miscegenation sentiments with the following, presumptively unanswerable query: 'Would you like to have your daughter marry a Negro?'[7] It is telling, of course, that the question usually concerned the matrimony of one's 'daughters', rather than one's 'sons', or even 'children', as whites were primarily concerned about the mythic potency of black male sexuality directed towards white females. Myrdal argued that this mantra revealed the overarching importance that many whites attached to forestalling any chance of interracial intimacy: 'The kernel of the popular theory of "no social equality" will, when pursued, be presented as a firm determination on the part of the whites to block amalgamation and preserve "the purity of the white race"'.[8] Ironically, Myrdal believed that it was white Americans' commitment to egalitarian rhetoric that compelled them to advance dubious arguments against social equality and interracial sex rather than to advocate straightforwardly for second-class citizenship for blacks. As Myrdal contended: 'The persistent preoccupation with sex and marriage in the rationalization of social segregation and discrimination against Negroes is … an irrational escape on the part of the whites from voicing an open demand for difference in social status between the two groups for its own sake….'[9]

It is a testament to how deeply entrenched notions of black inferiority were that even Myrdal, who portrayed blacks quite sympathetically in the context of the times, thought that the white loathing of blacks was not wholly irrational. 'In attempting to understand the motivation of segregation and discrimination,' Myrdal wrote, 'one basic fact to be taken into account is, of course, that many Negroes, particularly in the South, are poor, uneducated, and deficient in health, morals, and manners; and thus not very agreeable as social companions.'[10] If Myrdal, whose commitment to eradicating racial segregation was plain, deemed

[6] Myrdal, *An American Dilemma*, 587.

[7] Myrdal, *An American Dilemma*, 587.

[8] Myrdal, *An American Dilemma*, 586.

[9] Myrdal, *An American Dilemma*, 591.

[10] Myrdal, *An American Dilemma*, 582.

many blacks socially disagreeable, one can only imagine how people who took a less sanguine view of integration regarded the prospect of blacks as 'companions'—to say nothing of sexual partners.

A central way in which white Americans responded to their sexual insecurity, Myrdal contended, was by lynching black men. 'Lynching is a way of punishing Negroes for the white Southerner's own guilty feelings in violating Negro women, or for presumed Negro sexual superiority,' Myrdal contended.[11] Concerns about black male sexuality were—as they often have been—inextricably intertwined with societal advancements by blacks. Myrdal argued that blacks who were somehow perceived as 'uppity' seemed to fall prey to lynching more often than lower-class black men: 'The incident is usually some crime, real or suspected, by a Negro against a white, or merely a "racial insult", such as when a Negro buys an automobile or steps beyond the etiquette of race relations in any way.'[12] (Similarly, in his book on lynching, NAACP Secretary Walter White wrote: 'Lynching is much more an expression of Southern fear of Negro progress than of Negro crime.')[13]

Charles E. Wyzanski Jr, a United States district court judge in Massachusetts, wrote a six-page review of Myrdal's *American Dilemma* in the *Harvard Law Review* that played a major role in bringing the book attention in the legal world.[14] Wyzanski challenged whites to get beyond the notions that black people are 'less moral', 'improvident', malodorous, and that there was 'an innate physical repulsion to the

---

[11] Myrdal, *An American Dilemma*, 562.

[12] Myrdal, *An American Dilemma*, 564.

[13] Myrdal, *An American Dilemma*, 563, quoting Walter White, *Rope and Faggot: A Biography of Judge Lynch* (1929), 112, New York: Knopf. Historians continue to endorse White's assessment of the motivations for lynching. Philip Dray argues in an insightful history of lynching that fear of miscegenation operated as a galvanizing force for mob violence against African Americans: 'The anxiety over interracial sex was so great, it fostered the related notion that sex with white women was the real objective behind all black aspiration, that money, education, accomplishment of any kind were for black men mere stepping-stones en route to the bedroom and the ultimate nirvana of intimacy with white women.' Philip Dray, *At the Hands of Persons Unknown* (2002), 60, New York: Random House.

[14] Charles E. Wyzanski, review of *An American Dilemma, the Negro Problem and Modern Democracy,* by Gunnar Myrdal, *Harvard Law Review* 58 (1944): 285–91.

black race'.[15] Wyzanski closed his review by discounting the notion that African Americans' main objective in life was to sleep with whites, contending that blacks desired the following goals in descending order of preference: 'abolition of economic discrimination, abolition of legal discrimination, political enfranchisement, the absence of discrimination in schools, churches and other public facilities, the lowering of barriers against social intercourse such as eating and drinking together and, at the very end of the list, if at all, inter-marriage'.[16] Wyzanski's effort to diminish the importance of interracial marriage among the priorities of African Americans demonstrates how large this issue loomed in the minds of even relatively enlightened whites.

II

A primary reason that many Southern whites despised the National Association for the Advancement of Coloured People (NAACP) was that they believed that the organization's chief goal—after cutting through all of the lofty rhetoric about rights and education—was to bed white women. This thinking attained such prominence that Yale Professor Charles Black—a white Texan who worked with the NAACP Legal Defense and Education Fund, Inc. (LDF)—joked that he joined the effort so that he could gain access to the organization's fabled room that contained the keys to the bedroom doors of white women located throughout the South. LDF's leader, Thurgood Marshall, knew well the taboo of black men dating white women, and it caused him intense personal discomfort. As an undergraduate student at Lincoln College in the 1920s, he attended a debate at Harvard University, which was followed by a dinner at the Harvard Club. Years later, he recalled the deep unease he felt at being seated next to a white female student: '[At that dinner] I was the most uncomfortable son of a bitch in the world.'[17] The very discomfort that Marshall felt—as a young black man—being seated in such close proximity to a white woman would eventually serve as a guiding force in shaping his legal approach in the pursuit of racial equality in general, and in the school desegregation cases in particular.

---

[15] Wyzanski, review of *An American Dilemma*, 290.
[16] Wyzanski, review of *An American Dilemma*, 290.
[17] Juan Williams, *Thurgood Marshall: American Revolutionary* (1998), 43. For Charles Black's elaborate quip, see Kluger, *Simple Justice*, 644–45.

LDF's strategy of defusing accusations that its principal goal was interracial sex is illustrated by the organization's reluctance to defend black men accused of raping white women. Marshall feared that NAACP members would not approve of their money being dedicated to causes that could all too easily be misconstrued as defending the myth of black male hyper-sexuality because such defences might impair the organization's larger quest for racial liberation.[18] Marshall, for instance, once famously declined to participate in a lawsuit charging grand jury discrimination in a case where a black man was convicted of raping a white woman. After the Supreme Court subsequently issued a ruling that found discrimination in selection of the grand jury, a friend kidded Marshall for passing on the victorious case. Tellingly, Marshall responded, 'It is necessary that we at all times look out for the reputation of the Association. It is not a question of just trying to win cases.'[19] Similarly, in 1955, one year after the first decision in *Brown*, Marshall hoped that Emmett Till's lynching in Mississippi would not receive inordinate media attention because he regarded the underlying advance of a black male teenager towards a white woman, which supposedly precipitated the violence, to be distasteful.[20] The NAACP's march towards racial equality, in sum, exhibited a remarkably cautious approach when interracial sexuality was believed to animate particular disputes.

In the 1940s, Marshall demonstrated deep uncertainty over whether to prioritize desegregation in the realm of either transportation or education. According to his close colleague Robert Carter, Marshall initially believed that transportation should be pursued first because 'the question of social equality is least likely to be introduced to confuse the court's thinking'.[21] Social equality, of course, was a euphemism for sexual intimacy.

Though Marshall ultimately decided to pursue desegregation first in the educational realm, LDF strategically selected educational institutions and even plaintiffs to minimize anxieties regarding interracial sex. Marshall and his colleagues elected to challenge segregation in graduate schools before challenging segregation in grade schools in an effort to avoid provoking the most intense opposition to interracial

---

[18] Mark Tushnet, *Making Civil Rights Law: Thurgood Marshall and the Supreme Court, 1936–1961* (1994), 29, New York: Oxford University Press.

[19] Tushnet, *Making Civil Rights Law*, 59.

[20] Williams, *Thurgood Marshall*, 241.

[21] Tushnet, *Making Civil Rights Law*, 126.

relationships. Today, readers might instinctively believe that having adults of different races be educated together would have evoked greater animosity, as older students would be more likely to engage in sexual activity than younger students. Defenders of segregation believed, however, that keeping younger students racially separated was of paramount importance, so that during their most impressionable ages, white students would not grow accustomed to being in close proximity with black students. Segregationists hoped, in other words, that their early lessons in segregation would remain with white students throughout their educations and their lives.

Rather than selecting young black male plaintiffs, who opposing attorneys and judges might construe as sexually aggressive, NAACP attorneys consistently chose older black males and often females to act as lead plaintiffs in desegregation cases involving education. When Marshall sought a plaintiff to challenge segregation at the University of Oklahoma's graduate school of education, he selected George McLaurin from among eight potential plaintiffs because, at 68 years of age, it would be difficult to portray McLaurin as a sexual predator.[22] William T. Coleman Jr, who worked closely with LDF, recollected that Marshall once called 'the ... elderly McLaurin', without exception, 'the perfect plaintiff' because his profile 'was free of the sexual undercurrents often at play in desegregation cases, where white parents feared their perception of the social intermingling of their young daughters with testosterone-charged adolescent boys of color'.[23] In challenging segregation at the University of Texas School of Law, moreover, Marshall selected Heman Sweatt, a middle-aged postal carrier with a receding hairline.[24] When Sweatt first applied to the University of Texas, many accused him of wishing to attend law school solely as a subterfuge for trying to court white women. In response to such volatile allegations, Sweatt authored an article in a university publication affirming his true motivations, and disclosing that he was already married. 'I want to get a legal education at the university,' Sweatt explained, 'not a wife.'[25] In addition, LDF

---

[22] Kluger, *Simple Justice*, 266.

[23] William T. Coleman Jr, *Counsel for the Situation: Shaping the Law to Realize America's Promise* (2010), 118, Washington D.C.: Brookings Institution Press.

[24] *Sweatt v. Painter*, 339 U.S. 629 (1950).

[25] Heman Sweatt, 'Why I Want to Attend...,' *The Texas Ranger*, September 1947, 40.

often selected female plaintiffs, who would be less likely than black males to stoke fears of sexual aggression. Among the many female plaintiffs in race and education cases, Autherine Lucy was selected to challenge segregation at the University of Alabama, Lois Sipuel did the same at University of Oklahoma, and the *Brown* suit itself was brought on behalf of a girl, Linda Brown, rather than a boy.

Given the expressed concerns of some Supreme Court justices in the 1950s, LDF appears to have been shrewd in dedicating tactical energy to inoculate itself against the miscegenation charge. During the court's internal deliberations about *Brown*, Justice Stanley Reed was the last member of the court who agreed to invalidate school segregation.[26] It is scarcely surprising, then, that Reed, a native of Kentucky, also evinced the starkest concerns about interracial intimacy. When the justices first spoke about the case at Conference, Reed even noted Thurgood Marshall's fair complexion as proof of miscegenation.[27] When, during the same term that the Court decided *Brown*, it considered whether segregation should be permitted in a Washington, DC, restaurant, many of his colleagues noticed that Reed, who lived at Washington's Mayflower Hotel, demonstrated great apprehension at the prospect of integrating local restaurants. Upon exiting the Conference, Reed is reported to have quizzically exploded, 'Why—why, this means that a nigra can walk into the restaurant at the Mayflower and sit down to eat at the table right next to Mrs. Reed.'[28]

In a memorandum that Justice Tom Clark circulated to the Conference as the court considered *McLaurin* and *Sweatt,* he emphasized a desire to keep graduate school desegregation distinct from the question of desegregation in elementary and secondary schools.[29] 'There would be no "incidents",' Clark wrote, 'if the cases are limited to their facts, i.e., graduate schools. Oklahoma was frank enough to admit this. Its concern was the extension of the doctrine to the elementary and secondary schools.'[30] Not surprisingly, Justice Clark orally articulated

---

[26] Kluger, *Simple Justice*, 698.

[27] Dennis J. Hutchinson, 'Unanimity and Desegregation: Decisionmaking in the Supreme Court, 1948–1958', *Georgetown Law Journal* 68, no. 91 (1979) (quoting Conference notes of Justice Clark on the Segregation Cases (13 December 1952)).

[28] Patterson, *Brown v. Board of Education*, 55.

[29] Hutchinson, 'Unanimity and Desegregation', 89.

[30] Hutchinson, 'Unanimity and Desegregation', 89.

these same points when the justices considered *McLaurin* and *Sweatt* at Conference.[31]

Several other Supreme Court justices agreed with Clark that limiting the initial desegregation decisions to graduate schools was vital. Justice Robert Jackson, for instance, expressed concern that no party in *McLaurin* or *Sweatt* had articulated a logical distinction between graduate schools and grade schools.[32] Justice Hugo Black echoed the feelings of Jackson, noting that if they were to extend the holding to elementary schools, it would tap into a 'deep seated antagonism to commingling' in the South, which he thought would close its schools 'rather than mix races at grade and high school levels'.[33] Black called segregation 'Hitler's creed', but nevertheless indicated that the South 'may never accept that view until [the] races amalgamate as they do when they live side by side'.[34] Justice Frankfurter, too, expressed concern about identifying a limiting principle to desegregation in education. He prevailed upon Chief Justice Fred Vinson to alter one of the lines in his *McLaurin* opinion, changing the broadly-formulated claim that segregation 'handicaps … effective education' to the more targeted claim that segregation 'handicaps … graduate instruction'.[35]

In the *Brown* opinion itself, the Supreme Court consciously decided to avoid confronting the subject of interracial marriage and interracial sex even though the issue arose several times, both privately and publicly, throughout the case. Solicitor General Philip Perlman confided to his assistant Philip Elman that the nation was not yet prepared to accept school desegregation because of the issue's link to miscegenation. In language that bears a striking resemblance to President Eisenhower's admonition to Chief Justice Warren, Perlman remarked, 'You can't have little black boys sitting next to little white girls. The country isn't ready for that.'[36] At the trial court level, T. Justin Moore, attorney for Virginia's Prince Edward School Board, asked a black witness whether he thought that the state should abolish its laws against intermarriage. LDF attorney Robert Carter quickly objected that no one had made that proposal. Fortunately, for foes of segregation, the objection was

[31] Tushnet, *Making Civil Rights Law*, 144.
[32] Tushnet, *Making Civil Rights Law*, 141.
[33] Tushnet, *Making Civil Rights Law*, 142.
[34] Tushnet, *Making Civil Rights Law*, 142.
[35] Tushnet, *Making Civil Rights Law*, 145.
[36] Tushnet, *Making Civil Rights Law*, 173.

sustained. During an emotional appeal at the *Brown* oral arguments before the Supreme Court, John W. Davis drew the court's attention to the prevalence of laws—then found in 29 different states—that barred interracial marriage in his effort to defend school segregation in South Carolina.[37] Despite the presence of the interracial sex issue (in both the text and subtext) of the *Brown* litigation, Warren declined to address the matter and limited the decision's reach solely to matters of education.

III

While Chief Justice Warren aimed to write an opinion that would not inflame white Southerners, *Brown* nevertheless elicited angry reactions from many quarters, as critics consistently raised the reviled prospect of interracial sex. South Carolina governor James F. Byrnes, the only living former justice of the Supreme Court, argued that *Brown* had exceeded the judiciary's authority. Byrnes, writing in *U.S. News & World Report*, forthrightly acknowledged that the 'fundamental objection to integration' stemmed from whites' 'fear of mongrelization'.[38] 'Southerners fear that the purpose of those who lead the fight for integration in schools,' Byrnes explained, 'is to break down social barriers in childhood and the period of adolescence, and ultimately bring about intermarriage of the races.... To prevent this, the white people of the South are willing to make every sacrifice.'[39] The very thought of interracial sex left no room for compromise and, indeed, was sufficiently disconcerting that a former justice felt compelled to take the highly unusual step of condemning the Supreme Court in a national publication.

Byrnes, however, was hardly alone in believing that the Supreme Court's decision to desegregate schools would inexorably lead to interracial sex. Among his fellow politicians, Senator James O. Eastland of Mississippi contended that fighting *Brown* was necessary to maintaining white racial purity: 'Generations of Southerners yet unborn will cherish our memory because they will realize that the fight we now wage [against *Brown*] will have preserved for them their untainted racial heritage, their culture, and the institutions of the Anglo-Saxon

---

[37] Kluger, *Simple Justice*, 672.

[38] James F. Byrnes, 'The Supreme Court Must Be Curbed', *U.S. News and World Report*, 18 May 1956, 50, 56.

[39] Byrnes, 'The Supreme Court Must Be Curbed'.

race.'[40] Eastland's colleague from Mississippi, Senator John Stennis, advanced a slightly softened version of this same argument, contending that school segregation would preserve the racial integrity of both blacks and whites alike. 'One of the most compelling reasons is the deep realization that placing the children side by side over the years, in primary, grammar and high-school grades, is certain to eventually destroy each race,' Stennis said. 'I don't know how many generations that would take. And we all believe that the bloodstream—the racial integrity of each group—is worth saving. And this is one of the main, basic reasons why our people will oppose the mixed schools.'[41] Similarly, Senator Strom Thurmond of South Carolina asserted that black students sought admission to white schools even though, according to Thurmond, black schools actually had greater financial resources than white schools. The push for integration in the face of these facts, Thurmond averred, revealed that the lawyers representing black South Carolinians 'are interested in something else. The "something else" they are interested in is the mixing of the races'.[42]

Such claims also appeared in media outlets following *Brown*. The editor of Mississippi's *Jackson Daily News*, for example, claimed that '[school] integration is merely the first step, or an opening wedge, towards mixed marriages, miscegenation, and the mongrelization of the human race'.[43] In an *Atlantic Monthly* piece titled 'Mixed Schools and Mixed Blood', South Carolina native Herbert Ravenel Sass argued that white Southerners' aversion to miscegenation lies 'at the heart of our race problem, and until it is realized that this is the South's basic and compelling motive, there can be no understanding of the South's attitude'.[44] Sass further contended: 'The underlying and compelling reason for the South's refusal to operate mixed schools—its belief that mixed schools

---

[40] See Dan Wakefield, 'Respectable Racism', *Nation*, 22 October 1955, 339.

[41] 'The Race Issue: South's Plans, How Negroes Will Meet Them', *U.S. News & World Report*, 18 November 1955, 86, 89.

[42] 102 *Congressional Record* 4461 (1956) (statement of Senator Strom Thurmond).

[43] Thomas R. Waring, C.P. Liter, and Frederick Sullens, 'Interviews with Southern Editors: Race, Trouble to Grow in South: No Mixed Schools Yet', *U.S. News & World Report*, 24 February 1956, 40.

[44] Herbert Ravenel Sass, 'Mixed Schools and Mixed Blood', *Atlantic Monthly*, November 1956, reprinted in Jane Dailey, *The Age of Jim Crow* (2009), 271, 273, New York: W.W. Norton & Company.

will result in ultimate racial amalgamation—has been held virtually taboo....'[45]

Opponents of miscegenation often placed white females on pedestals in order to justify their disapproval of school desegregation. In a book published just two months after the *Brown* decision titled *Black Monday*, Mississippi Judge Tom P. Brady extolled the sanctity of white females. 'The loveliest and the purest of God's creatures,' Brady wrote, 'the nearest thing to an angelic being that treads this terrestrial ball is a well-bred, cultured Southern white woman or her blue-eyed, golden-haired little girl. The maintenance of peaceful and harmonious relationships, which have been conducive to the well-being of both the white and Negro races in the South, has been possible because of the inviolability of Southern Womanhood.'[46] Brady, a graduate of the Lawrenceville School and Yale University, intimated that it is only the prohibition on black males dating white females—enforced through lynching and violence—that allows blacks to resist these heavenly creations.

Many commentators embraced the mirror image of the angelic white female in the form of the demonic black male—a beast-like figure possessed by uncontrollable sexual urges that would be unleashed once they were placed in integrated classrooms. Shortly after *Brown* appeared, Alabama State Senator Sam Engelhardt Jr charged: 'Desegregating the schools will lead to rape! .... The nigger is depraved! Give him the opportunity to be near a white woman and he goes berserk!'[47] In *The Sin or Evils of Integration*, Reverend Louis E. Dailey of North Carolina agreed that black males were preternaturally libidinous. 'White people of the South know that a large number of Negro teenage boys are nearly sex maniacs.... Only under the protection of a school heavily guarded by police officers would they have any peace of mind for the safety of their daughters from the attacks of such Negro boys.'[48] Some

---

[45] Sass, 'Mixed Schools and Mixed Blood', in Dailey, *The Age of Jim Crow*, 276.

[46] Tom P. Brady, *Black Monday: Segregation or Amalgamation...America Has its Choice* (1954), 45, Winona: Association of Citizens' Councils.

[47] J.W. Peltason, *Fifty-Eight Lonely Men: Southern Federal Judges and School Desegregation* (1961), 38, Urbana: University of Illinois Press.

[48] Louis E. Dailey, *The Sin or Evils of Integration* (1962), 38, New York: Carlton Press. For a thoughtful exchange on whether whites typically drew upon religion to attack Jim Crow or to prop it up, see David L. Chappell, *A Stone of Hope: Prophetic Religion and the Death of Jim Crow* (2004), Chapel

observers dressed up their biological beliefs with sociological explana-tions. 'Negroes are … generally more retarded in school than white children', one newspaper editor explained, '[so that] a Negro of 14 may be in the fourth grade with a white girl of 10 or 11, and the Negro is a fully developed man, sexually'.[49]

Relatedly, in addition to arguing that blacks were uncontrollably libidinous, many white opponents of desegregation contended that blacks possessed looser sexual morals than whites. Expressing concern about the rates of illegitimacy and venereal disease among blacks, Thomas R. Waring argued: 'Many white persons believe that morals among their own race are lax enough as it is, without exposing their children to an even more primitive view of sex habits.'[50] Where Waring's use of the word 'primitive' is a thinly-veiled effort to conjure the 'nature' of blacks, Austin Earle Burges argued that it was black culture that accounted for the supposed deficiencies in black sexual norms. 'Negroes are notoriously lax in their sex morals,' Burges wrote, 'and children from Negro homes come to school imbued with the attitude toward sex morality which they have learned at home or absorbed by contact with the neighboring children.'[51] While Burges's comments could scarcely be construed as progressive, his willingness to view blacks as people who were at least theoretically capable of improvement, alas, distinguished him from many of his contemporaries who were firmly wedded to notions of black genetic inferiority.

Not all published reactions of Southern whites to *Brown* assumed such alarmist, openly aggressive tones. Yet, even white commentators who wished to avoid the most reactionary arguments against school desegregation often proved unwilling to support interracial dating. In an effort to explain the position of Southern moderates, for example, news-paper editor C.A. McKnight admitted that fear of miscegenation drove a good deal of the resistance to school desegregation.[52] While he sought

---

Hill: University of North Carolina Press; Jane Dailey, 'Sex, Segregation, and the Sacred after *Brown*', *Journal of American History* 91, no. 1(2004): 119.

[49] Waring et al., 'Interviews with Southern Editors', 42.

[50] Thomas R. Waring, 'The Southern Case Against Desegregation', *Harper's Magazine*, January 1956, 43.

[51] Austin Earle Burges, *What Price Integration?* (1956), 5, Dallas: American Guild Press..

[52] C.A. McKnight, 'Troubled South: Search for a Middle Ground', *Collier's*, 22 June 1956, 26.

to cast doubt on whether, in Sass's terms, mixed schools would actually lead to mixed blood, McKnight never questioned whether mixing blood would be a horrific eventuality. Likewise, even Hodding Carter, a moderate Mississippian who was among the few whites to advocate economic and political equality for blacks, blanched at the prospect of interracial romance. Carter argued that granting blacks economic rights would enable them to have greater respect for their 'ethnic integrity'.[53] Ralph McGill, the liberal editor of the *Atlanta Constitution*, described— though did not necessarily endorse—the aversion that his fellow white Southerners displayed towards interracial sex. 'Deep in the instincts of many Southerners is a fear of what might happen "when children all drink out of the same bucket",' McGill explained. 'Many of these people are entirely sincere when they say that nonsegregation means a "mongrelized" race. They will die before they will agree, they say. And they mean it.'[54]

Commentary on the connection between education and interracial sex was not confined to the South. William F. Buckley Jr, editor of the *National Review*, argued that the Southern loathing of blacks was simply too intractable to be addressed by a Supreme Court decision. 'In the South', Buckley instructed, 'the acceptance of racial separation begins in the cradle. What rational man imagines this concept can be shattered overnight?'[55] Relatedly, in Norman Mailer's 1957 essay 'The White Negro: Superficial Reflections on the Hipster', the Brooklyn-bred and Harvard-educated novelist argued that reactionaries more accurately understood school desegregation than liberals because the former group grasped that 'the deeper issue is not desegregation but miscegenation'.[56] Perhaps most surprisingly, even the *New York Times* editorial board, in a piece published one day after *Brown*, approvingly interpreted the opinion to leave statutes prohibiting interracial marriage completely untouched. 'It is true, of course, that the court [in *Brown*] is not talking

---

[53] Hodding Carter, *Southern Legacy* (1950), 181–2, Baton Rouge: Louisiana State University Press.

[54] Ralph McGill, 'The Angry South', *Atlantic Monthly*, April 1956, 34.

[55] Quoted in James Jackson Kilpatrick, *The Southern Case for School Segregation* (1962), 220, New York: Crowell-Collier Press.

[56] Norman Mailer, 'The White Negro: Superficial Reflections on the Hipster' (1957), excerpted in *The Time of Our Time* (1998), 228, New York: Random House.

of that sort of equality which produces interracial marriages,' the *Times* commented. 'It is not talking of a social system at all.'[57]

IV

Fears of the connection between schools and interracial sex persisted within the federal judiciary long after the initial shock of *Brown* subsided. In 1956, two years after *Brown*, the Supreme Court made clear that it would not quickly extend its anti-segregation principle to interracial relationships. In *Naim v. Naim*, Ruby Elaine Lamberth, a white woman, sued to annul her marriage to a Ham Say Naim, a Chinese-American man, because the marriage violated the Racial Integrity Act, as Virginia's anti-miscegenation statute was called.[58] Relying on *Plessy v. Ferguson* and *Pace v. Alabama*, Virginia's Supreme Court agreed to annul the marriage.[59] Focusing on the 'corruption of blood' and the prospect of a 'mongrel breed of citizens', the court reasoned: 'Both sacred and secular history teach that nations and races have better advanced in human progress when they cultivated their own distinctive characteristics and culture and developed their own peculiar genius.'[60] The Virginia court further concluded that nothing in the US Supreme Court's recent cases invalidating racial segregation in education required striking the Virginia law.

When *Naim* reached the US Supreme Court, Justice Felix Frankfurter wrote a memorandum imploring his colleagues to avoid issuing a substantive decision in the case.[61] Frankfurter warned of the 'important public consequences' that would accompany making such a decision and noted the 'deep ... moral and psychological presuppositions' that individuals bring to the idea of interracial marriage.[62] Frankfurter closed his message to the Conference by directly invoking *Brown* and suggested that invalidating Virginia's statute would jeopardize the nation's school desegregation efforts.[63] One unnamed justice is reported to have

---

[57] 'All God's Chillun', editorial, *New York Times*, 18 May 1954, 28.
[58] *Naim v. Naim*, 87 S.E.2d 749 (1955), *cert. denied*, 350 U.S. 985 (1956).
[59] 136 U.S. 537 (1896); 106 U.S. 583 (1883).
[60] *Naim*, 87 S.E.2d at 754.
[61] Hutchinson, *Unanimity and Desegregation*, 93.
[62] Hutchinson, *Unanimity and Desegregation*, 93.
[63] Hutchinson, *Unanimity and Desegregation*, 94.

captured the thrust of Frankfurter's memo with concision: 'One bomb-shell at a time is enough.'[64]

The justices who thought that the nation would be better off without a decision legitimating interracial marriage in the mid-1950s found an unlikely ally in Thurgood Marshall. He did not support Ham Say Naim's entreaty to the Supreme Court because he believed that such a ruling would undermine *Brown*.[65] Marshall's decision to withhold support in *Naim* underscores the depth of LDF's commitment to avoiding moves that may stoke anxieties about interracial sex. Just as the organization demonstrated great reluctance to support defendants who had been accused of rape, the organization—at least in the immediate aftermath of *Brown*—sought to avoid the perception that school desegregation efforts were mere pretexts for gaining access to sexual relations with whites.

Given that resistance to *Brown* was driven in large part by concerns about interracial sex, some opponents of the decision broached the pos-sibility of integrating public schools by race, but simultaneously separat-ing them by gender. With that technique, black girls and white girls would attend schools together, just as black boys and white boys would do the same, but the most dreaded sexual combination of white females and black males could safely be averted. The initial idea to segregate students by sex in order to limit the effects of racial desegregation sur-faced quickly after *Brown*. In 1957, for example, the Tennessee General Assembly enacted a statute urging school boards to 'provide separate schools for persons of the male sex and persons of the female sex'.[66] Two years later, Congressman Brooks Hays of Arkansas wrote a book—titled *A Southern Moderate Speaks*—where he suggested that the 'establishment of schools segregated by sex' may be one way to accomplish racial inte-gration 'without loss of values deemed vital by the white majority'.[67]

The actual adoption of such practices, however, did not pick up steam until the late 1960s, after the Supreme Court made it apparent that the time for deliberation in the name of 'all deliberate speed' had elapsed.[68]

---

[64] Walter F. Murphy, *The Elements of Judicial Strategy* (1964), 193, Chicago: University Of Chicago Press.

[65] Kennedy, *Interracial Intimacies*, 270.

[66] Tenn. Code Ann. § 49-2-108(a) (West 2003).

[67] Brooks Hays, *A Southern Moderate Speaks* (1959), 228, Chapel Hill: University of North Carolina Press.

[68] See, for example, *Green v. County School Board of New Kent County*, 391 U.S. 430 (1968).

Many Southern federal lower courts nevertheless blessed these devious efforts to preserve racial segregation in the intimate sphere over the course of many years. Indeed, federal courts preserved this arrangement until the astoundingly late date of 1977, more than two decades after *Brown II*, when an appellate court finally eliminated this rearguard technique. As one black school board member in Amite County, Mississippi, explained at that time, with evident irritation: '[Separating schools by sex] has always been a racial issue. The idea is to keep the black boys from having any contact with the white girls—pure and simple.'[69] Perhaps the most astonishing aspect of this dispute is that the white president of Amite County's school board publicly affirmed this account of the board's motivation. When a journalist asked why Amite County did not introduce single-sex public schools before 1969, the board president replied, 'We didn't have integration then. We had one school for whites and one school for coloreds, that's why.'[70]

V

Despite what should by now be clear is the prominent place that anti-miscegenation played in the *Brown* litigation and its attendant controversies, this subject has received insufficient attention in the standard account of the twentieth century's most celebrated decision. What accounts for this relative paucity of attention? Though explaining this disregard necessarily requires entering the realm of speculation, I propose two central reasons why *Brown* is not today typically understood as a dispute that was crucially informed by fears of miscegenation.

First, the United States has long exhibited a surprisingly potent puritanical streak, which—outside of a few specialized academic

---

[69] Merrill Sheils, 'Segregation by Sex', *Newsweek*, 19 September 1977, 97.

[70] Helen Dewar, 'Blacks Boycott Sex-Segregated Schools', *Washington Post*, 4 September 1977, A32. See *United States v. Hinds County School Board*, 560 F.2d 619 (5th Cir. 1977) (invalidating sex-segregated public schools in Amite County, Mississippi). For an early article examining the constitutionality of such sex segregation, see Robert B. Barnett, Comment, 'The Constitutionality of Sex Separation in School Desegregation Plans', *University of Chicago Law Review* 37 (1970): 296. For an incisive historical treatment of the topic, see Serena Mayeri, 'The Strange Career of Jane Crow: Sex Segregation and the Treatment of Anti-Discrimination Discourse', *Yale Journal of Law & the Humanities* 18, no. 2 (2006): 187.

fields—may have caused some mainstream commentators to shrink, almost reflexively, from frank discussions about sexuality and its importance to society. Not long ago, to place sex and sexuality at the centre of scholarship risked having work dismissed as both unserious and unsavoury. The general squeamishness about sexual matters may have assumed particular urgency in the context of school desegregation, as some researchers could well have feared that even mentioning the stereotype about black male hyper-sexuality—an idea that has hardly vanished within the United States—would risk instilling that pernicious idea deeper into the American psyche. While this impulse may certainly be understandable, it is also regrettable. To hope that simply ignoring an ugly stereotype will succeed in making it vanish is to participate in the sheerest of follies. The more promising method of disabling stereotypes is not to bury them, but to confront them. Notions of black male hyper-sexuality continue to haunt (and enthral) American society. To take only one recent example, Dylann Roof, who killed nine black parishioners at a South Carolina church in 2015, explained his racial violence in part by stating that black men 'rape … 100 white women a day'.[71] But it is precisely because such notions continue to lurk within the United States today that makes it essential to grapple openly with how those attitudes shaped a central event in American legal history.[72]

Second, while *Brown* has been examined from many different vantage points during the last several decades, relatively few authors have endeavoured to explore the controversy in a manner that places white Southerners and their concerns at the forefront. It is when one examines the language of those who fought *against* integration, rather than *for* integration, that the centrality of the anxiety over miscegenation becomes most readily apparent. To study the concerns of white Southerners who opposed *Brown* is not, of course, to sympathize with those concerns. One can simultaneously detest an ideology and seek to understand its animating frameworks, as—if nothing else—studying the opponents of integration will yield sharper insights into decisions made by the proponents of integration. In recent years, fortunately, scholars have begun to examine the antagonists in the *Brown* drama in

[71] See Kevin Sack and Alan Blinder, 'Jurors Hear Dylann Roof Explain Shooting in Video: "I Had to Do It,"', *New York Times*, 9 December 2016.

[72] See Wesley Morris, 'The Last Taboo: Why Pop Culture Just Can't Deal with Black Male Sexuality', *New York Times Magazine*, 27 October 2016.

greater detail. As the miscegenation issue vividly illuminates, however, that work must continue apace if we wish to understand more fully the nation's constitutional confrontation over school segregation.[73]

[73] For my own work examining the various legal manoeuvres made by signatories of the Southern Manifesto, see Justin Driver, 'Supremacies and the Southern Manifesto', *Texas Law Review* 92, no. 5 (2014), 1053–135.

4

Four Types of Racism

Emilio Comay del Junco[*]

'*video meliora proboque, deteriora sequor*'
I see the right, and I approve it too, Condemn the wrong—and yet the wrong pursue
—Ovid, Metamorphoses, vii.20 (trans. John Dryden)

You might convince me that you're right, but you'll never convince me that I'm wrong.
—James Weldon Johnson, Autobiography of an Ex-Colored Man

It is commonplace in political philosophy to distinguish between formal and substantive conceptions in some domain—justice, freedom, rights, whatever. The distinction is invoked to make the point that while a given social organization may formally recognize a principle (equality, say), it may at the same time fail to ensure that it is actually implemented. Consider, for example, the current state of racial justice in the United States of America. For the last 50 years or so, the United States has had legal anti-discrimination provisions and has adopted (admittedly

[*] Many thanks to William M. Burton, César Cabezas, Emily Dupree, Korey Garibaldi, Sheehan Moore, and Martha C. Nussbaum for their comments on and discussions of earlier versions of this chapter.

less wide-ranging) positive measures, such as affirmative action, with the aim of guaranteeing racial equality. Yet despite formal protections, racial inequality remains.[1] (The claim that contemporary racial inequality in America is unjust is taken to be axiomatic for the remainder of the chapter. I hope that a reader sceptical of this claim might be led to revise their judgement, but I do not argue for it directly.)

There is a psychic corollary to the split between formal and substantive racial justice. In the last half century, the proportion of Americans holding to explicitly racist beliefs has dropped precipitously. And yet, not only does racial inequality persist, but support for redressing such inequality is lacklustre at best. The following chapter might thus be thought of as an investigation into the psychic dimension of the failure of formal guarantees in providing substantive justice.

Let us start with the following bit of casual practical reasoning (the 'normative non-racist argument'):

(1) All humans are deserving of respect, opportunities, and basic welfare. ('We hold these truths to be self-evident....')
(2) Black people (or members of any historically oppressed racial group) are human.
(3) Therefore, black people (or members of any historically oppressed racial group) are deserving of respect, equal opportunities, and basic welfare.

While this argument is by no means—certainly not in historical terms—universally accepted, it will, happily, elicit very widespread assent in the contemporary American context.

Now let us add another simple bit of argument (the 'racial justice argument'):

(4) If a person or group of people is lacking in equal respect, opportunities, and basic welfare, then other people or the state have some responsibility to redress this (general principle of social justice).
(5) Black people in the United States lack equal respect, opportunities, and welfare.

---

[1] Both equality of opportunity and of outcome are lacking. For present purposes, I do not take a stance on whether equality of opportunity is sufficient for justice. (It isn't, but that would take us too far afield.)

(6) Therefore, other people or the state have a responsibility to ensure that black people in the United States get the respect, opportunities, and basic welfare they deserve.[2]

The second argument is based on propositions likely to elicit less universal assent. Indeed, it seems plausible to think that both arguments taken together move from more to less widely accepted propositions—even if the first three remain basically taboo to deny in public.

Despite the greater demandingness of the second argument, the distinction between the two arguments does not track a distinction between formal and substantive concerns. The second argument, like the first, is formal. Note first the utter generality with which these premises and conclusions have been formulated. I have said nothing about the causes of racial inequality. I have left the basic entitlements entirely unspecified and left to the side any assumptions about what sort of 'something'—which might include anything from privatized school vouchers, to reparations for slavery and segregation, to the seizure and redistribution of the means of production—ought to be done to alleviate racial inequality in the United States.

This is not because I do not have opinions on how to answer this question, nor is it born out of any desire to appeal to as broad an ideological audience as possible. It is rather because, while I will have something to say at the very end about the positive demands of racial justice, it is not my primary concern here. My primary aim is rather to capture some key premises and inferences that I believe would be endorsed by many—perhaps most—white Americans.[3] The two syllogisms are not, however, meant to be immune to objections or universally endorsed. They are rather meant to capture something like an 'ideal type' of liberal reasoning about race. What follows can be read in two ways. First, it can be read as a diagnosis of a failure to live up to liberal ideals and a call to

---

[2] I have framed these arguments in terms of humans, rather than citizens, to reflect the kind of humanistic natural rights doctrine underlying documents like the American Declaration of Independence. However, it could equally be reframed in terms of *citizens*, which might elicit slightly more widespread acceptance in a contemporary context, especially for the racial justice argument, with its more demanding conclusion.

[3] They may also be endorsed by many people of colour; that this is the case need not make the present inquiry any less of a contribution to the investigation of 'whiteness'.

those who espouse them to redress this failure. But it may also be read as an indictment of such ideals as inadequate for substantive justice, precisely because of their proponents' failure to live up to them. My focus, as the title suggests, is very specifically on *racism* itself and more specifically on its cognitive, emotional, and social structure.

The rest of this chapter examines failures of practical rationality with regard to race: how supposedly banished stigmas about African Americans creep back into our reasoning at various points. My focus is on American anti-black racism and black–white inequality. Most of the examples I draw on from history, literature, sociology, and psychology have to do with this specific brand of racism, in part because it is perhaps the most historically and currently salient example, but also because it is arguably the most varied and the most studied.[4] That said, many of the theoretical points I make may nonetheless be salient in the analysis not only of other forms of racism, but also other forms of out-group discrimination, for example, caste, religion, ethnicity, and perhaps also less obviously analogous cases like class, gender, and sexuality—that is, in contexts where deep material inequality and unequal treatment coexists with strong taboos on the expression of explicit prejudice.

I shall proceed by following the structure of the normative non-racist argument and the racial justice argument and locating various places in which practical reasoning breaks down. The two sections of the first part detail failures to accept the various premises of the arguments, which I shall argue correspond to distinct forms of racism informed by distinct brands of racial stigma. But insofar as my account is innovative, this comes in the second part, where I shall argue that even practical agents who endorse the entirety of both arguments may nonetheless fail to translate their reasoning into practice. One sort of such a failure is frequently explained in terms of 'implicit' or unconscious bias. But I also identify another kind of failure to act, which, borrowing the philosophical term of art for actions performed willingly against an agent's better judgment, I term 'racial akrasia', or 'akratic racism'.[5] My central claim is

---

[4] Racism against indigenous people in the United States has a good claim to being equally prominent and virulent; however, I do not focus on it directly because its ideological tropes and material bases are significantly distinct from anti-black racism and would need an extended analysis of their own.

[5] The first term, 'racial akrasia', appears to have been coined by the political theorist and Chicanx studies scholar Edwina Barvosa, though she understands it differently than I do, using it to denote psychic tensions between a subject's

thus that, even when people sincerely hold to normative non-racism and racial justice, they knowingly act in ways that perpetuate unjust racial inequality: they see and endorse the better, yet at the very same time pursue the worse.

Failing to See the Better—Hatred and Neglect

Hatred (against Normative Non-Racism)

The first place that the normative non-racist argument can fail is, rather predictably, in its first premises: that is, one may simply deny that human beings are universally worthy of respect and basic goods or alternatively deny that members of other races are human beings (usually in a moral sense, although in the most extreme form of scientific racism, the denial of humanity extends to a denial of a common biological identity). Historically, this is not an uncommon position.

This second sort of departure from normative non-racism also includes a common reading of certain strains in American republicanism.[6] The affirmation of the universal rights of man in the 1776

---

multiple racial/ethnic identifications. However, while racism appears frequently as an example of akrasia in philosophical literature (see Lionel MacPherson, 'The Banality of White Supremacy (In and Beyond Philosophy),' interview by Meena Krishnamurthy, *Philosopher*, 30 September 2016, https://politicalphilosopher.net/2016/09/30/featured-philosopher-lionel-mcpherson/), Barvosa is the first (and only) instance of this precise phrase I could locate and is also the only author I have read who uses akrasia to think about racism rather than vice versa. See Edwina Barvosa, *Wealth of Selves* (College Station: Texas A&M University Press), 2008.

[6] This is the reading usually ascribed to Frederick Douglass in his speech 'What to the Slave is the Fourth of July?' in which he faults the pre-Civil War republic for endorsing the correct ideals of equal rights for all (that is, affirming premise 1) but simultaneously failing to recognize that black people (and women of all races—Douglass was an early proponent of women's suffrage) ought to be included in the set. Hence, the question: Are 'the great principles of political freedom and of natural justice, embodied in that Declaration of Independence, extended to us [slaves]?' Douglass answers in the negative—'The rich inheritance of justice, liberty, prosperity, and independence bequeathed by your fathers is shared by you, not by me.' See Charles W. Mills, 'Whose Fourth of July? Douglass and "Original Intent"' in *Blackness Visible: Essays on*

Declaration can be read as an endorsement of premise 1. And the 1789 Constitution's failure, under the influence of the slaveholding South, to grant these rights to enslaved people of African descent can either be interpreted as withholding assent to premise 2 (that is, denying black people's humanity) or as an inferential failure to draw the conclusion 3, from 1 and 2, that black people have a claim to respect, opportunity, and basic welfare.[7]

The most extreme form of type 1 racism is the conceptual territory of national socialist racial ideology, which denies both premises 1 and 2. It denies 1 by denying that human beings have any rights or moral standing *qua* human (for example, by accepting some brand of social Darwinism or vulgarized 'Nietzscheanism') but also, for good measure denies premise 2 by consistently stigmatizing members of racial outgroups as *non*-human, for example, the stock comparisons of Jews in Nazi propaganda with rats, cockroaches, and viruses. The emotional structure of this first kind of racism includes not only generalized aversion, but highly detailed and richly patterned varieties of disgust as well as fear.

This failure to publicly endorse *any* of the premises of normative non-racism is far outside the bounds of acceptable public discourse in the United States. Since my focus is on the everyday and ubiquitous, rather than *extraordinary* instances of racial stigma, I will not devote significant space to analysing this explicit and radical denial of humanity. Nevertheless, it is important to note that even if it is a fringe view, this kind of racism has not only never quite disappeared from sight, but appears to be resurgent in a way that dispels too easy narratives of its complete disappearance.[8] And it is also important to remember that, in the American context, explicit denial of human status has often been the private (or masked) counterpart to public racial paternalism.

Philosophy and Race (Ithaca, NY: Cornell University Press, 2007), 167–200. Mills argues that Douglass is overly charitable in his analysis of the Declaration and Constitution.

[7] Note that the opening of the American Constitution explicitly refers to 'welfare' as a natural right.

[8] See, for example, the Southern Poverty Law Center's database of hate groups (the vast majority of which are white supremacist): 'Hate Map,' Southern Poverty Law Center, https://www.splcenter.org/hate-map. Or indeed many of the recent appointments working in the White House.

Neglect (against Racial Justice)

I have argued that, in a comparative historical sense, *explicit* denials of equal humanity are rare (though certainly not non-existent) in contemporary American discussions of race. More common are failures to show concern for the well-being of racial minorities, which I shall argue can and should properly be considered a denial of equal humanity, but an implicit rather than explicit one. Thus, we might say: neglect, understood as *the failure to show equal concern in equivalent cases of need*, is an implicit denial of equal humanity.

This, perhaps, is the most familiar brand of contemporary American racism. It takes the form of denying that black people are worthy of intervention to improve the material conditions of their lives, because of an underlying devaluation of people's worth based on racial identity. Sometimes, it is itself a way of expressing racial animus, as with the political strategy that emerged almost immediately along with the establishment of anti-racist expressive norms in public life in the late 1960s. In place of *explicitly* arguing that non-whites are inferior, this brand of racism relies not only on creating links between racialized groups and politically unpopular positions, the very unpopularity of certain programmes—welfare, public housing, less punitive criminal sanctions—is bound with their associations with racial subgroups. Because of the strength of these associative links, for example, between black women and welfare, racially charged tropes can be expressed in a superficially race-neutral packaging. An exemplar of this kind of rhetoric is the trope of the 'welfare queen'—a (fantasy) inner city woman supposedly growing rich on fraudulently cashed benefit cheques—deployed by Ronald Reagan during the 1976 presidential election.[9] Nowhere in the description of the welfare queen is it *spelled out* that she is black, but the associations are clear based on a variety of racially correlated attributes, above all the very fact of being on welfare (but also neighbourhood, car make, and so on). Unlike the elaborate and highly specific emotional structure

---

[9] In addition to Martin Gilens, *Why Americans Hate Welfare: Race, Media, and the Politics of Antipoverty Policy* (Chicago: University of Chicago Press, 1999), see Patricia Hill Collins, *Black Feminist Thought* (New York and London: Routledge, 2000), and Wahneema H. Lubiano, 'Black Ladies, Welfare Queens, and State Minstrels: Ideological War by Narrative Means', in *Race-ing Justice, En-Gendering Power*, ed. Toni Morrison (New York: Pantheon, 1992), 323–63, for black feminist critiques of the trope of the 'welfare queen'.

of hate racism, this second variety of racism is less characterized by clearly articulable varieties of disgust and more by generalized feelings of mistrust based in fear and, above all, as we shall see, resentment.

There is, to be sure, a certain class of American conservatives likely to deny that people in unfortunate circumstances *deserve* anything be done, regardless of race—who will deny that 'something' ought to be done to improve their lot, that any aid rendered is purely supererogatory, and that an end to suffering and deprivation should and, indeed, can, only come about through hard work. Thus, it is only because of a general opposition to providing aid that there is particular opposition to providing aid to non-whites. Yet it is seriously doubtful whether this opposition is ever quite so universal in reality. Indeed, it seems likely that much of the opposition to rendering aid to others—manifesting itself as, for example, hostility towards social programmes like welfare or subsidized healthcare—is, in fact, motivated by prior hostility towards racial minorities who are likely to be recipients of such aid. This is not to deny that many people indeed sincerely feel themselves to be hostile to any form of government-subsidized aid, regardless of the recipient's race. Rather it is to suggest that the stigmatization of poverty and welfare in the United States is driven to a significant degree by *racial* stigma 'rubbing off' on it.[10] (The phenomenon of a neutral object becoming negatively charged because of an association with stigmatized groups is central to the social theory of stigma going back to Erving Goffman's notion of 'vicarious' stigmatization.[11]) Moreover, I have already mentioned that the creation of these associative links between already stigmatized groups and apparently race-neutral measures is, in the American context, at least partly intentional.[12]

[10] Thanks to William M. Burton for helping me clarify this point. See Gilens, *Why Americans Hate Welfare*. See also Jim Sidanius, Felicia Pratto, and Lawrence Bobo, 'Racism, Conservatism, Affirmative Action and Intellectual Sophistication: A Matter of Principled Conservatism or Group Dominance?', *Journal of Personality and Social Psychology* 70, no. 3 (1996): 476–90 for a social psychological analysis. Compare with Barbara Fields and Karen Fields, *Racecraft: The Soul of Inequality in American Life* (London and New York: Verso Books, 2012), 278.

[11] Erving Goffman, *Stigma: Notes on the Management of Spoiled Identity* (New York: Prentice-Hall, 1962), 134.

[12] Consider the frank—and by now infamous and well-known—statements given by Republican strategist Lee Atwater in 1981 about the so-called 'Southern strategy': 'You start out in 1954 by saying, "Nigger, nigger, nigger."

But the failure to show concern for the racially unequal distribution is not only the province of those espousing strict laissez-faire ideology. Those who endorse premise 4 ('people lacking respect, opportunities, and decent conditions deserve redress') in general terms may fail to apply it in practice when the people in question are members of stigmatized groups. Two metaphors help make this point clear: naturalization and obliviousness.

Someone committed to racial equality (1–3) and to the general idea of intervening when people are doing badly (4) may fail to join this with the particular observation that a given group is doing poorly in some area and therefore something ought to be done, precisely because of a prior association between the group in question and the negative situation. If we are in the habit of assuming that a given class of people is in a certain state—if we see this state of affairs as *natural*—we are less likely to think intervention necessary. Glenn Loury argues along these lines in the specific context of the dramatic over-representation of African Americans in the prison population relative to their share of the American population at large: 'Dramatic racial disparity in imprisonment rates does not occasion more public angst, I claim, because this circumstance does not strike the typical American observer at the cognitive level as being counterintuitive.'[13] Or, many whites are *oblivious* to instances of suffering and injustice when those wronged are black. As Cory Greene, an anti-mass incarceration activist who himself was formerly incarcerated, put it in a recent interview, race 'makes it easier, cognitively and emotionally, to send people there'—in this case to prison, but 'there' could equally refer to any number of instances of degraded and degrading conditions disproportionately experienced by people of colour.[14] (Substitute 'keep' for 'send' as appropriate—as in 'keep people there, in poverty.') And,

---

By 1968 you can't say "nigger"—that hurts you, backfires. So you say stuff like, uh, forced busing, states' rights, and all that stuff, and you're getting so abstract. Now, you're talking about cutting taxes, and all these things you're talking about are totally economic things and a byproduct of them is, blacks get hurt worse than whites....'

The quote can be found in any number of sources. See Lee Atwater, interview on the 'Southern Strategy', 1981, audio, https://www.thenation.com/article/exclusive-lee-atwaters-infamous-1981-interview-southern-strategy/.

[13] Glenn C. Loury, *The Anatomy of Racial Inequality* (Cambridge and London: Harvard University Press, 2002), 81.

[14] *13th,* directed by Ava DuVernay (Los Gatos: Netflix, 2016), film, at 1:16

in addition to the *lack of concern* shown when stigmatized groups like African Americans are suffering, we can add the aforementioned hostility expressed by many whites towards even race-*neutral* measures that might mitigate inequality.

Note that this is not a claim about the genesis of racial inequality. I think it is certainly highly plausible—as an inference to the best explanation and drawing on specific social-scientific research—that the compounded historical effects of slavery, segregation, legal discrimination by private actors, and the historically unequal distribution of the limited American social welfare system,[15] continued though now illegal discrimination, would ultimately need to be a major part of the causal story about the persistence of racial inequality. This causal claim has been contested,[16] but I am not arguing for it here.[17] Indeed, Loury is one of those sceptical about it, and part of my motivation in quoting him is the desire to construct an argument which does not include claims about the specific genesis of racial inequality. Rather, I am claiming (and on this, Loury might agree) that the general *indifference* on the part of whites

[15] For example, the New Deal institution of Social Security excluded farm and domestic workers—two categories in which black people were over-represented—an explicit concession by Roosevelt to Southern segregationist Democrats. Following the war, the GI Bill, which gave veterans access to credit to buy property, was effectively closed to black people because of redlining. See Ira Katznelson, *When Affirmative Action Was White: An Untold History of Racial Inequality in Twentieth-Century America* (New York: W.W. Norton, 2005), for a historical account of the way that the post-War American welfare state produced and reproduced racial inequality.

[16] William Julius Wilson is the originator and most prominent defender of the view that racism is largely irrelevant in explaining contemporary racial inequality. See William Julius Wilson, *The Declining Significance of Race* (Chicago: University of Chicago Press, 1978) for the classic statement. Loury is also somewhat sympathetic to this view in Glenn C. Loury, *One by One from the Inside Out: Essays and Reviews on Race and Responsibility in America* (New York: Free Press, 1995).

[17] It is a claim, however, that ought to be argued for; my reasons for not doing so are due in large part to the constraints of space. Recent economic research suggests that black–white income inequality has actually *increased* over the last 35 years and that this is primarily explained by (illegal) discrimination in labour markets: see, for example, Valerie Wilson and William M. Rodgers III, *Black-White Wage Gaps Expand with Rising Wage Inequality*, (Washington, DC: Economic Policy Institute, 2016), 1–66, epi.org/101972.

towards patterns of racial inequality—whatever their causes—first of all perpetuates these patterns, and second, constitutes an implicit failure to extend equal humanity and is thus normatively problematic. The argument that contemporary racial inequality is the result of race-neutral forces alone seems susceptible to the critique that it focuses only on *instituting* and not at all on *perpetuating* a state of affairs. It is certainly true that no black Americans alive today were enslaved, and a decreasing number were themselves victims of Jim Crow-style discrimination. (Though insofar as (a) wealth is transmitted over generations and (b) health, education, and the like depend to a large degree on wealth, there is a direct link between historical regimes of legalized racism and current inequalities.) But the *perpetuation* of racial inequality depends crucially on the society in which it exists *consenting to its continued existence.* Insofar as the United States is content to allow black people to suffer deprivations which it would intervene to prevent in analogous cases of white suffering (or would be more *likely* to, at least, for there is no question that many poor white Americans have suffered enormous neglect), current racial inequality can be said to be at least *perpetuated by* racially discriminatory determinations of what situations merit intervention.

Writing in the wake of the 'war on drugs' and the punitive response to the rise of crack, Loury makes a similar point via a counterfactual scenario in which white Americans are the ones suffering: 'If there were a comparable number of young European-American men on beer drinking binges, or anorexic teenage girls starving themselves to death, and if these were situations in which the same degree of human suffering was engendered as is being produced in this case, it would occasion a most profound reflection about what had gone wrong, not only with *them,* but with *us*.'[18]

The point being made here is that when—or if—racially stigmatized groups are not the ones suffering, it would seem unthinkably callous to wipe one's hands of the situation, to deny that anyone but the immediately impacted people had any responsibility to intervene. Loury's examples, presumably, are meant to be ones in which the white teenagers would intuitively be assigned some degree of responsibility for their situation *even as* the public extended compassion and resources. Indeed, we might see Loury's prediction partially realized by comparing the generally quite humanizing media coverage of the 'opioid epidemic' gripping rural and suburban (white) America with past and present coverage of

[18] Loury, *The Anatomy of Racial Inequality*, 82.

similar social phenomena perceived as 'black', for example, the 'crack epidemic' in the 1970s and 1980s—now explained in terms of 'disease', then in terms of 'crime'.

This second type of racism, then, which looks more like neglect than hatred, might also be viewed in terms of differential ascriptions of *blame*: the same situations in which white Americans are thought not to bear personal responsibility, and hence for which intervention and aid is merited, are seen, when the agent is a member of a racially stigmatized group, as the result of personal failings. Yet, cleanly inverting the racial categories like this is impossible in practice. The United States is both punitive and individualistic towards poor whites, especially those who commit 'crimes', and has been for a long time. But because of the equally long-standing associations between poverty, crime, and race (particularly blackness), it is impossible to determine how much of the focus on punishment and so-called individual responsibility is truly race-neutral. That is, the reluctance of white Americans to endorse premise 4—even when doing so cuts against their own material interests—may be strengthened by the reluctance to apply it to black people in premise 6 (that is, they reject the premise in order not to be forced to accept the conclusion).[19]

Seeing the Better, Doing the Worse—Implicit Bias and Racial Akrasia

Acting against One's Principles

So far, I have described ways in which people reject the normative non-racist argument by rejecting one or more of its premises. We began with racial hatreds such as those of national socialism or the Ku Klux Klan, which deny the first two premises, namely, that humans are equally worthy of respect and basic rights, regardless of race, and that black

---

[19] Indeed, one might note that social welfare programmes have often needed to demonstrate that they are going to benefit primarily *white* people. Consider the New Deal compromise in excluding most black people by leaving domestic workers and farm workers outside the scope of the emerging welfare state and labour laws. See, in addition to Katznelson, *When Affirmative Action Was White*, Ira Katznelson, *Fear Itself: The New Deal and the Origins of Our Times* (New York: Liveright, 2014) or the ways in which 1930s era art and literature are careful to depict nobly suffering *white people* as those in need of a helping hand (for example, John Steinbeck's novels or Dorothea Lang's famous photo portraits).

people and other racially stigmatized groups are indeed humans. We then moved on the subtler—and more prevalent—form of racial thinking which accepts the *general* premises of human equality and equal humanity, but which denies that the various forms of material racial inequality in the United States are cause for intervention. I suggested that this constitutes an implicit denial of equal humanity to members of racial minorities: that the indifference shown by white Americans towards the vastly inferior life chances of African Americans and other people of colour would be unconscionable if applied to whites. This is racism expressed (publicly, at least) as neglect rather than as hatred.[20]

In both of these cases, stigmatizing conceptions of racial Others as subhuman or undeserving led to agents denying one or more of the premises in the two arguments we began with. But what about those who endorse both the normative non-racist argument and the racial justice argument in toto?

As I have noted, racially prejudicial beliefs (and to a somewhat lesser extent, behaviours) are something of a stock example in philosophical discussions of acting contrary to one's better judgment or professed beliefs.[21] Moreover, the phenomenon of behaviour systematically reflecting racial biases even in the absence of any professed racist beliefs—indeed in subjects who profess vehement *anti*-racist beliefs—has also been the subject of significant experimental research in social

[20] Macpherson, 'The Banality of White Supremacy.' The philosopher Lionel MacPherson puts the point about racism-as-neglect very clearly in a recent interview: 'Relatively few White Americans today seem viciously anti-black: they just don't care enough about the lives of Black Americans to do or give up much, if anything, to correct anti-black injustice and inequality.'

[21] Authors who explicitly refer to racism in discussions of akrasia include: Agnes G. Callard, 'Ignorance and Akrasia Denial in the Protagoras', *Oxford Studies in Ancient Philosophy* 47 (2014): 31–80; Graham Hubbs, *The Rational Unity of the Self* (PhD Thesis, University of Pittsburgh, 2008); Lubomira Radoilska, *Addiction and Weakness of Will* (Oxford: Oxford University Press, 2013).

Other authors cite racism as an example of closely related phenomena, such as 'acting contrary to professed beliefs': Eric Schwitzgebel, 'Acting Contrary to Our Professed Beliefs or the Gulf between Occurrent Judgment and Dispositional Belief', *Pacific Philosophical Quarterly* 91 (2010): 531–53; Tamar S. Gendler, 'Alief in Action (and Reaction)', *Mind and Language* 23, no. 5 (2008): 552–85; T.M. Scanlon, *Moral Dimensions: Permissibility, Meaning, Blame* (Cambridge, MA and London: Harvard University Press, 2008).

psychology, which claims to demonstrate persistent 'implicit bias' in experimental subjects who do not endorse racist norms.[22] Now, because there are strong norms governing the expression of racist sentiments in public, there will be many people who endorse not only the general normative non-racist argument, but also the more robust racial justice argument 'in bad faith'—that is, who do *not* believe some or all of the propositions, though they are willing to publicly endorse them. Such cases are properly described as lying,[23] exemplified by the tactical adoption of race-neutral race baiting by the Republican party.[24] The familiar sentence opener 'I'm not a racist, but….' is similarly a tactical adoption of (usually very superficial) anti-racism in order precisely to legitimize racist beliefs. Rather, the case that I want to focus on is the one in which a person may *sincerely endorse* every single one of premises 1 through 6 and yet be systematically racially prejudiced in their behaviours. In this third category of racism, the underlying emotional structure will be seen to be once again less articulate—though still powerful. Here, fear combined with a sense of moral indifference seems to motivate people to violate their own better judgements in racially invidious ways.[25]

The basic conflict in such an agent can be described in a variety of ways: between egalitarian beliefs and prejudicial emotions,[26] between conscious and unconscious beliefs (psychoanalysis), and between explicit

[22] See the overview in Mazharin R. Banaji and Anthony G. Greenwald, *Blindspot: Hidden Biases of Good People* (New York: Random House, 2013).

[23] In the *absence* of action, whether or not this kind of deception is desirable or not is another question which would need to be considered at some length: Is it better for people who hold racially stigmatizing beliefs to express them or to censor themselves?

[24] See Lee Atwater, interview on the 'Southern Strategy'.

[25] For a social psychological account of the extent of racially based fear responses, see Sophie Trawalter, Andrew R. Todd, Abigail Baird, and Jennifer A. Richeson, 'Attending to Threat: Race-based Patterns of Selective Attention,' *Journal of Experimental Social Psychology* 44, no. 5 (2008): 1322–7.

[26] Emotions need not be understood mechanistically and may or may not themselves include beliefs or indeed be a sort of belief—see Martha C. Nussbaum, *The Upheavals of Thought: The Intelligence of the Emotions* (New York: Cambridge University Press, 2001). This work argues for the emotions as a kind of belief, (albeit with a much broader account of belief, that is, 'seeing X as Y' [p. 28] than the psychological literature, which tends to limit belief to consciously endorsed propositions).

beliefs and implicit biases (cognitive social psychology). To this list, I wish to add the notion of racial akrasia.

Implicit Bias and Racial Akrasia

However, in addition to simply adding a new term, I mean to locate a division within the broader realm of action performed contrary to an agent's principles. On one side, there are beliefs or emotions (these may be treated interchangeably for present purposes) that are fully unconscious, even if they may still lead to actions with perfectly real consequences. This is the realm of implicit bias research. On the other side, there are beliefs/emotions which may be fully disavowed which nevertheless lead to action, which action, importantly, the agent is conscious of undertaking. This second way of acting contrary to one's better judgements is what I want to analyse—when the action is a racially invidious one—as an instance of racial akrasia, or a racially akratic action.

Akrasia is the ancient Greek term for lack of self-control. But more important than its historical pedigree is what it is taken to mean today. Namely, it has been borrowed from Plato and Aristotle by contemporary philosophers to describe a situation in which an agent *freely* acts contrary to their *complete* better judgement. The emphasized words are necessary to understand why the phenomenon has been the object of such philosophical consternation: the agent is neither forced to do something they don't want to, nor do they act the way they do because of countervailing stronger reasons. A situation in which a person choses option A over option B even though they think B is superior to A in some metric (for example, in terms of cost) is not acting akratically if there is another metric, which they prioritize more highly, in which A ranks more highly than B (for example, in terms of health—there is nothing ipso facto puzzling about choosing a healthier lunch over a cheaper one if I rank healthiness as more important than cost in my deliberation about which lunch to choose).

But why add akrasia to our lexicon? My aim is to highlight cases that do not fall simply into place as instances of unconscious or implicit bias, at least as they are usually understood. What is significant about an akratic person is that they are in some meaningful sense *aware* of what they are doing and of the fact that it violates their principles. It is not (entirely, at least) unconscious. Similarly, discriminatory conduct by those who disavow racist beliefs is not only a matter of purely unconscious behaviours and motivations.

An akratic agent may thus feel guilty about their bad action, while this seems ruled out in the case of one who is *implicitly* biased precisely because of the unconscious character of the beliefs leading to racist behaviour. Racial akrasia allows us to get into focus the extreme sense of unease and guilt which characterizes so much interaction between even sincerely non-racist white Americans and people of colour. And it also explains the significance of post hoc rationalization. A self-professed believer in racial justice crosses a street to avoid a group of black teenagers. Then they tell themselves that they would have done the same with a group of white teenagers, then that there was an interesting plaque on a building. Then that you saw a passer-by who looked like a friend, then that it was shadier, then that it was sunnier. Kettle logic, in short, to quell a palpable sense of guilt.

This may not be the kind of clear- or open-eyed akrasia that, because of its vague air of paradox, commands much attention in philosophical investigation. Medea, the speaker of my first epigraph, as she chooses to pursue an infatuation with Jason that will end in tragedy, declares that she knows what she is doing is bad for her and those around her, but at the same time remains fully committed to the act. (Not much of a sense of guilt.) But not all akratics are like Medea, and I submit that the kind of unease or guilt about one's behaviour that accompanies many accounts of implicit bias is a sign of akrasia, even if muddy-eyed.

The gulf, moreover, between racial akrasia and discrimination motivated by implicit bias may not be a large one. For even if an agent is moved by unconscious *forces*, they may nevertheless become aware of a conflict between their judgments and their *actions* in the moment that they act. Even in the limit case of fully unconscious attitudes—where bias is completely submerged and does not even rise partially above the surface—the experience of cognitive dissonance characteristic of acting knowingly against one's judgements may become manifest, not in a consciously available conflicting attitude, but in the action itself.

Nevertheless, racial akrasia as I have characterized it—that is, as accompanied by a sense of guilt or shame—is crucially different from implicit bias, at least as the latter is commonly understood. In the latter case, it is not infrequently held that agents are motivated to act by beliefs, of which, were they conscious, they would feel a deep sense of shame: 'On the view of implicit racism, it is much more likely that if … agents were pressed to give an account of their racial views, many would be upset to learn their judgments were unmistakably racially motivated.'[27] But in cases of akrasia, the agent is *already* aware and, I contend, may indeed already feel ashamed or guilty. And, as I have suggested, this sense of unease seems, as often as not, to lead people to justify or rationalize, after the fact, actions they know to be wrong. A set of positive prescriptions is beyond the scope of this chapter, yet it seems clear that simply alerting people to their unconscious biases or constructively trying to instill a sense of shame will be inadequate in cases in which people are already both aware and ashamed.[28]

However, at the level of social theorizing, conceptual tools like implicit bias and racial akrasia share a common focus on the millions of mundane decisions that pile up to reproduce a system of rigid racial stratification: the barely conscious choice not to sit next to classmates of other races in a university lecture or to cross the street when a group of black teenagers approaches, the methodical but unreflective choice of romantic/sexual partners exclusively from high-status racial groups, the decision where to live, where to send a child to school.

What of the more egregious sorts of racially harmful acts? Police shootings, in particular, of African Americans have rightly galvanized protest and popular outrage in the last few years. They have, moreover, been explained in terms of implicit bias. But given what we know about the culture of police departments in the United States, are they not particularly well explained by appeals to tacit, rather than overt, racism?[29]

---

[27] Christopher J. Lebron, *The Color of Our Shame: Race and Justice in Our Time* (New York: Oxford University Press, 2013), 44. Lebron starts his book with the observation that 'we tend to fall away from our ideals when blacks come into view,' (p. 27)—a way of framing the issue that fits very closely with my argument. However, his project of a productive deployment of shame as a way of closing the gulf between our principles and our actions would likely need to be re-evaluated in light of my contention that in the case of akratic racism, something like shame is already at play, with far from salutary effects.

[28] A separate issue is whether a sense of shame—when not redirected towards defensive and self-justifying narratives—might not end up, perversely, becoming the mark of one's anti-racist bona fides. See Sara Ahmed's critique of the politics of shame, and disavowal more generally, in her 'Declarations of Whiteness: The Non-Performativity of Anti-Racism', *borderlands e-journal* 3, no. 2 (2004), http://www.borderlands.net.au/vol3no2_2004/ahmed_declarations.htm.

[29] Some accounts of the racism—both structural and attitudinal—endemic to American police can be found in the series of reports on individual departments. The federal Department of Justice has compiled quite shocking reports

Deadly violence and routine humiliation by precisely those agents entrusted with protection may be the ultimate expression of the devaluation of black lives in the United States, but the root of this failure lies in more mundane context. That is, they are the horrific symptom of racial inequality, but not its cause. This is not only the realm of an economic and social policy that has singularly failed to promote racial equality, but also the more informal realm of individual actions and omissions that uphold an unjust racial order.

***

This may seem like an odd focus for reflections on racism and racial stigma. Surely such people are not worth spending time on, one might say. Those who fail to *make*, rather than fail to *make good on*, the normative non-racist and racial justice arguments are surely the bigger concern. The white neo-Nazi who murdered nine black churchgoers two years ago in South Carolina is certainly not a racial akratic or, it might be added, a self-deceived racist. But while spectacular acts of racial violence should not be ignored, insofar as one regards them as connected to less spectacular forms of racial oppression and inequality, they also must not be the exclusive focus of an investigation of racism.

Another objection may be pressing. First, some readers may find this method hopelessly psychologistic, individualistic, too focused on the intentions and decisions of particular agents, and not putting enough emphases on social structures and institutions. Three replies, I think, can be made to this charge. The first and most important is that my analysis of racism in terms of defective practical reasoning is not *only* meant to capture certain habits of thought characteristic of individual white Americans. Rather I want to suggest that we can learn about patterns of social and institutional decision-making and (ir)rationality by analogy with individual reasoning.[30] Thus my hope is that the kinds of defective reasoning that can be adduced in individual practical agents can, once

---

on abuses in the police departments in Ferguson (MO) Baltimore, and Chicago (2015, 2016, and 2017, respectively) and a local commission has issued a similarly damning report on the Chicago Police Department.

[30] One might think of this suggestion as a reversal of Plato's in the *Republic*: where Socrates proposes that we understand the soul on the model of the city, I am proposing that we can understand certain social and political decision patterns on the model of individual ones.

we have got a grip of the simple cases, also start to be recognized in contexts where multiple individuals are engaged in joint reasoning. Second, the cases of practical irrationality with regard to race do not simply concern person-to-person interactions; indeed, most of the examples that I discuss concern people's judgements about broader social and political questions. They are thus salient in political, and not merely interpersonal terms, *even if* one accepts a rigid distinction between public and private. Third, though this approach accepts some form of methodological individualism in the explanation of social facts, it is weak enough to readily admit that the kinds of stigma, biases, and impaired cognition that I have discussed do not exist independently of unequal social or economic structures. Indeed, getting rid of stigma may require profound shifts not only in our inner worlds, but in both material and social relations.

Whereas this broadly structural objection raises the worry that my argument veers too far into individualism and, in particular, moralism, another critic might raise the worry that a focus on implicit bias or unconscious prejudice is too exculpatory: that it locates the genesis of racial inequality in unintentional choices and behaviour patterns for which blame cannot reasonably be assigned. It is, in fact, this sort of worry that lies behind my desire to highlight the possibility of racism as akrasia or weakness of the will—actions which the agent is meaningfully aware contradict their own better judgments.

At the same time, the fact that racism as akrasia takes place in individuals does not mean that it is to be—or indeed can be—overcome by these individuals alone. Eliminating racial inequality may involve close attention to the psychological structures that generate and enforce it, but this does not make anti-racism simply a white man's burden. Gunnar Myrdal, the Swedish economist commissioned by the Carnegie Foundation to make a study of American 'race relations' in the mid-twentieth century, made this mistake in *An America Dilemma*. Moving from the largely accurate thesis that American white supremacy sat in psychological conflict with certain egalitarian norms underpinning American republicanism (whether these are sufficient for justice or not), he came to the largely inaccurate conclusion that only a working-out of these psychological conflicts in the individual and collective psyches of *white* Americans could lead to an amelioration of the racial order. But racial akratics do not simply let racially stigmatizing affect overwhelm their sincere egalitarian judgments because of faults in their character for which they and they alone are responsible. Racial stigma may manifest itself in individual actions, but it is also the product of large-scale social forces and may indeed only be overcome through large-scale social change.

Though I have stressed the conceptual distinctness of akrasia and implicit bias, a glance at social-psychological research on eliminating implicit bias suggests that contact with members of racial out-groups is the most significant factor in reducing racially patterned inequalities in behaviour and it seems that this would hold true of less implicitly prejudicial attitudes. But Americans have very little contact with members of other races, and when they do, it tends to be in positions of social inequality—for example, white people interacting with black people primarily as those performing relatively low-status tasks. Contact does not ipso facto mean that people are being treated as equals.[31] Thus, even if we were to limit ourselves to the aim of overcoming entrenched stigmas in order to eliminate unconscious discrimination (that is, without taking on more substantive material equality as an end), this may only be possible given substantive integration to bring people into real contact as equals.[32] Taking seriously the possibility of discriminatory conduct in conflict with an agent's sincerely held beliefs points to a more general hypothesis about racial inequality: namely that the elimination of formal discrimination (that is, equality of opportunity) is inseparable from a more substantively egalitarian vision (that is, equality of outcome).

It is beyond the scope of this chapter to develop a more detailed account of what is to be done. But we can start by recognizing that, viewed from the level of individuals, the perpetuation of racial inequality—material and social—in the United States today is due as much to emotional forces as it is to intellectual ones. Advancing anti-racist arguments will only go so far if it is possible to see and approve the better and do the worse.

---

[31] This is, of course, the standard criticism of the conception of discrimination as simply a preference for less contact, as articulated most famously by Gary Becker. For a good discussion on substantive *integration*, as opposed to mere contact, see Elizabeth Anderson, *The Imperative of Integration* (Princeton: Princeton University Press, 2004). Two examples of groups in very close contact but without any corresponding evidence of egalitarian attitudes are (a) white and black people in the pre-Civil Rights south (where the latter were commonly employed as domestic servants) and (b) men and women (who have lived in the closest and yet most unequal circumstances more or less everywhere and always).

[32] For example, in the form of government-mandated or incentivized integration in housing, education, labour, and so forth

5

A Social Location Theory of Gender
How Gender Borders Create the Category 'Woman'

*Emily Dupree**

Gender stereotypes of women are both ubiquitous and extremely resistant to change: strikingly similar stereotypes found across the globe continue to be endorsed by a majority of the global population (despite dramatic increases in women's labour force participation, educational attainment, and social status in those countries whose gendered beliefs have been studied in detail).[1] Women are consistently associated with a narrow set of subservient personality traits, social roles, and civic capacities, and those who deviate from these

* I am grateful to Martha C. Nussbaum and Emilio Comay del Junco for their valuable comments on earlier versions of this chapter, and to Vidhu Verma and the other participants of the conference that gave birth to this volume, whose comments helped shape and expand my ideas on the subject.

[1] John E. Williams and Deborah L. Best, *Measuring Sex Stereotypes: A Thirty-Nation Study* (Beverly Hills: SAGE Publications, 1990). See also Megumi Hosoda and Dianna L. Stone, 'Current Gender Stereotypes and Their Evaluative Content', *Perceptual and Motor Skills* 90, no. 3 (2000): 1283.

constraints are often subject to gender discrimination, hostility, and extreme violence.

A common background assumption in analyses of this phenomenon is that women marked by these stereotypes are women in virtue of some stereotype-independent property that they all share. Some look to biological sex, others look to gender identity. But the ontological independence of women is not often questioned—women are women, and their subordination in a gendered class system is in virtue of that status. I want to offer an alternative understanding of gender stereotypes, in which they reveal to us that there are no 'women' conceptually prior to the gender borders which these stereotypes track. Rather, women are simply those people who occupy a gendered underclass. This shared location is the only thing that women have in common *as women*.

As members of this subordinate gender class, women find themselves to be the 'Other'. The creation of an Other who is imagined to possess unwanted or devalued characteristics, and then subordinated on the basis of that imagined way of being, is essential to all class-based systems of power. Race, gender, economic class, sexuality, and caste, among other social markers, all rely in some way on an Other who exists as a counterpoint to dominant norms (of which the centring is essential to the consolidation of power and wealth among those deemed 'us'). In the case of women, the stereotypes reveal the borders of a two-class socio-political and economic arrangement that entrenches power in the hands of gender-conforming men by exploiting women's labour and resources.

This shift in understanding what it is to be a woman is incompatible with the view that biological sex or gender identity independently defines the class known as 'women'. However, I will argue that both of these likely candidates for class membership have serious conceptual errors, and a social location-based definition is free from these errors. Furthermore, a social location definition of 'women' allows us to have more intuitive and effective normative recommendations for gender justice. As a starting point, this view shows us that we must work to eradicate gender-based stigma and stereotype in all of its forms. But it also shows us that advocating for counter-normative gender-based behavioural changes is not enough if that advocacy does not also involve undermining the very class differences that make counter-normativity possible. Thus, the class system known as gender must itself be abolished in a comprehensive gender justice programme.

Gender Stereotypes

Stereotypes against women exist in every country today, and they are remarkably similar given the diversity of cultures in which they are found.[2] These stereotypes manifest both at the individual level, in sex-traits stereotypes that characterize women as having distinct psychological and behavioural traits, and at the social level, in sex-role stereotypes concerning the appropriateness of various roles and activities for women generally.[3] The individual-based stereotypes often do double duty, both in allegedly justifying the belief that women are inferior to men based on inherent qualities, and as allegedly justifying the rigidity of sex-role differences society-wide based on the unsuitability of those qualities for roles coded as masculine.

An exhaustive study of gender stereotypes in 25 countries revealed that the content of these stereotypes tends to cluster around three main categories: the family as a private sphere, heteronormative marriage and women's subservience to men, and women's fitness for emotional and care labour.[4] A close analysis of these cross-cultural stereotypes reveals a complex web of deeply held beliefs, all of which hang together to create a portrait that functions as both an alleged description of a gendered landscape and an active prescription for women's lives. And because these three categories overlap in mutually reinforcing ways, the beliefs associated with them are especially difficult to change. The following is a close analysis of these stereotypes.

The Family as a Private Sphere

The first cluster of stereotypes against women involves the notion of the family as a private sphere. However, the perniciousness of these beliefs is often not visible until they are contrasted with the stereotypes of men. In all but three of the countries studied, men are associated with the role of the 'critical parent' and the 'adult', understood as the family

---

[2] Williams and Best, *Measuring Sex Stereotypes*.

[3] Williams and Best, *Measuring Sex Stereotypes*,16.

[4] Participants' beliefs about gendered stereotypes were studied in Australia, Bolivia, Brazil, Canada, England, Finland, France, Germany, Ireland, India, Italy, Israel, Japan, Malaysia, Netherlands, New Zealand, Nigeria, Norway, Pakistan, Peru, Scotland, South Africa, Taiwan, Thailand, Trinidad, the United States, Venezuela, and Zimbabwe.

member who 'criticizes, controls, and reflects the rules of society' and engages in realistic problem solving.[5] Furthermore, men are believed to need leadership roles in groups, the ability to act autonomously and independently of others, and access to publicly recognized achievement.[6] Taken together, stereotypes of men paint a picture of a person who is uniquely suited for rational thinking, civic participation, and problem-solving. When family comes into this picture, it is always in terms of control over the family in such a way that the family unit conforms to the prevailing social norms that men themselves had a hand in creating.

The stereotypes of women, once the above is in view, show that women are understood as subservient participants in this system. In all but one of the countries studied, women are strongly associated with the role of the 'nurturing parent', understood to be the parent who nurtures and promotes growth within the family.[7] They are believed to be socially impotent, prioritizing affiliations of friendship over achievement, and comfortable in subordinate roles in relationships with others.[8] And women are more often associated with the ego state of the 'adapted child' rather than the 'adult'—the adapted child is under the domination of authority figures in the family, engaging in conforming and compromising behaviours rather than autonomous and critical behaviours.[9] Furthermore, women are believed to be inherently superstitious, disqualifying them from forms of public participation that require reason-based thinking.[10] Thus, women in every culture studied are believed to be most suited for life within the family. And the family is understood to be a sphere of male control in which women carry out the orders of men and facilitate male participation and achievement in the public sphere.

This picture is extremely troubling when viewed in light of theories about the role the social institution of the family has in larger systems of gender-based power and control. Susan Moller Okin convincingly argued against the idea that the family is somehow beyond justice precisely because she saw that the family was, instead, one of the primary

[5] Williams and Best, *Measuring Sex Stereotypes*, 227.
[6] Williams and Best, *Measuring Sex Stereotypes*, 228.
[7] Williams and Best, *Measuring Sex Stereotypes*, 227.
[8] Williams and Best, *Measuring Sex Stereotypes*, 228.
[9] Williams and Best, *Measuring Sex Stereotypes*, 227.
[10] Williams and Best, *Measuring Sex Stereotypes*, 227.

vehicles for gender *in*justice.[11] The unequal distribution of unpaid labour in the family, justified by women's 'natural' suitability for such labour, disadvantages women and taxes their efforts to enter the paid workforce (as they encounter both hostility and the notorious 'double shift'). It also consigns women to forms of labour that they do not necessarily consent to, solely in virtue of their female 'nature' (whatever that concept might mean)—the family is assumed to be a 'realm of private life in which the reproductive and nurturant needs of human beings are taken care of'.[12] The assumption here, of course, is that the caretakers are women, and the care-receivers are adult men and children (though even female children begin assuming the role of caretaker in both play and real life at an early age). The family has thus been theorized as an institution that extracts labour from one class of people for the benefit of the other, without pay, and justifies this extraction as both necessary for social function and rooted in the 'natural' dispositions of men and women. And stereotypes about women, at minimum, reinforce this dynamic: if women are naturally determined to be subservient participants in this system, then any deviation from it will be deemed 'unnatural' and therefore impermissible.

The family is also believed to be immune from justice-based critique because of its role in a larger public–private distinction that permeates liberal theories of justice as well as lay understandings of our social order. Okin describes this as the distinction between 'the "public" world of political life and the marketplace and the "private" domestic world of family life and personal relations'.[13] The stereotypes described earlier certainly match this distinction: cross-culturally, men are believed to be suited for the public world and women are believed to be suited for the private. And yet the family contains power dynamics, the 'distinguishing feature of the political'.[14] These power dynamics manifest in a variety of ways, including domestic violence, coercion, and imbalanced decision-making. But the idea that the family is political goes against deeply rooted stereotypes. As a result, the very women who seek to politicize their family life and/or enter the marketplace are believed to fundamentally misunderstand the scope of the 'political' and their role in it, and

[11]   Susan Moller Okin, *Justice Gender and the Family* (United States: Basic Books, 1989).

[12]   Okin, *Justice Gender and the Family*, 75.

[13]   Okin, *Justice Gender and the Family*, 111.

[14]   Okin, *Justice Gender and the Family*, 128.

thus are believed to display the very disqualification for civic participation that consigns them to family life to begin with. Stereotypes against women are an integral component to this phenomenon: they portray women's personalities and needs as uniquely suited to flourishing in the private sphere, and they trace the boundary of the private sphere such that any exit from it will automatically be deemed unnatural.

Heteronormative Marriage and Women's Subservience to Men

Stereotypes against women cluster around a second, related theme: heteronormative marriage and women's subservience to men. The family, as described earlier, is understood to be a sphere of private life revolving around a central, heterosexual marriage. In the majority of countries studied, women are strongly associated with heterosexuality (though men were not), where that was understood to mean that women seek the company of men and derive emotional satisfaction from relationships with men.[15] These relationships, however, are believed to be composed of two partners with highly asymmetrical psychological needs. In every country studied, men are believed to need opportunities for dominance and aggression, while women are believed to need opportunities for abasement and deference.[16] When these beliefs about women's alleged psychological need to seek subordinate roles in relationships are combined with the beliefs about women's satisfaction in heterosexual relationships, a picture emerges wherein women are believed to experience satisfaction in their own subordination (because they are 'inherently' submissive, and thus naturally fit to be dominated by men).[17]

These stereotypes contribute to the perception that any deviation from a heteronormative marital arrangement is normatively suspect. Lesbian, bisexual, and queer women who enter into same-sex relationships are, in virtue of doing so, rejecting heterosexual marriage and subservience to men in their family lives. Importantly, their relationships are remarkably egalitarian when it comes to the distribution of power and unpaid labour in the household. And yet current studies show that these women are doing worse than heterosexual women on every metric of well-being, including physical and mental health, susceptibility to violence, and

---

[15] Williams and Best, *Measuring Sex Stereotypes*, 227.

[16] Williams and Best, *Measuring Sex Stereotypes*, 227.

[17] Williams and Best, *Measuring Sex Stereotypes*, 227.

rates of discrimination.[18] It is plausible that much of lesbian, bisexual, and queer women's disadvantage stems from the constant hostility and violence they encounter in a world in which most people endorse these stereotypes. In particular, bisexual women in relationships with men are doing even worse than either lesbians or heterosexual women—giving lie to the idea that somehow bisexual women are privileged relative to their queer counterparts when they participate in relationships with men.[19] To the contrary, they are disadvantaged both by the constraints of heteronormative marriage and by the constant stress of a sexuality that deviates from stereotypical heterosexuality.

Conforming to heteronormative marital expectations is not much better, though. As Okin writes about marriage, and as the stereotypes discussed confirm, it is an institution of asymmetric vulnerability. Women are made vulnerable by a disproportionate share of unpaid domestic labour, financial dependence, minimal interpersonal power, and few exit options.[20] When they nonetheless conform to this arrangement despite its fundamental unfairness, they are saddled with a tremendous amount of work (which is barely acknowledged *as work*). But when women combat this unfair distribution within their marriages, they are highly likely to encounter hostility from their husbands: marital conflict rises in direct proportion to the amount of housework the male partner is asked to do. [21] This is not true of women's housework. As a result, women who are married to men often must choose, from a position of vulnerability, marital arrangements that are in all likelihood going to further solidify their own vulnerability going forward.

These stereotypes, when combined with the realities of marriage for women, show us that the institution of heterosexual marriage is one in which a woman is expected to both carry out the will of her husband and also take on the reproductive labour associated with her husband's life—she must cook, clean, bear and raise children, and make herself

[18] G. Gonzales, J. Przedworski, and C. Henning-Smith, 'Comparison of Health and Health Risk Factors Between Lesbian, Gay, and Bisexual Adults and Heterosexual Adults in the United States', *Jama Intern Med.* 176, no. 9 (2016): 1344–51.

[19] 'Invisible Majority: The Disparities Facing Bisexual People and How to Remedy Them', *Movement Advancement Project*, September 2016.

[20] Okin, *Justice Gender and the Family,* 149.

[21] Philip Blumstein and Pepper Schwartz, *American Couples* (New York: Morrow, 1983), 312., as cited in Okin, *Justice Gender and the Family,* 154.

deferentially available to her husband's sexual desires. What's more, she is believed to do this happily. John Stuart Mill made note of this in the late nineteenth century, writing: 'Men do not want solely the obedience of women, they want their sentiments.'[22] And the conditions that existed when he was writing *The Subjection of Women* are largely consistent with the stereotypes that endure to this day: women are believed to have inherent personality traits and needs that are perfectly tailored to be satisfied by deferring to men, serving men, and carrying out the will of men. One manifestation of this is through heterosexual marriage. But the epidemic of sexual violence against women, both within and outside of marriage, is a symptom as well. If women are believed to be inherently *for men*, then it is no wonder that so many men derive satisfaction from extracting this subservience from women who do not willingly display it. This epidemic is particularly devastating for transgender women, who encounter rates of sexual and physical violence at even higher rates than cisgender women.[23] Their vulnerability to violence is doubled—they encounter hostility both because they are gender-nonconforming and because they are women. The result is that they are the most vulnerable women among us.

Emotional and Care Labour

Finally, stereotypes about women in all countries surveyed cluster around women's fitness for performing emotional and care labour. As described earlier, women are believed to be uniquely suited for child-rearing, involving the almost nonstop administration of care, support, and attention to their growing children. Appeals to reproductive biology (that is, most women's childbearing and nursing capacities) are used to justify traditional sex-based family roles. And women in every country surveyed are believed to derive satisfaction from the act of nurturance, 'engaging in behavior extending material and emotional benefits to others'.[24]

Women are also expected to perform a disproportionate amount of emotional and care labour in the workforce. They are much more likely to

[22] John Stuart Mill, *The Subjection of Women* (Indianapolis: Hackett Publishing Company, 1988), 15.

[23] 'Hate Violence Against Transgender Communities', National Coalition of Anti-Violence Programs, http://www.avp.org/storage/documents/ncavp_transhvfactsheet.pdf, accessed on 27 February 2017.

[24] Williams and Best, *Measuring Sex Stereotypes*, 228.

perform jobs that require emotional labour and cheerful deference to men (primarily service-oriented jobs).[25] And the vast majority of in-home care workers in the United States (such as nannies and aids to the elderly) are women.[26] Even within jobs that do not primarily revolve around care work, women workers nonetheless take on a greater share of the informal, daily care work that arises (such as mentoring and service within academia).[27]

This segregation of women into care-dominant professions (or tasks within the non-care-based profession) tracks the general invisibility and devaluation of care labour in society. As one report summarized it, 'the very fact that women comprise a large majority of care workers contributes to the relatively low-paid nature of these jobs.'[28] And often these devalued jobs are not seen as *labour* at all, 'precisely because [care] work relies on qualities such as empathy, patience, and the ability to establish an emotional bond—qualities that women are often assumed to have acquired naturally rather than through rigorous work—it is seen as different from other paid labor and, therefore, undeserving of the same monetary rewards'.[29]

Of course, care and care labour is an integral part of any community, and much of feminist ethics has been centred on its importance for justice and progressive moral theory.[30] But care labour persists as

[25] Amy S. Wharton, 'The Sociology of Emotional Labor', *Annual Review of Sociology* 35 (2009): 147–65.

[26] See Jane M. Henrici, *Improving Career Opportunities for Immigrant Women In-Home Care Workers* (Washington, DC: Institute for Women's Policy Research, 2013), https://iwpr.org/publications/improving-career-opportunities-for-immigrant-women-in-home-care-workers/, accessed on 27 February 2017.

[27] See, for example, Marcia L. Bellas, 'Emotional Labor in Academia: The Case of Professors', *The Annals of the American Academy of Political and Social Science* 561 (January 1999): 96–110, for a discussion of women professors' disproportionate work in teaching and service, rather than research and administration, and the gendered reward structures of the profession.

[28] Cynthia Hess, *Women and the Care Crisis: Valuing In-Home Care in Policy and Practice* (Washington, DC: Institute for Women's Policy Research, 2013), https://iwpr.org/publications/women-and-the-care-crisis-valuing-in-home-care-in-policy-and-practice/, accessed on 27 February 2017.

[29] See Hess, *Women and the Care Crisis*, citing Paula England, Michelle Budig, and Nancy Folbre, 'Wages of Virtue: The Relative Pay of Care Work', *Social Problems* 49, no. 4 (2002): 455–73.

[30] See, for example, Alison M. Jaggar, 'Caring as a Feminist Practice of Moral Reason', in *Justice and Care: Essential Readings in Feminist Ethics*, ed. Virginia Held (Boulder, CO: Westview Press, 1995).

a devalued and invisible form of labour outside of these theories, and women are disproportionately performing this work. As a result, they constitute a class of people believed to be inherently suited to unpaid or underpaid work (depending on where it is performed) without the full recognition of having actually *worked*. In the United States, many care workers lack access to even the minimal worker protections afforded to other forms of labour (such as unionization and paid leave), consigning many of them to poverty wages and financial insecurity. These results are surely true in many of the other countries analysed earlier. Care has been segregated from productive society, asymmetrically distributed within the household, and demeaned as a form of labour. Already vulnerable women bear the brunt of this system.

Insights from Gender Stereotypes

Analysing these three stereotype clusters generates the following picture: women are believed to be inherently suited for forms of labour that are necessary to the reproduction of men's lives, involving both species reproduction via childbearing and individual reproduction via cooking, cleaning, and caring. And the people surveyed around the globe all move from this general descriptive belief to the normative one that women *should* be engaged in these sex-segregated roles, and that opting out is failing to give men the labour and access to which they are entitled. This theoretical step is not justified by the beliefs themselves, yet it motivates much of the hostility and violence that women encounter—gender-nonconforming women, transgender women, and women who reject heteronormativity or simply demand equality are made more vulnerable to male violence the moment they cross the gendered boundaries that these stereotypes map. And all women must contend with expectations of subservience, demeaned status, and compromised personhood. Taken together, these stereotypes show us that one of the essential features of womanhood around the world is to occupy a second-class status, understood in both material and ideological terms.

Women as the Other

The dominant global stereotypes against women reveal to us the borders of a gendered class system in which women's lives and labour are systematically exploited for men's benefit. I want to also argue that these stereotypes reveal that gender borders actively create a gendered underclass through the imagined relevance of neatly ordered sexed bodies. Women, far from being a natural biological kind, are members of a subordinate gender class, and their membership in that class is deemed 'natural' and therefore justified by the persistent gender stereotypes described above. But this 'naturalness' is a fiction, and so too is the idea that there are any women conceptually prior to the class system in which they find themselves.

In this way, women are members of a gendered underclass in a system that conforms to what is described in the social scientific literature as *othering*. Through this process, not only does a dominant group 'define into existence an inferior group', but the dominant group also constructs an ideology that both marks members of the class and justifies their membership in it. [31] What is important about this phenomenon is that the difference between the groups is a difference of power rather than a difference of ontological status—among all the various manifestations of *othering*, including the othering of racial minorities, religious minorities, and the 'poor', there is no pre-social characteristic that defines the group and justifies its subordination. Rather, the dominant group projects a pathologically and morally inferior status onto the Other, and then subjugates them on the basis of that fantasized difference.[32]

In particular, *othering* typically prioritizes the idea that some observed or imagined difference is a normative deficit.[33] In the stereotypes discussed earlier, we saw that women are widely believed to be superstitious, irrational, better suited to devalued emotional and care labour, and socially impotent. This differs substantially from beliefs that men are rational, socially effective, and powerful. Since these latter capacities are valued in a gendered class system, women's imagined deviance from such characteristics is viewed as a normative deficit. As a result, their normative deficit is believed to be grounds for subordination. This subordination, in turn, is maintained by symbolic classification schemes and identity codes 'whereby members of a group know what kind of self

[31] Michael Schwalbe, Sandra Godwin, Daphne Holden, Douglas Schrock, Shealy Thompson, and Michele Wolkomir, 'Generic Processes in the Reproduction of Inequality: An Interactionist Analysis', *Social Forces* 79, no 2 (2000): 419–52.

[32] Gayatri Chakravorty Spivak, 'The Rani of Sirmur: An Essay in Reading the Archives', *History and Theory* 24, no. 3 (October 1985): 247–72.

[33] Schwalbe et al., 'Generic Processes in the Reproduction of Inequality', 423.

is signified by certain words, deeds, and dress'.[34] This is a hallmark of oppressive *othering*, as it 'entails the creation of identity codes that make it impossible for members of a subjugated group to signify fully creditable selves'.[35] The very characteristics that women are marked with make it impossible for them to be viewed as full persons within this symbolic order—they are not autonomous but dependent and subservient to the will of men.

Along with *othering*, boundary maintenance is one of 'the key forms of joint action through which inequalities are reproduced in small groups, complex organizations, communities, and societies'.[36] Although stereotypes against women rest on the myth of natural gendered difference; in fact, a tremendous amount of work goes into maintaining and policing these gendered boundaries, which serve to 'limit Others' access to valued resources'.[37] This occurs in three ways: controlling the transmission of cultural capital; controlling access to networks of power; and the use of violence or the threat thereof to ensure that women remain in their gendered roles.[38] From early childhood, the intergenerational transmission of cultural capital within the family is influenced by gender norms, as boys and girls receive quite different informal education at home. Entering adulthood, cultural capital is further segregated by confining women to the home and to the work of the family—in some instances, women are simply not as familiar with the norms of navigating public and civic society. But even women who do work outside the home are shut out of this transmission—either they are employed in care professions that do not develop publicly recognized cultural capital, or men in their workplace hoard resources, leaving women to fend for themselves as they attempt to progress through their career.

Networks of power are controlled in similar ways, often locking women out of crucial social networks that give members access to

---

[34] Schwalbe et al., 'Generic Processes in the Reproduction of Inequality', 424.

[35] Schwalbe et al., 'Generic Processes in the Reproduction of Inequality', 424.

[36] Schwalbe et al., 'Generic Processes in the Reproduction of Inequality', 422.

[37] Schwalbe et al., 'Generic Processes in the Reproduction of Inequality', 430.

[38] Schwalbe et al., 'Generic Processes in the Reproduction of Inequality', 430.

wealth-building and power-gaining opportunities. Recent controversies surrounding men-only social clubs at Harvard University and other elite American universities show that these issues are still present,[39] but so too does the ordinary exclusion women experience in social networks that serve as springboards for men's employment opportunities. And even *after* gaining access to groups that discriminate on the basis of cultural capital, women continue to experience barriers (such as the 'glass ceiling' encountered by women in corporate settings). These further barriers, which determine the distribution of status and rewards within the group, ensure that the women who make it into male-dominated fields remain low-level outliers rather than the high-achieving norm. Women's status as an Other is maintained, even as they gain access to spaces that would otherwise render them a member of the 'in-group'.

Finally, violence and the threat of violence is one of the most salient ways gender boundaries are policed and maintained. Sexual and physical violence against women is an epidemic in the United States and around the world, and often gender-nonconforming women (bisexual, lesbian, queer, and transgender) are at the highest risk of sexual and physical violence by men. In the United States, 17 per cent of heterosexual women report having been raped at some point in their life, 13 per cent of lesbian women, and 46 per cent of bisexual women (note, again, the dramatic increase in victimization for bisexual women).[40] And a staggering 69 per cent of transgender women report having been the victim of rape at least once in their lifetime, almost always citing their transgender status as one of the reasons motivating their perpetrator.[41] Other studies have

[39] See Harvard Dean Khurana's statement: 'The most entrenched of these spaces send an unambiguous message that they are the exclusive preserve of men. In their recruitment practices and through their extensive resources and access to networks of power, these organizations propagate exclusionary values that undermine those of the larger Harvard College community.' From Ramsey Fahs, 'In Historic Move, Harvard to Penalize Final Clubs, Greek Organizations', *The Harvard Crimson*, 6 May 2016, http://www.thecrimson.com/article/2016/5/6/college-sanctions-clubs-greeklife/, accessed on 27 February 2017.

[40] S.G. Smith, J. Chen, K.C. Basile, L.K. Gilbert, M.T. Merrick, N. Patel, M. Walling, and A. Jain (2017). 'The National Intimate Partner and Sexual Violence Survey (NISVS): 2010-2012 State Report'. Atlanta, GA: National Center for Injury Prevention and Control, Centers for Disease Control and Prevention.

[41] G.P. Kenagy, 'Transgender Health Findings from Two Needs Assessment Studies in Philadelphia', *Health and Social Work* 30, no. 1 (2005): 19–26.

shown that men use violence and the threat of violence to 'control the social lives of their female partners', and employ degrading and threatening sexual harassment tactics against colleagues and women in public in order to 'keep them in their place'.[42] As a result, violence, the fear of violence, and the anticipation of harassment 'limit[s] women's access to people and places from which might be acquired the resources needed to challenge men for power'.[43] What these statistics show is that violence against women has a unique political character—it both circumscribes women into a set of gender-normatively acceptable behaviours, and also degrades the quality of women's lives, once circumscribed, so as to establish and perpetuate their second-class status.

Otherness and Women's Ontological Status

Women are the gendered Other, and they are made so by an interconnecting network of beliefs, behaviours, customs, and institutions. I have foregrounded the dominant beliefs about women in this chapter because of the extent to which these beliefs influence and are influenced by the behaviours, customs, and institutions that exist in all the countries investigated. As one study described it, 'the reproduction of inequality, even when it appears thoroughly institutionalized, ultimately depends on face-to-face interaction, which therefore must be studied as part of understanding the reproduction of inequality'.[44] These face-to-face interactions, which of course populate our daily lives, occur against a backdrop in which women are believed to be the subordinate Other. These background beliefs, far from being *caused by* a pre-existing gendered order, instead contribute substantially to its production and reproduction they constitute an ideology that both establishes social distances between the self-appointed 'us' and the subordinate Other, and justifies the subordinate status of the Other by appealing to 'nature'.

But an essential point about this status is that it is not a natural kind—the Other is something that is created, or that emerges, in sociopolitical interaction. And it always goes against fundamental values of

---

[42] Schwalbe et al., 'Generic Processes in the Reproduction of Inequality', 434.

[43] Schwalbe et al., 'Generic Processes in the Reproduction of Inequality', 434.

[44] Schwalbe et al., 'Generic Processes in the Reproduction of Inequality', 420.

equality and dignity, as the Other is imagined to be normatively inferior, and thus deserving of subordination, on the basis of some observed or imagined difference from the dominant group. One result of this understanding is that those that are othered in a particular way, in this case in a gendered way, often do not have some fundamental property that they share *apart from* living in a world in which they are the Other. The properties that women are imagined to inherently possess, such as meekness, maternal tenderness, and heterosexuality, are just that—imagined. Once these are revealed to have no necessary relationship to the designation 'woman' (as much of feminist work attempts to show), the very definition of what makes a woman begins to look hollow. My proposal is that, before we attempt to fill this void with alleged *properties* that all women might have in common, we should look instead to the sociopolitical situatedness of women. Doing so reveals that the dominant network of gendered beliefs, behaviours, and institutions do more than simply subordinate a pre-existing group in the world—they determine who counts as eligible for membership in this group to begin with. Thus, women are simply those people who are subordinated in this gendered order. And they are subordinated not because they are women; rather, they are women because they are subordinated in this particular way. Although this reverses the dominant understanding of what it is to be a woman, especially given the development of modern feminist thought, it appears to be the only tenable option for such an understanding.

This is made more clear by pausing to consider other possible answers to the question: What makes a woman? Many people will answer that women are female-bodied people—this is the independent, pre-social characteristic that marks the group, and the subordination women experience is derived (historically, conceptually) from this starting point. Such a view exists in numerous forms: we often hear anti-feminists appeal to women's female bodies when justifying their beliefs about women's proper role as domestic caregivers; but feminist philosophers, too, have endorsed the view that being female is an essential (though not entirely explanatory) feature of womanhood. Simone de Beauvoir and those influenced by her begin with what they see as a fact of women's (female) bodies at birth, which then determines their placement in the complicated caste system of gender; and radical feminists writing during the 1970s in the United States, among other places, defined women as simply a subordinated sex class.[45]

---

[45] Simone de Beauvoir, *The Second Sex* (Vintage Books: New York, 2011 [1949]). See also Shulamith Firestone, *The Dialectic of Sex: The Case for Feminist Revolution* (New York: Farrar, Straus, and Giroux, 1970).

To be sure, some conception of the 'female body' is closely linked to women's subordination. In virtue of their reproductive capacities, cisgender women are imagined to be an embodiment of animality in ways that cisgender men are not, and this proximity to animality triggers disgust. Menstruation, childbirth, and lactation involve unexpected, smelly, and difficult-to-contain fluids; many gender norms about decency require women to hide away at precisely the moment such disgusting possibilities might encroach on the clean, sanitized world of men. And cisgender women's bodies that deviate from stereotypical femininity elicit tremendous disgust—fat women, women with non-sanctioned body hair, and disabled women are expected to hide from public view lest their disgusting corporeality infringe on a public space that demands adherence to gender norms.

The 'female body' is also deeply relevant to gender designations. Girls are labelled 'girls' at birth, because in most cases, their external genitalia match what is classified as 'female'. And using 'female' as a proxy for picking out all the women will be, on the whole, quite accurate (though its inaccuracy has lasting negative consequences for intersex and transgender people of all genders). One can't simply deny then that, in many cases, women are those people whose bodies have something to do with the status of being female. But what is this relationship? It is that their bodies are deemed uncomplicatedly female—and this designation of non-complication is a gendered designation. By centring a particular type of body as paradigmatically female (and indeed by considering it a *type* at all), and then assigning that body to the paradigmatic woman, these women are made to fit into a heterosexual order in which their ontological status is necessarily interwoven with their reproductive capacities. Put differently, the designation 'female' is not in reference to a self-contained characteristic of an individual body, but to the relative proximity of that body to a heteronormative centre.

Thus, while we can recognize that some notion of biological sex is a fairly accurate proxy for women, we must also recognize that the accuracy of this proxy perpetuates the idea that these women, in virtue of their 'female' bodies, are the ones who must carry out the reproductive labour associated with the lives of gender-conforming men. Species reproduction via childbearing is one such task, but so too is cooking, cleaning, and the emotional labour described in detail above. Of course, the performance of this labour does not make someone a woman. And I argue that the capacity does not, either—the capacity to bear children that inheres in the status of being uncomplicatedly female is not what *makes* someone a woman. We should not mistake the accuracy of a proxy for an ontological explanation.

Instead, we must look to what women have in common now, which is a shared residence in the social location of 'woman'. This social location, and the ideology that constitutes its boundaries, lends itself well to origin stories of women that draw a necessary connection between them and their female status. We must resist these origin stories, or at least understand them in their appropriate historical context, if we are to maintain an understanding of women that takes seriously their status as the Other and all that it entails.

There are, of course, other serious problems with the attempt to ground women's status in a binary biological sex framework, even if one rejects the above arguments for the tenuous ontological relationship between sex and gender. To begin, the idea that biological sex is either male or female is a highly oversimplified understanding of the biological classification of bodies into sexes. Sex determination is, in fact, best understood as a holistic process that considers multiple metrics (including our genetics, cell composition, hormones, genitals, and secondary sex characteristics[46]), and it does not always produce results that conform to a binary sex framework. People deemed 'female' can nonetheless carry a mosaic of cells considered both male and female, or can have hormone levels inconsistent with the typical female person. And intersex people can have both 'male' external genitals and 'female' internal reproductive organs, illuminating the spectral rather than binary character of biological sex. But intersex people are not outliers of an otherwise binary sex framework, to be disregarded in our theories—rather, they are at the heart of the spectrum of biological sex and must be seriously considered when analysing the relationship between sex and gender.

Furthermore, the treatment of intersex people by the medical establishment undermines the presumption that biological sex is somehow a pre-social characteristic of bodies onto which the social construct of gender is projected. Children born with clear intersex traits almost always undergo surgery in the United States to 'normalize' their genitals. This normalization process brings the child's body into line, as much as possible, with the expected morphology of bodies in a binary biological sex system. But we must see that this surgery is not an assignment of

---

[46] Claire Ainsworth, 'Sex Redefined', *Nature Magazine*, 18 February 2015, http://www.nature.com/news/sex-redefined-1.16943, accessed on 27 February 2017.

gender; it is an assignment of sex so that the eventual gendering process will not be thwarted by an ambiguous body. These surgeries, objected to as human rights violations by intersex activists, show us that even the sex of children is subject to social and medical intervention well before their gendered behaviour can be subject to the same sort of intervention which has been described in detail earlier.

Judith Butler's *Gender Trouble* helps locate these claims in feminist theory: 'Gender ought not to be conceived merely as the cultural inscription of meaning on a pregiven sex (a juridical conception); gender must also designate the very apparatus of production whereby the sexes themselves are established.'[47] Put differently, sex itself is an integral layer of a gendered process that relies on the imagined existence of a 'politically neutral surface'[48] for its purchase on the world. The medical intervention on intersex bodies shows us this, but so too does the subtler belief that we can use a single metric to determine biological sex when, in fact, a holistic approach calls into question the very possibility of this determination. What can it mean, then, to define women as 'the subordinate sex' when sex is neither binary nor pre-hierarchical? Such a definition cannot give us the resources we need in a feminist theory because its normative recommendations will leave too many women behind. Transgender women and intersex women are not considered women in this theory (or at best, they are peripheral women), and yet they are some of the most vulnerable targets of gender-based violence.

In response to these concerns, many feminists have argued that we must shift away from sex-based classification and towards gender-identity classification. Influenced by Butler and other post-modern theorists, many feminists claim that *gender identity* is the independent characteristic that determines the group of women who are then subordinated on that basis. And yet the concept of gender identity is both conceptually confused and politically incomplete. Popular understandings of gender identity focus on an internal, subject-dependent feeling about the gender that best 'fits' with oneself. Individual feeling is prioritized over medical designation of sex; gender identity need not conform to the binary of 'man' or 'woman'; and gender identity is importantly related to one's self-conception. On these definitions, a woman is someone who identifies as a woman—that is, as someone who has an inner sense of being a woman (or alternatively, as someone

[47] Judith Butler, *Gender Trouble* (New York: Routledge Classics, 2006), 10.
[48] Butler, *Gender Trouble*, 10.

who feels most aligned with femininity, or who is most comfortable in the gender role 'woman'). It is a strength of these definitions that they include transgender and intersex women and eschew the fiction of neatly ordered bodies.

And yet the definitions themselves contain seeds of an ideology that feminism has been unearthing and debunking for centuries. First, the popular understanding of gender identity comes close to positing an essential 'femininity' which is felt by all women. Not only is this empirically false (as many women feel no such kinship with femininity), it is not clear what it could even mean. Is this a physical sensation? A deeply held belief? All such accounts of what it is to 'feel like a woman' reify gender in a way that is unacceptable from a feminist standpoint.[49] Furthermore, the idea that being a woman means being most comfortable in the gender roles assigned to women betrays all of the feminist work that has gone into protesting the tyranny of these very roles. And it erases the fact that many people remain in these roles not because they feel comfortable in them, but because of the violent boundary maintenance that a system of gender oppression exerts.

More troubling, the idea that gender identity is the central characteristic that defines a woman radically individualizes gender. It suggests that there is some empirical fact about each individual which is discovered as we age, and that the priority of gender justice should be to facilitate the expression of this gendered discovery. Such a refocusing of the priorities of gender justice ignores the ways in which gender is imposed at birth and maintained through coercive and violent means. It ignores what Nancy Fraser calls the 'injustice of maldistribution', that is, the unequal distribution of resources and primary goods.[50] And it ignores that even gender expression, and the injustice of gender misrecognition, is an 'institutionalized social relation, not a psychological state'.[51] In this way, the focus on gender identity to understand what makes a woman is politically incomplete. Its recommendations cannot go beyond the

[49] For a similar take on this point, see Talia Mae Bettcher, 'Trans Women and the Meaning of "Woman"', in *The Philosophy of Sex: Contemporary Readings*, eds Nicholas Power, Raja Halwani, and Alan Soble (United Kingdom: Rowman and Littlefield, 2013).

[50] Nancy Fraser, 'Heterosexism, Misrecognition, and Capitalism: A Response to Judith Butler', *Social Text* (special issue on Queer Transexions of Race, Nation, and Gender) 0, no. 52/53 (1997): 280.

[51] Fraser, 'Heterosexism, Misrecognition, and Capitalism', 280.

politics of recognition, leaving feminists without a comprehensive theory to critique gender-based material inequality.

On the other hand, understanding women as the gendered Other, inhabitants of a socio-political location rather than bearers of some intrinsic property, gives us the resources for understanding the ways in which gender creates a class system that concentrates power and resources in the hands of gender-conforming men through the exploitation of women's labour and lives. It also gives us the resources for both including and centring transgender women in our definition of women and for understanding how it is that they are most vulnerable to gendered forms of violence. Admittedly, it does not answer the biographical question of what makes any particular woman cisgender, transgender, or some other nonbinary category. But much of this curiosity about the personal origins of gender identity is itself rooted in the way gender identity builds in the assumption of a readily accessible biographical explanatory history. Once we abandon the notion of a gender identity grounding one's status as a woman, historical-biographical questions lose their relevance. And, more importantly, abandoning both gender identity and biological sex as the ontological ground for gender allows us to generate a theory with normative recommendations that include the dissolution of the gendered class system as we know it.

Towards Gender Abolition

Once gender is understood as a class system that entrenches power and wealth in the hands of gender-conforming men by exploiting women's labour and lives, it is clear that justice requires class abolition. Class abolition, in this case, is a gender abolition. What might this mean? To begin with, we must work to eliminate the pervasive stereotypes against women that trace the boundaries of their class. Counter-normative behaviour is one way to achieve this goal—women working in male-dominated fields, men taking on a meaningful and equal share of emotional and care labour, and all people refusing to structure their relationships according to heteronormative values will do some work in reforming people's attitudes. But studies show us that these beliefs are remarkably intransigent even in the face of the enormous strides towards gender equality that have been made in the last 50 years. Equality, then, and especially equality achieved through counter-normative behaviour, is clearly not enough.

Abolition is one step past liberal equality—it is the proposal that gender justice requires us to recognize not just that men and women, and all genders, are equal with respect to our basic dignity and worth, but that respecting this dignity requires us to eventually cease understanding ourselves, and treating one another, as gendered beings. No justice can come from a theory that does not critically examine and move past the category of the gendered Other. The socio-political location 'woman' must be eliminated, and with it the idea that anybody *is* a woman. And of course, so too the location of 'man'. This is not to say that differences in sex will cease to matter, or that the disproportionate burden that reproduction imposes on some bodies will cease to matter, or that sexual dispositions towards some bodies and not others will cease to matter (though on this last point, it is likely that rigid notions of sexual orientation will dissipate). The gender abolitionist collective 'Xenofeminism' summarizes it thus: 'Let a hundred sexes bloom! "Gender abolitionism" is shorthand for the ambition to construct a society where traits currently assembled under the rubric of gender no longer furnish a grid for the asymmetric operation of power.'[52]

It must be noted, however, that the abolition of gendered categories is a *goal* of feminist liberation on this account, and not an avenue towards it. Given the current state of affairs around the world, simply refusing to acknowledge gender will be an instance of the same obtuseness that motivates proponents of the failed 'colour-blind' policies in the racial arena. There is still much work to be done about gender injustice, past and present, and a vivid awareness of the way gender norms and gendered violence impacts women's lives is essential to this project. Looking forward to the construction of a gender-just society, though, will likely entail a radical transformation of not only gendered forms of power, but also gendered forms of labour and labour relations.[53] Our analysis of the stereotypes against women shows how deeply these views are interwoven with views about the different categories of labour ('paid' and 'unpaid') and women's fitness for the latter category. Transformation in this arena, both ideological and material, holds the promise for moving us forward

---

[52] 'Xenofeminism: A Politics for Alienation', Laboria Cuboniks, 2016, http://www.laboriacuboniks.net/, accessed on 27 February 2017.

[53] See Christine Delphy, *Close to Home: A Materialist Analysis of Women's Oppression* (Amherst, MA: University of Massachusetts Press, 1984), for an analysis of this possibility.

in this project. And transformation in this arena requires us to see that what women have in common is not some intrinsic property held by each individual in the group, but rather a shared social position in which their labour and resources are exploited. This social insight is the key to understanding both women's ontological status and the way forward.

On this view, women's solidarity can continue to be a force for feminist mobilization and change. But it is important that we understand this solidarity in the right way—a shared membership in the social location of 'woman' must be the source of political community and inspiration for gendered change. From this socio-political vantage point, a rich feminist vision can emerge in which the politics of othering, including its dehumanization and violent boundary maintenance, can be exposed from the point of view of those whom it targets. This will require us to give up the body dimorphism that has mobilized much of feminist thought for so long. But what we lose in connection to past feminist movements, we gain in conceptual clarity and solidarity with *all* who are dehumanized by gendered borders. Importantly, this shift preserves our ability to advocate for the differing forms of care and support that are demanded by differences among our bodies. The only change is that these differences will not map onto gender categories in such a way that they will be used as evidence of the naturalness of those very categories. As a result, feminist solidarity will have the conceptual tools to move past our current gendered order, and towards a social order in which our individual and collective flourishing is facilitated, rather than undermined, by our socio-economic and political landscape.

6

Gender and Anti-Discrimination Laws in India

Modesty, Honour, and Defiled Bodies

Vidhu Verma

The idea of framing gender discrimination as a problem worthy of examination goes back to the Indian Constitution.[1] In the constituent assembly, equality proponents spoke of their moral and legal commitments to a system in which women and men stand as equal individuals under the law. Various strategies were used by the constitutional

[1] Women's organizations played a crucial role in supporting universal franchise before the drafting of the Constitution. Sarojini Naidu would declare that women ask for the vote, 'not that we might interfere with you in your official functions, your civic duties, your public place and power, but rather that we might lay the foundation of national character in the souls of children that we hold upon our laps, and instill in them the ideals of national life'. Cited in Geraldine Forbes, *Women in Modern India* (New Delhi: Cambridge University Press, 2004), 94. Others like her reasoned that the best way for women to participate in public life was for them to start reasoning like men through better education.

feminists to favour the goal of equal treatment over special treatment of women. Their attack was on differences codified in existing equal protection jurisprudence as well as on the stereotypes that justified them. They argued that any recognition of difference or argument for special treatment would work to the disadvantage of women.[2] This tension, though not framed in such precise terms, gave rise to one of the most enduring arguments in feminist jurisprudence which is also a subject of this chapter.

It was a crucial turning point in our history when the Constitution incorporated ideals of equal citizenship and social justice as central to our political culture. For the first time in history, women in India extracted from law a rights framework to fight social inequalities they were trapped in and undermined appeals to biological determinism as a justification for social discrimination. However, when we reconsider this development from a historical vantage point and its moral and legal character, it becomes apparent that, by appealing to constitutional equality, we effectively assumed that a quasi-juridical notion of equality would guarantee a good society. Since then, policy debates have taken place to overcome women's exclusion and discrimination. Social media has stimulated a new form of dialogue in the space of democratic governance by bringing women's rights issues to the attention of a more comprehensive public.[3] But critiques of discrimination have not yet achieved widespread currency as for long it was not considered a problem worthy of scholarly analysis and intervention. Gender discrimination has uncomfortable overtones of group rights, which stands in tension with widespread notions of individual rights and merit that threaten to upset the accepted concepts and categories of liberal feminism. Although the eventual integration of gender discrimination into ordinary speech marked a watershed in society's conceptualization of sexuality, both the word and construction it signifies have limitations and the parameters of justice remain vague.

Early conceptions of gender equality and the rights framework did not address the exclusion of women in workplaces based on the principle

[2] In 1946, most of the women members in the Indian constituent assembly argued against reservation of seats which they considered an 'impediment to their growth and an insult to their intelligence and capacity'. See Renuka Ray, *Constituent Assembly Debates (CAD), vol. iv. Friday 18 July 1947* (New Delhi: Lok Sabha Secretariat, 2003), 668.

[3] William H. Dutton, *The Oxford Handbook of Internet Studies* (United Kingdom: Oxford, 2003).

of equality of opportunity. Subsequently, a primary aim of gender justice was to make valid distinctions between men and women to revoke arbitrary differences between them. When women asked for equal status to men as right-holders at the workplace, they had to challenge simplistic notions of equality with sameness. For women to assert claims of inequality, it had to be proven that they were in similar circumstances to men but were mistreated because they were women.

Jurisprudence on discrimination against women in the workplace raised questions of efficiency rules, as in the case of airlines in India that expected female flight attendants to fulfil the requirements of a physical appearance they also defined as medical fitness.[4] Before solemnizing marriage, a woman officer had to obtain written permission, a rule that Justice Krishna Iyer described as 'misogynist'. The two provisions, namely 8(2) and 18(4) of the Indian Foreign Service Rules 1961, were subsequently challenged as they practically barred married women from entering the Indian Foreign service till 1979.[5] Efficiency arguments were made to defeat equality claims in cases of promotion, as suitability for a particular post was in conjunction with appropriate behaviour according to baseline norms keeping in mind the male perspective on decency, morals, and decorum.[6] It explains why for very long Indian sex discrimination jurisprudence failed to consider pregnancy benefits by Articles 15 and 16.[7] Only recently, the Delhi High court acknowledged pregnancy-based discrimination in denial of seniority benefits as a form of sex discrimination which brought it under the non-discrimination guarantees in the Constitution.[8] Thus, implementing the principle of gender justice

---

[4] *Air India v. Nergesh Meerza and Others* AIR 1981 SC 1829. The courts read the regulations as 'unreasonable and arbitrary' and as against the spirit of Article 14.

[5] See *C.B. Muthamma v. Union of India* AIR 1979 SC 1868. In another case, a married woman was disqualified from being selected to the post of district judge. *Radha Charan v. State of Orissa and ANR*, 28 February 1969. Ori 237.

[6] *R.S. Singh v. State of Punjab and Others* AIR 1972 Punjab and Haryana 117.

[7] For defects in the usage of sex discrimination, see Ellen Frankel Paul, 'Sexual Harassment as Sex Discrimination: A Defective Paradigm', *Yale Law and Policy Review* 8, no. 2 (1990), http://digitalcommons.law.yale.edu/ylpr/vol8/iss2/9.

[8] *Inspector (Mahila) Ravina v. Union of India*, W. P. (C) 4525/2014, August 2015.

as giving each their due questions the principle of non-discrimination or equal treatment of all persons found in the Constitution.[9]

Second, the opinion that the 'woman's question was primarily a "welfare" question or a "social question", that it had little to do with the nature of government and political development' persists and represents one of the important tendencies till now.[10] Generalizations about differences between men and women continue to uphold the classifications on the ground that women require protection, more than men. Many court decisions reflect stereotypical thinking about women's inert nature and need for protection that perpetuates the very stereotypes that have kept women in a subordinate position.[11]

Finally, though current welfarism aims to improve the situation of disadvantaged groups, it is different from a type of welfare sought by the state in ensuring an equal distribution of resources or opportunities to equalize people's chances of fairly competing for valued outcomes. The Hindu Succession Act, for example, celebrated for being progressive, is found on closer scrutiny to be inadequate for protecting rights of Hindu married women. The rationale behind the devolution of property owned by a Hindu woman appears to be that property should revert to its source as the common assumption is that women do not create property out of their earnings or wealth.[12]

Given these legal shortfalls, several questions emerge: If the laws emphasize deontological moral theory, that is, duties of women in the family, does it reflect societal values, buttressing and reinforcing them? Can Indian law develop relations of evidence and procedure to protect legal deliberation from invalid assumptions? As a woman's legal identity remains bound up with her duties to the state as wife and mother, within

---

[9] See debates on reasonable classification in Article 14 in *Vijay Lakshmi v. Punjab University and Others*, 23 September 2003.

[10] Vina Mazumdar, *Women's Participation in Political Life* (New Delhi: United National Educational, Scientific and Cultural Organisation, 1983).

[11] See *Smt Sowmithri Vishnu v. Union of India* AIR 1985 SC 1618, where the appellant complained that section 497 on adultery is an instance of gender discrimination. Also, *Anil Kumar Mahsi v. Union of India* 20 July 1994, which upheld gender-based divorce laws because of the 'muscularly weaker physique of the woman, her general vulnerable' condition.

[12] I am grateful for this point to Sujata Mehra, advocate, Delhi High Court, for raising the inequity in section 15 on inheritance rights of a Hindu woman. See the Hindu Succession (Amendment) Act, 2005, no. 39 of 2005.

the traditional heterosexual family, is a release from this identity a condition for recognition of women as equal and free persons? To raise these questions means to challenge the well-entrenched myths of liberal legalism: the legal person is genderless, one's life course is by self-determining actions, and the law has universal application. All these lead to further complex issues in the currently fractured modernity of the post-colonial state that I can only partially address here.

In what follows, I begin by presenting some methodological clarifications to my research. Then I discuss the Indian jurisprudence on sexual harassment and assault. I then briefly focus on the right to temple entry and 'honour' crimes and the legal responses to them. I argue that forms of discrimination faced by women are not only a feature of our social structure but their disadvantaged status is due to the moral status assigned to them in the legal-juridical framework. The persistence of gender discrimination in the wider societal sphere is expressed by the unevenness that marks women's access to the legal system, given their low levels of education and economic status in India.

I argue that legal campaigns and initiatives on violence against women have done little to displace the dominant sexual norms which invade the law. In fact, these efforts have reinforced the negativity about sex and sexuality and have failed to dislodge the conservative cultural moorings that anchor issues of sexuality in law.[13] The circulation of stereotypes impact sentencing in cases and shift from adjudicating to another site of law that is not accountable. I argue that a criterion of modesty has been very central in sexual offense in the past and stands upon the patriarchal bedrock refusing to recognize the concept of individual autonomy and bodily integrity. This criterion relies on inspecting the victim's history and sexual behaviour; further, women's bodies in Indian jurisprudence are seen as repositories of community honour or familial shame leading to the dichotomy between virtue and suspect women. For legal feminists, the law remains a site of discursive struggle where dominant meanings come to inform not only juridical categories but also the social world that defines our concepts and practices. The dilemma of preserving difference in law and yet not having disadvantageous effects to unequal parties remains.

[13] Dawn Currie, 'Feminist Encounters with Post-Modernism: Exploring the Impasse of Debates on Patriarchy and Law', *Canadian Journal of Women and Law* 5, no. 1 (1992): 63–86.

Methodological Issues

To focus on the concerns of this chapter, I must grapple with some methodological and normative concerns that arise from my claim that existing laws are reflective of male bias; stereotyping of women occurs as they are members of a particular group or category of which there are structured sets of beliefs. By focusing on differences between men and women, whether socially constructivist or biological, this argument is directed at law reforms addressing the different and inferior position women occupy in society. My attempt could then be seen to focus on trying to change male bias in law or arguing that, as judgments vary, so will the social order. Furthermore, my advocating an overhaul of the legislature and courts could be an argument for drafting and interpretation of laws that could be more gender-friendly.

This chapter rests on the premise that legal deliberation on women's rights is easily distorted by attitudes that reflect gender and caste bias. Some of these prejudices are outside ordinary conscious awareness. Once I accept that stereotypes, not intentional discrimination, make up the primary source of harm, then I must admit that the primary source of conduct is unconscious, not intentional; the cause of injury lies principally in senseless acts of misogyny. We must have evidence of stigmatic harm in the form of negative regard and relegation of women to inferior status, which prevents them participating in society. But with this argument, many readers might also assume that judges should increasingly be directed, in a defendant's treatment, to consider a variety of variables that include socio-economic status, marital status, gender, age, family, and neighbourhood characteristics to overcome the limitations of their unconscious conduct.[14] This takes me to the debate on statistical discrimination or use of group tendencies as a proxy for individual characteristics—as a permissible justification for constitutionally forbidden discrimination. In response to this reading, I would argue that since the Indian Constitution is not blind to group identity, the approach in this chapter on socially constructed meanings grounded in society's power relations might help in highlighting conditions of stigmatized groups. While I agree to tolerate statistical generalizations as a remedy in specific contexts for disadvantaged groups, a defence of classifications in

---

[14] Popularly referred to as legal terrorism, social media has raised the case of misuse of rape laws or dowry cases by women.

all cases, triggering heightened legal scrutiny, is not something I would support.

As a corollary of the above, there is a substantive meaning to a virtue ethical approach to adjudication in a democratic society limited to western philosophical thinking about law. A virtue-centred approach sees adjudication by judges as the problem, not rules or principles. Robust character traits in developing virtue ethics or assigning an important role to the judge's affective state are central to this approach.[15] What are 'judicial virtues' in the Indian context? The virtues needed for judges to live up to the demands of their role are framed by a legal system that is continually evolving. The idea of leaving these matters to ethics imply that definitions will vary across the length and breadth of the country and lead to arbitrary judgments when confronting the social realities of caste prejudices and communal conflicts.[16] As will be evident in the following sections, if women citizens who participate in a legal procedure are to be given their due, then primacy to a particular set of judicial virtues are significant. However, given the limited scope of this chapter, I will not discuss these virtues in detail even though they deserve a more detailed exploration.[17]

This chapter argues that several of these suggestions could be taken much further through a revised framework for thinking about gender. This context is inspired by feminist scholars who have developed versions of virtue epistemology that are agent-centred. I find Miranda Fricker's account of two types of epistemic injustice—testimonial and hermeneutical—very useful.[18] The central cause of both types of injustice involves identity prejudice or prejudice against someone because of their social identity. For Fricker, a testimonial injustice occurs when 'prejudice causes a hearer to give a deflated level of credibility to a speaker's word'. But frequently we can rise above social prejudices of our day, and we can do so by exercising what Fricker calls 'testimonial justice'—this virtue

[15] For a critique, see R.A. Duff, 'The Limits of Virtue Jurisprudence', *Metaphilosophy* 34, nos. 1–2 (2003): 214–24.

[16] For debates on the role of the judge, which is not merely to interpret the law but to lay new norms of law to the changing social and economic scenario, see *C. Ravichandran Iyer v. Justice A.M. Bhattacharjee* 1995 SCC (5) 457.

[17] See Amalya Amaya and Ho Hock Lai, eds., *Law, Virtue and Justice* (Oxford: Hart Publishers, 2013).

[18] Miranda Fricker, *Epistemic Injustice: Power and the Ethics of Knowing* (Clarendon: Oxford University Press, 2010), 1–2.

calls for 'reflective critical awareness of the likely presence of prejudice'. Hermeneutical injustice is when there is a gap in our share tools of social interpretation. This injustice occurs when a society lacks the interpretative resources to make sense of important features of a speaker's experience because he or she or members of their social groups have been prejudicially marginalized in meaning-making activities. For example, before the concept of sexual harassment or sexual assault was inserted into public discourse, people tended to interpret women's discomfort as hysterical reactions. They lacked interpretive resources to make sense of the injustice they were suffering.

Sex, Modesty, and Indian Jurisprudence

Over the last several decades, from the array of possible interpretive possibilities, one particular conception of the meaning of these three ideals—the rule of law, rights, and formal equality—has achieved a remarkable degree of dominance in legal theory and strikingly in the, often unstated, significant assumptions of our pedagogy. This dominant interpretation has both an internal logic, or coherence, and an external vision as they hang together as a set of ideas, and rest comfortably with a political insight about the role of the state in individual and community life. In what follows, I will delineate the outlines of this dominant interpretation of legal justice and will argue that this conception is flawed in a way that it restricts the conversation to nature of injury or harm. It should be concerned not only with the meanings of conduct but rather with the meanings associated with gender. As such, this concept of legal justice stands as a real impediment to progressive law reform that can give us gender justice.

Judicial grappling with gender is instructive not only about the lack of women's rights but also the complex relations between cultural norms and doctrinal developments. One of the places where Indian legal theory has made an impact is a proper ground for sentencing where it is justified by a defect in the character attributes of the defendant. Such positions substantiate my argument that the appropriate end of jurisprudence is to cultivate moral virtues in women and keep intact the central values of society.

It has been more than 15 years since sexual harassment, seen as a juridical category of crime, was for the first time recognized by the Supreme Court as a human rights violation and gender-based systemic discrimination. No one argued till the Vishaka judgment in 1997 that sexual harassment foregrounds the issue of women's civil and human rights, that it asserts women's right to work and their right to a safe environment.[19] It was not until 2013 that the Protection of Women against Sexual Harassment at Workplace Bill was presented to the Indian Parliament.[20]

Before 1997, there were laws in the Indian Penal code (henceforth IPC) that could be evoked when a woman was sexually harassed, but these were framed as offenses that amount to 'obscenity' in public or seen to violate a woman's 'modesty'. Many accused persons in a rape or sexual assault got acquitted or received a minor sentence. Sometimes, the sexuality of the victim was considered as responsible for the sexual assault, and sometimes, the past sexual history or character of the victim was taken into consideration.[21] Cases of sexual harassment came under a popular category of 'eve teasing' in section 509 of the Indian Penal Code (IPC) where it was treated as a joke that only trivialized and ridiculed women. Before the Vishaka case, women who faced sexual harassment had to lodge a complaint under section 354 of the IPC that deals with criminal assault of women to outrage a woman's modesty or section 509 that punishes an individual for using words that insult the modesty of a woman.

The first cases of discrimination and assault were mostly governed by an idea of 'modesty' which was seen as an attribute of womanhood. The framing of a harassment case failed to raise it as a violation of women's right to equality. All women, irrespective of their age, possessed 'modesty' that is capable of being outraged. However, 'outraging a woman's modesty' is not defined in the IPC. While the term 'sexual harassment' changed usage after 1997, the Rupen Deol Bajaj case in 1995 saw contestations of 'outraging of modesty' provision. Justice J.M.K. Mukherjee, in this case, dwelt on the meaning of the term 'modesty'. The courts interpreted it as referring to 'womanly propriety of behavior; scrupulous chastity of thought, speech, and conduct'. It was defined as including any 'act done to or in the presence of a woman', which was

---

[19] *Vishaka and Others v. State of Rajasthan and Others*, 13 August 1997. AIR 1997 Supreme Court 3011, https://www.iiap.res.in/files/VisakaVsRajasthan_1997.pdf, accessed on 24 September 2017.

[20] It received the president's assent on 22 April 2013.

[21] *Raju v. State of Karnataka* 1995 I SCC 453 in which the sentence was reduced as the rape victim had consented to sleep in the same room with the accused.

clearly suggestive of sex 'according to the common notions of mankind' being gauged by contemporary societal standards. Drawing on these assumptions about modesty, the high court which had quashed Bajaj's first information report (FIR) observed: 'In the present case there were about 48 more persons present, 24 ladies and equal number of gentlemen, it sounds both unnatural and unconscionable that the petitioner would attempt or dare to outrage the modesty of the author of the FIR in their very presence inside the residential house of the Financial Commissioner (Home).'[22]

In an earlier case of 'causing injury to the vagina' of a seven-month-old girl, there was a discussion of whether a woman possesses modesty from birth, or is the essence of a woman's modesty her sex. The judges debated whether 'a female child of that age was possessed of womanly modesty'.[23] The fact that the law was apparently inadequate to deal with cases of sexual assault and sexual abuse was highlighted in later instances when there was no penetration as it was not considered rape under section 376 or when there was a failed attempt at rape.[24] In this way, they ignored contemporary understanding of rape but also the larger issues of humiliation, degradation, and violence that occurred when foreign objects invaded body parts of a woman. Gender bias and prejudices persisted in a case when the accusation of rape of a three-year-old girl by her father, raised by the mother, was seen as false and also as part of an act of revenge by the mother on her husband for an 'unhappy marriage'. The Supreme Court pointed to the 'seemingly incredulous nature of the accusations against a father' and added that the wife's attitude to the petitioner 'was vengeful'. Professed disbelief motivated the court's judgment that such crimes could take place.[25]

Recalling the publicized case of Rupen Deol Bajaj, we find that her complaint was ridiculed as the 'butt slapping case' for many years. Once she challenged the high court ruling which had allowed Mr Gill's petition, all this changed. This ruling had quashed both the FIR and complaint, as the allegations were unnatural and nature of harm did not entitle her to complain. The press stood solidly behind K.P.S. Gill during this episode, even though it was a clear case of sexual abuse of

---

[22] *Rupan Deol Bajaj and Others v. Kanwar Pal Singh Gill and Others* 1988; *Rupan Deol Bajaj v. K.P.S Gill* AIR 1996 SC 309 pp. 314–15.

[23] *State of Punjab v. Major Singh*, April 1966.

[24] *Ankariya v. State of Madhya Pradesh*, 1991, Cr.L 786.

[25] *Satish Mehra v. Delhi Administration and Another*, July 1996.

power in which people in a supervisory position exploit their authority and influences to compel a subordinate to submission and unwanted attention. Instead, Gill, a super-cop known for handling the insurgency in Punjab, was the mighty hero who had committed a momentary lapse but who ought to be pardoned on the grounds of state loyalty. The act of teasing a middle-class woman after imbibing a few drinks was looked upon with indulgence. It was after this incident that Gill went on to win a Padma Shri award.[26]

Caste, Class, and Gender

While research on social inequality is prevalent in India, interest in stigma and discrimination emanating from caste bias is recent. Inquiry into the effects of caste on identity indicates that a substantial amount of stigma and markedness is bestowed upon the lower classes as they are in lower-grade service occupations. It is hard to engender self-respect because of an emphasis on occupational status as a primary basis for social esteem. A landmark case challenged these to realize the effects of class and caste on social identities.

It was Bhanwari Devi's intervention in court that raised the question of 'testimonial injustice' that I mentioned in the earlier section when judges were not appropriately open to the truth of the testimony given by women. In 1992, Bhanwari Devi, a Dalit woman employed as a *sathin* (friend, soulmate) in a government programme to combat child marriage in Rajasthan, was gang-raped in front of her husband, by five upper-caste landlords. These individuals were acquitted with the judge stating that since 'rape is usually committed by teenagers, and since the accused are middle aged and therefore respectable, they could not have committed the crime. An upper-caste man could not have defiled himself by raping a lower-caste woman.'[27]

The Vishaka judgment in the words of a noted scholar 'is significant at a symbolic level for its validation of the problem of sexual harassment and its recognition of the fact that it is an experience many women are

---

[26] K. Kannabiran and V. Kannabiran, *De-eroticising Assault: Essays on Modesty, Honour and Power* (Kolkata: Popular Prakashan, 2002), 71. The title of this chapter is inspired by the book's theme.

[27] Human Rights Watch, *Broken People* (USA: Human Rights Watch, 1999), 175.

routinely subject to in the workplace'.[28] But the three-judge bench of the Supreme Court that delivered the Vishaka judgment on 13 August 1997 did not give justice in the case of sexual assault, as rape was viewed as a subject matter of a separate criminal action under the IPC. Under the astute leadership of Justice Verma, the court focused on the hazards to which working women may be exposed. Although such incidents resulted in a breach of fundamental rights, it was more a violation of Article 19 which allowed individuals to practice any profession. The judgment raised the responsibility for ensuring 'safety and dignity' of women through suitable legislation. In the absence of a domestic law and any legislative measures, the contents of international conventions and norms, such as Convention on the Elimination of All Forms of Discrimination against Women (CEDAW), were seen as instructive. Justice Verma also quoted the Beijing Statement of Principles of the Independence of the Judiciary (1995) as representing the minimum standards necessary to be observed for maintaining the independence of the judiciary to guide them in the absence of any law.[29]

Bhanwari's journey from being a gang-raped, abused, humiliated, and threatened woman paints a terrifying picture of the law. Cases have the potential to be influenced by the judge's perceptions of caste and gender that are brought to bear in assessing the credibility of evidence or the likelihood of guilt. The preceding case material and in the following sections illustrates the atmosphere of prejudice that women face both as Dalits and as non-Dalits. In the Indian context, since the core ingredient of the definition of harassment is that the sexual conduct is unwelcome, the complainant's sexual past and mode of dress is included. In this way, feminists cautioned that waitresses, barroom dancers, and performers become vulnerable to such claims as the definition provides scope for reinforcing assumptions about women's sexuality.[30] However, in the post-colonial context, it simultaneously reproduces discourse about women's sexual conduct based on cultural idealizations of women as guardians of cultural values and, hence, entitled to legal protection. Even if women have obtained a professional status or highly skilled occupation, either by inherited class privilege or social mobility, they

---

[28] Ratna Kapur, *Erotic Justice. Law and the New Politics of Postcolonialism* (New Delhi: Permanent Black, 2005), 38.

[29] See Justice Verma's response to the writ petition in *Vishaka and Others* AIR 1997 Supreme Court 3011.

[30] Kapur, *Erotic Justice.*

are unable to escape stigma because of the inferior status that society, including legal judgments, accords to them.

The Right to Temple Entry and the Right to Love

The ban on women accessing places of worship contravenes the right to equality. This prohibition raises questions of discrimination and exclusion justified under the garb of traditional religious practices in the guise of a biological determinism of purity and pollution as far as women are concerned. Article 25(2) of the Indian Constitution questions unfair, discriminatory practices within religious customs and is committed to purging them. The controversial Kerala Hindu Places of Public Worship (Authorisation of Entry) Rules 1965 (KHPPW) was born out of this constitutional prerogative. Many questions arise: Can a denominational right undermine the individual right to religion under Article 25 to manage internal affairs of a religious institution? Can any authority governing a place of public worship be empowered to prohibit women from entering?

In the 1950s, many provincial legislatures enacted laws to reform religious institutions and their practices restricting entry or worship in Hindu temples. The temple entry movement was a long and cherished part of the struggle against the caste system historically excluding ex-untouchables of the Hindu community. The rule 3(b) prohibiting women was enforced under KHPPW, which was initially meant to facilitate temple entry for all social groups. A public interest litigation (PIL) was filed by a devotee of Lord *Ayyappa* in the 1990s, in the Kerala High Court to restrict entry. In 1991, the Kerala High Court upheld the ban and advised the Travancore Devaswom Board to implement it after the following conclusion: 'The restriction imposed on women aged above 10 and below 50 from trekking the holy hills of Sabarimala and offering worship at Sabarimala Shrine is in accordance with the usage prevalent from time immemorial.'[31]

Since the 1950s, the Supreme Court, through its various judgments on similar cases, developed a doctrine of 'essential' religious practice to identify practices that enjoyed constitutional protection; any change in

---

[31] See details of Justice Marar's response to the PIL filed in the Kerala High Court in 1991 in *S. Mahendran v. the Secretary, Travancore*, 5 April 1991. AIR 1993 Ker 42.

contested practices will alter the existence of the sect and its core belief system fundamentally.[32] At the same time, the Constitution subjected beliefs and practices to test to allow regulation where public order, health, and morality were threatened. The Kerala High Court in its judgment supported the rights of the temple authorities to decide what was 'essential religious practice' and to inquire to what extent custom prevailed in excluding women. The court examined Ravivarma Raja of the Pandalam royal family, to which the temple belonged. Arguing that the restriction was based on age and not women as a class, Justices K. Paripoornan and K.B. Marar held that the prohibition imposed on women worshippers, by the Travancore Devaswom Board, was not violating the equality provisions of the Constitution or the KHPPW Act: 'The position that emerges is that a religious denomination or organization enjoys complete autonomy in the matter of deciding as to what rites and ceremonies are essential according to the tenets of the religion.' Citing Article 26(b) that gives freedom to the religious denomination to manage internal affairs in matters of religion, the court upheld the ban. The judgment further explained that 'women who are not by custom and usage allowed to enter a place of public worship shall not be entitled to enter or offer worship in any place of public worship'. Restriction and entry are prohibited only in respect of 'women of a particular age group and not women as a class'.[33]

In 2006, the Indian Young Lawyers Association filed a writ petition (civil) in the Supreme Court to challenge these rules and made a plea to lift the ban on entry of women to Sabarimala temple. They questioned the constitutional validity of Rule 3(b) of the KHPPW and the notification issued by the Travancore Devaswom Board on the grounds that they violate the right to religion of women devotees and the right to equality and non-discrimination.[34] However, the arguments from the state continued to assert Article 26 which deals with rights of a religious denomination to prevail over Article 25 guaranteeing freedom of conscience. The ban increasingly focuses on subtle reasons for the persistence of gender discrimination, including the assault on separate spheres in which constitutional protection of religious rights insulates women within the private sphere.

---

[32] *Commissioner, Hindu Religious Endowments, Madras v. Sri Lakshimindra Thirtha Swamiar of Sri Shirur Mutt* April 1954 SCR 1005.

[33] See footnote 30.

[34] For more, see *Indian Young Lawyers Association and Others v. State of Kerala and Others*, 2016.

Shorn of all the legal and ethical constrictions, the justifications for denying entry into places of worship based on custom rest on a supposed inferiority of women. Whether such an argument is linked to menstruation, the weakness of physical frame, or some other attribute of women, the arguments offered for restricting women's entry are a brute exercise of patriarchal power. A common thread that runs through these bans is patriarchy, which is premised upon the notion of women's inferiority that becomes a justification for their subordination. The other is the perception that women are evil seductresses who have the power to undermine custom even while men are engrossed deeply in prayer and worship. Finally, hatred towards women and fear of their sexuality is deeply ingrained in most religions and discrimination against women is observed in religious worship and practice. The prospect of menstruating women is terrifying and threatening, capable of contaminating the celibate God.[35] In this situation, the state and the law have become a mute spectator. Even though the Supreme Court has pronounced that such a prohibition is unconstitutional, the government's stand to defend the ban on the entry of women in Sabarimala temple is surprising. Since the Travancore Board is an autonomous body and derives its income from administration of the temple, the Kerala government argued that beliefs and customs of its devotees cannot be changed through a judicial process.

Accepting the court's strict adherence to the primacy of religious norms over women's rights has raised questions about secularism as an ideal state policy and the way liberalism with its promise of equality and freedom holds different consequences for men and women. While men gain the right to equality and freedom in the public sphere and right to practice their religion in the private domain under Article 25(1), women are excluded from the public domain and subjugated in their private sphere due to their religious affiliation. The relationship between religion and the state of Kerala in this instance affects women's rights, and direct intervention by the central government is the only means for creating conditions for gender justice.

Apart from denying entry to temples, women are often deprived of the right to love. Even though they all confront patriarchal arrangements,

---

[35] Radhika Sanghani, 'Indian Women Protest Temple that Wants to Scan them for Impure Periods', *Telegraph*, 23 November 2015; S. Saxena, 'Shani Shingnapur Protests', *Indian Express*, 28 January 2016.

the nature of discrimination varies according to their position in the class and caste hierarchy. Thus, there arise precise regional disparities in gender relations as hierarchies of class, caste, and ethnicity intersect the hierarchies of gender. In many parts of rural India, the caste system is sustained by the power of the upper ranks to enforce caste-based codes and norms within the village. There is a particular kind of male control over female sexuality, rooted in patriarchy, which gets manifested in territorial and caste group control. One of the principal means to enforce caste rules is through endogamy that applies rules of marriage within a specified caste. In this way, the principles of marriage rituals and practices based on continuity of the male descent line get intimately connected to the principles of caste hierarchy. The control over reproductive powers of women and female sexuality are crucial in maintaining the boundaries between castes and in perpetuating the caste system. Within the community, women are the repositories of family honour. Thus, the purity of women is crucial to maintaining the blood purity of the lineages and the family's position within the wider social hierarchy.

Khap panchayats (caste assemblies) play an important part in punishing caste transgressions in love marriages perceived as violating the caste norms of permitted sexual relationships. The violence towards such self-chosen marriages is explained by the challenge they pose to the dominant caste communities by 'lower' castes, which have begun to prosper with the help of educational and employment opportunities. Many brutal killings of couples have taken place for the community's honour when they transgress caste norms. A host of issues related to property and maintenance of caste purity is a reason for the opposition to intra-*gotra* and inter-caste marriages. There is no definition of 'honour crime', no legal recognition of the various aspects of the crime, no protections afforded to couples in self-chosen partnerships, and no punishment for such crimes. After all, it is hard to identify a killing in any given community, since the reasons often remain a closely guarded matter showing criminality at its worst; women in the household and the community are usually complicit in these killings. Caste panchayats play an active role in running a parallel legal system, giving orders on their own or in connivance with the family members, making it difficult to pinpoint the culprits. They ultimately get their orders implemented through the killing of innocent couples.[36] The Supreme Court has expressed outrage

[36] Although different in nature, recent cases of honour killings are of Manoj and Babli in 2007, and Nitish Katara in 2002.

in courts in India, and described these crimes as 'barbaric, brutal, committed by bigoted persons with feudal minds,' but the law is often slow in convicting those who committed these crimes.[37]

Three Challenges: Intersectional Identities, Laws, and Civic Failure

I realize the account presented above can be criticized for generalizations that set the tone of its analysis. It is time now to consider some cases which give me more difficulty. I argued that debates on equality and freedom in the constituent assembly assumed that law would be one of the important instruments that could bring about social change. Despite the emphasis on rights, the constitutional approach is criticized for the failure to confront unjust gender norms through cases on modesty, honour, and defiled bodies. Since stigma, prejudice, and discrimination are multifaceted and very complex phenomena, they are present, not only in the law, state, or private institutions but also in civil society in general. Through a gamut of legal decisions, I claim that institutional sexism and the implicit bias of judges enforce women's subordinate position by constructing them as weak and in need of protection.

Our analysis needs to address three specific challenges. The first site of strong contestation could be to my reliance on the homogenization of the category 'woman'. I claim that the stigma of harassment, assault, or rape is borne by the victim/survivor for the remainder of her life whatever her class, caste, or religious background. Caste, gender, and identity categories are treated in liberal discourse as negative frameworks which should eventually be of little social significance. At the centre of this analysis is gender discrimination, but not the multiple discriminations faced by women of disadvantaged communities. To highlight subtle discrimination, social stereotypes, and stigmas, we need to establish how the argument we presented can avoid essentialism and consequently incorporate a more diverse set of women's experiences into the analysis.

Of particular relevance for my response is to recall that rape and sexual harassment are increasingly 'public' events sanctioned by the law and focus of regulation. In December 2012, the Nirbhaya rape case in Delhi became a watershed moment for reporting of sexual assault and

---

[37] *Bhagwan Dass v. State (NCT) of Delhi*, 9 May 2011. Since then, convictions have taken place; see footnote 36.

illustrated the tension between different levels of caste and class. A sharp contrast exists between the way law constructs sexual harassment of middle-class women and the way in which sexual assault of poor women is imagined. I agree with this sharp critique and on the need to address intersectionality in gender discrimination as the law against harassment speaks for a particular class of women, along with age, ethnicity, and a level of educational attainment. Many of the legal regulations emerged from the experiences of the middle-class women who entered the labour force in the 1960s.

While the rape law itself is problematic and I will not discuss this here, custodial rape by the police has been treated as 'routine cases' in the past and for which sentencing was inadequate. Women were likely to be believed if they were single and virginal or married and chaste. Further, working-class women were seen as sexually available, as they were less secluded and consequently less respectable than 'middle-class' women, a point I take up in the final section. Despite changes in custodial rape law following the 1983 amendment, we find that judicial interpretations remained centred on the character of the 'complainant'.[38]

As most of the cases of custodial rape are perpetrated against working-class women, class assumptions regarding sexuality are apparent. Many times, the judgment acknowledges the force inflicted on the woman but adds in defence that 'no woman of honor will accuse another of rape since she sacrifices thereby what is dearest to her'.[39] Recalling the infamous Mathura rape case, we find that the session court disbelieved the Dalit girl's testimony and termed her a liar and acquitted the policemen who raped her.[40] She wouldn't fit into the category of 'good girl' status that the society has normalized. The session judge held that Mathura was a 'shocking liar' whose testimony is 'riddled with falsehood and improbabilities'. The court concluded that she had sexual intercourse while at the police station; rape had not been proved given that she was habituated to sexual intercourse. The outrage created by this judgment triggered the anti-rape movement and the much-needed rape law amendment.

[38] See Criminal Law (Amendment) Act, 1983 for changes in section 275.

[39] See J. Krishna Iyer, in *Rafiq v. State of Uttar Pradesh*, August 1980.

[40] After the Bombay High court sentenced the accused to imprisonment, Justice Jaswant Singh and Koshal of the Supreme Court reversed the decision and acquitted the accused policemen. See *Tuka Ram and Others v. State of Maharashtra* 1978, 1979 AIR 185.

The theory of 'mandatory minimum punishment' as part of the criminal jurisprudence meant that a judge had to give reasons for awarding less than the minimum prescribed.[41] In the Suman Rani custodial case in Haryana, the Supreme Court refused to apply the minimum ten-year sentence to the police officers charged because of the Dalit woman's 'questionable character'. According to Justice Pandian and Justice B.C. Ray, the medical officer was of the opinion that the fact that the victim Suman Rani 'had not complained of the alleged rape said to have been committed at the police station by these two appellants to anyone (till five days after the incident) shows that the present version is not worthy of acceptance'. The court ultimately held that the case did not warrant the imposition of the minimum ten-year sentence. Instead, they invoked provision 376(2) which allows the judge to use discretion in reducing the minimum sentence.[42] In 2013, when the rape law was amended, this legal maxim was altered and a mandatory minimum punishment was prescribed. If a judge were to award less than the minimum, the judge was bound to give reasons for the same.[43]

In the Khairlanji rape and murder case, in 2006, four members of a Dalit family were brutally murdered in a village in Maharashtra. At the end of the lengthy trial, the session court ruled that the offense of the rape was not proved, though some of the accused were awarded death penalty for murder. After a four-year wait for justice, Bhaiyyalal Bhotmange's family got little satisfaction since the basis for the violence against his family was sought to be eliminated. In 2010, the court said that the murder of his wife and three children were an act of revenge which had nothing to do with the fact that the victims were Dalits. The failure of the law against the atrocity of Scheduled Castes is that caste violence is not easy to prove because the extent of evidence required to invoke the Atrocities Act seems to be far more challenging than what is needed in case of homicide.[44]

[41] See *Prem Chand and Others v. State of Haryana*, 31 January 1989, 1247.

[42] K.S. Tomar, 'Atrocities against Rajasthan Women on the Rise: Report', *Hindustan Times*, 28 May 1998.

[43] Justice J.S. Verma, Justice Leila Seth, and Gopal Subramanium, *Report of the Committee on Amendments to Criminal Law*, 23 January 2013, http://www.prsindia.org/uploads/media/Justice%20verma%20committee/js%20verma%20committe%20report.pdf, accessed on 11 February 2014. For recent debates on consent, see *Mahmood Farooqui v. State (Government of NCT of Delhi)* (25 September 2017).

[44] Lyla Bavadam, 'Gaps in the Story', *Frontline* 27, no. 16 (July–August 2010).

In all these cases, the deterrent value of legal enactments is apparently negligible as the judgments rest on problematic assumptions about women's sexuality. Error confounds the interpretation of these laws due to influence of invalid generalizations about male and female gender roles, and sexuality. From these cases, I would argue that stigma is intimately tied to the reproduction of social difference and social exclusion; the representation of a Dalit or tribal woman, or minority woman is anchored in histories of poverty, exclusion, and policing.[45] Apart from the intention, an implicit bias is present in the judges in both litigation and policy discourses on honour and shame. One noted scholar is of the view that 'combatants and other state agents rape to subjugate and inflict shame upon their victims, and by extension, their victims' families and communities. In other words, women are raped precisely because the violation of their protected status has the effect of shaming them and their communities.'[46] Hence, the existing legal frameworks on caste and gender should reach out to include intersectional experience.

A second challenge comes from a greater focus on the meaning and dangers of carceral feminism; the tendency for middle-class feminists in liberal democracies to tie legal victories to campaigns that privilege law and coercive mechanisms despite the contradictory nature of the court's reasoning. Many feminists argue for using criminal law more effectively to address sexual violence, caste stigma, and structural discrimination.

These punitive responses of the state take place within what has been termed as 'governance feminism'. The latter refers to the 'incremental, but now quite noticeable installation of feminists and feminist ideas in actual legal-institutional power'.[47] It is the phenomena by which gender is activated within political institutions. In particular, Indian feminism in the 1990s entered a governance mode with the growing incorporation of non-state actors such as non-governmental organizations and civil society experts, in light of the following three parameters: an increased reliance on criminal law, a deep commitment to a highly gendered reading of sexual violence, and a diluted oppositional stance against the state power.

---

[45] On religious minorities, see Haider Naqvi, 'Muzaffarnagar after Three years', *Hindustan Times*, 17 February 2016.

[46] Amrita Basu, *The Challenge of Local Feminisms: Women's Movements in Global Perspective* (Colorado: Westview, 1995), 136.

[47] J. Halley, *Split Decisions* (Princeton: USA, 2006); J. Halley and C. Thomas, *Governance Feminism: A Two Book Publication* (Minnesota: University of Minnesota Press, 2013), 13, 15, 17–22. See www.lawschool.cornell.edu.

These feminisms are seen as situated alongside the rise of neoliberal global governance, characterized by the 'contract/crime paradigm', where 'legal structures that seek to preserve freedom of the market exist alongside and reinforce the heightened surveillance and policing of citizens'. [48] The neoliberal economy has incorporated women's rights into the vocabulary of human rights, focusing on reforms that allow women to participate fully in the economy, thereby making their labour more available to capital and intensifying its exploitation. So an argument for policing and stringent law to overcome implicit bias in jurisprudence can also be seen as producing 'carceral feminism'. Are the worries that feminists express justified?

While advocating proposals for governance feminism for a better work environment, child care, maternity leave, health, and education, legal feminism concentrating on punitive responses to sexual violence needs a detailed response. Much debate has gone on within this context following the tragic case of Nirbhaya in Delhi. Many activists' focus on government's failure to protect women gets referenced to women's dressing inappropriately and for taking safer public transport. Many argue for efficient judicial and medical procedures to be in place in the future. Feminists are concerned that the Justice Verma Committee Report, while welcome, did not go far enough in some areas. I would argue that we need to be aware of the unintended consequences of feminist legal reform while seeing that there are dangers in abandoning the legal sphere altogether. Groups mobilizing for women's rights bear a troubled relationship with the law which has frequently been an agent of patriarchal violence.[49] Feminist groups are aware that, despite being a free space, the legal domain excludes many underprivileged sections. Abandoning the law remains an impossibility for those who are looking for justice and scepticism of the state policies is an option that feminists in countries like India cannot afford. The Verma committee recommended many changes of the IPC; the maximum punishment for rape resulting in the death of the victim was modified to include the death penalty, but it still does not alter the present 'modesty' language of sections 509 or 354. The committee also did not consider marital rape as a criminal offense. At the same time, the power of the law to change societal attitudes cannot to be overlooked. Laws are a valuable tool when seeking to bring about

[48] Halley, *Split Decisions*.
[49] Geetanjali Gangoli, *Indian Feminisms: Law, Patriarchies, and Violence in India* (UK: Ashgate Publishers, 2007).

social change for disadvantaged groups who have no access to rights, and in gradually increasing the scope of these groups to gain their agency.

A third contestation addresses the drawbacks of the rule of law in liberal legalism to demonstrate the problem of grounding the law in values so that both government officials and citizens are bound to act consistently with the law. This challenge casts light on the connection between the jurisprudence on constitutional rights and that of civic virtue. Although these are, formally speaking, distinct principles, it is not surprising that the same state fails in its legal obligations even as it claims a commitment to an idea of personal freedom. Government and public officials must ensure that investigations and prosecutions in cases are pursued without undue delay to deliver justice. This point is raised by Judith Shklar when she talks of passive injustice, as 'refusal of both officials and private citizens to prevent acts of wrong doing when they could and should do so'. She defines it as more than habitual indifference to the misery of others as it is 'specifically civic failure to stop private and public acts of injustice'.[50] In the Indian context, this opens a challenging discussion on what kind of bonds of human community we should cultivate to overcome this civic failure. Feminists protest that the conception of the legal person has a masculine individualistic orientation and that law disregards women's identities. Carol Gilligan's book argues that the sense of connection women have entails a path of moral development and a view of the world which sharply contrasts with that of men. Care ethics in her view serve as an essential basis for the civic duty to address injustices. Setting forth a solution to the politics of similarity, Martha Nussbaum maintains that the politics of humanity includes 'both respect and imagination, and imagination understood as an ingredient essential to respect itself'.[51] She argues that emotions such as anger and compassion serve important functions in liberal states. If the 'politics of disgust is all about separation from those who disgust, then the 'politics of humanity' is about association.

***

This chapter discusses how the dominant rhetoric of universality of rights in constitutional feminism is inadequate to grapple with the

[50] Judith Shklar, *Faces of Injustice* (CT: Yale University, 1990), 5–6..

[51] Martha Nussbaum, *From Disgust to Humanity: Sexual Orientation and Constitutional Law* (New York: Oxford University Press, 2010), XIX.

deep-rootedness of prejudice and historical discrimination. I mean to challenge its belief that legal justice can be built across fields of social difference through similar treatment. Assuming that the goal of anti-discrimination provisions is to promote the social and economic integration of stigmatized groups, the problem of sex discrimination lies in its concrete construction in a patriarchal society. In this chapter, I claim that law enforces women's subordinate position by constructing them as 'weak' and in need of protection. Through a gamut of legal cases, I argued that judicial decisions have thwarted the notion of differences within women for social policies. Over the years, the courts have emphasized the distinct virtues of women rather than premising its decision of civic responsibility as an element of liberty and respect. If unconscious harm is the cause of women's subordination, our inquiries must account for 'truth finding' in the legal process against distortion by erroneous assumptions. Hence, the judges are unable to overcome invalid assumptions or address patriarchal attitudes towards modesty, honour, and defiled bodies.

The progressive nature of Indian law derives from a constitutional recognition of discrimination suffered by disadvantaged groups and a commitment to rectify these through affirmative action. However, that it does not acknowledge any moral responsibility for the grave injustice perpetrated on women is precisely what leaves it open to many judicial interpretations. In recognizing the limits of the law, this chapter, through a wide-ranging discussion of the pitfalls of the law, acknowledges three main challenges of multiple and intersecting oppressions, legalization of feminist struggles by the state, and the civic failure to stop injustice. All these and others, I argue, can be addressed by a critical awareness to depart from deterministic sex stereotyping and by evolving new norms for institutional structures. Drawing upon three challenges, I would argue that a new understanding of the qualitative difference of intersectionality and the focus on stigma be activated in judicial decision-making. By some cases, I argue for the thesis that liberal conception of the person does not do justice to women of disadvantaged communities. To avoid the bias, for legal feminists, the identity that must be recognized is not that which corresponds to the traditional understanding of their role in the family, but one that acknowledges a self-determined identity. Second, the courts need to adopt a position on whether gender-based classifications show regard for autonomy or do they eventually reduce liberty. Finally, despite the presence of constitutional-centred legislations that cover specific aspects of equality or the lack of it, India nevertheless needs an all-encompassing anti-discrimination law that would extensively address the varied dimensions of gender inequality, including laws of inheritance.

7

Regulating Retirement and Wrinkles in an Age of Prejudice

Saul Levmore

Stigma and Benefit

Non-discrimination law in many places forbids or discourages asking questions about marital status, ethnicity, caste, religion, and other matters in order to make discrimination more difficult. But age is a bit different, if only because everyone ages, and almost everyone eventually finds it hard to hide. In the employment context, where discrimination law might matter most, most employers are eager to know an applicant's experience, and it is difficult to convey information about education and work experience without giving strong clues about age. Second, age is often valued positively. When we emphasize stigma, we risk overlooking the advantages of age profiling, and certainly the private rewards from some stereotyping. Older people do, on average, have less stamina than younger ones; some employers would be rational to eliminate older ones in their hiring processes. But other jobs and employers might profile in favour of age. Profiling is inevitable and if there are categories (including age) where the gains are as likely as the losses, then perhaps we should be slow to fight the practice of statistical discrimination. Law may do more harm than good when it intervenes in the cause of ageing. This chapter develops this claim about non-intervention with respect to retirement and then through attention to the problem, or cost, of hiding age and battling prejudice through invasive cosmetic procedures. The discussion develops a connection between retirement and cosmetic surgery; law and social norms may be too interventionist with respect to retirement age and too accepting when it comes to anti-ageing cosmetic surgery.

It is tempting to think of both topics as dealing with autonomy. With respect to retirement, US law protects the individual who wants to keep working, while other legal systems try to make the entire class of ageing people better-off. Arguably, autonomy is more widely protected when it comes to anti-ageing cosmetic procedures, because individuals with enough money can avail themselves of these procedures even if, by comparison, it makes many more people look relatively older. Somewhat similarly, both topics can be examined through the lens of prejudice or stigma. Age discrimination law in a few countries protects people who fight the generalization that older people are less productive. But other countries might fight the stigma by encouraging or forcing retirement at an age when most people will envy the retirees, and regard them as having earned a reward for many years of productive work. Moreover, if older workers are allowed to determine their own retirement ages, some will inevitably be subpar workers and that might exacerbate negative stereotypes about ageing. And in the realm of cosmetic surgery, it is unclear whether anti-ageing procedures fight or exacerbate any stigma associated with looking old. In sum, stigma and autonomy arguments can be advanced for or against legal intervention with respect to retirement and cosmetic surgery. The chapter begins with retirement policies and then turns to anti-ageing procedures. The final section offers some concluding observations.

Retirement Age Policies

Variety in the Legal Treatment of Retirement Ages

In a very few countries—including the United States and Australia—age discrimination law bans forced retirement. In other countries, however, progressives press for *lower* retirement ages and accomplish this by structuring national and private pension systems to pay out retirement benefits at ever younger ages. In essence, the structure of national pension plans often compels retirement. Moreover, if retirement benefits are relatively generous, there is little political pressure to allow older workers to continue on. The only people who would complain about mandatory retirement are those who are highly paid and love their work, and these workers do not usually attract much political sympathy.

In contrast, the American system promises relatively low (public pension) retirement benefits, so that there is more support for an age-discrimination-centred approach, in which workers get to choose when to retire; employers who try to force them out are vulnerable to age discrimination lawsuits. The system is costly to some employers, and also to many younger employees, as discussed presently, but it can also be costly to those employees who remain on the job in their later years. Anti-discrimination law can, in other words, have unintended consequences, adding to stigma rather than reducing it.

Rethinking the American Ban on Compulsory Retirement

It is unlikely that I will be as good at my job at age 75 as I was at age 55, and yet my employer might be stuck with me because of US law, under which an employer cannot require an employee (with some exceptions such as airline pilots) to retire, even at a respectable age such as 70, and even through a mutually agreed upon contract. Although a great majority of workers do retire by age 68, the fact that they need not do so surely causes employers to hesitate to hire middle-aged and older workers because they fear that these employees will not retire if and when their productivity begins to drop. Moreover, productivity must be compared to compensation; in many jobs, compensation rises with seniority even if productivity falls. Not only am I likely to be less useful to my employer at 75 than I was at 55, but also my compensation at the older age will greatly exceed what it was at 55. Employers correctly fear that if they decrease or even flatten the salaries of ageing employees, they will trigger age discrimination suits. Employers are thus worse off, as are younger workers who would fill the slots vacated by retiring workers.

With some exceptions, such as state court judges, strict mandatory retirement was never common in the United States. On the other hand, *permissive* mandatory retirement, brought about by private, contractual arrangement, was once common. Modern age discrimination law now forbids these contracts, or stated retirement ages, but an employer can legally encourage retirement in ways that make the pattern of employment and retirement reasonably predictable. The employer is motivated not only by the advantages of predictability but also by the opportunity to avoid the substantial cost of meeting law's requirement that an ageing employee was let go for a *very* good reason relating to the employee's misbehaviour or failure to perform work duties; subpar performance is an insufficient cause. The most effective method has been to design retirement plans that encourage voluntary departure from the workforce. Many employer-designed pension plans made it financially unattractive for workers to stay on the job past age 58 or 60, the age at which various employers seemed to think that retirement was desirable. But for a variety of tax law and other reasons, these retirement plans are becoming obsolete, as most retirement savings now takes the form of individual accounts that the workers build, often aided by their employer. Each worker's account has a market-determined investment value, and the worker can choose to retire and withdraw from this tax-favoured account at any age above 59.5. These individual accounts do not particularly encourage early retirement.

Retirement is not just a matter of finances. It becomes more attractive when there is a critical mass of retirees. If only a small minority live long lives, these survivors are likely to be dispersed and integrated into family life. They are unlikely to have saved for what we now call retirement, and unlikely to have the political power to secure state-sponsored retirement plans. Retirement communities in the Unites States seem to have started in the 1920s, when there was just such a critical mass that found it attractive to engage in leisure activities without a surrounding majority of younger, working people. Private pension plans also became popular, perhaps because they began to receive tax-favoured treatment, but most of these plans provided only a modest fraction of pre-retirement income. It is plausible that part of what makes many countries comfortable with compulsory retirement is that when there is both a critical mass as well as virtually universal retirement (at a set age), then retirement seems natural and welcome, rather than a choice that might lead to disapproval or prejudice.

Dramatic increases in life expectancy, pension benefits, and overall affluence steadily *reduced* the age of most retirements throughout the 1900s. By the turn of the century, however, improved health, less-strenuous jobs, and other factors increased the number of working years per person and reversed the drift; the median retirement age has since risen from 58 up to 62. Voluntary retirement is at a higher age for men than for women and, interestingly, better health, financial status, and more education are all correlated with *later* retirement. Nevertheless, only a small percentage of

Americans—between 5 and 10 per cent—works full-time beyond age 70. Still, even if an employer can expect most workers to retire by age 70, it may be risky to hire a 50-year-old both because that employee may stay on long after 70, and because even by age 70, productivity is likely to be flat or declining while wages are expected to increase. The employer might be willing or eager to hire this 50-year-old person (and not younger people) with a contract that limited employment to five or ten years, but that would surely violate current age discrimination law in the United States. The situation is quite different from what we find in some other countries, where it is poor people who look to work into old age.

Retirement is also a function of job type. Even in the United States, teachers, police officers, and many union workers retire between ages 57 and 62. These workers face a system very much like that found in European countries because, in addition to the relatively modest federal retirement benefits available through the Social Security system, they have been included in *defined benefit* pension plans offered by their employers. These plans specify the payouts to beneficiaries or, more accurately, the formula that will determine these payouts; they are usually a function of salary earned in the final years leading up to retirement. The benefits are in this way 'defined', in the sense of being known within a modest range and not directly affected by investment returns. An employer offering such a plan sets aside some fraction of payroll each year in order to invest and build up reserves to finance the promised, future benefits. Workers who anticipate significant pension-plan benefits from an employer-provided plan will be influenced in their retirement decisions by the combination of these benefits and Social Security (a national, mostly mandatory pension system). Many of these defined benefit plans strongly encourage 'early' retirement at an age *below* that associated with the availability of Social Security benefits. They do so by capping benefits, by requiring contributions from those who continue to work, and by diminishing benefits for those who stay at work beyond the desired retirement age. In a typical plan affecting government or union employees, the most profitable retirement age from the worker's perspective is a bit below 60. This can be sensible for the employer because, at that age, the retiree is likely to draw a much larger salary than that required by his or her replacement. It can also save the employer the substantial effort and risk associated with dismissing employees who become less productive as they age, or who would otherwise expect wages to continue to rise even as their own productivity plateaus or declines.

It should be plain that a defined benefit plan can be designed to be a near-perfect substitute for (permissive) mandatory retirement, so long as there is opportunity to reshuffle compensation in the manner desired by the employer. But why might employers prefer the early retirement, and even the forced retirement, of their workers, including some who are marvellously productive? Employers did not lobby for the end of mandatory retirement, and they did not play a dominant role in the design of Social Security. Conventional (and insightful) wisdom is that when employees receive training in their early years at a firm, they must be 'overpaid' later on in order to keep them from moving to other firms that did not bear the cost of training and that will try to hire them away from the employer that provided training. The first employer might underpay during the training years, and then overpay during the employee's mid-career years in order to prevent defection. At some point, the workers might shirk or just stay on the job past their most productive years in order to continue to collect these back-loaded, high wages. To combat this problem, employers could structure wages so that they increase with seniority, but then start decreasing when the worker is mature and when diminished productivity is likely, or lateral hiring is unlikely. But modern laws against age discrimination make such plans ill-advised.

The important thing here is the idea that mandatory retirement is but one way of ensuring that workers do not remain with their employers too long, especially at high wages, even as employers are not discouraged from training them in the first place. A concerned employer can structure a defined benefit pension plan to encourage retirement by shifting compensation dollars from wages to retirement benefits, and by scheduling these benefits around an ideal retirement age. If fixing a retirement date is prohibited, then employers can recreate its desirable effects with defined benefit plans. The result is especially appealing because extraordinary workers are left some choice regarding retirement.

There is nothing unusual in law about depersonalized age cut-offs. Thus, law, as well as private parties, uses age minima for driver's licenses and other rights. When we require drivers to be at least 16 years old, it is because it is costly to make case-by-case determinations of maturity and other valuable characteristics. There are surely mature 14-year-olds, just as there are excellent 80-year-old employees, but at both ends of the spectrum, it is sometimes useful and reasonable to allow categorization. We worry less about discrimination when the group is very broad. Just as we were all young, we will all be old, and in such cases, law is usually less concerned with discrimination against discrete minorities. Indeed, discrimination against young drivers is more troubling than it is against older workers, because the former group has less political power.

When compulsory retirement is forbidden, even when agreed to in a contract, employers can try to unlink compensation from seniority, as is naturally the case in industries where workers earn commissions, but I have already suggested that there are problems with paying workers less as they age or even as their productivity declines or stays constant as wages rise with seniority. The process can be demoralizing for the worker and costly for the employer. When unproductive older workers stay on, younger workers and customers develop unhealthy attitudes towards older people; hidden from view is the fact that the superior mature employees have moved to other workplaces because they were underpaid at this one.

In the era before Social Security and large-scale pension plans, employers could dismiss workers as they liked. Once union and other protections took hold, they could no longer just dismiss veteran workers, but there was a wage and pension system in place that made retirement virtually inevitable, even before the Social Security age, or the age of any mandatory retirement agreement. With these contracts, little changed when age discrimination law came into effect. An unintended consequence of the demise of defined benefit plans is that employers have lost the primary tool for encouraging voluntary retirement at an age structured by the employer's plan.

Of course, some workers are fantastic at their jobs well past any age we could specify. There are 85-year-olds who are or would be extraordinary managers, and requiring them to retire would impose serious private and social costs. Some law firms, for example, go to great lengths to keep these few marvels on the job. But there are also many workplaces in which it is awkward or even harmful to suggest to someone that he or she ought to retire, and if workers can continue forever, then more such conversations are required. It is easy to see why some employers might prefer to have a rule requiring retirement at a specified age, even though the rule comes with a cost to some employees as well as to the employer. Contractual retirement of this sort also makes room for new employees and new ideas. Nothing stops the retiree from opening a business or looking for work elsewhere, because nothing requires all employers to mandate retirement; the idea is that compulsory retirement would be of the permissive, contractual, and agreeable kind.

It is plausible that such contractually forced retirement would reduce rather than encourage any stigma attached to ageing. If everyone in a workplace must retire at age 70, there is the danger that persons above 70 will be seen as over the hill, even away from the workplace. But there is the alternative and rosier possibility that retirees will be understood as having agreed to a scheme in which they benefitted from the retirement of their predecessors, and they now agree to make room for their successors. A rule requiring retirement can be less of a taint than multiple drawn out and uncomfortable processes in which ineffective senior workers are shown to be liabilities and then pushed out. In the current system, the employer has an incentive to employ these processes if wages rise over time.

It is likely that if law were (once again) to allow employment contracts to specify a retirement age, employers might find middle-aged and even older employees more attractive. At present, employers must not discriminate against older job applicants, but it is difficult to bring a successful lawsuit on behalf of persons *not* hired. Age discrimination lawsuits are almost all about the dismissal of older workers rather than about the failure to hire them. An employer might readily hire someone at 55 if that person could promise to retire at age 65, but employers are advised by their attorneys that such a contract would be unenforceable and would make the firm vulnerable to age discrimination suits. If the average employee is less useful after age 70, then the rational employer might not want to be in the business of discerning which employees should be dismissed. However, if the entire pool could be counted on to retire by age 70, it would make more sense to hire middle-aged applicants.

Many employers have developed retirement incentives that are accepted by a significant percentage of eligible employees. An employer who cannot demand retirement by some age might have a standing offer that any employee at age 65 can agree to retire at age 68 and, in return, receive a payment equal to one year's salary. If these plans remain in effect for many years then, eventually, the employees who accept or reject these payments will no longer be those who received a windfall from the elimination of compulsory retirement. It is plausible, therefore, that no great change in law is needed from the employer's perspective. Employers will simply have shifted from at-will employment contracts (allowing them to dismiss workers without fear of lawsuits) to mandatory retirement to defined benefit plans and now to severance contracts. A less optimistic story is that employers have learnt to be very careful before hiring employees who can overstay their welcome, with the threat of lawsuits in the air. I will not overclaim and say that the surge of part-time workers comes as much from the inability to contract about retirement as it does from the cost of healthcare and other benefits, but there is probably some cause-and-effect relationship between the end of compulsory retirement and the bringing-on of more part-time workers. In universities, the substitution to part-time instructors is dramatic.

Public Choice and the Regulation of Retirement Age

If the ban on mandatory retirement contracts in the United States is costly to employers, and therefore to many employees, why do we not see pressure to change the law? Law might, for example, allow private contracts with set retirement ages. Current employees would oppose this change, and it would likely be necessary to protect them against the possibility that an employer would simply terminate them, and then offer to rehire them under the terms newly permitted by law. Moreover, employees might fear that they will be terminated in order to make room for new employees who could be signed to these new, mandatory retirement contracts. But if set retirement terms are only permitted in new contracts with new employees, then there will be very little political pressure to pass such laws. Employers will have little to gain because they will not enjoy the benefits of the new law for many years; they must 'pay' for law now but profit from it far in the future—assuming the law does not change back meanwhile. With an ageing population, the centre of political gravity is likely to oppose anything that can be seen as limiting the options of senior citizens. If the ban on mandatory retirement is ever to end, reform will need to come in steps that anticipate the objections of powerful groups.

One strategy would be for law to promise that no age discrimination suit could be brought by anyone over a specified age, such as 68. Social Security and other retirement plans would provide income for retirees, and it would be a part of the strong statutory default for retirement. Some employers could offer employment contracts that, as described earlier, provide that compensation drops 5 per cent for every year after age 68. (Automatic decreases prior to that age would need to survive age discrimination suits.) Other employers might simply structure contracts so that employment ceased at age 68, perhaps the same age that maximum Social Security benefits became available, but the employer and employee could choose to negotiate a new contract for work beyond that age, and at any wage they agreed upon. In a job like mine, retirement would come at age 68, if my employer so desired, whereas there is now no retirement age. Again, my university could choose to offer me a job beyond that age for any number of years it liked, and at a wage that was (or was not) unrelated to the wage earned before age 68. In some countries, retirement is regulated in this sort of way, with the presumptive retirement age tied to the age at which retirement benefits become available. In Israel, for example, the retirement age is 67 for men and 62 for women (though at present the government is in the process of raising these ages in steps to 70 and 64, respectively). At age 67, a man's employment comes to an end, whether in the public or the private sector, and he begins to receive retirement income from the state. His employer, or another employer, is free to engage him for pay beyond that age, but these contracts are rare. The same would be true in the United States, under the proposal sketched here, except that one age (68 perhaps) applies to both sexes, and given our relatively ungenerous retirement system, there would likely be a significant minority of workers rehired beyond that age.[1]

A ban on mandatory retirement is just the sort of thing that an interest-group-driven democracy is likely to create and then find very difficult to undo. Rules against age discrimination are appealing, and many voters will think they stand to gain from the anti-discrimination law. When the rule extends to an outright ban on mandatory retirement provisions, millions of voters immediately think they are better-off. At

---

[1] It might seem surprising that law in many countries provides retirement benefits to women at a younger age than it does to men. The typical difference is five years. This differential was introduced in the post-World War II period, but has now been eliminated in many countries. Women everywhere tend to outlive men, but in no country is the pensionable age higher for women than for men. Women tend to retire at *younger* ages than men, even in places like the United States where retirees qualify for pensions at set ages, regardless of sex. On the other hand, because women are more likely to be caregivers, it is very common to require fewer years of contributions than are required of men. Proposals to raise the retirement age, which is to say the age at which a full pension is available, are often opposed most vociferously by women. The obvious reason for this objection is the expectation of earlier retirement, but it is also the case that lower-income workers have more to lose, in relative terms, by a postponement of the retirement age, and that women, on average, have lower incomes than men.

first the law had several exceptions, so that it was difficult for opponents to point to obvious cases where ageing workers were liabilities. Voters would be likely to underestimate the difficulty of proving that someone was no longer able to perform a job. Few employers would invest in efforts to oppose the ban because they could encourage retirement quite effectively with defined benefit plans. Indeed, when the ban on mandatory retirement went into effect, most employers had defined benefit plans, and their workers were therefore retiring at ages below the focal point created by Social Security. By now, things have changed; the median retirement age is rising, but the major tool for encouraging earlier retirement has been made obsolete, and partly so by law. Many workers will stay on the job well beyond the point where their productivity justifies their compensation. Employers will suffer, as will younger workers who will not be hired until these older workers retire. At the same time, the median age of the population has increased and seniors have considerable political power. Any assault on the ban on mandatory retirement, or any attempt to make it easier for employers to dismiss underachieving employees (protected by age discrimination law), will arouse the fierce opposition of this powerful group. Younger workers are unlikely to support change with matching intensity because members of this potential interest group do not really know whether they will individually gain from legal change. An identifiable group of potential losers will normally be much more active and successful in the political arena than will a group of dispersed, unidentifiable, potential winners. It is unlikely that younger workers and voters can undo the ban on compulsory retirement—even where employees voluntarily agree to such terms.

Anti-Ageing Procedures

Social Attitudes towards Cosmetic Surgery

Just as retirement is more attractive when a large fraction of one's peer group is retiring, so too external indicia of age are more acceptable, and less stigmatizing, when one is in good company. Wrinkles are like retirement, we might say. It may be human nature to find youth attractive, but it is not too wild to imagine a world in which wrinkles are seen, not as abhorrent and a sign of the approaching end of life, but rather as a proxy for wisdom, humour, and companionability. Many modern societies show a strong preference for youth and therefore, individually, for bodily interventions that preserve the appearance of youth. In India, for example, there has been a dramatic upsurge in plastic surgeries and other age-camouflaging interventions. Mumbai has become a centre for cosmetic surgery; the market was at first dominated by medical tourism, but now half the customers are domestic. India has joined the United States, Italy, Taiwan, and Japan as the leading places where affluent people try to purchase the appearance of youth.

It is pointless to argue that all body improvements are objectionable. Healthy eating, exercise, and some attention to fashion, hygiene, and make-up are normal for most well-adjusted people. It is therefore a stretch to insist that a Botox injection or a facelift is entirely different from everyday body adjustments. If law were to try to overcome the collective action problem of ageing appearances, it would have trouble sensibly specifying forbidden or taxed treatments. Indeed, Brazil subsidizes cosmetic surgeries through its tax system, in part because it has the same difficulty distinguishing cosmetic from medically required interventions. And yet, there is something troubling about a society with a high rate of elective surgeries. Americans now spend some $13 billion a year on cosmetic surgery—much more if we add in eye surgery, tattoos, cosmetic dental work, and hair transplants. Law regulates but does not outlaw many cosmetic procedures, but the focus here is on social norms rather than legal prohibitions. The question is whether bodily interventions in the cause of youthful appearance are objectionable. As a first approximation, if these interventions help reduce discrimination, in the workplace or elsewhere, then we ought to hesitate to condemn them.

Anti-Ageing Procedures

Some cosmetic surgeries, like rhinoplasty and piercings, are popular with young people and unrelated to ageing. Others, most notably breast augmentation, are common for women in their 20s through 50s, and while available to older people, not especially associated with a desire to look younger. At present, the most common cosmetic surgical procedures for people over 65 are facelifts, necklifts, and eyelid surgery. Even these decline sharply after middle age. Non-surgical procedures (such as injectables) also drop considerably once people are in their 70s. It is possible that the demographics of cosmetic surgery will change, because the generation that created a boom in this business will maintain these preferences and spending habits as it ages. Plastic surgeons and pharmaceutical companies can be expected to adjust their practices to meet the demand. But if the preference for body interventions in the cause of youthful appearance reliably diminishes with age, so that it continues to be the case that relatively few 75-year-olds yearn for altered faces or breasts, then we might conclude that older people are simply more comfortable in their own skins, as presently constituted. An economist might say that these investments are less appealing as one ages, because for the same cost, there are fewer years left in which to experience or benefit from the change. But that seems wrong, both because ageing can create a sense of urgency and because many cosmetic procedures require updating, so that the useful life of the investment is not very different for the young and the old.

There are other procedures that ought to be counted as anti-ageing body interventions. Lasik and other eye-correcting surgeries begin at age 20 and then decline with advanced age, but this is largely because the problems of ageing eyes are unresponsive to such surgeries. In any event, the desire to see better without corrective lenses has only an indirect connection to youthful appearance. Hair restoration, including transplants, is more obviously an anti-ageing procedure. As with breast augmentation, it is most popular with people in their 30s and 40s, when hair loss seems to have the greatest impact on appearance for men. In all these areas—female breast augmentation, male hair transplants, and eye and dental procedures—law allows individual choice. We are free to do almost anything we want in order to look better—and younger. The fear of fraud and exploitation that drives so much regulation of cancer drugs is nearly absent where ageing and cosmetic surgery is concerned. In the United States, the Food and Drug Administration keeps an eye on safety, but allows consumers and their doctors to decide what is efficacious. If people in the 60–80 age range do not begin to dominate the market for facelifts and other cosmetic surgeries, it will be because they choose to forego these interventions. Entertainers and politicians, male and female alike, are expected to have their faces refreshed in their 60s. Nipping and tucking is probably a good strategy, though in some surveys, a modest share of supporters say they would not vote for someone who had a facelift.

The dramatic increase in cosmetic surgery is centred on young and middle-aged adults, but there is an unmistakable increase among older patients. This increase can be associated with a larger pool of seniors, increased affluence, and a more aggressive cosmetic surgery industry. There remain physicians who discourage breast augmentation in healthy

80-year-olds, as if the surgery is more necessary for someone half that age, but demographics and economics guarantee an increase in these and other surgeries for older patients.

A hyper-rational economist or evolutionary biologist finds many things about self-presentation difficult to understand. We comprehend mating rituals, like peacocks' displays, as proxies for fitness. It takes effort to present plumage to an audience of peafowl and then to hold the display, and so the competition among the males makes sense, if only after the fact. If a teenage boy successfully displays a fancy sports car or rock-solid abs, we can think of him as signalling financial security, competitiveness, health, or rebelliousness, and each of these might be a desirable trait in a partner. Similarly, if a young woman has beautiful long hair, well-toned arms, or the most fashionable clothes, she might signal affluence, health, effort, or other desirable qualities. But why would people undertake these costs when they are beyond the age of reproduction? Perhaps the behaviour is ingrained and not easily abandoned at an advanced age. For thoughtful people, able to overcome primitive instincts, physical attraction is a kind of door-opener. A gorgeous model must always wonder whether suitors like the inner person, or are too easily attracted to physical attributes. Whether the attraction is primitive or competitive (the suitor wants to win in the competition for attractive mates), the attractive person must be anxious that, with ageing, the partner will lose interest. She (let us assume) cannot simply reason that her suitor will also take steps against the danger that he (assuming a male suitor) is overly swayed by her appearance, because he can exit the relationship and redeploy whatever qualities he has. It is youthful attraction—thick hair, firm breasts, smooth skin, and so forth—that presumably does the work, and these attributes will depreciate, while power and wealth will remain valuable to the imagined suitor.

As we age, we no longer compete for reproductive partners; if there is competition, it is for companions or even future caregivers. Virility still matters, but it is rational to look for signs of—and then to avoid—dementia and decrepitude. Anti-ageing procedures remain useful as a signal of health, but mobility and various life habits are increasingly important attractors. It is easy to understand why some plastic surgeries decline in importance among people over 50, while great attention is given to hair-styling, cleanliness, and fitness. These become more important than uplifted breasts and the battle against baldness, to take one example for each sex. Hair care is especially interesting because it might be a proxy for one's ability and inclination to care for oneself, and be a ready companion rather than a burden.

A visit to a town with many retirees casts some light on the effect of comparison groups on anti-ageing procedures. Plastic surgeons are in evidence in Sun City, Arizona, as they are in Boca Raton and The Villages in Central Florida—all places with substantial populations of retired people—so that it is obvious that the demand for plastic surgery does not completely subside when competition in the workplace or mating market comes to an end. The photo galleries on these doctors' websites show face and neck work on 64- to 74-year-old women, but nationwide in the United States, only 4 per cent of surgical cosmetic procedures are performed on patients over 64. Liposuctions and tummy tucks, for example, are very popular, but not, or not yet, among older people. If non-surgical cosmetic procedures are included, the percentage of procedures involving patients over age 64 is higher, but it is still only 10 per cent. Nationwide, more than 90 per cent of cosmetic procedures are performed on women, and this is true in every age group and in virtually every country. The places with relatively highest numbers of plastic surgeons per capita, including Beverly Hills, Miami, San Francisco, and Mumbai, do not have disproportionate elderly populations. Indeed, a couple of these hotspots for cosmetic surgery suggest that demand increases when the surrounding population is young.

Women in retirement communities seem to spend much more time on their hair and on being sociable and pleasant than they do on body interventions. Perhaps at some age it feels foolish to try to look 'young', as many 40- to 50-year-olds do. Older people in retirement communities often seem, at long last, comfortable in their own skins. I confess that at times I find their wrinkles glamorous. At some age, a weathered and wrinkled face seems more beautiful to me than does smooth and clear skin. The person behind the skin seems more interesting for the wrinkles and, if the eyes sparkle, I find myself engaging the person in conversation, rather than looking over the person's clothes, accessories, or body features. I want to believe that the lower rate of cosmetic surgeries within this age group reflects an increasing comfort in one's own (changing) skin. Both baby skin and aged skin are beautiful in their own ways; the former hints at promise or perfection, while the latter suggests experience and wisdom. Once we are mature adults, most of us would rather be wise than promising. Perfection would be nice, but we know it is out of reach.

Anti-Ageing Prejudices and Peer Groups

As we age, we think differently of ourselves, depending on the demography of the group in which we are embedded. An attractive person can easily seem (and feel) dowdy and even misshapen in a room full of models. In a retirement community, most people look and feel quite normal; distinctions might be based on mobility or one's connection to an oxygen machine, but wrinkles, hair volume, abdominal muscles, and breast shape can seem less important to the residents than they do to comparable people who live among the population at large. Some ageing people insist that they want to live in a 'normal' community, where people of all ages circulate. Leaving aside economics and politics and focusing only on appearances, it becomes clear that, for many people, the opposite is the case, and subconscious comparisons might be key. It is not just that a retirement community offers activities and neighbours looking to play golf or cards. For some residents, these communities offer a peer group that makes it easier to feel attractive. Some 75-year-olds might feel compelled to look younger if they lived in a world with people many years younger; they feel more comfortable when the comparison group is also wrinkled. This is the sort of thinking that leads to practices, or even laws, against super-thin models; everyone can be better-off if no one can starve themselves.

The importance of the comparison group has implications for cosmetic surgery. Imagine, for example, that we find much more plastic surgery among 80-year-olds in a retirement community than within the same age group dispersed in a city. We would have two ready explanations for the difference. First, the demand for cosmetic surgery is fuelled or dampened by the peer group. This group spreads information about the availability and effectiveness of something like a new skin resurfacing technique or a good doctor, and then more individuals join in or imitate the practices of their friends and neighbours. Alternatively, the peer group might bring about serious internal competition for youthful appearance. If the 80-year-olds in a retirement community compete for status or romantic partners, then they might engage in a kind of arms race, in this case by patronizing plastic surgeons. On the other hand, if we find fewer cosmetic surgeries among residents of a retirement community, reasonable but different explanations would come to mind. Residents may be in frequent contact with one another, and may not need special means of initially attracting one another in order to overcome inertia. Thus, it would not surprise me if, holding age constant, people lied about their age less in retirement communities than elsewhere. A second explanation for a lower rate of body alterations in a retirement community brings us back to the comparison group. In such a community, a 70-year-old is relatively young, and is surrounded by people who are considerably older. It may be that when the comparison group has plenty of older-looking people, there is less demand for cosmetic procedures because it is actually easier to feel relatively young than it is when one is living on the outside, where even a 70-year-old person can sometimes feel old. Age is, in part, a matter of self-perception, and it is influenced by the available comparison group. I wish I could report that one of these arguments about the demand for cosmetic surgery in and out of retirement communities is better than the other, but in fact, it is hard to get fine-grained data on cosmetic procedures. Doctors classify their patients by procedures and then by age groups and minority status, but there are no ready data by retirement communities or even by zip codes. My very inadequate and prying questions lead me to think that invasive surgeries are, unsurprisingly, more common than average in some retirement communities, and then lower than average in others. It would be nice to aggregate and then know on average whether living among peers drives the rate of cosmetic surgery up or down, but unfortunately we just do not know. Moreover, if we did know, would we be sure that a higher rate of one anti-ageing strategy meant a higher rate for others? I have already suggested that cosmetic surgery and deception about one's age may be substitutes rather than complements. Similarly, a low rate of cosmetic surgery might be correlated with a *high* rate of exercise, hair transplantation, consumption of peptides and antioxidants, and so forth. And note that these anti-ageing strategies might be positively correlated for a community, but negatively correlated at the individual level. If Smith gets a facelift, her neighbour, Jones, might be more inclined to exercise or try a skin resurfacing procedure, whether or not Smith is also more likely to exercise or opt for more cosmetic surgery.

In a crowd of older people, nice eyes, smiles, and neat hair can make someone look very inviting. In a crowd of tall statuesque models, all of us mortals look distressed. And yet a subway car with many older, well-coiffed men can look much better to someone accustomed to older men without hair. In lower Manhattan, where young people congregate, even a 55-year-old can look out of place, and the observer's brain notices stiffness, thinning hair, and hearing aids. But in a room full of mature adults, once the observer's brain is accustomed to various qualities that

are now plentiful, wrinkles begin to look interesting. My brain interprets them as signals of depth or wisdom. The same logic that causes
middle-aged people who work in Silicon Valley or Hollywood to rush to
plastic surgeons in order to look young, might allow older people who
are surrounded by contemporaries to forego these interventions and to
feel comfortable as they are.

I do not want to push the glamorous or wise wrinkles thing too far.
I doubt that any 60-year-old intentionally chooses to present as wiser
on an online dating site by using a photo that is brushed to look older
rather than younger. The presentation is aspirational and understood to
mean: 'I wanted you to agree to meet me and then to judge for yourself
my "true" age and qualities.' People do not like to be profiled, at least
when the stereotype is negative, and so we allow some room for creative
expression. I wonder whether people who undergo cosmetic surgery are
more likely to understate their age or claim senior discounts. Eventually,
I hope they find that their deepening wrinkles are attractive and worth
keeping.

***

It is interesting that law in the United States intervenes more where retirement is at stake than where adults' body interventions are concerned. In
the case of retirement, the law aims to empower older workers who need
or simply wish to continue working, and it does this by characterizing
any long-term agreements, or legal requirements, to retire by a certain
age as illicit discrimination. But in the cause of ending discrimination
based on age, law creates many sympathetic losers. Law's unintended
consequences include the difficulty middle-aged workers face in finding
employment or switching jobs, and the likelihood that young workers
have diminished opportunities because older workers have something of
a property right in jobs, even though their wages exceed their value to
employers. Most legal systems have made other choices, and encourage
or force retirement, but do so with relatively higher guaranteed income
for retirees. In terms of stigma, it is plausible that there would be less
rather than more negative profiling if compulsory retirement were permitted in the United States. This is because people understand or intuit
that employers are virtually forced to keep underperforming older workers on the payroll, so that older workers are often seen as beneficiaries of
law rather than as valuable assets. Compulsory retirement might disadvantage a number of older workers, but it would likely raise the status

of many more. American law probably has this one wrong; however, for reasons explained earlier, it is not an easy law to change.

In contrast, law allows adults and their physicians to do more or less as they like. When older people compete with younger ones, they often feel pressure to appear younger themselves. The growing number of anti-ageing interventions is thus a bit troubling, because it reflects the stigma and negative profiling attached to age. Wealthier people are better able to hide age in this way than are less financially secure peers, so that inequality is likely increased as anti-ageing interventions become more commonplace. It would be absurd to suggest that compulsory wrinkling is as desirable as compulsory retirement, but the point made here is that a great many people would be better-off if law stayed out of employer–employee retirement arrangements with respect to age. Indeed, legal intervention is more likely to do some good for the majority of people, and for the less affluent among us, if it constrains anti-ageing medical interventions rather than employment contracts. Botox is for the affluent and, as it becomes popular, the less fortunate look older *and* society is less likely to think that their weathering reflects wisdom. Fortunately, the growth of retirement communities may slow down the rate of increase in anti-ageing procedures, and allow both old and young to view wrinkles and sags as signs of experience rather than some dreaded stage of life.

8

Ageing, Stigma, and Disgust

Martha C. Nussbaum

> *But was there ever any domination which did not seem natural to those who possessed it?*
>
> —John Stuart Mill, *The Subjection of Women*

Ageing people have suffered from social discrimination and stigma ever since there were enough of them alive to be noticed as a group.[1] Stigma and prejudice are, in fact, the focus of the first surviving philosophical work on ageing in the Western philosophical tradition—still the best— Cicero's *De Senectute*, written in 45 BCE, when Cicero was 62. Because

---

[1] Much of the material in this chapter is taken, in modified form, from Martha C. Nussbaum and Saul Levmore, *Aging Thoughtfully* (New York: Oxford University Press, 2017). This book contains a detailed analysis of the Cicero work, as well as more extensive discussions of legal issues connected to age discrimination. As always, I am very grateful to Saul Levmore for his comments. I would also like to thank Douglas Baird, William Birdthistle, and Emily Dupree for their valuable comments on the book manuscript. The original paper was presented as a plenary address at the 2016 meeting of the Human Development and Capability Association in Tokyo, where it received valuable comments from Flavio Comim.

the literary structure of the work is part of its attack on stigma, I must pause to describe it.

Cicero, both statesman and philosopher, composed the work during the chaotic events of the Roman civil wars, as he attempted to defend the dying Roman Republic, an effort for which he was assassinated a year later. He dedicates the work to his best friend Titus Pomponius Atticus, noting that its purpose is to divert both men from the anxiety of the political struggle. And how is he diverting them? By writing a philosophical dialogue on old age, the *De Senectute*. Cicero frames ageing, then, not as a hideous horror story but as a lighter topic than the all-too-present theme of the impending loss of political liberty. As he immediately observes, he and Atticus (then 65) are not elderly men yet, but they are on their way, so they had better look ahead and scout the territory. The lead character in the dialogue, Cato (a real historical figure) is 83 at the time of the dialogue's dramatic date, 150 BCE, and he is depicted, accurately, as playing an active role in politics, writing several books, learning new languages, and enjoying friendships both with people of his own age and with many people who are younger.

Unlike Western philosophical tradition's other major work on ageing, the relentlessly depressing *La Vieillesse* by Simone de Beauvoir, published in 1970—a work stuffed full of every social stereotype known to the twentieth century, in which these stereotypes parade as necessary universal truths—the *De Senectute* exhibits a refreshing determination to confront stereotype and stigma. First of all, two young men in their twenties, the other characters in the dialogue, are depicted as enjoying Cato's company. They have sought him out, because, as they note, they would quite like to get to be that old, and in case they do, they would like to know more about what that time of life is like. They feel that Cato is doing very well, so they want to know why, given the negative reputation attached to that time of life. In response, Cato gracefully, cogently, rebuts four charges commonly made (he says) against his time of life: that ageing people are inactive and unproductive; that they have no physical strength; that they no longer enjoy bodily pleasures; and that the nearness of death makes them prone to debilitating anxiety. Particularly striking is his 'use it or lose it' philosophy: by continued disciplined activity, both mental and physical, one remains strong and active.

As Cicero uses Cato to rebut the common charges, he is clearly having some fun himself: for he portrays Cato as mentally and physically impressive, but also as having at least one or two mildly annoying traits commonly associated with old age. Cato talks too much and listens too little, he is fond of long digressions about his own past, and he focuses too much on his own pet hobbies, without considering the interests of his audience. In this case, Cato, the real-life author of a very boring work about farming, *De Agri Cultura*, bores the two young men, and the reader, by long digressions about mulching and ploughing, and there's an especially hilarious passage about the miraculous properties of manure. Some Romans found these topics interesting, but we know that Cicero did not, so the portrait is playful. On the whole, then, old age isn't perfect; but it acquits itself very well, rebutting stigma.

I'll return to Cicero's arguments frequently in what follows, but for now I repeat: smart people knew already in 45 BCE that ageing was the subject of denigrating and inaccurate stereotypes, and that these stereotypes caused real harm to ageing people, marginalizing them and diminishing their lives. And they knew already that one way philosophy can contribute to human development is to question those stereotypes with good arguments—and, let's hope, also with a sense of humour.

In this chapter, I follow Cicero's lead, though by a different route, examining the particular stigma attached to the ageing body, its origins, its relationship to and difference from other types of stigma, and its powerful effects. Cato has good arguments, but his case for ageing lacks an underlying psychology of prejudice, which I shall attempt to supply. Finally, I shall propose some directions for public policy.

I have long argued, as a legal theorist, for a theory of stigma and group discrimination that makes the operations of disgust central. I developed it in *Hiding from Humanity* using results in cognitive psychology to show how disgust operates in a wide range of types of discrimination, including anti-Semitism, racism, sexism, and homophobia.[2] I then made the normative argument that disgust is never a sufficient condition to make an act illegal when it causes no harm to non-consenting parties. In 2010, in my book on sexual orientation and constitutional law, I developed the theory further and then connected it empirically to recent discrimination against gays and lesbians.[3] Here, then, I must begin by summarizing my theory, before looking more closely at the stigma attached to ageing bodies.

---

[2] Martha C. Nussbaum, *Hiding from Humanity: Disgust, Shame, and the Law* (Princeton: Princeton University Press, 2004).

[3] Martha C. Nussbaum, *From Disgust to Humanity: Sexual Orientation and Constitutional Law* (New York: Oxford University Press, 2010).

What is disgust, and why is its social role troubling? The emotion has recently been the subject of some important research by a team of US experimental psychologists, led by Paul Rozin.[4] All humans appear to share an acute discomfort when confronted by their own bodily fluids, excretions, and smells, and also by the decay of the corpse. I use the term 'primary disgust' for a shrinking from contamination by such objects and by other objects that closely resemble them in smell or feel (such as insects and animals that are slimy, smelly, and the like). Primary disgust, though not present at birth, is culturally universal and is probably grounded in inherited tendencies. Although this aversive reaction may in some cases protect people from real danger (and perhaps that was its evolutionary origin), Rozin shows that its cognitive content is quite different from that of fear: it is about contamination, not danger; it is a reaction to the animality and decay of the human body, and it is both under-inclusive and over-inclusive for real danger. (Many dangerous things are not disgusting—think of poisonous mushrooms—and people feel disgust even when they are rationally convinced that danger is absent, as with many experiments done with sterilized cockroaches and other non-dangerous but disgusting creatures.) Rozin concludes that in disgust we are rejecting something about our own animality. Although he is not specific enough at this point, it is evident from his research that we do not reject all signs of our kinship with the other animals: not traits such as strength, speed, and beauty. What we reject is all that is associated with decay and mortality: we are rejecting our own animal weakness and vulnerability.

All that might be harmless enough, although I would argue that it is always problematic to encourage this sort of self-loathing. In all known societies, however, people do not stop there and we arrive at what I call 'projective disgust'. People seek to create a buffer zone between themselves and their own animality, by identifying a group (often a powerless minority) who can be targeted as the quasi-animals and projecting onto that group various animal characteristics, which they have to no greater degree than the ones doing the projecting: bad smell, animal sexuality, and so on. The so-called thinking seems to be: if those quasi-animal humans stand between us and our own animal stench and decay, we are that much further from being animal and mortal ourselves. There is no society in which we do not find subgroups, to whom, irrationally,

[4] See references to and discussion of the work of Paul Rozin and his colleagues in Nussbaum, *Hiding from Humanity*.

properties of smelliness, sliminess, hyper-sexuality and in general hyper-animality are imputed.[5]

There are many varieties of disgust stigma. In European anti-Semitism, Jews were depicted as hyper-bodily, smelly, and hyper-sexual, but also as crafty and intelligent.[6] They were regarded with fear and envy, as well as disgust. African Americans, by contrast, were, and unfortunately at times still are, imagined as hyper-sexual and also smelly, bestial, and stupid. They were regarded with both disgust and bodily fear, but not with envy. Another contrast involves strength: African Americans are imagined as physically powerful and aggressive. To upper Hindu castes who observed untouchability, by contrast, untouchables were foul, weak, and not particularly aggressive.

In misogyny, women in so many cultures have been imagined as disgusting—and yet that disgust is frequently combined with sexual desire and arousal, in such a way that no less an authority than Sigmund Freud argued that disgust is an inevitable part of sexual arousal. Feminists are surely right to see in this disgust (so oddly linked with attraction) a linchpin of gender-based denials of moral and intellectual equality—and yet the reaction of disgust does not lead to avoidance of intimacy, but, rather, to an intimacy and domesticity characterized by anxious attempts to police female sexuality. It's not that women are never avoided as contaminating: taboos surrounding menstruation in many cultures testify to the power of misogynistic stigma. And that polite and sophisticated observer of morals, Adam Smith, observed that males like to avoid females after sexual desire is gratified: 'When we have dined, we order the covers to be removed.'[7] Contemporary US legal scholar William Ian Miller concurs, arguing that such male reactions are tenacious and will always impede gender equality.[8] All this disgust, of course, is fully compatible with sharing a dwelling, food, and a bed.

To continue to another case, in contemporary homophobia, gay men are imagined as hyper-sexual and also as disgusting—and as not sexually

[5] See the longer version of these arguments in Nussbaum, *Hiding from Humanity*.

[6] See references to the historical literature in Nussbaum, *Hiding from Humanity*.

[7] Adam Smith, The Theory of Moral Sentiments, Book I, ed. D.D Rafael and A.L. Macfie (Indianapolis: Liberty Classics, 1982).

[8] William Ian Miller, *The Anatomy of Disgust* (Cambridge, MA: Harvard University Press, 1998).

desirable to the homophobic men who have these reactions. Straight homophobic men seek not just subordination but also segregation.[9] (The violent type of disgust stigma associated with homosexuality is more or less entirely directed at gay men: lesbian acts were never illegal in Britain, and in the United States, lesbian sex is rarely central to the political mobilization of hatred.) The mobilization of disgust against gay men typically focuses on anal sex, imagining the mingling of bodily fluids, as, allegedly, semen, faeces, and blood all stir around together.[10] (It is striking that, in India, the legal struggle over sodomy laws has prominently recognized the role of stigma and disgust: discrimination against gay men has been explicitly compared to discrimination on the basis of caste.[11]) Gay men, like Jews, are usually imagined as quite intelligent, and as potentially successful, so disgust here often mingles with envy and competitive anxiety. These differences in stigma are important, but a common set of threads runs through all.

An interesting puzzle is class. At times, class-based stigma appears to involve a form of bodily disgust, as elites imagine lower-class bodies as smelly, sweaty, gross, and dirty. George Orwell argues that the upper classes will always feel disgust for the living conditions of the lower classes—citing, however, conditions that are ubiquitous in British housekeeping in all classes.[12] William Miller reaches a similar conclusion, considering an instance of his own interaction with a manual labourer.[13] On the other hand, class relations involve many rational differences about policy, and are not solely mediated by disgust. Moreover, in nations with reasonable social mobility, class is a temporary status.

Now we begin to arrive at the heart of the matter, for our current purposes. Two instances of disgust stigma are different from the others,

---

[9] Nussbaum, *From Disgust to Humanity*.

[10] See Nussbaum, *From Disgust to Humanity*, for illustrations from the pamphlet literature.

[11] Martha C. Nussbaum, 'Disgust or Equality? Sexual Orientation and Indian Law', *Journal of Indian Law and Society* 6 (2016): 1–24.

[12] George Orwell, *The Road to Wigan Pier* (New York: Harcourt, Brace, 1958 [1937]).

[13] Miller, *The Anatomy of Disgust*. The example is peculiar, since Miller's negative interest in the worker (who was repaving his driveway) is initially aroused, he tells us, by the fact that his wife evidently found the worker attractive and was flirting with him. It is only later that he maintains that he always found the man's body (with its beer belly) disgusting.

and interestingly similar to one another. Disgust for people with physical and mental disabilities is directed at weakness and inability—seen, very likely, as a lot potentially open to all human beings. It is not linked to any type of envy, and not to any type of fear except the fear of becoming like that. Disgust for the bodies of ageing people (who are often also members of the category of the disabled) has a similar flavour: there is no envy, no fear of superior power or intelligence, not even fear of ungovernable sexuality or a propensity to rape others—just a kind of horror at the prospect of being broken down and (allegedly) decaying, close to death, in that way. For 'able-bodied' people, there's an uneasy comfort, in looking at the bodies of the people with disabilities: they are different, and I'm not like that. With ageing bodies, no such comfort is available; however much a younger person tries to 'other' the ageing, at some level, they know that this is them in the future—unless they meet the yet worse fate of premature death.

Projective disgust always leads to some type of avoidance of bodily contact. Again, the type and extent vary. African Americans were forbidden to use white people's drinking fountains, swimming pools, lunch counters, hotel beds—and, of course, sexual contact was strictly forbidden and was considered to be a felony in many states (widely though, white men had sexual relationships with, and sexually abused, black women). Yet, an African American might prepare and serve food for a white family. An Indian untouchable, by contrast, could never serve food in an upper-caste family, and, as noted, Dalits also could not share lodging or drinking taps. The crazy irrationalities of these ideas are manifold. As for gay men in America, given the reality of the closet, no ban on shared restaurants, lodgings, drinking fountains, or even swimming pools could realistically be imposed, but straight men still often find gay men creepy and seek to avoid any possible advance from them. Women have often been segregated from male discussion and deliberation, as though their sexuality bore a kind of contagion.

As for people with mental and physical disabilities, they have often been denied access to mainstream spaces, public and private. Sometimes these denials are covered by the claim of expense: how costly it would be to make buildings fully accessible to people using wheelchairs. (No more expensive than to make them inaccessible, of course, if we are starting de novo, but dominant groups tend to forget how they have formed the world, excluding others.) How costly it would be to keep the sidewalks repaired so that people who are blind could use them in safety. As the blind law professor Jacobus tenBroek observed in a famous article, the very standard of due care in tort law denies people like him 'the right to be in the world'.[14] Meanwhile, children with disabilities have typically been excluded almost from birth. Many have been relegated to institutions; most, until recently, have been denied access to integrated education; most until recently have lacked meaningful access to public spaces, whether recreational or utilitarian (busses, trains, and the like). The testimony that led to the passage of the Americans With Disabilities Act shows that a common 'justification' offered for such exclusions was that 'normal' people found it upsetting to look at people with disabilities.

Now let us zero in on age. Projective disgust always targets imputed (and often fantasized) characteristics that are thought to be contaminating to the disgusted person, reminders of an animal nature that has not been embraced. What is special about the prejudice against ageing bodies?

First, the shrinking from contact appears to be somewhat less mediated by culture than in most of our other cases. The stigma attached to wrinkles, drooping skin, and other signs of age seems to be culturally universal in some form, and pre-verbal children already show avoidance behaviour when given a choice between an ageing and a non-ageing person. It seems plausible that an aversion to ageing bodies is based on an evolutionary tendency that is connected to reproductive fitness. Even if children's disgust is far from totally innate, getting many cues from surrounding culture, at least a part of it may be based on innate tendencies.[15]

Second, the stigma has at least some truth and is not a total fantasy. Ageing people are indeed closer to death, on average, than younger people (though the peak age for homicide death is a very young age, 21–4), and at least some of the stigmatized characteristics (drooping skin, age spots, wrinkles) are indeed signs of this nearness, although they are exacerbated by lack of exercise and self-care. Racial stigma and caste stigma, by contrast, rest entirely upon fantasy: the bodies of these groups smell no different from bodies in the dominant group, nor is the sexuality of the stigmatized group more 'animal' than any other instance of human sexuality. Gender is somewhere in the middle: some rather complicated

[14] Jacobus TenBroek, 'The Right to Be in the World: The Disabled and the Law of Torts', *California Law Review* 54 (1966): 841–919.

[15] Becca R. Levy, 'Mind Matters: Cognitive and Physical Effects of Aging Self-Stereotypes', *Journal of Gerontology: Psychological Sciences* 58B, no. 4 (2003): 204.

and not binary underlying biological realities, and over top a set of binary social stereotypes that are basically fictive. Disability, a category that overlaps considerably with that of ageing, is more like ageing—a good deal of biology, but also a good deal of fantasy and stereotyping.

As Cato says, however, most of the stereotype of ageing people is not based on truth. The ageing are widely believed to be less competent along all parameters, and to be incapable of understanding normal speech—explaining why medical personnel typically use a high-pitched hyper-articulate baby speech called 'elderspeak' to address them.[16] Like people who use wheelchairs, who are often addressed in baby talk even though no mental impairment is present, ageing people are assumed to be less competent as a class and across all life functions, without assessing the abilities of the individual. And this is surely wrong. The admixture of truth only feeds the fantasy.

Cicero's Cato is on to this area of stigma, and he rebuts it eloquently by pointing to the many instances of high achievement in ageing people. Particularly lovely is the story of how the heirs of the poet Sophocles tried to get him declared incompetent so that they could get their hands on his money. They hauled him into court—where he read to the jury some speeches from the *Oedipus at Colonus*, which he had just been writing (at the age of around 90).[17] He then asked the jury whether they thought this the work of a mentally incompetent person. He won.

Cato's argument does not give us statistics, it simply points to a group of cases, but the point is that the existence of such cases means that we need to examine the individual. And he addresses the distributional point by observing that the Roman Senate is actually named after old men, *senes*, because it is full of them, and even Romans concede that deliberation and wisdom are virtues of ageing men.

More generally, says Cato, the difference between competence and incompetence, whether mental or physical, is largely made, as one ages, by daily habit and practice. Some activities that require a lot of physical strength are on average harder for people as they age, but even here habit makes a huge difference: he regularly does farming and rides horseback. And intellectual and deliberative pursuits do not diminish at

---

[16] Laura L. Carstensen and Christine R. Hartel, eds, *When I'm 64*, Committee on Aging Frontiers in Social Psychology, Personality, and Adult Developmental Psychology (Washington, DC: National Academies Press, 2006).

[17] Sophocles was born in 497/6 and died in 406; the play was produced posthumously.

all, if people exercise their mental faculties by reading and learning new things. He concludes:

> My young friends, we should resist old age; we should compensate for its defects by watchful care; we should fight against it as we would fight against a disease; we should adopt a regimen of health; we should do regular moderate exercise; and we should eat and drink just enough to replenish our strength, not so much as to crush it. Nor, indeed, should we give our attention only to the body. Much greater care should be given to the intellect and the mental faculties. For they too, like lamps, grow dim with time, unless we keep them supplied with oil.

(I note that it is very striking that Cato has never heard of Alzheimer's disease. In this otherwise highly realistic work, he would have had to discuss it if it had been a well-known social reality. I think this absence indicates that Alzheimer's has environmental causes, but to say more would take me too far from my argument.)

The third distinctive fact about age prejudice is indicated in the very structure of Cicero's dialogue, which depicts the younger men as seeking out Cato in order to inquire into their own future. Namely, the stigma is associated, from very early on, with the felt inevitability that one will enter the stigmatized group, if one lives long enough. It is the only out-group into which each and every member of the in-group of the young will inevitably move, if he or she lives long enough. This future, however distant, inflects the shrinking from the start. As time advances, it becomes not just a projection but a partial or total self-ascription. The self-ascription is characteristically mingled with uncertainty and vague dread. Unlike the progress of childhood, which, while hardly uniform in all, is uniform enough for age-related generalizations and bright-line rules to make at least some sense, the progress of ageing is both hugely variable among individuals and different across the different aspects of human life. One may be mentally acute with one or more physical disabilities; one may be bad at sprinting while having undiminished ability to play the piano or (as Cicero's Cato notes) to give public orations. Even the mind is plural: one may have problems remembering names without any difficulty talking about politics or culture. So, the anxiety about whether the stigma applies to oneself ramifies to embrace the rich plurality of zones of life: as many activities as life contains, so many sources of anxiety about metaphorical or literal wrinkles and sag.

In short, disgust is always at some level self-disgust, as one perceives animality in others and shuns it in oneself. But with ageing, the truth is front and centre: it is really for oneself that one fears. Stigma learnt early and towards others gradually becomes self-stigma and self-exclusion, as one's own ageing body is seen as a site of decay and future death—by oneself, as well as by others.

What has recent research shown us? We have not progressed very far beyond Cicero. One thing that is constantly said is that more research is needed, so all these findings should be regarded as provisional.[18] Still, several seem reasonably solid.

First, stereotypes about ageing people are in part explicit, in part implicit. As in other areas of bias research, it is now clear that the bias against ageing operates powerfully at a non-conscious level, as prompts associated with ageing (words like 'old' and 'aged') elicit negative reactions even when the subject is not aware of having any such bias.[19] Implicit bias towards the ageing is likely to be based on childhood learning, deeply internalized; it will, therefore, be difficult to eradicate.[20]

The stereotype involves aversive reactions to ageing bodies as such; but it also contains more specific beliefs. One is that all ageing people have declining cognitive capacity and memory. Thus, the very same mistakes and instances of forgetfulness that are ascribed to normal human frailty when a younger person makes them, are ascribed to age when an ageing person makes them.[21] Similarly, the same physical problems that are ascribed to treatable disease in younger people are ascribed to the inevitable effects of ageing when the patient is older.[22] Since such stereotypes of inevitability have reigned for so long, we actually do not know very much about what the baseline of health is for people at various ages, in a variety of performance areas. Ignorance then supports further stereotyping, both about others and, often, about oneself. Cato is on to this problem too, and remarks that if one thinks decline inevitable, one will not work hard, and then one will really decline.

---

[18] Carstensen and Hartel, *When I'm 64*.

[19] Becca R. Levy, 'Stereotype Embodiment: A Psychosocial Approach to Aging', *Curr Dir Psychological Sci.* 18, no. 6 (2009): 332—6. See also B.R. Levy and M.R. Banaji, 'Implicit Ageism', in *Ageism: Stereotyping and Prejudice Against Older Persons*, ed. T.D. Nelson (Cambridge, MA: Massachusetts Institute of Technology Press), 2002.

[20] Levy, 'Mind Matters', 203.

[21] Carstensen and Hartel, *When I'm 64*.

[22] Carstensen and Hartel, *When I'm 64*.

Even when the stereotype contains a positive element, the positive often contains hidden negativity. Thus, the positive stereotype of an ageing man emphasizes 'wisdom'—not analytical ability or skill, or subversive challenges to existing norms. And women are denied even 'wisdom'—the positive female stereotype is of the 'perfect grandmother', which probably connotes nice subservient behaviour and not anything associated with professional excellence or challenging ideas.

We should pause here to observe that these stereotypes involve what, in an important recent book, philosopher Miranda Fricker has called 'epistemic injustice'.[23] That is, ageing people are systematically downgraded and disparaged as knowers. Their testimony, their insights, their interventions in discussion, and even, as I have noted, their reports of their own health conditions, are taken to be weak, like the contributions of children. Ageing people share epistemic disadvantage with many other marginalized groups. Women, in particular, have long and ubiquitously been at an epistemic disadvantage in law and more generally in society, and this sort of testimonial disadvantage applies to other marginalized groups as well. But the epistemic disqualification of the ageing is unusually acute, since women and African Americans are rarely addressed with baby talk, as is common for the ageing. And it is more acute in today's United States than in at least some times and places, as Cato's observations about the Roman Senate make clear. Senators were taken to be good at arguing, not just sources of grandfatherly wisdom, and Cato seems to have been right about this. At least ageing men, then, were treated with some epistemic deference—though not always, as Cato's analysis shows. In today's United States, this deference rarely exists. One has to have significant signs of external authority, such as fame and reputation, or high office, for one's epistemic contributions to gain the respect that they merit. Thus, ageing philosophers such as Amartya Sen (83), Jürgen Habermas (87), and Noam Chomsky (87) are taken very seriously, but less famous people of similar age are not. Moreover, if even a famous ageing intellectual (or judge or politician) has a bad day or writes a bad article, it is immediately imputed to age: 'She's losing it.' Now, in fact, people write some bad articles, and probably the people who make such criticisms have themselves done so. But when they are ageing, the bad article is almost invariably imputed to age. In the case

---

[23] Miranda Fricker, *Epistemic Injustice: Power and the Ethics of Knowing* (New York: Oxford University Press, 2007).

of my dear friend, the late Hilary Putnam, one of the great philosophers of the last century, who died in 2016 at age 89, nobody could say with a straight face that anything he wrote was bad, so they found another way to disparage him agistically (to coin a term). Namely, Putnam wrote a good deal about the philosophy of religion in his later years, so those who wanted to disparage his age did so by disparaging his choice of topic, as if it were 'easy' or even 'empty,' never mind the fact that he was simultaneously coming up with new insights about Carnap.

As one might predict, both explicit and implicit biases have real effects on the behaviour of ageing people themselves. Where health is concerned, stereotypes prevent ageing people from seeking treatment for treatable weaknesses and diseases; should they seek treatment, they may not get what they need, if medical personnel, influenced by stereotypes, believe the condition is just 'normal ageing'. Mental performance has been experimentally shown to be directly affected by stereotypes: people do worse on tests of memory and other cognitive abilities when 'primed' by references to stereotypes of ageing.[24] And as Cato observes, one will simply stop working on one's body and one's mind if one thinks work is futile. Furthermore, the stress imposed by carrying around negative stereotypes about oneself has direct effects on health and well-being.[25]

Sometimes, ageing people cordon themselves off from the ill effects of stereotyping by refusing to identify themselves with the denigrated group: retaining an idea of oneself as young and able has good effects.[26] On the other hand, this strategy forfeits the usual good effects of in-group solidarity.[27] In other cases of deprived groups suffering from stereotyping—racial, gender, and sexual orientation groups, and also disability groups—group solidarity has been important for revolutionary movements seeking better treatment from the world and seeking to enhance their own self-image. But the age stereotype has such a grip on people's self-perception that many people refuse to acknowledge group membership despite its evident benefits. This is changing. The AARP (American Association for Retired Persons) has surely promoted a useful type of group solidarity and self-respect by making definite progress on many issues. Other nations have lagged behind the United States in fighting age discrimination, largely because of the political work of this lobby group.

---

[24] Carstensen and Hartel, *When I'm 64*. See also Levy, 'Mind Matters', 206.

[25] Carstensen and Hartel, *When I'm 64*. See also Levy, 'Mind Matters', 207.

[26] Cartensen and Hartel, *When I'm 64*.

[27] Levy, 'Mind Matters', 204.

But what about group segregation for a range of different activities? It seems that many seniors enjoy senior fitness classes, and in many sports, a type of voluntary group segregation seems to improve enjoyment. (I note, however, that in the half-marathons that I run, extremely slowly, I always end up finishing along with a group of younger people who probably have not trained to maximize their potential, and I find their company fun and happy. It is much better than finishing with most of the women my own age, who are typically hyper-competitive and much faster than I am: self-selection at work.) In the athletic case, the group segregation is all right, to the extent that it is, because it helps ageing people avoid shame and stigma—if they chose that mode of participation, and the presence of choice is important. And it is also helpful in the way that AARP is helpful, because the ageing body, to be productive, needs specialized attention. One of the nicest parts of the incipient pro-senior revolution is that physical trainers do not tell ageing people to do less. They typically tell them they need to do more. Thus, when I have some typical runner's injury, whether a hamstring strain or Achilles tendinitis, I am given specific therapy for that problem, but I am also told firmly that I ought to be doing more core exercises and more exercises for foot tendons, which don't need so much specific attention earlier. So that is a way in which group segregation can promote achievement and useful activity.

But there are also many cases in which the segregation itself embodies a pernicious stereotype and seems likely to produce both lowered self-esteem and diminished performance. What would we think of a work-in-progress workshop for 'older law professors'? Opera and symphony performances for 'older audiences'? (Well, all too many of those end up that way, because of lack of outreach to new and younger audiences, but that is a different problem.) Voting by age group, with different age groups having different political representatives? Segregation of politicians or voters by age would be not just grotesque, but, by this point in our history, deeply unpopular.

One part of life that can be especially damaged by stigmatizing segregation is that of friendship. Families have the advantage that they promote continued contact between the generations. This contact, however, is not always benign: it can reinforce the stereotype of the non-threatening grandmother, the wise patriarch—rather than promoting attention to the capacities and preferred activities of the individual. Ageing people whose only context for friendship is family are vulnerable to a narrowing of their perceived social role. Workplace friendships are more promising:

another reason to oppose compulsory retirement is that it deprives active ageing people of continued friendships with people of many different ages, shunting them off onto the stigmatized track of the 'retired' or 'emeritus (a)'. Choosing friends in a variety of different age groups works against complacency, keeps one open to challenges of many types, and prevents stigmatizing segregation and self-segregation.

***

What conclusions may we draw for policy? The first one is that ageing people need a political movement, indeed a national and international human rights movement, akin to the disability rights movement that has made so much legal progress. Such a movement exists in the United States, where the AARP, as I have mentioned, is one of the most powerful lobby groups ever, but in other modern democracies, although lobbying based on class, race, sex, caste, and even disability is acceptable, there is not yet a strong political movement composed of and working on behalf of people who are ageing. I believe part of the reason for this is that people in Europe, at least, have a strong social safety net and are therefore to a degree less vulnerable than their US counterparts. Another issue is that strong labour movements want a low retirement age and do not bother to distinguish between permission and requirement. But surely part of the issue is shame and the internalization of damaging stereotypes.

The feeling that discrimination against older workers is just 'natural' and is not discrimination at all is extremely widespread among both older and younger people. A comprehensive study of discrimination against workers over the age of 55 in the United States shows that it is very widespread, as has been experimentally confirmed by tests in which fake résumés are submitted: some suggested age, others did not.[28] The study concludes that people simply do not see this type of discrimination as unjust—it is just natural.

I began this chapter with John Stuart Mill's remark that all forms of domination seem natural to those who exercise them. We should now pause to ponder this obvious fact. Feudalism made elites think that serfs were by nature a different type of human being. It took revolution to change consciousness. Racial discrimination and discrimination against women, as Mill notes, have been similarly rationalized by a belief, no doubt

---

[28] 'As More Older People Look for Work', *New York Times*, 18 August 2016, 3.

sincere, that this discrimination was based upon nature. Discrimination against people with disabilities was not recognized as the social evil it is, because for a long time so-called normal people just thought it was natural that society catered to their needs (including their weaknesses) and kept 'the handicapped' outside. Age is the last frontier, and because the stigma is always a self-stigma, it is perhaps the most difficult to fight. Armed with this insight, let me turn to my central policy conclusion.

This conclusion is that compulsory retirement should be rejected by us all, as a form of unjust discrimination, just as unjust as racial discrimination in hiring, or the exclusion of women from the workplace, or the segregation of children with disabilities in 'special' classrooms. We must carefully distinguish, here, the age at which retirement is *allowed* with full pension and the age at which retirement is *required*. The United States has made this distinction, and compulsory retirement has not been legal since I entered the workforce, and thus my generation has expectations and a sense of self that are not shaped by this pernicious practice.

This is a long topic, and I have written on it at length elsewhere, but several points can be briefly made. The greatest advantage of ending compulsory retirement is the same advantage Mill claimed for ending discrimination against women: namely, the advantage of basing central social institutions on justice rather than injustice. But we may mention other advantages, in particular the fact, now widely acknowledged but seen already by Cato, that work is very important for health and happiness. Among the important dividends of the US regime is the wonderful fact that people by now do not care how old their colleagues are, and there is the joy of looking ahead to the next day's interactions with colleagues who are themselves of varying ages, thus nourishing non-stigmatic mixed-age friendships. This was Cicero's smartest point—for the young men visit Cato, look up to him, and enjoy his company. Cicero knows how valuable cross-generational friendships are for both older and younger persons, and often alludes to his own ageing mentors. I note that we imitate this Ciceronian practice in our Human Development and Capability Association, which was founded with the deliberate intent of bringing older and younger researchers together.

On the 'con' side, we must face, first, the inevitable reply that such policies are too costly. In addition to observing that keeping people productive rather than supporting them through social security might be thought to be a savings, not a cost, we should reply that when it is a matter of extending to a group equal respect and the equal protection of the laws, expense cuts no legal ice. When that same argument was made against including children with disabilities in integrated public-school classrooms, the courts said that the financial shortfall of the school district that was griping about including extra children must not be permitted to weigh more heavily on an already disadvantaged group than on the majority. This was the correct response.

And just imagine the response if people were to say, let us exclude women and minorities from the workplace, because there are not enough jobs for everyone—or, more pointedly, because 'they' are taking 'our' jobs. People of reason would rise up, objecting that the full inclusion of all qualified workers on a basis of equality is an urgent issue of justice. Not all people are people of reason, and this so-called argument is the main force behind the movement supporting Donald Trump, such as it is. But fear of popular anger should not stop us from doing what is just, any more than the huge violence of the civil rights era stopped the struggle for racial equality.

To the objection that ageing people require special treatment, mentally and physically, we should make Cato's reply: it all depends on your habits. Many do not require anything special at all. Furthermore, suppose they do: under the Americans with Disabilities Act, employers are required to make reasonable accommodations for workers with a range of disabilities; so even the extra expense of accommodation is acknowledged as a requirement of justice. But suppose job-related competence really does slip badly, despite all accommodation. Employers under the US system may lure people into retirement, and outside of the academy, people can be fired for cause. What is forbidden is (a) refusal to accommodate, and (b) termination simply on grounds of age. This is as it ought to be, since there is such great variety, as Cato observed, among ageing lives. Compulsory retirement, the leading form of age discrimination, is one of the great moral evils of our time, the next 'frontier of justice' that any theory of human capabilities must address.

The stigma attached to the ageing body is real and it has real, baneful effects. Work is a great help, friendship is a great help, but in most movements for social justice, stigmatized people have also felt the need of a more informal anti-disgust movement that creatively reshapes the stigma into something to be embraced. The formal civil rights movement was accompanied by the slogan 'black is beautiful', and a widespread social movement around that idea. The women's movement in my youth invented the slogan 'Our Bodies, Ourselves', and set about reclaiming the female body as a site of curiosity and love, rather than stigma and disgust. There are many reasons to think that ageing people need, in addition to the good political work of AARP, a movement akin to the feminist Our Bodies movement: a movement against self-disgust. I believe this, in the end, was the deeper goal of Cicero's little treatise—to bring a despised topic into graceful and zestful social discourse, and make people study it, have fun with it, love it.

Following my argument, this movement would be best imagined as integrative rather than self-segregating—since, after all, the stigma against ageing is lodged in all of us, regardless of age. There is little hope of limiting its harmful influence unless one begins with the young. The stigma is, at its core, a stigma about our embodiment and our mortality, so we ultimately will need to shift attitudes towards the body in order to counter stigma effectively. The Our Bodies movement was partly about autonomy. We said, we will not let doctors take over our bodies and extract the babies, we will be awake and active, and give birth as ourselves. But it was also very much a rebellion against the idea that the female body is disgusting, a staple of misogyny the world over. Whether we read the poetry of Walt Whitman or not, we were Whitmanians, saying 'I sing the body electric', that triumphant denunciation of all the shames and disgusts that Whitman saw behind the social phenomena of racial aversion, misogyny, and homophobia.

Whitman knew that we will not be able to love one another unless we first stop hiding from ourselves—meaning our bodies, which are not Platonic, which change and age like all bodies. For, as he says: 'If the body were not the soul, what is the soul?'[29] If we can love our own bodies, we may possibly also love 'the likes of [them] in other men and women.' In a bold crescendo of anti-disgust, Whitman then enumerates all the parts we might come to love—starting with the ones we already like pretty well, like 'head, neck, ears', then continuing on to the trunk, but its rather pleasing outer parts such as 'palm, knuckles, thumb, fore-finger', and on down to the strong thighs supporting the trunk. But then he delves within, caressing with his words 'the lung-sponges, stomach-sac, the bowels sweet and clean … the thin red jellies within you or within me'. These, he says, are actually poems, and they are his poems. 'O I say these are not the parts and poems of the body only, but of the soul. / O I say now these are the soul.' It is because we still shrink from Whitman's invitation to self-love that we permit the hideous wrongs of age discrimination to deform our societies.

[29] Walt Whitman, 'I Sing the Body Electric', *Leaves of Grass* (self-published, 1855).

9

Disgust or Equality? Sexual Orientation and Indian Law

*Martha C. Nussbaum**

Come you Outcaste, dispelled be the burden of all insults, ...
With holy water made sacred by the touch of everybody
On the shore of this Bharat's ocean of the great Humanity.
　　　　　　—Rabindranath Tagore, song composed in June 1910[1]

* I am grateful to Joseph Harper and Nethanel Lipshitz for research assistance on the US side and to Wendy Doniger for comments on an earlier draft. This chapter was delivered as the M.K. Nambyar Lecture at the West Bengal National University of Juridical Sciences (NUJS) in Kolkata in March 2015, and subsequently published in the *Journal of Indian Law and Society*. I am grateful to Justice Ruma Pal and Justice Altamas Kabir for comments on the occasion of the Nambyar Lecture, to Vice-Chancellor Ishwara Bhat for his most generous hospitality, to Vasujith Ram for his research assistance, to an anonymous referee for valuable comments, and to the journal for permission to reprint. This chapter was also delivered as the Herbert Morris Lecture at UCLA Law School in February 2015. I am grateful to Herbert Morris, Seana Shiffrin, and others for challenging comments on that occasion.
　　[1] English translation by Kalpana Bardhan.

Same-Sex Law: A Time of Astonishing Change

The landscape of same-sex laws around the world has been changing rapidly. In the United States, although sodomy laws were not thrown out until 2003,[2] marriage equality recently became the national norm.[3] In the Republic of Ireland, a referendum conducted on 22 May 2015 legalized same-sex marriage, despite the opposition of the Catholic Church. In Luxembourg, where same-sex marriage became legal on 1 January 2015, Prime Minister Xavier Bettel became the first European Union leader to celebrate a same-sex marriage by marrying his partner Gauthier Destenay in May 2015. In Korea, by contrast, although sodomy has never been illegal, gays and lesbians encounter great stigma and hostility and same-sex marriage is not likely in the near future, largely on account of the influence of conservative Christian churches.[4] In India, despite the decriminalization of sodomy in 2009 by the Delhi High Court, the criminal statute has recently been reinstated by the Supreme Court. Each country, in short, has its own story. Because of my long-standing focus as a legal scholar on Indian constitutional law as well as my long association with the Lawyer's Collective, I am delighted by the opportunity to assess these Indian developments and their history, several years after having published a book on sexual orientation and constitutional law in the United States.[5]

[2] *Lawrence v. Texas*, 539 US 558 (2003), overruling *Bowers v. Hardwick*, 92 L Ed 2d 140: 478 US 186 (1986).

[3] *Obergefell v. Hodges*, 2015 SCC Online US SC 6: 576 US (2015).

[4] Martha C. Nussbaum, preface to the Korean translation of *From Disgust to Humanity: Sexual Orientation and Constitutional Law* (New York: Oxford University Press, 2010).

[5] Nussbaum, preface to the Korean translation of *From Disgust to Humanity*. At the time of publication of that book, only five states—Massachusetts, Connecticut, Iowa, Vermont, and California—had legalized same-sex marriage and in California, Proposition 8 had undone what the courts had done. By January 2015 however, same-sex marriage had been legalized by referendum in three states, by legislation in six, by a complicated combination of litigation and government action in two, and by state court action in six. State-imposed bans on same-sex marriage have been struck down by a long list of federal court actions; particularly notable and interesting is *Baskin v. Bogan*, 766 F 3d 648 (7th Cir 2014), where the majority opinion by Richard Posner has attracted worldwide attention. The net result as of January 2015 is that same-sex marriage is legal in 35 states, the District of Columbia, some jurisdictions in Missouri, and 21 Native American tribal jurisdictions. Furthermore, the Defense of Marriage

I have long argued, as a legal theorist, for a theory of stigma and group discrimination that makes the operations of disgust central. I developed it in *Hiding from Humanity*[6] using results in cognitive psychology to show how disgust operates in a wide range of types of discrimination, including anti-Semitism, racism, sexism, and homophobia. I then made the normative argument that disgust is never a sufficient condition to make an act illegal when it causes no harm to non-consenting parties. That general argument had been made by the great British legal philosopher Herbert Hart, responding to the conservative jurist Lord Devlin, who opposed the decriminalization of sodomy, saying that the disgust of the average person was a sufficient condition to make an act illegal, even if it caused no harm to others.[7] (Their debate continued the nineteenth-century exchange between conservative James Fitzjames Stephen and liberal John Stuart Mill).[8] I argued, however, that a close analysis of the particular cognitive structure of disgust—which none of these theorists had attempted—was crucial to understanding just why it was so unsuitable as a basis for law. In 2010, in my book on sexual orientation and constitutional law,[9] I developed the theory further and then connected it empirically to recent discrimination against gays and lesbians. I suggested that the legal notion of 'animus', used in both *Lawrence v. Texas*

Act (DOMA) was struck down in 2013 in *United States v. Windsor*, 2013 SCC Online US SC 86: 570 US (2013). The outlier was the Sixth Circuit, which in *De Boer v. Snyder*, currently on appeal to the US Supreme Court, upheld state bans on majoritarian grounds.

[6] Martha Nussbaum, *Hiding from Humanity* (Princeton, MA: Princeton University Press, 2004).

[7] Patrick Devlin, *The Enforcement of Morals* (1959; reprint, Oxford: Oxford University Press, 1970), passim (see my analysis of his argument in Nussbaum, *Hiding from Humanity*). See also Herbert Hart, *Law, Liberty and Morality* (Stanford: Stanford University Press, 1963), 51 (attacking Devlin's position); and Ronald Dworkin, 'Lord Devlin and the Enforcement of Morals' (faculty scholarship series, Yale Law School Legal Scholarship Repository, 1 January 1966).

[8] See J.S. Mill, *On Liberty* (London: J.W. Parker and Son, 1859), arguing that harm to non-consenting parties is a necessary condition of the legal regulation of conduct; See also James Fitzjames Stephen, *Liberty, Equality, Fraternity* (London: Macmillan and Co., 1874), arguing for a conservative tradition-based theory of legal intervention.

[9] Nussbaum, preface to the Korean translation of *From Disgust to Humanity*.

(invalidating the sodomy laws) and *Romer v. Evans*[10] (invalidating a law that prevented gays and lesbians from getting protection from anti-discrimination laws), was best understood as an allusion to disgust above all. I tried to show how my theory supported the decisions and reasoning in those two cases. I also argued that, despite the surface absence of disgust from arguments against same-sex marriage, disgust was a driving force, as with earlier opposition to interracial marriage. I supported this claim by a study of the pamphlet literature that had circulated at the time, in which appeals to disgust were prominent.[11]

Here I propose, first, to summarize my theory of disgust, and then to turn to the recent developments in India, where much of my work as a political and legal theorist has taken place, and where same-sex law is currently the scene of a fascinating struggle. These cases are not only fascinating and of urgent human significance, they are also theoretically significant: they appear to confirm my disgust-based theory.

Because India is a common-law country with a written constitution containing a detailed section of Fundamental Rights, it is easy to compare to the United States—and its similarity to the US Constitution reflects a deliberate choice on the part of the Constitution's primary architect, B.R. Ambedkar, who believed that vulnerable groups needed protection from majority tyranny.[12] Knowing what majorities were capable of, through a childhood of appalling discrimination and brutality, Ambedkar insisted on a Bill of Rights that could not be trumped by majority sentiment, and his views play a central role in the recent debate.

We shall see that what is precisely at issue in the recent struggle over same-sex rights is the tension between fundamental rights and majoritarianism, when disgust enters the picture. To set the stage, let me mention some of the things that Ambedkar, as he tells us, encountered as

---

[10] *Romer* v. *Evans,* 134 L Ed 2d 855: 517 US 620 (1996).

[11] I also discussed disgust at length in Martha C. Nussbaum, *Political Emotions: Why Love Matters for Justice* (Cambridge, MA: Harvard University Press, 2013).

[12] I discuss his role and his ideas in detail in Martha C. Nussbaum, 'Ambedkar's Constitution: Implementing Inclusion, Opposing Majority Tyranny', in *Assessing Constitutional Performance*, eds. Tom Ginsburg and Aziz Z. Huq (Cambridge, MA: Cambridge University Press, 2016). See also Martha C. Nussbaum, review of 'Annihilation of Caste,' by B.R. Ambedkar, *The New Rambler Review* (online), August 2015, http://newramblerreview.com/book-reviews/religion/untouchable.

a wealthy, middle-class Dalit child.[13] At school, he was not allowed to sit with the other students; he had to sit in a special corner by himself. Other students sat on communal mats. Ambedkar had to sit on a special mat that could not be touched by any other student and he had to take that mat home at the end of the day. While all other students could drink from the public tap, he could not—unless a servant first turned the handle for him. Travelling to meet his father along with his two sisters, all being well-dressed children with lots of cash, they were not admitted into any lodging.[14]

When I hear this story as an American, I think immediately of our struggle against racism and racial segregation and this is not an inappropriate comparison. It is that denial of basic equality and dignity, inspired by bodily loathing and irrational fears of contamination, that Ambedkar set out to stymie by ensuring that the Constitution had a strong and explicit commitment to fundamental rights and equal protection, even when majority sentiment was beastly, as it was. As we shall see, the memory and, to a distressing extent, the current reality of these horrible caste practices inform the reasoning of Indian courts concerning same-sex law, just as an analogy to laws against interracial marriage often inform the treatment of sexual orientation in US law.

Disgust and Constitutional Law

Let me now summarize my theory of disgust, drawing (as I did in 2004) on the research of a team of first-rate US experimental psychologists.[15] All humans appear to share an acute discomfort when confronted by their own bodily fluids, excretion, smell and by the decay of the corpse. I use the term 'primary disgust' for a shrinking from contamination by such objects and by other objects that closely resemble them in smell or feel (such as insects and animals that are slimy, smelly, and the like). Primary disgust, though not present at birth, is culturally universal and is probably grounded in inherited tendencies. Although this aversive reaction may, in some cases, protect people from real danger (and perhaps that was its evolutionary origin), Rozin shows that its cognitive

---

[13] For all references to his autobiographical writings, see Nussbaum, *Hiding from Humanity*, Chap. 11 (discussing Ambedkar's critique of caste).

[14] Nussbaum, *Hiding from Humanity*, 366.

[15] See references to the work of Paul Rozin and his colleagues in Nussbaum, *Hiding from Humanity*.

content is quite different from that of fear—it is about contamination, not danger. It is a reaction to the animality and decay of the human body and it is both under-inclusive and over-inclusive of real danger. (Many dangerous things are not disgusting and people feel disgust even when they are rationally convinced that danger is absent.) Rozin concludes that, in disgust, we are rejecting something about our own animality.

All that might be harmless enough, although I would argue that it is always problematic to encourage this sort of self-loathing. In all known societies, however, people do not stop there and we arrive at what I call 'projective disgust'. People seek to create a buffer zone between themselves and their own animality, by identifying a group (often a powerless minority) who can be targeted as the quasi-animals and projecting onto that group various animal characteristics, which they have to no greater degree than the ones doing the projecting: bad smell, animal sexuality, and so on. The so-called thinking seems to be—if those quasi-animal humans stand between us and our own animal stench and decay, we are that much further from being animal and mortal ourselves. There is no society in which we do not find subgroups to whom irrationally, properties of smelliness, hyper-sexuality, and, in general, hyper-animality are imputed.[16]

There are many varieties of disgust stigma. In European anti-Semitism, Jews were depicted as hyper-bodily, smelly, and hyper-sexual, but also as crafty and intelligent.[17] African Americans, by contrast, were and, unfortunately at times, still are imagined as hyper-sexual and also smelly, bestial, and stupid. Again, African Americans are imagined as physically powerful and aggressive. To upper Hindu castes who observed untouchability, untouchables were foul, weak, and not particularly aggressive. These differences are important and yet a common set of threads run through them all.

What about the propaganda that links disgust with same-sex acts? I studied a lot of US pamphlet literature that attempts to whip up animosity towards gays and lesbians (though above all, gay men) and found prominent use of the tropes of projective disgust. The standard way of doing this is to focus obsessively on anal sex and to describe it in terms apt to elicit revulsion. All sorts of abstract claims are made, for example,

---

[16] See the longer version of these arguments in Nussbaum, *Hiding from Humanity*.

[17] See references to the historical literature in Nussbaum, *Hiding from Humanity*.

claims that gays eat faeces and drink raw blood. (I heard Will Perkins, proponent of Colorado's Amendment 2, testify under oath in Denver, in the bench trial of *Evans v. Romer*, that he had circulated pamphlets making that claim.) A related trope is the idea that gays travel a lot and thence bring germs into America—fascinatingly reminiscent of Nazi propaganda linking Jews to a variety of diseases.[18] India, as we shall see, is no different here.

Projective disgust always leads to some type of avoidance of bodily contact. Again, the type and extent vary. African Americans were forbidden to use white people's drinking fountains, swimming pools, lunch counters, hotel beds, and of course, sexual contact was strictly forbidden and was considered to be a felony in many states (widely though, white men had sexual relationships with and sexually abused black women). Yet, an African American might prepare and serve food for a white family. An Indian untouchable, by contrast, could never serve food in an upper-caste family and as noted, Dalits also could not share lodging or drinking taps. The crazy irrationalities of these ideas are manifold.

As for gay men in America, given the reality of the closet, no ban on shared restaurants, lodgings, drinking fountains, or even swimming pools could realistically be imposed, but the desire to impose one crops up in weird places such as the symbolic aversion to shared showers in the military. I say symbolic, because it is well known that all gyms have a fairly high proportion of gay members and yet I know of no attempt to oust gays from the locker room, which, of course, would be both impossible and very bad for business. Still, straight men often fantasize that the very gaze of a gay man could penetrate and thus sully them; where they could use this to exclude gays, they did.

With regard to the legal side of the issue, my general normative conclusion was that close study of the operations of disgust should give us reasons not to base laws upon it—even if we remain sceptical of J.S. Mill's argument that harm to the non-consenting is a necessary condition for the legal regulation of conduct. Of course I agree with Mill, but I think that we can give new support to many of his positions by the study of disgust. (Such a study may convince people who still want to maintain some regulations of what Mill called 'self-regarding acts' in

---

[18] Robert N. Procter, *The Nazi War on Cancer* (1997; Princeton: Princeton University Press, 2000). Extensive references to the pamphlet literature are given in Nussbaum, *Hiding from Humanity*.

areas such as gambling and perhaps hard drugs, where the operations of disgust seem less easy to see and may even be absent.)[19]

[19] What reasons, if any, do we have to think that Justice Kennedy had such phenomena in mind when he wrote that laws occasioned by 'animus' do not pass the rational basis test? We may begin by noting that it is always a bad idea to impute much theoretical sophistication to Supreme Court justices in matters outside their domain. Particularly when sex is in question, confusion is apt to reign. (See Tom Grey, 'Eros and the Burger Court', *Law & Contemporary Problems* 43, no. 3 (1980): 83–100. As Judge Richard Posner noted, judges are selected for their relative lack of sexual experience, so it is not altogether surprising that they are ignorant about sexual variety. Richard A. Posner, *Sex and Reason* (Cambridge, MA: Harvard University Press, 1992). Justice Kennedy is surely no careful student of research into sexuality or the political emotions. Still, there are several reasons why we ought to think that disgust, if not the only possible reading of the term 'animus', is at least firmly in the background.

First, it is simply there in the facts of *Romer*. Amendment 2 was indeed campaigned for with pamphlets aimed at creating disgust and the trial record showed this. (See my discussion in Nussbaum, *Hiding from Humanity*, concerning the testimony of Will Perkins, which I heard in person.) This is less obvious but also true of the sodomy laws at issue in *Lawrence*, as my research into the pamphlet literature shows (Nussbaum, *Hiding from Humanity*). On that topic, furthermore, we can turn to our next point.

Second, then, disgust is there in the influential legal theory in the history of the question. Every judge knows Lord Devlin's scathing attack on the report of the Wolfenden Commission recommending the decriminalization of sodomy. Disgust is the emotion on which Devlin most centrally relies for his anti-Millean contention that conduct that harms no non-consenting party can still be criminalized. The disgust of the 'man on the Clapham omnibus' is a famous legal entity, and here it is the sodomy laws that are at issue. It is difficult to believe that Justice Kennedy was not informed at some level by the debate about Devlin's ideas, which every law student studies. Closer to his time, moreover, the influential US conservative Leon Kass, head of the President's Council for Bioethics established in 2001, had influentially supported Devlin's line in a 1997 article and later pamphlet, entitled 'The Wisdom of Repugnance'. Although Kass's argument was actually very different from Devlin's (see references and analysis in Nussbaum, *Hiding from Humanity*), the differences tended to be ignored, and his influential advocacy gave new life to Devlinism. So, disgust was prominent in US public policy at the time of *Romer*.

Third, disgust was at least somewhere in the two precedents most important for the denials of rational basis in *Romer* and *Lawrence*, the two Supreme Court cases that had found laws to lack a rational basis on the ground that they were prompted solely by negative emotion. *City of Cleburne v. Cleburne Living*

Center, 87 L Ed 2d 313: 473 US 432 (1985) denied the rational basis of a zoning ordinance that attempted to screen out a home for people with mental retardation. Although the case spoke of 'irrational prejudice', 'antipathy', and 'invidious discrimination', and did not use the word 'disgust', it's easy enough to see it in the way in which people sought to avoid the stigma of contact with people whose bodies so vividly (to the dominant group) emblematize the lowness of animality. Obviously, the emotion was not fear and it did not seem to be hatred either. Furthermore, it just seems true that our dealings with people with mental retardation are overwhelmingly infected with disgust. As the concurring opinion says, people with mental retardation are seen as 'pariahs' who do not belong in the community.

The other important precedent, *United States Dept. of Agriculture v. Moreno*, 37 L Ed 2d 782: 413 US 528 (1973) spoke of the 'bare desire to harm a politically unpopular group', and did not allude to disgust. Moreover, since my colleague Geof Stone, who was then clerking for Justice Brennan, wrote the relevant portions of the opinion, I know that he did not have concrete thoughts about the sort of negative emotion involved. Still, the group in question, hippie communes, were the objects of a kind of phobic disgust for the allegedly promiscuous sex acts that would transpire there. Hippies were typically portrayed as hyper-animal, associated both with bodily fluids and with unsanitary living conditions. To say that disgust was in fact involved is not to say that Justice Kennedy found it there. But in combination with our first two reasons, it does help us to conclude, very cautiously, that thought about disgust is around somewhere, in the reason in *Romer* and *Lawrence*.

More recent cases make the role of disgust explicit. Discussions of same-sex marriage almost always use the parallel of anti-miscegenation laws, which were obviously based upon disgust and irrational fears of contamination. The Supreme Court of Connecticut engages in a detailed analysis of disgust prejudice against gays and lesbians in its same-sex marriage opinion:

> Beyond moral disapprobation, gay persons also face virulent homophobia that rests on nothing more than feelings of revulsion toward gay persons and the intimate sexual conduct with which they are associated ... Such visceral prejudice is reflected in the large number of hate crimes that are perpetrated against gay persons ... The irrational nature of the prejudice directed at gay persons, who 'are ridiculed, ostracized, despised, demonized and condemned "merely for being who they are"' ... is entirely different in kind than the prejudice suffered by other groups that previously have been denied suspect or quasi-suspect class status ... This fact provides further reason to doubt that such prejudice soon can be eliminated and underscores the reality that gay persons face unique challenges to their political and social integration. (*Kerrigan v. Commr. of Public Health*, 289 Conn. 135)

While the court seems quite wrong to say that similar issues of revulsion have not been involved in racial prejudice and misogyny, they are certainly right to find it here.

India: Bodily Freedom, Bodily Disgust

To set the stage for the current legal struggle, I must discuss its background in Hinduism, since it is there and not in India's minority religious communities—Muslim, Christian, Parsi, Jain, Sikh, Jewish, and Buddhist—that the struggle over purity and disgust rages, although it gets a lot of help from Victorian Christianity. This summary is unavoidably brief and over-simple but it provides a useful orientation, especially for international readers.

Among all the world's major religions, Hinduism is the one that most unequivocally celebrates the body and its pleasures. Sexuality has a central and positive place. Thus, the three arts that one must know in order to live well are the art of morality (dharma), the art of political/economic management (artha), and the art of pleasure (kama). To each of these arts is devoted a major religious text. Westerners think that Kama Sutra is a type of pornography, but it is actually as solemn as the other two key religious texts. The sexuality that is celebrated is not a narrow type: rather, women are encouraged to take sexual initiative and same-sex relationships are celebrated without stigma.[20] The ancient epics are a little more judgemental, but they too give many examples of the gods and heroes having a wide range of desires and relationships. Traditionally too, hijras (transgender people, most of them male at birth, who identify as neither male nor female and who often take a receptive role in sex with men) were not stigmatized but were regarded as auspicious. Since that community played an important role in recent litigation, I shall say more about them later.

On the other hand, Hinduism of a later period ossified into a form in which some bodily functions are heavily stigmatized. As the caste hierarchy developed out of an earlier system of four 'varnas', the idea of untouchability became extremely prominent. Untouchability was closely connected with disgust at faeces and corpses and attached above all to those whose occupations connected them to those matters (including leather tanners, since they deal with animal corpses). A whole ideology of disgust developed; it was thought to be contaminating to share anything with such people.

Untouchability focused on faeces and decay, and for some time, it coexisted with the celebration of sexual pleasure. Stigma was also attached increasingly to non-marital sexuality and, to some extent, to

[20] Mallanaga Vatsayana, Kama Sutra, trans. Wendy Doniger and Sudhir Kakar (New York: Oxford University Press, 2009).

sexuality itself. This development, already suggested in some traditional texts, was greatly egged on by Victorian British puritanism. The British had a horror of India's sexual freedom. Clearly, they had a fascination too and an early era saw a lot of intermarriage.[21] But as the Victorian era arrived, the British in India connected their puritanism to a new shrinking from the overt sexuality and sensuousness of Indian religion. The received British view was that the Hindu religion was filthy. Typical, and giving authority to the received view, was Winston Churchill, who remarked in 1942, 'I hate Indians. They are a beastly people with a beastly religion.'[22]

As time went on, reacting to this affront, some Hindus began to internalize the Victorian critique and to ape Victorian puritanism in order to deflect criticism.[23] While emphasizing an aggressive conception of masculinity in preference to the sensuousness of earlier traditions, they also emphasized sexual purity more and more, along with the traditional strictures attached to caste.

Thus, Hindus struggled with the body, becoming increasingly anxious about representations of joyful and sensuous bodily life. Some progressive leaders, and of course Gandhi, led the way, crusaded vehemently against untouchability, and Gandhi was famous for insisting that his followers perform tasks that were traditionally performed only by Dalits, such as cleaning latrines. But Gandhi combined his progressivism with a famous emphasis on dietary and sexual purity that, while it surely had some Hindu roots, was in many ways extremely alien (Gandhi always counted Tolstoy as among his key intellectual influences and he had by then spent many years in Christian circles, in Britain and elsewhere). Far from urging that all people accept their bodily nature and learn not to feel disgust at bodily functions, he expressed a powerful loathing of sexuality in all its forms, sought to extirpate it in himself, and expressed in harsh terms his moral judgment on the sexual lives of others.

Gandhi loathed all sexual acts, but same-sex acts come in for particular emphasis—perhaps because, unlike opposite-sex acts, they did

---

[21] William Dalrymple, *The Last Mogul* (New Delhi: Penguin Books, 2007).

[22] In conversation with Leo Amery, Secretary of State for India, and reported in Amery, *The Leo Amery Diaries*, eds. John Barnes and David Nicholson, vol. 2 (London: Hutchinson, 1980), 832.

[23] For one good account, see Wendy Doniger, 'India: Censorship by the Batra Brigade', *The New York Review of Books*, 8 May 2014.

not even have the redeeming virtue of procreation.[24] A student of Rabindranath Tagore once asked Gandhi what he thought of the role of arts in society and Gandhi immediately replied that artists can be highly immoral, citing the example of Oscar Wilde. The fact that Wilde, who went to prison for same-sex conduct, is the first example of immorality that came to his mind seems significant.[25] So Gandhi, while asking his followers to repudiate bodily disgust in one area, caste, ramped it up in another, sex, and he created a puritanism that, in some respects, reinforced the Victorian critique.

One note before we proceed: someone might opine that the Indian aversion to same-sex acts reflects Muslim influence. This would be utterly wrong. Babur, the first Muslim ruler of India, celebrated his sexual relations with males in his memoirs,[26] and in general, that group of Muslims was distinguished by its outstanding tolerance in all matters. In more recent times, it has been shown that pertinent variations in gender norms are regional rather than differing between the religions.[27]

Disgust had its determined opponents.[28] Rabindranath Tagore, the great poet, novelist, philosopher, composer, choreographer, dancer, and educator, held the view that free and equal citizenship in the nation of the future, required finding joy and pride in the human body. He

---

[24] Biographer Joseph Lelyveld has opined that Gandhi felt powerful same-sex desire towards the German architect Herman Kallenbach, with whom he shared a house for some time. See Joseph Lelyveld, *Great Soul: Mahatma Gandhi and his Struggle with India* (New York: Knopf, 2011). Lelyveld's argument is quite unconvincing; when Gandhi noticed himself feeling desire, he always expressed guilt and self-loathing, as he did several times concerning women, but never about Kallenbach. I review Lelyveld's book very critically in Martha C. Nussbaum, review of *Great Soul: Mahatma Gandhi and his Struggle with India*, by Joseph Lelyveld, *The Nation*, 31 October 2011, 27–32.

[25] See reference and discussion in Martha C. Nussbaum, *The Clash Within: Democracy Religious Violence, and India's Future* (Cambridge, MA: Harvard University Press, 2007), Ch. 2.

[26] See Babur, *The Baburnama: Memoirs of Babur, Prince and Emperor*, trans. W.M. Thackston (New York: Modern Library Classic, 2002).

[27] See Zoya Hasan and Ritu Menon, *Unequal Citizens: A Study of Muslim Women in India* (New Delhi: Oxford University Press, 2004), describing the results of their extensive and first-rate survey of attitudes and living conditions among Muslim women throughout India.

[28] I discuss Tagore's thought at greater length in Nussbaum, *Hiding from Humanity*, Chapter 4.

set about creating a style of education for the young in his school at Santiniketan that aimed at bodily reconciliation and love.[29] Students learnt in large part through dance and music—led by the example of Tagore himself, a superb dancer whose techniques as both dancer and choreographer are studied by modern dance leaders all over the world. The message Tagore continually sent, though still in a careful and controlled way, was that there could be no political freedom without bodily freedom and acceptance. His own style of dance in the many surviving photographs and accounts (especially the wonderful book by Amita Sen, *Joy in All Work*) was androgynous, and sensuously receptive rather than aggressive.

In Tagore's major philosophical work, *The Religion of Man* (1931), he ventures yet further into anti-Victorian terrain by citing the *Bauls* of Bengal as his prototype of the sort of love a good society needs at its heart. He gives the example further emphasis by appending to the book a learned (albeit somewhat evasive) essay on the Bauls by K.M. Sen, the great scholar of Hinduism (who was also Amartya Sen's maternal grandfather). The Bauls are countercultural minstrels who have left organized society to form their own marginal society based upon love. Although Tagore does not go into explicit detail for his British audience, they were well known to have countercultural sexual practices, both opposite-sex and same-sex, and to have initiation rituals that required the aspirant to taste all the fluids of the body, thereby repudiating disgust. Their creed was (and is) love of humanity and they believe that this love requires forming a loving relationship with all the parts and fluids of the body.[30] Tagore's own poetry and musical compositions are closely inspired by Baul lyrics and one of his most famous dance dramas was Rituranga, in which he himself danced the role of a blind Baul who breaks the fetters with which an uncomprehending society has shackled him. Here is Amita Sen's description:[31]

---

[29] I discuss Tagore's school in Martha C. Nussbaum, *Not for Profit: Why Democracy Needs the Humanities* (Princeton, MA: Princeton University Press, 2011), and with attention to the role of dance and the body, in Nussbaum, *Hiding from Humanity*, Chapter 4, here making use of Amita Sen's memoir.

[30] I discuss the Baul tradition, with references to modern scholarship, in Nussbaum, *Hiding from Humanity*, Chapter 4.

[31] Amita Sen and Pronoti Sinha, *Joy in All Work* (Calcutta : Bookfront Publication Forum, 1999).

Entering the stage, he sang as he walked:

My fetters will be broken, will be broken, at the time of departure/I am free, who can imprison me behind locked doors! / I go in the dark as the evening bell rings).

What a wonderful movement of strong hands breaking fetters! The free wayfarer advances, the joy of freedom ringing in his steps, and fearlessness in his clear voice. Even after he had left the stage, the sound of the evening bell echoed in the spectators' ears.

Here, a young woman sees in Tagore's body a powerful image of citizenship, in the not-yet-created Indian nation of the future. The image is drawn from a sexual counterculture.

Tagore, moreover, strongly connected the struggle against sexual disgust with the struggle against caste-based and race-based disgust. In his great novel *Gora* (1909),[32] the young hero (whose name means 'pale-face') decides that a rededication to traditional caste norms is the core of a renewed Hinduism and the best basis for Indian citizenship in the future nation. Gora accordingly refuses food his own mother has prepared, because she is not willing to ostracize a Christian maidservant who cooks for the family. (Christians typically were converts from the lowest castes. So, the idea of untouchability, not just Christianity, is clearly operative.) But the reader knows early on that Gora's project is doomed because, as his name suggests, he is actually not a Hindu at all, but the adopted child of an Irish mother who died in 1857 during the First War of Independence. His mother's liberal attitudes led her to adopt this baby and bring it up as her own. By the end of the novel, Gora has realized that the new nation must be based on the repudiation of caste disgust and the embrace of humanity in all people.

Where are same-sex relationships in Tagore? In many ways, he is a spiritual cousin of Walt Whitman and gestures towards the conclusion that India must also accept same-sex relationships even as it accepts the equality of all castes and the equality of women. This message is sent pretty clearly to those in the know, since the Bauls practice same-sex conduct. But he never makes the idea explicit; he really could not at the time; nor did he have any such relationships. But his style of dance does return to the older androgynous and sensuous idea of Hindu masculinity, part and parcel of which, originally, was openness to receptive

---

[32] Rabindranath Tagore, *Gora* (India: Rupa Publications, 2002 [1909]).

sexuality and perhaps to same-sex desire. Gandhi's Oscar Wilde remark may have been an allusion to this.

Today's India, in some quarters at least, has forgotten the joyful message of inclusion sent by Tagore. There is still a lot of puritanism and it targets both women's freedom and same-sex relationships.[33] The Hindu right has been around since the turn of the century, but it now dominates the cultural scene and it continues the post-Victorian emphasis on bodily purity. It has campaigned ceaselessly for years against the scholarly portrayal of Hinduism as a religion that prominently includes sensuousness and bodily delight. Many books have been targeted under a law that makes it a crime to 'outrage the feelings of Hindus', but especially virulent has been the assault on my colleague Wendy Doniger, the great historian of Hindu religion, for her two recent books[34] portraying, in a very positive light, the sexual aspects of early Hindu religion. Indeed, the lawsuit against Doniger's *The Hindus* makes it clear that one of the main objections is to the zest and humour with which Doniger portrays the sexuality of the gods and heroes. The plaintiff, Dinanath Batra, a proud member of the Hindu right-wing social organization Rashtriya Swayamsevak Sangh (RSS), describes Doniger in the brief itself as 'a woman hungry of sex'. Although the lawsuit was ludicrously weak and the case eminently winnable, Penguin India, fearing violence against its employees, agreed to settle and get rid of all copies of the book.

As for same-sex relations, the Gandhi biography by Lelyveld was banned in Narendra Modi's home state of Gujarat and was denounced by Modi and other leading Hindu right-wing politicians, none of whom seemed to have read it.[35] A national ban was considered but the law minister decided not to go ahead—only because he discovered by actually

[33] For an acute discussion of the cultural landscape, see Ratna Kapur, 'Out of the Colonial Closet, But Still Thinking "Inside the Box": Regulating "Perversion" and the Role of Tolerance in Deradicalising the Rights Claims of Sexual Subalterns', *NUJS Law Review* 2 (July–September, 2009): 381–96.

[34] Wendy Doniger, *The Hindus: An Alternative History* (New York: Penguin, 2009) and Wendy Doniger, *On Hinduism* (Oxford New York: Oxford University Press, 2014),

the former a general introduction, the latter a collection of essays. On the lawsuit, see Martha Nussbaum, 'Law for Bad Behaviour', *Indian Express*, 22 February 2014, http://indianexpress.com/article/opinion/columns/law-for-bad-behaviour/.

[35] See Nussbaum, review of *Great Soul*, for details of this campaign.

reading the book that Lelyveld had not actually imputed homosexual acts to Gandhi.

So there is a sex panic at large in some parts of the nation, and as we shall see shortly, the Hindu right and the Victorian past are once again joining hands to oppress and stigmatize.[36]

Indian Penal Code—Section 377 and the Naz Foundation Case

The British believed that they could govern best if both commercial and criminal law were uniform for all of India, while they strongly encouraged civil law, including property and family law, to be managed by the four major religions. This set-up continues. Thus, the criminal law of India and the related parts of Hindu family law, codified by the British and rarely updated, are, not surprisingly, Victorian and not particularly Indian. They contain some odd British artefacts: for example, the remedy (in the Hindu Marriage Act) of 'restitution of conjugal rights'—intelligible in the context of nineteenth-century British divorce litigation and long since abandoned. Today, the remedy is used by Indian males to curb an independent spouse and get her income. The remedy was rightly declared unconstitutional by an appellate court on grounds of sex inequality—until the Supreme Court reinstated it.[37]

---

[36] As for miscegenation, only five per cent of Indians say that they have married someone of a different caste. See Rukmini S., 'Just 5 percent of Indian Marriages are Intercaste', *Hindu*, 13 November 2014, http://www.thehindu. com/data/just-5-per-cent-of-indian-marriages-are-intercaste/article6591502. ece. Given the very large number of castes, this is a pretty amazing result. (Because caste is to a great extent regional, it would be very difficult to get a precise number. Even when mandatory quotas are concerned, as with the OBCs [other backward castes], state lists often differ from national lists. The national list of 'Scheduled Castes' recognizes 1108 castes, and the list of 'Scheduled Tribes' recognizes 744 such tribes. As for OBCs, the Central list recognizes 99 in West Bengal alone, and other states are similar.)

[37] *T. Sareetha v. T. Venkata Subbaiah*, 1983 SCC Online AP 90: AIR 1983 AP 356. Sareetha was married at age 16 and later became a famous movie star in the Telugu film industry. Her husband, who had left her only a few months after the marriage, claimed restitution five years later when she was independently wealthy. See my discussion in Martha C. Nussbaum, introduction to *Sex and Social Justice* (New York: Oxford University Press, 1999). Also see Chapter 1.

Another anachronistic Britishism is the criminal offence of 'outraging the modesty of a woman', which has been a very uneasy fulcrum for Indian feminists seeking redress against sexual harassment. It has proven divisive, advantaging 'modest' women of upper class and caste and disadvantaging those who are thought not to have 'modesty' in the first place, for example, because they perform manual labour.[38] 'Modesty' was defined in a 1998 Indian Supreme Court case (via several British dictionaries) as 'womanly propriety of behaviour; scrupulous chastity of thought, speech and conduct'.[39] These Victorian ideas are not very helpful, if what is wanted is gender equality.

Of course, the culture that has historically been Europe's most intensely homophobic, the culture that sentenced Oscar Wilde to three years of hard labour for oral sex with consenting partners, did not hesitate to insert its strictures on same-sex acts into the Indian criminal law as well. Section 377 of the Indian Penal Code reads as follows:

377. Unnatural offences: Whoever voluntarily has carnal intercourse against the order of nature with any man, woman or animal, shall be punished with imprisonment for life, or with imprisonment of either description for term which may extend to ten years, and shall also be liable to fine.

Explanation: Penetration is sufficient to constitute the carnal intercourse necessary to the offense described in this section.[40]

Even more than my other examples, this law bears the unmistakable stamp of antiquated Victorian piety.

It is crystal clear that this law is utterly foreign to India. India surely does have its disputes over marital property, hence interests in

---

[38] See Martha C. Nussbaum, 'The Modesty of Mrs. Bajaj: India's Problematic Route to Sexual Harassment Law', in *Directions in Sexual Harassment Law*, eds Catharine A. MacKinnon and Reva B. Siegel (New Haven: Yale University Press, 2004), 633–54. The plaintiff, a high-ranking civil servant, pronounced to the press that she was not a mere manual labourer, as if that meant that she could be harassed while other women could not.

[39] Nussbaum, 'The Modesty of Mrs. Bajaj'. Much debate ensued about who might be said to have modesty: in one case in which a man exposed himself in the presence of a young infant, it was held that modesty is innate, thus an infant can have it. But the fact that modesty doesn't have to be acquired never meant that it could not be lost.

[40] Indian Penal Code, Section 377.

'restitution'. It also has some ideas related to the Victorian ideas of modesty and chastity. But the idea of 'the order of nature' and of certain sex acts as offences against that 'order' is utterly Western and Christian in origin, with no foundation in (non-Christian) Indian traditions, as subsequent legal arguments rightly insist. Nor do (non-Christian) Indian traditions seek the legal regulation of same-sex conduct. India, indeed, was long a haven for British gay men seeking a greater liberty: E.M. Forster is just one of them.

This is not to say that Indian society in the twentieth century has been tolerant of same-sex conduct. It has not, and I have suggested that the reasons for this derive in part from the pain of British stigmatization and critique, and the desire of elites to emulate Victorian propriety—although they derive no doubt, as well, from some aspects or versions of indigenous traditions. But it is to say that the law itself, with all its Christian framing, is a very problematic one for any court in independent India to uphold. Moreover, like many sodomy laws in the United States, it is both under- and over-inclusive so far as same-sex conduct is concerned. It apparently applies to opposite-sex anal penetration as well as to same-sex, and it says nothing clear about oral sex or mutual masturbation. Case law had long grappled with these problems.

It was long felt that Section 377 was an anachronism and by late in the twentieth century, pressure began building to seek its repeal. This campaign gained momentum from the battle against HIV/AIDS. Groups grappling with the disease understood that criminal laws against gay sex were a strong deterrent to seeking testing, counselling, and treatment. Even many who had no particular sympathy with the lesbian and gay community joined the repeal campaign as a clear public health issue.

One part of the repeal strategy was protest, as a variety of intellectuals, activists, and literary figures spoke up against the law. Another arm was a legal challenge to the law's constitutionality. The Naz Foundation, an activist group working with same-sex issues, joined forces with Lawyer's Collective, India's premier legal non-governmental organization (NGO).[41] Founded by Indira Jaising and her husband Anand Grover, the Collective has two arms, one dealing with sex equality and the other with HIV/AIDS. Jaising's distinction as a lawyer led to her appointment as the first woman additional solicitor general, under the

---

[41] The Collective has argued many important gender-equality cases, including the Bajaj case—*Rupan Deol Bajaj v. Kanwar Pal Singh Gill*, (1995) 6 SCC 194.

recent Congress government, as well as other recognitions. Meanwhile, Grover's distinction was recognized worldwide when he was named special rapporteur for HIV/AIDS by the United Nations. So, the case could not have found a more prestigious team of advocates.

The challenge to Section 377 was initially filed in 2001, but in 2003, the Delhi High Court refused to consider it, concluding that the petitioners lacked standing because the law was rarely enforced. Petitioners appealed to the Supreme Court to reinstate the case and the Court agreed, sending it back to the Delhi High Court to consider it on its merits. The case was finally considered in 2008. The government was divided—as the High Court later said, a 'rather peculiar feature of this case'. The Health Ministry supported the petitioners on the ground that Section 377 was counterproductive in the fight against HIV/AIDS; the Home Ministry supported the law. The new law minister, Veerappa Moily (the same man who later refused to ban Lelyveld's Gandhi book because he actually read it), conceded that the law might be outdated. In July 2009, the Delhi High Court struck down Section 377, holding that it violates Article 14 of the Fundamental Rights section of the Indian Constitution, which guarantees all citizens equality before the laws and the equal protection of the laws, as well as Articles 15 (non-discrimination), and 21 (due process, right to life with dignity.)[42] (The law was invalidated only in its application to consenting acts between adults and it remained in force as regards non-consensual acts and acts involving minors). The case was heard by two of the High Court's most respected judges, Justice A.P. Shah and Justice Muralidhar, both known for the quality and progressive character of their opinions.

The Naz Foundation opinion is very long and unusually complex, given the number of distinct legal and factual issues involved. Because

---

[42] See Martha C. Nussbaum, 'Sex Equality, Liberty, and Privacy: A Comparative Approach to the Feminist Critique', in *India's Living Constitution: Ideas, Practices, Controversies*, Volume from conference on 50th anniversary of the Indian Constitution, eds. E. Sridharan, Z. Hasan, and R. Sudarshan (New Delhi: Permanent Black, 2002), 242–83. A shortened version published under the title 'What's Privacy Got to Do with It? A Comparative Approach to the Feminist Critique', in *Women and the United States Constitution: History, Interpretation, Practice*, eds, Sibyl A. Schwarzenbach and Patricia Smith (New York: Columbia University Press, 2003), 153–75. The history of substantive due process and the privacy right is extensively discussed by the Court in *Naz Foundation*.

the later reversal fails to confront these intricate details, we must now do so. In general, what is particularly impressive about the opinion is its thoroughness: it cites many social science findings and a huge number of legal judgments, both from Indian courts and from courts abroad, as well as a wide range of international treaties. This aspect of the opinion cannot be reproduced (the opinion is over a hundred pages long), but should be imagined. A succinct analysis of its major arguments is consequently useful.

Throughout the opinion, the acronym MSM is used for men who have sex with men, thus bypassing irrelevant debates about orientations and acts. The opinion is written as if the targeted group is male, and nothing at all is said about lesbians or whether Section 377 has ever been used to burden their rights. (In Britain, lesbian acts were never illegal.) I shall follow the logic of the opinion, though I note its narrowness. (It is also worth noting that bisexuality is completely ignored.)

History

The court repeatedly delves into the history of Section 377, insisting, correctly, that its foundation is Victorian and Christian, with no basis in Indian traditions. Because India was more liberal than Britain in matters of sexual orientation, the court notes, many people came to India to take advantage of this liberal atmosphere. Therefore in 1860, when Lord Macaulay drafted the Indian Penal Code, he felt a need to be harsh, introducing the idea of sexual offences 'against the order of nature'.[43] But the concept of an offence against the order of nature was simply absent from Indian society; it is essentially a Western concept,[44] 'based on a conception of sexual morality specific to Victorian era drawing on notions of carnality and sinfulness'.[45] In particular, it embeds an idea that sex is sinful unless its goal is procreation within marriage, and has been so interpreted in a 1925 opinion applying Section 377 to oral sex.[46] At this point, the court cites an Australian opinion by the distinguished Justice Michael Kirby, noting that a

---

[43] *Naz Foundation v. Government of NCT of New Delhi and Others*, WP(C) No. 7455/2001, 2 July 2009, 70, available at: https://www.escr-net.org/sites/default/files/Court_decision.pdf

[44] *Naz Foundation v. Government of NCT of New Delhi and Others*, 70.

[45] *Naz Foundation v. Government of NCT of New Delhi and Others*, 75.

[46] *Naz Foundation v. Government of NCT of New Delhi and Others*, 5.

similar law in Australia was 'imposed on colonial people'.[47] This history is not legally relevant without further argument, but it does prepare the reader to see a dissonance between India's own self-imposed Constitution and the vestiges of Empire that remain in the Penal Code. As the court said: 'There is no presumption of constitutionality of a colonial legislation.'[48]

Facts

Since the Supreme Court will subsequently overrule the Delhi High Court on the findings of fact, an unusual thing for a higher appellate court to do, we might expect to see sloppiness in the factual record. Nothing could be further from the truth. Buttressing its argument with wide-ranging citations from empirical and scientific studies (some of which were made available to the court in amicus briefs and some of which it apparently found on its own), the court draws three important conclusions:

- The illegality of consensual same-sex acts harms public health efforts to curb the spread of HIV/AIDS by discouraging MSM from seeking treatment or testing. This is the primary emphasis of the factual argument and detailed factual analysis was presented to the court in an affidavit from the National AIDS Control Organisation, affirmed by the government's Ministry of Health and Family Welfare. Further data were presented in an amicus brief from the Lawyer's Collective.[49] The court notes an opposing argument by the Home Office to the effect that criminalizing gay sex will help the struggle against HIV/AIDS by deterring homosexual acts, but it concludes correctly that there is no evidence for this contention and a great deal of evidence against it.[50]
- The illegality of same-sex acts has led to violence against gay men, including violence by the police. This section of the opinion draws on a wide range of affidavits, involving gang rape, police violence, custodial torture, and other offences.[51]

---

[47] *Naz Foundation v. Government of NCT of New Delhi and Others*, 70.
[48] *Naz Foundation v. Government of NCT of New Delhi and Others*, 105.
[49] *Naz Foundation v. Government of NCT of New Delhi and Others*, 12–17.
[50] *Naz Foundation v. Government of NCT of New Delhi and Others*, 59.
[51] *Naz Foundation v. Government of NCT of New Delhi and Others*, 18–19.

- The illegality of same-sex acts is associated with feelings of low self-esteem and humiliation.[52] This argument, buttressed by studies from many nations, lies on the border of fact and norm, but the fact of such feelings will later prove relevant in reaching the normative conclusion that dignity has been violated, so I include it here.

Constitutional Argument

The court makes three constitutional arguments. I begin with the two brief arguments that actually come later in the opinion, in order to dwell on the pivotal Article 21 argument. Addressing Article 14 (equality before the law), the court reviews the history of the requirement that a law's classification be founded upon an intelligible differentia and one that has a rational relation to the objectives of the law. Arbitrariness is excluded, as is an objective that is itself 'illogical, unfair, and unjust'.[53] But, argues the court, Section 377 does not take account of relevant factors such as consent and its classification is based upon 'disgust towards a particular social group' or 'animus'. Its classification is therefore 'both arbitrary and unreasonable'.[54]

As to Article 15 (discrimination), what needs to be argued is that discrimination on the basis of sexual orientation amounts to discrimination on the basis of sex, since sex, and not sexual orientation, is mentioned in the text. The view that sexual orientation discrimination is a form of sex discrimination has frequently been urged in legal literature.[55] After all, to criminalize a consensual act because its participants are two men rather than a man and a woman is in the most straightforward sense to discriminate on the basis of sex. The US Courts have typically been reluctant to accept this argument, but the Delhi court does accept it.[56] The court mentions that the Canadian Supreme Court agrees with this reasoning, but it then proceeds to offer an independent argument for the

---

[52] *Naz Foundation v. Government of NCT of New Delhi and Others*, 39.

[53] *Naz Foundation v. Government of NCT of New Delhi and Others*, 74.

[54] *Naz Foundation v. Government of NCT of New Delhi and Others*, 76.

[55] See Andrew Koppelman, 'Why Discrimination Against Gay Men and Lesbians is Sex Discrimination', NYU L. Rev. 69, no. 2 (1994): 197; Leslie Green, 'Sex-Neutral Marriage', *Current Legal Problems* 64, no. 1 (2011): 1–21. (Both authors argue that discrimination on grounds of sexual orientation is sex discrimination.)

[56] 81–5.

conclusion. First, a primary purpose of anti-discrimination norms is to prevent individuals from being judged by gender stereotypes; but that is exactly what Section 377 does. Furthermore, a series of prior cases, dealing with discrimination against women, contains language implying that all cases dealing with gender stereotypes must be subject to strict scrutiny (which Section 377 will not pass, as we shall see).[57]

Article 21 provides the court with its central line of argument. The basic idea is that if it is established that a law burdens a fundamental right, the law can only survive if the state can demonstrate a compelling government interest. (This basic tenet of Indian constitutional law was set forth very clearly in a series of cases that the court extensively cites.) There are two fundamental rights at stake: the right to privacy and the closely related right of life with dignity. (Much is said about the intimate relationship between privacy, especially sexual privacy, and full human dignity.) These rights are not explicit in the constitutional text but they have been recognized over the years through interpretation of Article 21.

Now we must provide some history, since Article 21, as written, says only this: 'No person may be deprived of his life or personal liberty except according to procedure established by law.'[58] No mention of privacy and none of dignity. At the time of the framing, India deliberately sought to limit due process to the procedural aspect, since Ambedkar had learnt from his study of the United States that substantive due process, as in the Lochner era, could be used against laws friendly to labour. So, in place of the words 'due process of law', the document reads 'procedure established by law'.

However, as time went on, the need for substantive due process began to be felt in three areas: (a) limits on police behaviour, since India's Constitution lacks an analogue of our Fourth Amendment; (b) limits on criminal punishment, since it also lacks any analogue of our Eighth Amendment; and (c) sexual privacy. India has gradually followed the United States in using due process to craft a privacy right that is used in all of these areas,[59] including the defence of some areas

---

[57] 86–90. For an illuminating argument that Article 15 incorporates a principle of swaraj, see Tarunabh Khaitan, 'Reading Swaraj into Article 15', *NUJS Law Review* 2, no. 3 (2009): 419–32.

[58] Constitution of India, Article 21.

[59] The punishment area gives rise to some oddities, as when the solitary confinement of death row prisoners is held to be a violation of the 'right to privacy' and 'privacy' is understood to involve a right to conversation with others. See Nussbaum, 'Sex Equality, Liberty, and Privacy'.

of sexual privacy—though with a somewhat uneven record.[60] The court in *Naz Foundation* goes into the details of this gradual recognition of a privacy right.[61] They then argue more briefly that Section 377 burdens this right, which they root in the word 'liberty' in Article 21. As for dignity, the word 'life' in Article 21 had long since been interpreted to mean 'life commensurate with human dignity'[62]—and the court gives this history as well. Then, by alluding to the factual record of stigma and discrimination, they argue that this right as well is burdened by Section 377.[63] They mention that both the right to equality and the rights to privacy and dignity belong to all—just in virtue of their humanity.[64]

A compelling state interest must therefore be found. Since the court has already disposed of the flimsy claim by the Home Office that Section 377 helps public health (which the Health Ministry denied), the only remaining interest is supplied by popular feeling. So, the court now argues that a compelling governmental interest cannot be supplied by a majority moralism that subordinates a class of persons. Popular morality, they note, is distinct from the morality embodied in the Constitution[65] and the Constitution makes the courts guardians of Fundamental Rights, including, and especially, 'the fundamental rights of those who may dissent or deviate from the majoritarian view'.[66] At this point, the court quoted the well-known words of Dr Ambedkar, against majoritarianism. Thus, the court reminds its audience of the way in which the heinous practice of untouchability was held in place by majority sentiment.

---

[60] Nussbaum.

[61] 28–35.

[62] Martha Nussbaum, 'India, Sex Equality, and Constitutional Law', in *Constituting Women: The Gender of Constitutional Jurisprudence*, eds Beverly Baines and Ruth Rubio Marin (Cambridge and New York: Cambridge University Press, 2004), 174–204. Key cases are *Francis Coralie Mullin v. UT of Delhi*, (1981) 1 SCC 608: AIR 1981 SC 746, cited in *Naz* and *Olga Tellis v. Bombay Municipal Corpn.*, (1985) 3 SCC 545: AIR 1986 SC 180.

[63] 44–50.

[64] 97. On these aspects of the case, see the detailed analysis in Pritam Baruah, 'Logic and Coherence in Naz Foundation: The Arguments of Non-Discrimination, Privacy, and Dignity', *NUJS Law Review* 2, no. 3 (2009): 504–24.

[65] 63.

[66] 99.

Disgust and Stigma

The legal situation in *Naz Foundation* is thus somewhat different from that in the US cases in which 'animus' played a leading role. In both *Romer v. Evans* and *Lawrence v. Texas*, the appeal to negative emotion was used to show that the laws in question lacked even a rational basis. As we have seen, that is what the court does with the notion of disgust in its Article 14 argument. But, as to Article 21, given that strict scrutiny has been held to be the appropriate level of review, the legal role of disgust could be expected to be less prominent. All the court needs to do is to knock down each claim of compelling state interest. However, given that the claim of public morality is the central claim, showing that the interest in criminalizing consensual gay sex acts is actually motivated by disgust and stigma helps to establish the constitutional unsuitability of the interest, in a nation committed to equality. At the same time, it helps show precisely how the dignity of a minority has been violated, a key part of showing that Section 377 violates Article 21. For both of these reasons and perhaps just understanding the importance of the issue, the court devotes a lot of attention to disgust and revulsion as putative justifications for maintaining the law. The term 'animus' is used once in the opinion, but 'disgust', 'revulsion', and 'repugnance' frequently.

I have already mentioned the court's indirect allusion to the caste hierarchy through its attention to Dr Ambedkar's criticism of public sentiment. One of the most interesting sections of the opinion is a very explicit reference to caste, in the form of a discussion of India's hijras, a group targeted by public disgust and revulsion and treated at times as untouchable.[67] No brief account can do justice to the complexity of this community, but, simply: hijras are a very ancient community of transgender people, most of them male at birth, who identify as neither male nor female and who often take a receptive role in sex with men, often also dressing in female dress. They are mentioned in *Kama Sutra* and it appears that, in ancient Indian traditions, they were respected and not found disgusting. They are blessed by Rama in Ramayana and given special functions at occasions such as childbirth and weddings. Now, however, forced by public stigma to live on the margins of society, hijras are subject in an extreme form to harassment and violence,

---

[67] 41–2. On this aspect of the opinion, see Siddarth Narain, 'Crystallising Queer Politics: The Naz Foundation Case and its Implications for India's Transgender Communities', *NUJS Law Review* 2 (2009): 455–70.

to denials of employment, and also to refusals of medical treatment (almost 30 per cent are HIV positive). The court discusses the history of this community, noting that the British displayed obsessive hostility to this group and even defined it as a 'criminal tribe', that is, as outlaws by nature, in 1871.[68] Indeed, the persecution of this community was British in origin. The court then reports that although Nehru called this stigmatization 'monstrous' in 1936, the classification as 'criminal' was not repealed until much later, and contemporary studies show that its ill effects have barely abated at all, as police feel free to mistreat members of the group and even torture them.

Now, of course, hijras are not the topic of Section 377, which sweeps much more broadly. But the court's intention is clear: this case, which most Indians will very likely agree to be 'monstrous', for the way in which human beings are singled out by public disgust and then subjected to extreme forms of violence and discrimination, is really the situation of MSM in India much more generally. It just is the same case. There is ultimately no difference but one of degree. Section 377 classifies all MSM as a criminal tribe. That is what the court clearly wants the reader to understand.

The court thus makes disgust and untouchability or quasi-untouchability central in its analysis, showing the depth of tension between Section 377 and the spirit of the Indian democracy, with its commitments to equality, dignity, and inclusiveness.

The court summarizes:

> If there is one constitutional tenet that can be said to be underlying theme of the Indian Constitution, it is that of 'inclusiveness'. This court believes that Indian Constitution reflects this value deeply ingrained in Indian society, nurtured over several generations. The inclusiveness that Indian society traditionally displayed, literally in every aspect of life, is manifest in recognizing a role in society for everyone. Those perceived by the majority as 'deviants' or 'different' are not on that score excluded or ostracized. Where society can display inclusiveness and understanding, such persons can be assured of a life of dignity and non-discrimination. This was the 'spirit behind the Resolution' of which Nehru spoke so passionately. In our view, Indian Constitutional law does not permit the statutory criminal law to be held captive by the popular misconceptions of who the LGBTs are. It cannot be forgotten that discrimination is

[68] 41.

antithesis of equality and that it is the recognition of equality which will foster the dignity of every individual.

In short, using public disgust as a weapon to pillory individuals was the way of the Raj. India has a different set of commitments and a different history.

This, I believe, is the deep insight *Naz Foundation* offers to the United States and other nations: rationalize 'animus' however you will, laws discriminating against gays and lesbians express a fear of contamination whose infamous prototype and core example is untouchability and whose damages to equal dignity are profound. If we think the practice of untouchability is heinous, and a US reader could quickly add the practices of the Jim Crow era regarding drinking fountains, swimming pools, lunch counters, and (of course) miscegenation, then we should think the same thing about our laws and practices where they discriminate on grounds of sexual orientation.

We are not at the end of the road. I must now turn to a sad recent development: the reversal of the Delhi High Court decision by the Supreme Court of India.

The Supreme Court Case: Ideology and Carelessness

On 11 December 2013, the Supreme Court of India reinstated Section 377, in the case of *Suresh Kumar Koushal v. Naz Foundation*.[69] The attorney general had refused to appeal. (The central government later filed a review petition against the Supreme Court, arguing that their reasoning was full of errors.) The appeal was therefore filed by Suresh Kumar Koushal, a private individual who runs an astrology centre in Delhi.[70] (The belief that Vedic astrology is a science is a cardinal tenet of India's Hindu Right, who want it to be taught in university science faculties.) The case was heard by a two-judge panel as is the normal practice.[71]

---

[69] (2014) 1 SCC 1.

[70] For his biography and his views, see Sangeeta Barooah Pisharoty, 'It is like reversing the motion of the Earth', *Hindu*, 20 December 2013, http://www.the-hindu.com/features/metroplus/society/it-is-like-reversing-the-motion-of-the-earth/article5483306.ece. There would appear to be a grave standing issue here, but when law gives a hearing to majority feelings, treating them as a real and legally cognizable harm, those issues tend to get lost.

[71] Nick Robinson, 'The Indian Supreme Court and Its Benches,' *Seminar* (2013), http://india-seminar.com/2013/642/642_nick_robinson.htm.

Thus, the judgment cannot be taken to represent the view of the court as a whole. There is no provision for *en banc* rehearing, however. There is a corrective mechanism known as a 'curative petition', and the Naz Foundation filed such a petition on 31 March 2014, asking for an oral hearing of the petition and an interim stay on the Koushal decision. This matter is still pending.

The Koushal opinion is also very long, but at that point, all resemblance to the Delhi opinion ceases. In terms of history, it bizarrely cites statements by Macaulay and other Victorian legal authorities as if they were 100 per cent suitable for independent India, not even addressing the historical contentions of the Delhi court.

As to facts, the major reason given for reversing is that the Delhi court erred in its findings of fact. To overrule a lower court on findings of fact is highly unusual and typically occurs only when the lower court's factual findings have been egregious. And yet, the Supreme Court simply asserts with no argument that the factual record concerning HIV/AIDS and the other burdens Section 377 places upon the gay community and upon public health workers is deficient. As we saw, that record was very detailed and from recognized authorities, including the National AIDS Commission and the Ministry of Health, with no factual evidence on the other side. Moreover, the Supreme Court itself extensively cites from Anand Grover's amicus brief, apparently granting him the status of a reliable authority. (At the time of the 2013 case, he had assumed his post as UN special rapporteur.) No discussion of violence against the gay minority is offered.

As for law, there is almost nothing there. First, there is an obvious standing issue that is not addressed at all. The case is similar to *Hollingsworth v. Perry* in the United States,[72] where private individuals brought appeal of the same-sex marriage decision, since the state of California refused to appeal. It should clearly have had a similar outcome, denying standing to the plaintiff, since the plaintiff had not suffered a legally cognizable harm. But this extremely important issue is not discussed at all. The key contention of the Delhi court, that majority preferences cannot trump fundamental rights, receives no reply. Indeed, the sloppiness of the entire text gives an impression of haste and pressure.

What happened? Of course, the practice of hearing Supreme Court cases in panels of two or three, with 28 justices total, means that

---

[72] 570 US __ (2013): 133 SCt 2652.

anything can happen.[73] But India itself had been changing, and on the eve of the landslide election of Narendra Modi, one would be hard-pressed to find evidence that India as such stands for inclusiveness and equal rights. One way or another, these two justices simply did not do their job, and the opinion does not compel respect. As mentioned, the central government filed a petition against it. Many influential intellectuals and artists have protested the ruling[74]. So have prominent world leaders, including UN Secretary-General Ban Ki-moon. If things are to change, the Parliament must act, which seems most unlikely. The best hope is the curative petition that has been filed by the Lawyer's Collective, and which the Supreme Court has agreed to hear. Since both the justices who originally heard the case have retired, the panel will be different, and very likely larger. Still, however, Section 377 remains law.

Two beacons of light can, however, be found. In the wake of the 2013 judgment, violence against the hijra community dramatically increased, including violence by the police. It was reported, as well, that the police were refusing to investigate reported instances of such violence. In a landmark ruling on 15 April 2014, in *National Legal Services Authority v. Union of India*,[75] the Supreme Court ruled that hijras and other transgenders should be treated legally as a third category, neither male nor female, and should also be entitled to affirmative action in education and employment. (Nepal has recently ruled similarly.) The case was heard by two justices, neither of whom was involved in the reversal of *Naz Foundation*. They have a very different mindset from their colleagues in *Naz*.

The judgment opens with a stern and eloquent repudiation of disgust and stigma:

[73] See my discussion of the pros and cons of this structure in Nussbaum, *Hiding from Humanity*.

[74] Sen's statement is available on YouTube. For an open letter signed by Seth, Soli Sorabjee et al., 'Section 377 Violates Fundamental Human Rights', *Outlook India*, 16 September 2006, http://www.outlookindia.com/ article/ Section-377-Violates-Fundamental-Human-Rights/232514. My own critique of the judgment was published in the *Indian Express* on 27 December 2013; see Martha Nussbaum, 'A law against Dignity', *Indian Express*, 27 December 2013, http://www.indianexpress.com/news/a-law-against-dignity/1212167/0.

[75] (2014) 5 SCC 438.

Seldom, our society realises or cares to realise the trauma, agony and pain which the members of Transgender community undergo, nor appreciates the innate feelings of the members of the Transgender community, especially of those whose mind and body disown their biological sex. Our society often ridicules and abuses the Transgender community and in public places like railway stations, bus stands, schools, workplaces, malls, theatres, hospitals, they are sidelined and treated as untouchables, forgetting the fact that the moral failure lies in the society's unwillingness to contain or embrace different gender identities and expressions, a mindset which we have to change.[76]

Whether this inclusive and tolerant view will dominate, or instead, the narrow, zealously Victorian mindset of the Hindu Right, remains uncertain.[77] A large step forward, however, was taken in August 2017, when a large panel of the Supreme Court, in a 9-0 vote, recognized that a right to privacy inheres in the Constitution, and connected that right with the equal dignity of gays and lesbians, declaring that *Koushal* is 'bad law'. The opinion authored by Justice Chandrachud rejected the argumentation in *Koushal*, insisting with particular vehemence that constitutional rights do not have their basis in majority opinion. The right of privacy does protect this minority from discrimination: 'Discrimination against an individual on the grounds of sexual orientation is deeply offensive to the dignity and self-worth of the individual. Equality demands that the sexual orientation of each individual in society must be protected on an even platform. The right to privacy and the protection of sexual orientation lie at the core of the fundamental rights guaranteed by Articles 14, 15, and 21 of the Constitution.'[78]

Because the challenge to *Koushal* is still pending before a larger bench, the Court did not formally overrule it, but it made its views exceedingly clear. In a most hopeful recent development, in January 2018, the Supreme Court has heard a fresh petition challenging the constitutionality of Section 377; and has definitively referred it to a five-judge bench for hearings on substantive issues. In effect the 'curative petition' has been allowed.

[76] (2014) 5 SCC 438.

[77] A positive step is the recent passage in the Rajya Sabha of a private member's bill promoting transgender rights (April 2015).

[78] *Justice K.S. Puttaswamy (Retd.) and Others v. Union of India and Others*, 24 August 2017, Paragraphs 124–7 at 126.

Whither Disgust?

Disgust is a powerful force in human life, and it creates tough obstacles to a politics of equal respect. I am with Tagore and Walt Whitman: it would be a great thing if we could bring up young people to be free of bodily disgust. It would improve relations with others and especially the all-important relationship with oneself. But even more important is inhibiting projective disgust, a primary force underlying discrimination.

If societies prove powerless to stop projective disgust entirely, however—since that would require a degree of control over religion and the family that most of us would reject—they can still refuse to listen to its voice when laws are made. The Delhi High Court has it right: laws against same-sex conduct are forms of caste hierarchy that identify a group as untouchable and stigmatize them as criminals by nature. Such laws have no place in any nation that pursues equality before the law. This wise opinion, together with the recent Supreme Court opinion about hijras, and the eloquent defence of privacy and dignity in *Puttaswamy*, can enlighten and guide us, even while those of us who love India must remain anxious about the still uncertain fate of such humane ideas.

10

The Rule of Disgust?

Contemporary Transgender Rights Discourse in India

Jeffrey A. Redding

The Supreme Court of India's 2014 decision in *National Legal Services Authority v. Union of India*[1] was a complex opinion coming at a complicated time for India's lesbian, gay, bisexual, transgender, and queer (LGBTQ[2]) community. Decided soon after the Supreme Court's controversial 2013 decision[3] to overrule the Delhi High Court's 2009 decision[4] invalidating Section 377 of the Indian Penal Code[5]—criminalizing

---

[1] *National Legal Services Authority v. Union of India*, (2014) 5 S.C.C. 438.

[2] I use this term cautiously, seeing that it relies on sexuality and gender categories popular in the United States, yet ones which are not nearly as widespread in India (or also many other places).

[3] *Suresh Kumar Koushal v. Naz Foundation*, (2014) 1 S.C.C. 1.

[4] *Naz Foundation v. Govt. of NCT of Delhi*, 160 (2009) Delhi Law Times 277 (DB).

[5] Section 377 penalizes 'unnatural offences' or, in other words, when someone 'voluntarily has carnal intercourse against the order of nature with any

'unnatural sexual offences'—*National Legal Services Authority* spoke to the empowerment of India's transgender communities, if not India's sexual minorities. Yet the Supreme Court's seeming distinction between the rights and welfare of transgender people in India, and the rights and welfare of sexual minorities, was not the only line-drawing that the Court engaged in with *National Legal Services Authority*. Indeed, the Court also seemed to draw a sharp distinction between transgender people and cisgender women and men, in the process not only cabining transgender persons as a 'third gender' but also, perhaps, carving off trans activism from feminism. After this opinion, in fact, it would not be entirely wrong to characterize the 'official view' in India of gender, transgenderism, and sexuality as one positing conceptual and ontological differences between these ideas, rather than coalescences.

This chapter aims to explore how something like disgust informed this set of legal line-drawing and, moreover, a kind of disgust which is difficult to sift out from other liberal legal practices. As a result, this is also a kind of disgust which will be hard to eradicate in liberal constitutional democracies devoted to the rule of law.

To be sure, to see disgust as embedded within the core of liberal constitutionalism does not mean that there are no advantages to this disgust or, indeed, liberal constitutionalism itself. A view of transgenderism and transgender rights as a separate line of inquiry from gender and feminism, and sexuality and lesbian, gay, bisexual (LGB) activism, can potentially accrue some benefits. For example, employment and educational reservations (or quotas) for transgender people,[6] differentiated from those for cisgender women (or gays and lesbians), create the possibility of increasing the total number of welfare-enhancing positions available for non-cisgender, non-heterosexual men—thereby chipping away at patriarchy and its privileges with more force. Conversely, collapsing the movement for transgender people's welfare into the movement

---

man, woman or animal'. India Penal Code, Section 377, http://ncw.nic.in/acts/THEINDIANPENALCODE1860.pdf, accessed on 2 March 2017.

[6] Towards this point, one of the directives issued by the Supreme Court of India in *National Legal Services Authority* ordered 'the Centre and the State Governments to take steps to treat [transgender persons] as Socially and Educationally Backward Classes of citizens and extend all kinds of reservation in cases of admission in educational institutions and for public appointments'. *National Legal Services Authority*, 5 S.C.C. 438 at 508.

for sexual minorities poses the danger that existing legal, cultural, and political roadblocks to sexual freedom can seep into and undermine the movement for transgender people. In some sense, this is a lesson that the United States teaches well, as the recent controversies over transgender access to bathrooms and locker rooms of persons' own choice/gender identification demonstrates.[7] Here, a previous generation's paranoia over what would transpire if gays and lesbians were to serve in the US military—with its close living quarters and non-private showers—has now played itself out again in relation to transgender people.[8]

Yet dangers also lurk with any separation impulse. For one, identities are certainly intersectional, especially in relation to women, sexual minorities, and transgender people. Indeed, homosexuality has long been indexed by non-normative gender performances, in India and elsewhere.[9] And as David Valentine reminds us about the US context, a certain kind of respectability politics—oriented around distancing 'outrageous' and 'embarrassing' queer, drag, and trans folk—has often accompanied mainstream gay and lesbian political efforts to achieve traction and 'acceptance' from US society.[10] Moreover, some 'transgender' people—for example, transgender women—simply identify as one of the binary genders—for example, women. As a result, separating out transgender women from women ('simpliciter') and feminism

[7] See generally Tessa Stuart, '17 Anti-Trans Bills That Could Become Law Next', *Rolling Stone*, 28 March 2016, http://www.rollingstone.com/politics/news/17-anti-trans-bills-that-could-become-law-next-20160328, accessed on 2 March 2017.

[8] This is a point that a former student of mine, John LeRoy, has aptly made and explored in a paper he wrote for my Comparative Law & Sexuality class at Saint Louis University School of Law. See John Leroy, 'This Rest Stop's Not for You: A Comparative Look at Transgender Bathroom Rights in the United States and India and How the Sexualization of Gender May Explain the Difference' (paper, Saint Louis University School of Law, 2016), on file with author. The history of gays and lesbians in the military—and worried discussions about them being in barracks and showers—has been a long one. For an example of this kind of worrying, see Daniel R. Plane, 'Don't Mess with "Don't Ask, Don't Tell"', *Marquette. Law Review* 79, no. 1 (1995): 386-7.

[9] For a discussion of this in the context of the United States, see generally David Valentine, *Imagining Transgender: An Ethnography of a Category* (Durham: Duke University Press, 2007), and especially his Chapter 1.

[10] Valentine, *Imagining Transgender*, 42–6.

begs fundamental questions similar to the ones raised by earlier feminist attempts to sideline lesbian 'women loving women'.[11]

Ultimately then, one can certainly identify both benefits and costs to the Supreme Court of India's separating moves in the context of discussions concerning transgenderism, sexuality, and gender. And it may be the case that a subtle and savvy sort of calculation of these benefits and costs informed the Supreme Court's actions in *National Legal Services Authority*, and also elsewhere. That being said, it is also arguably the case that a deeper and more inchoate set of motivations are operating here including, namely, the legalized operation of the political emotion of disgust—or, put another way, the 'rule of disgust'.

This chapter's suggestion is likely to be treated with some scepticism. This is especially the case given that political disgust often seems to get operationalized in a gross manner—and it would be difficult to characterize *National Legal Services Authority* in this way. Indeed, so horrific are common examples of political disgust in action—for example, the well-known historical instances of legalized slavery (and Jim Crow) in the United States, the German Holocaust, or the more recent Gujarat genocide[12]—one's reaction to these instances of political disgust is likely to be disgust itself. Quite simply, these 'disgust events' are often over the top, gruesome, and ugly. Conversely, and as will be discussed in greater detail below, the *National Legal Services Authority* opinion seems to be quite different and, indeed, rather sympathetic, sophisticated, and cosmopolitan.

To be sure then, this chapter's suggestion that one way of viewing the separation of conversations concerning transgender rights from LGB and women's rights alike as involving the political emotion of disgust begs the question of how we identify political disgust in the first instance. Here, we might specifically ask whether we need to be *personally* disgusted in order to diagnose *political* disgust. Alternatively, we might ask: Are there non-affect-laden, 'scientific' forms of political disgust (for example, the 'tolerance' that Wendy Brown has so memorably discussed and challenged[13]) that also require our concerted attention?

---

[11] For a brief discussion of earlier lesbian interventions vis-à-vis 'traditional' articulations of feminism in the United States, see Valentine, *Imagining Transgender*, 46–8.

[12] Martha C. Nussbaum, *The Clash Within: Democracy, Religious Violence, and India's Future* (Cambridge: Harvard University Press, 2007), 44–51.

[13] See generally Wendy Brown, *Regulating Aversion: Tolerance in the Age of Identity and Empire* (Princeton: Princeton University Press, 2006).

This chapter aims to suggest answers to these questions, building an argument across three parts. The first part explores the Supreme Court of India's decision in *National Legal Services Authority*, highlighting the ways in which it separates transgender rights issues out from LGB and (cisgender) women's rights. The second part then brings a multifarious set of theoretical perspectives to bear on the Supreme Court of India's recent line-drawing, in the process arguing that all legal line-drawing (and especially that engaged in by the state) embodies political perceptions and ambitions. Consequently, the kind of line-drawing engaged in by the Supreme Court of India in *National Legal Services Authority* is hardly 'innocent' or necessarily progressive—indeed, it quite likely harbours disgust, or at least something in continuity and conversation with it. The last part then concludes this chapter's discussions, in the process suggesting additional lines of query about law and disgust moving forward.

> A ... Bench of this [Supreme] Court in *Suresh Kumar Koushal v. Naz Foundation* has already spoken on the constitutionality of Section 377 [of the Indian Penal Code] and, hence, we express no opinion on it since we are in these cases concerned with an altogether different issue pertaining to the constitutional and other legal rights of the transgender community and their gender identity and sexual orientation.[14]

The Separate Trajectories of Transgender, Sexual, and Women's Rights after *National Legal Services Authority*

This part aims to explicate the Supreme Court of India's 2014 *National Legal Services Authority* opinion, while also situating its discussions alongside those found in the Court's 2013 *Suresh Kumar Koushal v. Naz Foundation* opinion concerning Section 377. In doing so, the goal is to highlight instances of line-drawing between transgenderism and sexuality, and also gender and transgender, made by the Supreme Court in *National Legal Services Authority*. To be sure, the Court was not univocal either between *Naz Foundation* and *National Legal Services Authority*, or within *National Legal Services Authority* itself. The first disjuncture is not entirely surprising given that the 2013 and 2014 opinions were written

---

[14] Justice K.S.P. Radhakrishnan, *National Legal Services Authority*, 5 S.C.C. 438 at 464.

by different and non-overlapping two-justice benches of the Supreme Court.[15] In other words, there were no authors or decision-makers in common between these two opinions, and there may also have been concerns by the authors of the 2014 opinion to not too overtly come into conflict with the earlier 2013 opinion written by fellow members of the Supreme Court. As to the second disjuncture, however, the Supreme Court bench that decided *National Legal Services Authority* often gave ambivalent or even contradictory signals within this single opinion itself as to how the bench viewed transgenderism and its relation to sexuality and 'gender simpliciter'. In short, there is much that is unclear within the more recent 2014 opinion, as subsequent (and controversial) attempts by the Government of India to implement it have amply demonstrated.[16] The main aim of this part, then, is to highlight those parts of the 2014 opinion, read in conjunction with the 2013 opinion, that seem to suggest a view of transgenderism and transgender rights distinct from sexuality and LGB rights, and gender and women's rights.

In all this, the question of *why* the 2014 *National Legal Services Authority* opinion separated transgender rights from other social justice concerns is certainly lurking. This part does not focus on offering *reasons* for this separating move, whether those reasons be salutary or pernicious. That being said, the actual significance and momentousness of this 2014 opinion's separating moves can perhaps be more readily appreciated by emphasizing here that the questions of gay and lesbian, or transgender rights, do not necessarily have to be dealt with under a paradigm different from (some forms of) feminism. In other words, it is important to see here that there is nothing 'natural' or 'inevitable' about the Supreme

---

[15]   For an excellent discussion of the internal structure and workings of the Supreme Court of India, see Nick Robinson, 'Structure Matters: The Impact of Court Structure on the Indian and U.S. Supreme Courts', *American Journal of Comparative Law* 61, no. 1 (2013): 173–208.

[16]   For example, after this opinion, Prime Minister Narendra Modi's government petitioned the Supreme Court, asking it to give clarity as to several aspects of the *National Legal Services Authority* opinion. It is important to note here that some commentators diagnosed insincerity in this petition, seeing it as an attempt to sow confusion and delay vis-à-vis the opinion's implementation. See Utkarsh Anand, 'Government Objects to SC Empowering Third Gender: Seeks Clarification on Quotas, LGBT Rights', *Indian Express*, 11 September 2014, http://indianexpress.com/article/india/india-others/government-objects-to-sc-empowering-third-gender/, accessed on 2 March 2017.

Court of India's separating moves in *National Legal Services Authority*—reasons or emotions of some sort likely underlay these moves.

Towards this point, and putting aside for the moment ethnographic[17] and historical[18] observations about the haziness of distinctions between (homo)sexuality, gender, and transgenderism as either ontological categories or day-to-day personal experiences, a number of jurists around the globe have suggested such distinctions do not necessarily have to (or should not) play a role in legal and constitutional argumentation. For example, unlike in India or Pakistan,[19] the US Supreme Court has not issued any sort of 'paradigmatic' decision on transgender rights.[20] Yet this 'silence' is not entirely surprising or necessarily lament-worthy given that the Court, back in 1989, issued an important decision concerning sex stereotyping and the legal actionability of employment discrimination on the basis of non-normative gender expression.[21] In short, the

[17] In India, the ethnographic evidence cuts even deeper against any attempt to cabin 'transgenderism'. Towards this observation, see Gayatri Reddy, *With Respect to Sex: Negotiating Hijra Identity in South India* (Chicago: University of Chicago Press, 2006), 30–4 for discussion of her discomfort at describing her research subjects as occupying gender-, sex-, or sexuality-based positionalities only.

[18] See, for example, Ruth Vanita and Saleem Kidwai, eds, *Same-Sex Love in India: Readings from Literature and History* (New York: St. Martin's Press, 2000).

[19] For more on recent developments in Pakistan, see Jeffrey A. Redding, 'From "She-males" to "Unix": Transgender Rights and the Productive Paradoxes of Pakistani Policing', in *Regimes of Legality: Ethnography of Criminal Cases in South Asia*, eds Daniela Berti and Devika Bordia (Delhi: Oxford University Press, 2015).

[20] One potentially paradigmatic case—concerning transgender bathroom access—was recently set for oral argument before the Supreme Court. However, this case was then returned to the lower courts. See Adam Liptak, 'Supreme Court Won't Hear Major Case on Transgender Rights', *New York Times*, 6 March 2017, https://www.nytimes.com/2017/03/06/us/politics/supreme-court-transgender-rights-case.html, accessed on 2 March 2017

[21] See *Price Waterhouse v. Hopkins*, 490 U.S. 228 (1989). And, indeed, something like the *Price Waterhouse* rationale got articulated at one point in *National Legal Services Authority* when the Supreme Court of India wrote: 'The [Indian] Constitution-makers ... gave emphasis to the fundamental right against sex discrimination so as to prevent the direct or indirect attitude to treat people differently, for the reason of not being in conformity with stereotypical generalisations of binary genders', *National Legal Services Authority*, 5 S.C.C. 438 at 488.

suggestion here has been that feminist legalism in the United States has been a capacious pursuit and, moreover, one that has not had to rely on any narrow or exclusive definition of what it means to be (or act like) a woman—or even what it means to have a gender in the first place. Similarly, when the US Supreme Court recently took up the question of the constitutionality of different American states' bans on same-sex marital unions, in *Obergefell v. Hodges*,[22] some legal commentators suggested that this should be an 'easy' question for the Court given the many precedents declaring sex discrimination unconstitutional under the Equal Protection Clause of the US Constitution.[23] Indeed, the argument was made that bans on same-sex marriage were paradigmatically and evidently *sex* discrimination—so much so that even conservative members of the Court could conclude thus!

All that being the case, *National Legal Services Authority* arguably decided to offer up a fenced-off constitutional legal terrain, at least vis-à-vis women, sexual minorities, and transgender people. Before entering that uneven and tricky terrain, it is worth emphasizing some of the other 'big picture' aspects of this opinion. Generally speaking, *National Legal Services Authority* was a broad-based decision, declaring multiple forms of social and governmental discrimination against India's transgender citizens to be unconstitutional. Indeed, commenting on the shortcomings of India's legal treatment of transgender persons living in India, the Supreme Court in this decision took sharp cognizance of how 'Indian Law, on the whole, only recognises the paradigm of binary genders of male and female, based on a person's sex assigned by birth, which [affects] the law relating to marriage, adoption, inheritance, succession and taxation and welfare legislations'.[24] Importantly, when thinking about how India's laws would have to change to more fully include and respond to the concerns of transgender people, the Supreme Court in its opinion looked to international and comparative legal discussions and precedents.[25] And ultimately, the Supreme Court's concluding

---

[22] *Obergefell v. Hodges*, 135 S. Ct. 2584 (2015).

[23] See, for example, Andrew Koppelman, 'The Supreme Court Made the Right Call on Marriage Equality—But They Did it the Wrong Way', *Salon.com*, 29 June 2015, http://www.salon.com/2015/06/29/the_supreme_court_made_ the_right_call_on_marriage_equality_%E2%80%94_but_they_did_it_the_ wrong_way/, accessed on 2 March 2017.

[24] *National Legal Services Authority*, 5 S.C.C. 438 at 484.

[25] *National Legal Services Authority*, 5 S.C.C. 438 at 465–80, 484–7.

directives to India's central and state governments vis-à-vis the reform of Indian practices were multiple and diverse, including commands for Indian state authorities to not only improve the formal legal situation of transgender people in India, but also their broader social and cultural position.[26]

The Supreme Court's varied conclusions and directives in *National Legal Services Authority* are not entirely surprising given that the plaintiffs involved in this public interest litigation were multiple and diverse. Indeed, these plaintiffs were representative of a variety of different gender communities within India, including hijras,[27] *kinnars*,[28] and—as the Supreme Court described one aggrieved person—a eunuch.[29] Moreover, this diversity of persons in front of the Court seemed to inform how the Court understood the issues at stake in this case. Towards this point, the Court summarized these diverse issues towards the very beginning of its opinion in the following manner:

> We are, in this case, concerned with the grievances of the members of transgender community (for short 'TG community') who seek a legal declaration of their gender identity [different] than the one assigned to them, male or female, at the time of birth and their prayer is that non-recognition of their gender identity violates Articles 14 and 21 of the Constitution of India. Hijras/eunuchs, who also fall in that group,

---

[26] For example, one of the concluding directives of the Supreme Court of India was that the 'Centre and State Governments should seriously address the problems being faced by hijras/transgenders such as fear, shame, gender dysphoria, social pressure, depression, suicidal tendencies, social stigma, etc. and any insistence for [sexual reassignment surgery] for declaring one's gender is immoral and illegal', *National Legal Services Authority*, 5 S.C.C. 438 at 508.

[27] The (impleaded) plaintiff in this respect was the well-known Indian activist, Laxmi Narayan Tripathy. See *National Legal Services Authority*, 5 S.C.C. 438 at 459–61.

[28] The Poojaya Mata Nasib Kaur Ji Women Welfare Society, representing kinnars, filed a separate writ petition (No. 604 of 2013) in this case. See *National Legal Services Authority*, 5 S.C.C. 438 at 459. The Supreme Court's opinion in *National Legal Services Authority* responded to this petition and the one filed by the National Legal Services Authority simultaneously.

[29] See *National Legal Services Authority*, 5 S.C.C. 438 at 462 (describing Siddarth Narrain as a 'eunuch' even though Narrain's statement quoted here described Narrain as identifying as a 'woman' who decided, as a teenager, to go live with a 'hijra' community).

claim legal status as a third gender with all legal and constitutional protection.[30]

One way of reading this summary of the case, then, is that the Supreme Court saw this case as involving the issues as to whether *some* transgender people in India should be able to traverse the male/female binary—from one dyadic gender designation given to them at birth, to the other available dyadic option—and also whether *other* transgender people (namely, hijras) should be able to officially identify as something different from male or female altogether.[31]

With either question, however, it is important to note that the Court here was not obviously identifying a more generalized right to choose one's gender identity as an issue. In short, for the Court, there were transgender people who may want to change their assigned gender identity, but there appears to be no fundamental problematizing of the (usually early childhood) assignation of gender itself.[32] In other words, deep questions as to who has the right to (ever) choose or designate another's gender—be that the state or parents—are not the fundamental questions of this case. Rather than these deep questions about gender— arguably relevant to cisgender and transgender people alike—we have a more limited Supreme Court inquiry about a demarcated group of people, namely 'transgender people'.

This demarcation was both linguistic and legal, but also visual. Towards this latter point, the Court also made the following observation in its opinion:

[30] *National Legal Services Authority*, 5 S.C.C. 438 at 459.

[31] A bit later in its opinion, the Supreme Court also mentioned (by way of description) one petitioner's claim that seemingly combined both of these positions. See *National Legal Services Authority*, 5 S.C.C. 438 at 460.

[32] Admittedly, the Court's emphasis, at times, on the importance of 'self-identification' of gender may indicate that it was worried about children being assigned a gender at or near birth. See, for example, *National Legal Services Authority*, 5 S.C.C. 438 at 492 (opining that '[g]ender identity as already indicated forms the core of one's personal self, based on self-identification, not on surgical or medical procedure'). See also *National Legal Services Authority*, 5 S.C.C. 438 at 465 (possibly problematizing the assignation of sex at birth). But see *National Legal Services Authority*, 5 S.C.C. 438 at 474 (discussing a UK House of Lords 'transsexual' case and noting how the woman whose identity was in question in that case was 'at birth ... correctly classified and registered as male').

Discussion on gender identity including self-identification of gender of male/female or as transgender mostly focuses on those persons who are assigned male sex at birth, whether one talks of hijra transgender, woman or male or male to female transgender persons, while concern voiced by those who are identified as female to male transsexual persons [is] often not properly addressed. Female to male unlike hijra/transgender persons are not quite visible in public unlike hijra/transgender persons. Many of them, however, do experience violence and discrimination because of their sexual orientation or gender identity.[33]

In not generalizing the 'problem of gender' to all people, and seeming to ascribe it only to transgender people, *National Legal Services Authority* arguably drew a line between transgenderism and transgender welfare, and gender ('simpliciter') and feminism. At times, this separating move seemed to get articulated with even more force as well. For example, at the beginning of its opinion, the Court described the hijra community in the following manner:

[Transgender] may also take in persons who do not identify with their sex assigned at birth, which include hijras/eunuchs who, in this writ petition, describe themselves as 'third gender' and they do not identify as either male or female. *Hijras are not men by virtue of anatomy appearance* and[,] psychologically, they are also not women, *though they are like women with no female reproduction organ and no menstruation. Since hijras do not have reproduction capacities as either men or women, they are neither men nor women* and claim to be an institutional 'third gender'. Among hijras, there are emasculated (castrated, nirvana) men, non-emasculated men (not castrated/akva/akka) and inter-sexed persons (hermaphrodites).[34]

The Court here was clearly struggling with how to conceive of hijras and gender alike. On the one hand, the Court was seemingly trying to defer to (at least some) hijras' personal identifications as 'not man, nor woman' and, instead, as an entirely different (third) gender category altogether. On the other hand, the Court also seemed to be operating with its own firm sense of what makes a 'normal' man or woman—namely the (at least theoretical) capacity to participate in copulative

---

[33] *National Legal Services Authority*, 5 S.C.C. 438 at 483–4.

[34] *National Legal Services Authority*, 5 S.C.C. 438 at 462 (emphasis added). But see *National Legal Services Authority*, 5 S.C.C. 438 at 491 for a more forceful articulation, perhaps, of the importance of hijra gender self-identification.

reproduction (even if some biological reason comes in the way of actual fertility). Ultimately, for the Court, it seemed that if gender can be chosen, it is only by people who are neither (cisgender) men nor (cisgender) women and, moreover, that 'biological' and reproductively capacious men and women are exemplars of the fact that some genders *cannot* be chosen. Or, put another way, that 'biological sex' is an unambiguous and unavoidable thing, even if gender (later) deviates from this 'natal fact'.

Transgender people were also distinguished from cisgender people—and also sexual minorities—in another important way in this opinion, namely, through a kind of 'indigeneity talk' deployed by the Court when describing India's transgender communities. For the most part, this happened in two different portions of the *National Legal Services Authority* opinion: in one section entitled 'Historical background of transgenders in India'[35] and in another entitled 'Indian scenario'.[36] In the first such section, the Court discussed the history of different Indian transgender communities, firmly situating them within the Hindu tradition. While the Court did mention that '[h]ijras ... played a prominent role in the royal courts of the Islamic world, especially in the Ottoman empires and the Mughal rule in the Medieval India',[37] this mention of non-Hindu, Indian transgenderism came after a more thorough summary of the Hindu tradition in this respect. For example, the Court recounted here how

> Lord Rama, in the [Hindu] epic *Ramayana*, was leaving for the forest upon being banished from the kingdom for 14 years, turns around to his followers and asks all the 'men and women' to return to the city. Among his followers, the hijras alone do not feel bound by this direction and decide to stay with him. Impressed with their devotion, Rama sanctions them the power to confer blessings on people on auspicious occasions like childbirth and marriage, and also at inaugural functions which, it is believed set the stage for the custom of *badhai* in which hijras sing, dance and confer blessings.[38]

In the Court's second discussion of the 'indigenous' nature of India's transgender communities, the Court offered up a taxonomy of the different kind of transgender people in India, including hijras, eunuchs,

[35] *National Legal Services Authority*, 5 S.C.C. 438 at 463–4.
[36] *National Legal Services Authority*, 5 S.C.C. 438 at 480–4.
[37] *National Legal Services Authority*, 5 S.C.C. 438 at 463.
[38] *National Legal Services Authority*, 5 S.C.C. 438 at 463.

*aravani*s and *thirunangi*s, *kothi*s, *jogta*s and *jogappa*s, and *shiv-shakthi*s.[39] While the Court's awareness of the diverse positionalities of India's trans- gender communities is admirable, this kind of discussion also sets these communities off from—if you will—'cisgender communities'. Notably, there was no discussion in this opinion of the 'history of *males*' or the 'Indian *female* scenario', much less any acknowledgment of the history and arguable indigeneity of Indian homosexuality.[40]

The indigeneity of homosexuality is often a point of discussion and contention in debates about the rights of sexual minorities. As a result, the focus in *National Legal Services Authority* on the indigenous nature of transgender communities in Indian can be seen as an implicit rebuke of any attempt to see or use this opinion for the benefit of India's LGB communities. As the excerpt that opens this part makes clear,[41] this cleaving off of LGB rights from transgender rights was also made explicit by the Supreme Court in *National Legal Services Authority*.[42] This is the case even if the Court's mention of the sexual orientation of transgender people in this opening excerpt—and also the Court's final holding in this opinion[43]—lends itself to some ambiguity as to what the Court was really saying about all this.

The final major way that the *National Legal Services Authority* opinion separated transgender rights and welfare out from legal and social discus- sions concerning gender and sexual minorities is through the remedies and directives that the Supreme Court issued in this opinion. While

---

[39] *National Legal Services Authority*, 5 S.C.C. 438 at 480–2.

[40] By way of contrast, see a brief discussion of this in *Naz Foundation v. Govt. of NCT of Delhi*, 160 (2009) Delhi Law Times 277 (DB) at 316.

[41] Justice K.S.P. Radhakrishnan, *National Legal Services Authority*, 5 S.C.C. 438 at 464.

[42] Elsewhere in this opinion as well, the Court remarked that 'gender iden- tity and sexual orientation … are different concepts', *National Legal Services Authority*, 5 S.C.C. 438 at 465.

[43] The lead opinion (written by Justice K.S.P. Radhakrishnan) in this Supreme Court opinion ends with the following declaration: 'We, therefore, conclude that discrimination *on the basis of sexual orientation* or gender identity includes any discrimination, exclusion, restriction or preference, which has the effect of nullifying or transposing equality by the law or the equal protection of laws guaranteed under our Constitution, and hence we are inclined to give vari- ous directions to safeguard the constitutional rights of the members of the TG community', *National Legal Services Authority*, 5 S.C.C. 438 at 493 (emphasis added).

there was much in these directives that spoke explicitly and otherwise to the goal of full social inclusion for transgender people in India—for example, the Supreme Court here urged Indian officials, at all levels, to generate 'public awareness so that TGs will feel that they are also part and parcel of the social life and ... not treated as untouchables'[44]—there were also ways that transgender people are separated out. This comes across perhaps most clearly in the Court's discussion of the toilet facilities that should be provided to India's transgender citizens. After observing that '[s]ince ... there are no separate toilet facilities for hijras/transgender persons, they have to use male toilets where they are prone to sexual assault and harassment',[45] the Court ultimately ordered the 'Centre and State Governments ... to ... provide them separate public toilets and other facilities'.[46] Similarly, the Court also ordered 'Centre and State Governments ... to operate separate HIV serosurveillance centres since hijras/transgenders face several sexual health issues'.[47]

Non-Disgusting Disgust and the Rule of Law

The decision in *National Legal Services Authority* seems a far cry from typical manifestations of disgust-oriented law and politics. Indeed, well-known and oft-discussed examples of the politico-legal operationalization of disgust (for example Nazi Germany, Jim Crow in the United States, the genocide of Muslims in Gujarat) are often compelling because they not only aptly identify how societies commonly deploy disgust to impute a 'gross' animality to these societies' 'Others', but also because these examples tend to demonstrate how all this boomerangs back on to societies. As a result, in discussions of them, 'disgustful' societies often enough get transformed into gross and savage monstrosities that we can all be disgusted with in turn. Put another way, and redirecting Martha Nussbaum's penetrating analysis, these examples and discussions are often compelling because they ask us to see how crude otherizing societies '*must be kept at a distance because of [their] animality [and because we] have nothing in common with them*'.[48]

---

[44] *National Legal Services Authority*, 5 S.C.C. 438 at 508.
[45] *National Legal Services Authority*, 5 S.C.C. 438 at 487.
[46] *National Legal Services Authority*, 5 S.C.C. 438 at 508.
[47] *National Legal Services Authority*, 5 S.C.C. 438 at 508.
[48] Martha C. Nussbaum, *Political Emotions: Why Love Matters for Justice* (Cambridge: Harvard University Press, 2013), 184 (emphasis in original).

This part takes a different approach to the politico-legal operation of disgust, namely, in its submission that a key technology of disgust—namely separation—does not, and often is not, accompanied by vitriol and rage, blood and other bodily fluids, or general grossness. As this part argues, the separating work of politics and law alike is often embodied, rather, in the 'elegant scientificism' of modern bureaucratic and legalistic thinking. Moreover, the argument here is that *National Legal Services Authority* harbours this kind of 'covert disgust'. In short, this part aims to highlight how disgust and ugliness can be delinked and, also, how we can find an example of this 'non-disgusting disgust' in *National Legal Services Authority*.

As just suggested, a leading analysis of the role of 'disgusting disgust' in contemporary politics and, moreover, one which has helpfully interjected a comparative analysis of this emotion in political action, is provided by Martha Nussbaum. In Nussbaum's recent pathbreaking work, *Political Emotions: Why Love Matters for Justice*[49]—and especially its Chapter 7, entitled '"Radical Evil": Helplessness, Narcissism, Contamination'—she asks us to move away from simplistic and 'optimistic'[50] accounts of human political behaviour, and to focus on the possibility of 'real evil',[51] which Nussbaum goes on to describe as 'deliberately cruel and *ugly* behavior toward others that is not simply a matter of inadvertence or neglect, or even fear-tinged suspicion, but which involves some active desire to denigrate or humiliate'.[52] Moreover, this denigration—specifically described as 'subordination'[53] later in the chapter—is described by Nussbaum as often deploying the emotion of disgust and, specifically, an awfully 'gross' kind of disgust. Nussbaum writes, '[a] key device of subordination is disgust: people in power impute animal properties that typically inspire disgust (sliminess, stickiness, bad smell, connection with decay or with bodily fluids and excrement) to other groups of people, whether African-Americans, women, lower castes, Jews, or gay men—and then they use that alleged disgustingness as a reason to refuse contact.'[54]

[49] Nussbaum, *Political Emotions*.

[50] Nussbaum, *Political Emotions*, 164.

[51] Nussbaum, *Political Emotions*, 165.

[52] Nussbaum, *Political Emotions*, 165 (emphasis added).

[53] Nussbaum, *Political Emotions*, 182.

[54] Nussbaum, *Political Emotions*, 182, 184.

As specific examples of all this, Nussbaum points to inter-caste discrimination in India,[55] and Jim Crow laws and policies in the United States.[56] Certainly, it is the case that the instances of political disgust described by Nussbaum were often marked by disturbing interpersonal violence—for example, the torching of Dalit residences by upper-caste Hindus in India, and the lynching of African-Americans by whites in the American South. It is also worth observing that even the formal state laws or governmental actions complicit in this subordination were often shockingly gross and crude. For example, one of the more famous anti-miscegenation laws in the United States, declared unconstitutional in the seminal US Supreme Court case of *Loving v. Virginia*,[57] did not simply criminalize 'interracial marriage'. Rather, the operative laws were marked—stained even—by crude and gross determinations of racial membership. One of these laws was Section 20-54 of the then-Virginia code, which read (in part) as follows:

Intermarriage prohibited; meaning of term 'white persons.' - It shall hereafter be unlawful for any white person in this State to marry any save a white person, or a person with no other admixture of blood than white and American Indian. For the purpose of this chapter, the term 'white person' shall apply only to such person as has no trace whatever of any blood other than Caucasian; but persons who have one-sixteenth or less of the blood of the American Indian and have no other non-Caucasic blood shall be deemed to be white persons.[58]

In this kind of disgustful world, then, the operation of political disgust not only imputes disgusting qualities to the victims of this disgust but also, often enough, makes the perpetrators of this disgust out to be crude and gross as well— which can be seen even in the drafting of these victimizers' 'legalistic laws'.

This kind of analysis of political disgust is certainly apt and compelling, but here I would like to suggest how it could also be supplemented by bringing other theoretical perspectives into conversation with it. Indeed, Nussbaum herself recognizes that not all political disgust is (to use her terms) 'motivational' and, rather, can also be 'institutional'.[59]

---

[55] Nussbaum, *Political Emotions*, 164.

[56] Nussbaum, *Political Emotions*, 164.

[57] *Loving v. Virginia*, 388 U.S. 1 (1967).

[58] *Loving*, 388 U.S. 1 at n.4.

[59] I have in mind here Nussbaum's discussion of and distinction between governments' 'motivational' and 'institutional' emotional work with, for

One place to begin such a discussion is with James Scott who, in his influential work *Seeing Like a State*, reminds us that '[e]very act of measurement [is] an act marked by the play of power relations'.[60] In this work, Scott traces the 'high-modernist'[61] project of governance, finding power plays embedded in everything from the modern state's description and management of forests and other landscapes, to similar moves made vis-à-vis human populations and communities.

In one particularly compelling discussion of all this, Scott explains the cultivation of contemporary forests by modern governments. Describing the development of 'fiscal forestry'[62] by modern Europeans, with this kind of forestry's intense focus on the production of commercial timber, Scott describes how 'the actual tree with its vast number of possible uses was replaced by an abstract tree representing a volume of lumber or firewood'.[63] Importantly, in this view of the forest, 'nearly everything was missing from the state's narrow frame of reference. Gone was the vast majority of flora: grasses, flowers, lichens, ferns, mosses, shrubs, and vines. Gone, too, were reptiles, birds, amphibians, and innumerable species of insects. Gone were most species of fauna, except those that interested the crown's gamekeepers.'[64]

Moreover, such a limited and unreal focus eventually led to efforts to *create* such bureaucratically imagined forests *in reality*.[65] And even more powerfully, Scott goes on to then describe how this kind of depleted forest became an aesthetic in itself: 'The visual sign of the well-managed forest ... came to be the regularity and neatness of its appearance. Forests might be inspected in much the same way as a commanding officer might review his troops on parade, and woe to the forest guard

---

example, there being the possibility that legal and other institutional norms can orient populations' thoughts and feelings. Nussbaum, *Political Emotions*, 20, 135. Nussbaum's focus in her 2013 work, however, is on governments' explicit motivational work through, for example, fostering the right kind of 'political rhetoric, songs, symbols, and the content and pedagogy of public education'. Nussbaum, *Political Emotions*, 20.

[60] James C. Scott, *Seeing like a State: How Certain Schemes to Improve the Human Condition Have Failed* (New Haven: Yale University Press, 1998), 27.

[61] Scott, *Seeing like a State*, 4.

[62] Scott, *Seeing like a State*, 12.

[63] Scott, *Seeing like a State*, 12.

[64] Scott, *Seeing like a State*, 12–13.

[65] Scott, *Seeing like a State*, 15.

whose "beat" was not sufficiently trim or "dressed".'[66] Through such a discussion, Scott powerfully demonstrates how even the seemingly mundane techniques and categories of modern governance—he is talking here about the production of a commodity, namely, lumber, after all—are inflected with deep power operations, affecting not only *what* we see but also *how* we want to be seen.

As mentioned earlier, Scott's analysis is not just limited to the modern management of things, but also human peoples and communities as well. For Scott, human beings are not only a terribly seductive target of modern states' bureaucratic governance techniques, but so can they be transformed—not only in others' eyes, but in their own perception—by these techniques. Moreover, for Scott, such governance techniques, when taken to their extreme, tend to produce a terribly abject sort of human life—one which we might consider, in fact, animal-like. Scott writes: 'I would argue that just as the monocropped, same-age forest represents an impoverished and unsustainable ecosystem, so the high-modernist urban complex represents an impoverished and unsustainable social system ... The point is simply that high-modernist designs for life and production tend to diminish the skills, agility, initiative, and morale of their intended beneficiaries. They bring about a mild form of ... neurosis.'[67]

The thought that state-authored bureaucratic forms of social ordering can end up thoroughly transforming the human populations (both in their own and others' eyes) that this ordering is directed at is also a point taken up, quite powerfully, by Sara Ahmed in her work on 'queer phenomenology'.[68] For Ahmed, however, the abjectness of overly state-managed human life is more unevenly distributed than what Scott describes, with his focus on more general state/non-state (or state/social) relations. Put another way, Ahmed's work focuses on the *uneven* terrains and spaces created by states, societies, and histories—with some people being created more precariously than others.

A central concern in Ahmed's work on queer phenomenology is how human beings get 'oriented' (or directed) in the ways that they are—whether that involves a sexual orientation, a gender (orientation),[69] or a

---

[66] Scott, *Seeing like a State*, 18.

[67] Scott, *Seeing like a State*, 348–49.

[68] See generally Sara Ahmed, *Queer Phenomenology: Orientations, Objects, Others* (Durham: Duke University Press, 2006).

[69] Ahmed, *Queer Phenomenology*, 60.

race (orientation).[70] For Ahmed, sexuality, gender, and race share simi-larities in that, for her, all involve a certain way of being situated—or oriented—in the world. Moreover, in all this, one of Ahmed's central concerns is exploring the political economies that draw us close to some things and (kinds of) people, and away from others. In one of her more haunting observations, Ahmed comments that her 'model of touch shows how bodies reach other bodies.... And yet ... not all bodies are within reach. Touch ... involves a [political] economy. Touch then opens bodies to some bodies and not others'.[71]

In these economies producing proximity and distance, social stratifi-cation and hierarchies emerge—with devastating effects for the socially marginalized. Towards this point, Ahmed re-narrates Frantz Fanon's account of the extreme self-consciousness that black bodies are made to feel in white spaces, noting how, in these spaces, '[r]acism ensures that the black gaze returns to the black body, which is not a loving return but rather follows the line of the hostile white gaze'.[72] Moreover, '[t]he disorientation affected by racism diminishes capacities for action'.[73]

Combining insights from the analyses of Scott and Ahmed presented here, one can perhaps begin to see how any state's attempt to neatly divide up its human citizens into different categories is prone to pro-ducing political disgust. As Scott urges us to realize, the modern state's measuring and demarcation exercises involve a certain peculiar way of seeing nature and people alike, and are also likely part of the state's efforts to gain leverage or even superiority vis-à-vis its otherwise unruly citizens. For Scott, in the state's *seeing* some aspects of its subject popula-tions, but not other aspects, the state is ultimately trying to advance certain state interests—for example, 'productivity, health, sanitation, education, transportation, mineral resources, grain production, and investment'[74]—amongst which justice or equality does not figure solely,

---

[70] Ahmed, *Queer Phenomenology*, 112.

[71] Ahmed, *Queer Phenomenology*, 107.

[72] Ahmed, *Queer Phenomenology*, 111.

[73] Ahmed, *Queer Phenomenology*, 111.

[74] Scott, *Seeing like a State*, 52. This is admittedly Scott's description of modernist states in the nineteenth century, but I believe it is still relevant to understanding states' priorities today. Scott notes later that 'high-modernist social engineering usually came cloaked in egalitarian, emancipatory ideas: equality before the law, citizenship for all, and rights to subsistence, health, education, and shelter'. Scott, *Seeing like a State*, 352.

or even necessarily highly. In turn, Ahmed's analysis then importantly reminds us that the social sight-lines created (or just 'blindly' reproduced) by the state are likely to produce uneven social effects, with some kinds of people being created more abjectly—more animal-like—than others.

Taking all of this into account, it should not be too difficult now to diagnose how *National Legal Services Authority*'s separating work not only created divisions between transgender people, cisgender people (and especially cisgender women), and sexual minorities, but has also potentially suggested a hierarchy between them measured in terms of abjectness, animality, and disgust. I will turn shortly to making this point more forcefully, but here I first want to emphasize that *National Legal Services Authority* is not unique in creating these hierarchies. Indeed, something like this has been on display in other jurisdictions' legal discussions concerning gender and sexuality as well. For example, in the US Supreme Court's recent *Obergefell* same-sex marriage decision, the Court dignified same-sex marriages, while it also 'happily' denigrated non-marital families. One example of all this is embodied in the Court's observation that 'excluding same-sex couples from marriage … conflicts with a central premise of the right to marry. Without the recognition, stability, and predictability marriage offers, [these same-sex couples'] children suffer the stigma of knowing their families are somehow lesser'.[75] In all this, the US state's marriage valorizing project was on full display, as was its conjoined project to make the non-marital family abject.

To mention another comparative example, and one perhaps more directly relevant to this chapter's discussion of India, one can also see gender and sexuality hierarchies being recently (re)created in Pakistan with its own recent discussion of transgender rights. In June 2009, four months after the filing of a legal petition in the Supreme Court of Pakistan concerning the rights and welfare of transgender people,[76] this Court issued one of the first of a series of orders in what would turn out to be a multiyear litigation of the various issues raised by this petition. As part of this initial order in this case, the Supreme Court ordered Pakistan's various provincial governments to conduct a census of the numbers, names, and locations of 'she-males' (as the Court initially

---

[75] *Obergefell*, 135 S. Ct. 2584 at 2600.

[76] For more on this petition, including its genesis and its consequences, see Redding, 'From "She-males" to "Unix"'.

termed them[77]) living in each province. Furthermore, evidencing a degree of hostility and suspicion towards the gurus who typically govern 'she-male' communities,[78] and giving voice to common stereotypes about the (sexual) predations of these gurus, the Court also directed the provincial governments to 'ensure that in future if any child is handed over to the 'Gurus', their particulars should be noted and intimated to the [provincial government] for the purpose of further probe with regard to the status of such child and also to know whether they are voluntarily handed over or under compulsion'.[79]

In ordering this kind of counting and accounting of Pakistan's transgender citizens, one cannot help but notice a post-colonial resonance with a well-known trope of colonial governance—namely, the census. Moreover, as Arjun Appadurai has noted, the colonial census was not simply about demography, but also embodied morality and, moreover, a morality that one can describe as embodying disgust. Towards this point, Appadurai notes how the colonial census (amongst other colonial governance techniques) resulted in 'new forms of categorization … which saw [colonial South Asia] as a museum or zoo of difference and of differences, and [a] project of reform [] which involved cleaning up the sleazy, flabby, frail, feminine, obsequious bodies of natives into clean, virile, muscular, moral, and loyal bodies'.[80] Arguably then, the gender counting conducted in 2009 in Pakistan has also been implicated in exoticizing, surveilling, and attempting to reform 'disgusting' transgender persons, as well as their 'distasteful' kinship/guru practices. At the very least, we can see in these Supreme Court-ordered census efforts a re-emergence of colonial-era tropes (and horrors) about transgender gurus 'reproducing' transgender communities through kidnapping and castrating young boys.

[77] See Redding, 'From "She-males" to "Unix"' (discussing how terminology referring to the non-normatively gendered individuals at the heart of this litigation changed over the course of the litigation).

[78] See Reddy, With Respect to Sex, 155–64 for a discussion of guru dynamics in a particular urban context in India.

[79] Human Rights Const. P. No. 63 of 2009, 16.06.2009 Order at 2 (on file with author).

[80] Arjun Appadurai, 'Number in the Colonial Imagination,' in *Orientalism and the Postcolonial Predicament: Perspectives on South Asia*, eds. Carol A. Breckenridge and Peter van der Veer (Philadelphia: University of Pennsylvania Press, 1993), 335.

Turning now to India, Appadurai's comments about the colonial-era census are not only relevant to post-colonial Pakistan but also post-colonial India, including the recent *National Legal Services Authority* opinion. For example, Appadurai's observations about how the colonial census viewed Indians as embodying a 'zoo of difference[s]'[81] are arguably on full display in *National Legal Services Authority* with its taxonomization (discussed earlier) of India's transgender communities. Notably, there is no comparable discussion in this opinion of India's 'cisgender communities'.

Beyond listing and describing India's transgender citizens in a way suggestive of their animality, other key aspects of *National Legal Services Authority* also resonate with Appadurai's observations, in particular for how these parts demonstrate a preoccupation with 'cleaning up'[82] ostensibly disgusting transgender practices and realities—and, moreover, ones which are made out to be discontinuous with those pertaining to either gender or sexuality in India more broadly. Towards this point, *National Legal Services Authority* seemed generally oriented towards viewing transgender people in India as living in a hellish landscape of pathos. In doing so, this opinion de-emphasized the ways in which transgender people enrich Indian society or might even cause it to joyfully reimagine its meanings and contours.[83] Notably, this kind of overarching pathos framework can be found in the very first sentence of *National Legal Services Authority*, where it was observed that '[s]eldom [does] our society realise[] or care[] to realise the trauma, agony and pain which the members of transgender community undergo'.[84]

This framework also revealed itself in the orders that the Supreme Court ultimately issued in this case including, notably, the order for 'separate HIV serosurveillance centres' for transgender people.[85] HIV was also a particular focus of the predecessor case to *Suresh Kumar Koushal v. Naz Foundation*, where the Supreme Court overturned the Delhi High Court's decision invaliding Section 377 and its criminalization of sexual minorities (amongst others). In this earlier 'LGBT-friendly' decision,

---

[81] Appadurai, 'Number in the Colonial Imagination,' 335.

[82] Appadurai, 'Number in the Colonial Imagination,' 335.

[83] For example, perhaps along the lines suggested by the Supreme Court's narration of the Ramayana tale and how it ended with the empowerment of hijras. See *National Legal Services Authority*, 5 S.C.C. 438 at 463.

[84] *National Legal Services Authority*, 5 S.C.C. 438 at 459.

[85] *National Legal Services Authority*, 5 S.C.C. 438 at 508.

the Delhi High Court expressed much concern about how Section 377 makes it harder to combat the prevalence of HIV in India's non-heterosexual communities.[86] Reading this opinion alongside *National Legal Services Authority*, one begins to understand the Indian state's view of India's transgender and sexual minority communities as steeped in anxieties about these communities' sexual health practices.[87] Moreover, one does not have to doubt the veracity of HIV prevalence in these communities to note how this framing of issues helps enact a kind of disgust-oriented gender and sexuality hierarchy. This hierarchy—and the cleaving off of discussions concerning transgenderism and sexuality from those of 'gender simpliciter' on which it is predicated—happens through an implicit imagining of immunity from HIV for India's cis-gender and heterosexual communities, and a fairly explicit attribution of animal-like (sero) abjectness for everyone else.

The Supreme Court's order in *National Legal Services Authority* that separate toilet facilities be created in India for transgender people can be seen in a similar light.[88] On the one hand, the Court can be commended for recognizing, in another part of its opinion, that transgender people (presumably women) 'are prone to sexual assault and harassment'[89] when they use male toilets. Yet ultimately, when devising a final order with respect to all this, the Court seems to have also decided that transgender (women) themselves pose some kind of risk to cisgender women—hence the Court's ordering the creation of altogether separate toilet facilities for transgender people. Moreover, in all this, it cannot help but be noticed that we are talking about toilets here—or, in other words, sites and spaces devoted to some of human beings' most evidently animalistic activities. In short, with the Supreme Court's efforts to separate transgender from gender in *National Legal Services Authority*, including the Court's specific order pertaining to toilets, the Court arguably created not only a decidedly uneven toilet terrain for India's citizens but also reinforced a cis/trans hierarchy premised in disgust.

[86] See generally *Naz Foundation* 160 (2009) Delhi Law Times 277 (DB).
[87] For a more detailed exploration of this point, see Aniruddha Dutta, 'An Epistemology of Collusion: *Hijras*, *Kothis* and the Historical (Dis)continuity of Gender/Sexual Identities in Eastern India', *Gender and History* 24, no. 3 (2012): 839–44.
[88] *National Legal Services Authority*, 5 S.C.C. 438 at 508.
[89] *National Legal Services Authority*, 5 S.C.C. 438 at 508.

These examples of how the Supreme Court of India's separating work in *National Legal Services Authority* embodied a complicated yet disgust-informed hierarchy of gender, transgender, and sexuality are not surprising in light of this part's discussions of the work of James Scott and Sara Ahmed, and also Martha Nussbaum. Yet this all paints a terribly dispiriting picture about the operation of law and liberal constitutionalism. Is there an alternative way to do or view things? The next and concluding part will very briefly turn to these questions, suggesting some subtleties and additional queries we must bring to the analysis of all this.

Conclusion

Disgust vis-à-vis marginalized groups can take a variety of forms. This chapter has attempted to demonstrate how the Supreme Court of India's 2014 opinion in *National Legal Services* embodied disgust of transgender people in India in bureaucratic and legalistic ways. This kind of disgust relied less on clear ascriptions of 'grossness' to the 'strange' (often bodily) practices that (some) transgender people engage in, and more on legal techniques of power that separated transgender people out from cisgender women (and men), sexual minorities, and also the general population.

In making this argument, however, a certain kind of pessimism might be engendered, and also a pressing question: How can law discuss the specific situation of a group of people, often historically marginalized and discriminated against, without re-enacting that marginalization and discrimination? One might also wonder whether this chapter's critique is too allied with 'conservative' views of equality predicated on the 'blind' application of law, and hostile to the kind of specific reservations and spaces—for example, special employment programmes and special toilets—that *National Legal Services Authority* orders. Perhaps most fundamentally, one might wonder whether the rule of law made out by this chapter is *too inherently* the rule of disgust.

These are important questions and ones that, for reasons of space, this concluding part can only begin to sketch out responses to. But in short, in all this, I believe we need to be highly attuned to distinctions between *perceiving* social difference and *ascribing* social difference, and then also *stigmatizing* difference. The latter two relations to difference are particularly problematic and, as this chapter suggests, deeply prone to the politico-legal operation of disgust. Moreover, whenever the state acts as an 'external actor' to society—as the state often does in post-colonial contexts[90]—it arguably has a special propensity (not always realized) to ascribe and then stigmatize social differences from the top down, rather than be truly responsive to the bottom-up demands of socially marginalized peoples.

To be sure, in all this, there are subtle but crucial distinctions to be made which, for example, the separate HIV-treatment and toilet facilities for transgender people that the Supreme Court of India ordered in *National Legal Services Authority* bring into high relief. Such separate facilities can be crucial refuges. But they also embody disgust-imbued exclusions. What these spaces are depends, in part, on who asked for them—a reality which a more ethnographic approach to the study of law and constitutionalism can help us better understand. But even here, it is important to realize that the meaning of separateness may change over time, or be different for different people at the same time. In all this then, this chapter's crucial point emerges, namely, that future transgender legal developments in India (and elsewhere) need to be attuned to the covert possibility of disgust, as well as its perils, and also the risks accompanying its non-angelic alternatives.

[90] For a thoughtful explication and analysis of this in the Indian context, see Mithi Mukherjee, *India in the Shadows of Empire: A Legal and Political History (1774-1950)* (Delhi: Oxford University Press, 2010).

11

Combatting Exclusions through Law

Rights of Transgender People in India

H.R. Vasujith Ram

In the Introduction to this volume, the editors emphasize that the
pervading theme is understanding prejudice and discrimination, which
in turn may indicate 'directions' for legal and social change. Two possibilities emerge. One, the 'normative irrationality' of emotions such as
projective disgust—and an understanding of its operation—ought to
give us reasons to *preclude* enactment of law based on the logic of such
disgust. Two, an assessment of prejudice and continuing discrimination
would call for positive legal and policy intervention efforts to displace
centuries of continuing discrimination. This chapter focuses on the second 'direction' of institutional response: that of legal and policy efforts
to remedy prejudice, stigma, and discrimination. More specifically, this
chapter evaluates the legal and policy action in *India* aimed at remedying
discrimination and recognizing the rights of *transgender*[1] *persons*. I begin

---

[1] Unless otherwise specified, I use the term 'transgender' as an adjective to
describe those persons whose gender position/s or identity/ies is at variance (in
the widest sense) from the one initially assigned at birth. This is not meant to

the chapter with an overview and discussion of the judgment in *National Legal Services Authority v. Union of India*[2] ('NALSA case'), and traverse a clarification petition, a government expert committee report, and three proposed bills.

The Nalsa Judgment

On 15 April 2014, a two-judge bench of the Supreme Court of India (SC) ruled on a petition (a public interest litigation[3]) filed by the National Legal Services Authority[4]. The prayer was to declare that the 'non-recognition of the Transgender Community's gender identity violates Articles 14 and 21 of the Constitution of India'.[5] Justice K. Radhakrishnan delivered the primary opinion, supported by a concurring opinion of Justice A.K. Sikri.

Opinion of Justice Radhakrishnan

Justice Radhakrishnan's judgment describes the term 'transgender' as an 'umbrella term' for 'persons whose gender identity, gender expression or behaviour does not conform to their biological sex'.[6] Turning to history, Justice Radhakrishnan opines that while transgender persons played a prominent role in social life in India historically, the colonial government instituted a regime that was regressive (with the example of the Criminal Tribes Act, 1871) and initiated discussion against transgender persons.[7] Interestingly, the opinion also cites the example of Section 377

---

serve as an objective or universalized definition, or to deny the possibility of intersectional identity/ies. I only adopt this usage for the sake of simplicity.

[2] (2014) 5 SCC 438. See the previous chapter for a more elaborate description.

[3] In India, the emergence of 'public interest litigation' has led to relaxation of rules of standing, allowing public-spirited citizens to bring constitutional claims to court on behalf of the marginalized.

[4] The National Legal Services Authority is constituted under the Legal Services Authorities Act, 1987. Other interveners, such as trans activist Laxmi Tripathi, were also parties to the case.

[5] *National Legal Services Authority*, 5 S.C.C. 438 at 459.

[6] *National Legal Services Authority*, 5 S.C.C. 438 at 462.

[7] *National Legal Services Authority*, 5 S.C.C. 438 at 463–4. See Laurence Preston, 'A Right to Exist: Hijras and the State in Nineteenth-Century India,'

of the Indian Penal Code, which the justice acknowledges has been used as an instrument of marginalization. However, the judgment expresses no opinion on the constitutionality of the provision.[8]

The opinion (with the support of various international instruments and principles) declares that 'discrimination on grounds of sexual orientation or gender identity' would constitute a violation of Article 14 of the Indian Constitution.[9] With respect to Articles 15 and 16, the opinion found violations of Articles 15(2)[10] and 16(2)[11] and recommended that transgender persons be provided reservations under Articles 15(4)[12] and 16(4)[13],[14].

The gender *expression* of transgender persons in terms of 'dress, words, action or behaviour' as well as 'personal appearance' was held to be protected under Article 19(1)(a).[15] It was also held that their legal recognition is mandatory since Article 21 enshrines the right to dignity and personal autonomy.[16]

The opinion concludes by directing that one's gender is to be determined by the person himself/herself/hirself, and that 'hijras/eunuchs (*sic*) have to be considered as Third Gender'.[17] Further, in the determination of gender, the 'psychological test'[18] is to be utilized instead of the

---

Modern Asian Studies 21, no. 2 (April 1987): 371–87 for an examination of the attitude of the British state towards hijras.

[8] *National Legal Services Authority*, 5 S.C.C. 438 at 463–4.

[9] *National Legal Services Authority*, 5 S.C.C. 438 at 487.

[10] The provision bars discrimination 'with regard to—(a) access to shops, public restaurants, hotels and places of public entertainment; or (b) the use of wells, tanks, bathing ghats, roads and places of public resort maintained wholly or partly out of State funds or dedicated to the use of the general public'.

[11] Discrimination in public employment.

[12] Reservations for socially and educationally backward classes.

[13] Reservations in public employment for backward classes.

[14] *National Legal Services Authority*, 5 S.C.C. 438 at 488–9.

[15] *National Legal Services Authority*, 5 S.C.C. 438 at 488–9.

[16] *National Legal Services Authority*, 5 S.C.C. 438 at 491.

[17] *National Legal Services Authority*, 5 S.C.C. 438 at 492.

[18] Psychological test refers to principles evolved in cases like *Department of Social Security v. SRA*, (1993) 118 ALR 467 and *AB v. Western Australia*, 2011 HCA 42 (Aust), that 'gender should not be regarded merely as a matter of chromosomes, but partly a psychological question, one of self perception, and partly a social question, how society perceives the individual'.

'biological test' under the *Corbett* principle.[19] Calling for equality and non-discrimination, the opinion decries the binary notions of gender in various legislations such as the Indian Penal Code, 1860, and the National Rural Employment Guarantee Act, 2005.[20]

Opinion of Justice Sikri

Justice A.K. Sikri begins his concurring opinion stating that he is 'entirely in agreement' with Justice Radhakrishnan's judgment.[21] Justice Sikri divides the 'core issue' into 'two facets':[22]

- Whether a person who is born as a male with predominantly female orientation (or vice versa), has a right to get himself to be recognized as a female as per his choice, more so, when such a person after having undergone operational procedure, changes his/her sex as well;
- Whether transgenders, who are neither males nor females, have a right to be identified and categorized as a 'third gender'?

Justice Sikri then 'hastens' to add: 'it is the second issue with which we are primarily concerned in these petitions'.[23]

On the first issue, the opinion states: 'If a person has changed his/her sex in tune with his/her gender characteristics and perception, which has become possible because of the advancement in medical science, and when that is permitted by/in medical ethics with no legal embargo, we do not find any impediment, legal or otherwise, in giving due recognition to the gender identity based on the reassigned sex *after* undergoing SRS'.[24]

On the second issue, it is clarified that it does not concern transgender persons interpreted in its 'wider' meaning, that is, as an umbrella term. Instead, it concerned 'transgender persons' in the restrictive meaning of

---

[19] *National Legal Services Authority*, 5 S.C.C. 438 at 492. The Corbett principle refers to the principle established in *Corbett v. Corbett,* (1970) 2 All ER 33, that biological factors—chromosomal, gonadal, and genital tests—are key determinants of one's gender.

[20] *National Legal Services Authority*, 5 S.C.C. 438 at 492.

[21] *National Legal Services Authority*, 5 S.C.C. 438 at 493.

[22] *National Legal Services Authority*, 5 S.C.C. 438 at 493.

[23] *National Legal Services Authority*, 5 S.C.C. 438 at 493.

[24] *National Legal Services Authority*, 5 S.C.C. 438 at 501. Emphasis mine.

the term, that is, members of the transgender community who consti-tute a distinct class in India. These, according to Justice Sikri, are 'Hijras, eunuch, Kothis, Aravanis, Jogappas, Shiva-Shakthis, etc.'[25] The opinion then concludes that the members of the community must be recognized as being members of a 'third gender'. It is stated that treating them as male or female would constitute 'denial of constitutional rights'.[26]

Joint Declaration

The judgment concludes with a joint declaration (issued by both jus-tices) which forms the operative portion. It declares that:[27]

- Hijras are to be treated as the 'third gender'.
- Transgender persons' right to decide their self-identified gender is to be upheld and that governments must recognize their gender identity as male, female, or transgender.
- Transgender persons are to be treated as 'socially and educationally backward' classes, entitled to reservations.
- Governments must operate HIV sero-surveillance centres for trans-gender persons or hijras facing sexual health issues.
- Governments are to recognize problems such as 'fear, shame, gender dysphoria, social pressure, depression, suicidal tendencies, social stigma' faced by the community.
- Any insistence for sex reassignment surgery (SRS) for declaring one's gender is 'immoral and illegal'.
- Governments are directed to take measures to provide appropriate medical care to transgender persons in hospitals and provide *separate* toilets and other facilities.
- Governments are to take steps to frame social welfare policies.
- Governments are to take public awareness campaigns and other mea-sures for an inclusive society.
- Expert Committee of the Ministry of Social Justice and Empowerment are to examine issues in light of the declarations in this judgment, and governments to implement the report of the Expert Committee within six months of the date of the judgment.

---

[25] *National Legal Services Authority*, 5 S.C.C. 438 at 501.
[26] *National Legal Services Authority*, 5 S.C.C. 438 at 505.
[27] *National Legal Services Authority*, 5 S.C.C. 438 at 508–9. The declara-tions are not quoted verbatim.

Vacillation and Incoherence: A Critique of the Judgment

When the judgment in the NALSA case was delivered, the ruling was hailed as 'extraordinary',[28] as 'progressive in the best sense of the term',[29] 'important on a global level',[30] and as a 'ray of hope'.[31] Martha Nussbaum called the judgment a 'gleam of light'.[32] The judgment is certainly landmark, and is a progressive outlier considering the record of the court in closely related civil liberties cases such as that of the Suresh Koushal case.[33] Studies also suggest that the judgment has had some positive effects.[34] However, a careful scrutiny reveals many flaws and opens scope for criticism of the judgment. Here, I discuss some of these criticisms.

Constructing Identities

First, the judgment's treatment of definitions is highly problematic.[35] Justice Radhakrishan's judgment labels the term 'transgender' as an umbrella term, 'whose gender identity, gender expression or behaviour does not identify with their sex assigned at birth'. However, Justice Sikri's judgment states that the court is 'primarily concerned with' members of

[28] Vishnu Varma and Nida Najar, 'India's Supreme Court Recognizes 3rd Gender', *India Ink* (blog), *New York Times*, 15 April 2014 (quoting Colin Gonsalves).

[29] Gautam Bhatia, 'The Supreme Court on Transsexuals, and the Future of *Koushal v. Naz*', *Ind. Con. Law. Phil.* (Blog), 15 April 2014.

[30] 'Transgenders Hail SC Verdict, Seek Respect from Society', *Deccan Herald*, 15 April 2014.

[31] Manjeet Kumar Sahu, 'Case Comment on *National Legal Services Authority v. Union of India and Others*: A Ray of Hope for the LGBT Community', *BRICS Law Journal* 3 (2016): 164.

[32] Martha C. Nussbaum, 'Disgust or Equality? Sexual Orientation and Indian Law,' *Journal of Indian Law and Society* 6 (Winter 2015) 1–24.

[33] *Suresh Kumar Koushal v. Naz Foundation,* (2014) 1 SCC 1, upholding the constitutionality of Section 377 of the Indian Penal Code.

[34] International Commission of Jurists, *"Unnatural Offences": Obstacles to Justice in India Based on Sexual Orientation and Gender Identity* (Geneva: International Commission of Jurists, 2017), 25–6.

[35] Aniruddha Dutta, 'Contradictory Tendencies: The Supreme Court's NALSA Judgment on Transgender Recognition and Rights', *Journal of Indian Law and Society* 5 (2014): 225.

the transgender community under its 'restrictive' meaning, that is, *only* those transgender communities considered distinct and unique to India (and other neighbouring countries). Thus, although Justice Sikri states that he is in agreement with Justice Radhakrishnan, his opinion seems to offer a different (and restrictive) definition of the term. Consequently, there is no clarity whether the benefit under the judgment is to be extended only to these distinct communities that Justice Sikri refers to.

The communities listed exclude transmen or transgender persons who were assigned female at birth.[36] Revathi, a trans activist, contends that such exclusion renders invisible a minority within a marginalized group. She says that the 'judgment is based heavily on the testimonies and experiences of the HIV/AIDS sector ... [whose focus is] almost exclusively on male to female transgender individuals'[37].

As a related concern, the judgment also uses obsolete notions to construct identities. Hijras are described by Justice Radhakrishnan as those who 'are not men by virtue of anatomy appearance and psychologically, they are also not women, though they are like women with no female reproduction organ and no menstruation. Since hijras do not have reproduction capacities as either men or women, they are neither men nor women.'[38] In another place, he adds, 'hijras do not identify as female because of their lack of female genitalia or lack of reproductive capability'.[39] Justice Sikri's description of a transwoman is as follows: 'It may ... happen that though a person is born as a male, because of some genital anatomy problems his innate perception may be that of a female.'[40] Such descriptions, couched in reductionist biological terms, only serve to reify existing stereotypes.

Notably, the judgment also imposes the 'third gender' on hijras and other Indian transgender persons. There is no consideration of the possibility that some may prefer to identify as a transman or a transwoman,[41] nor of the complexity of the transgender identity in India (discussed

---

[36] *National Legal Services Authority*, 5 S.C.C. 438 at 483–4, however, does explicitly mention transmen.

[37] A. Revathi, *A Life in Trans Activism* (New Delhi: Zubaan Publishers, 2016), loc. 2903 of 2985, Kindle.

[38] *National Legal Services Authority*, 5 S.C.C. 438 at 462.

[39] *National Legal Services Authority*, 5 S.C.C. 438 at 491.

[40] *National Legal Services Authority*, 5 S.C.C. 438 at 494.

[41] Gee Imaan Semmalar, 'Gender Outlawed: The Supreme Court Judgment on Third Gender and its Implications', *Round Table India*, 19 April 2014.

later). Justice Sikri states: 'In order to translate the aforesaid rights of [transgenders] TGs into reality, it becomes imperative to first assign them their proper "sex".'[42] Ironically however, as Semmalar points out, this imposition of 'third gender' may affect their rights[43] under various laws such as election and inheritance laws where the third gender is neither mentioned nor recognized.[44] Consider a recent example—in light of 'demonetization', where the Indian government withdrew certain high-value currency notes from circulation, gold purchases shot up. Thus, the Finance Ministry and the Central Board of Direct Taxes were forced to issue clarifications regarding the cap on gold holdings. While different figures were given for 'married lady', 'unmarried lady', and 'male', there was no mention of 'third gender' made.[45]

Such 'contradictory tendencies'[46] in the SC judgment has led to further confusion in the judgments of High Courts. In *Ashish Kumar Mishra v. Bharat Sarkar*,[47] the Allahabad High court examined the interpretation of the National Food Security Act, 2013. Under Section 13, women above 18 years of age are deemed to be the head of the household for collection of ration cards. The court held that Section 13 could be interpreted to include transgender persons. What is troubling, however, is the High Court's observation: 'The SC observed that *since transgenders are neither male nor female*, treating them as belonging to either of these categories, will be a denial of their constitutional rights.'[48] The Madras High Court decision in *Nangai v. Superintendent of Police*[49] presents another interesting case in point. The petitioner was assigned female at birth and self-identified as a woman. In 2009–10,

---

[42] *National Legal Services Authority*, 5 S.C.C. 438 at 504.

[43] Revathi points out that such an imposition may inadvertently exacerbate stigma and discrimination against transgender persons. Transwomen, for instance, may be asked to use *separate* toilets, and even if such separate toilets are constructed, they may be singled out for their difference. Revathi, *A Life in Trans Activism,* loc. 2918 of 2985, Kindle.

[44] Semmalar, 'Gender Outlawed.' See also 'International Commission of Jurists', *Unnatural Offences*, 31–2.

[45] Utkarsh Anand, 'In Gold Limits, Point Overlooked: What About Transgenders', *Indian Express*, 3 December 2016.

[46] Dutta, 'Contradictory Tendencies'..

[47] AIR 2015 All 124.

[48] *Ashish Kumar Mishra* AIR 2015 All 124, emphasis mine.

[49] (2014) 4 MLJ 12. Hereinafter referred to as 'Nangai case'.

she successfully applied for the post of a police constable. She was asked to undergo medical examinations, whose reports diagnosed her with 'partial androgen insensitivity syndrome' and 'male pseudohermophrodism' and stated (incorrectly) that she was 'transgender'. Thereafter, the petitioner was removed from service for utilizing the women's quota for recruitment and failure to disclose her transgender identity. Reading the NALSA case, the High Court opines that only 'MtF' (that is, male to female) transgender persons would be classified as belonging to the 'third gender'. Other transgender persons would have the freedom to opt for identification as man, woman, or a transgender person.[50] Thus, the NALSA case would not bind the petitioner, who, with intersex variations, identified as a woman.[51] The High Court gives its reasoning behind this interpretation: 'If these transsexuals are not treated either as males or females, while applying the laws, since there is no special law recognising the transsexuals as third sex providing them with special rights, the transsexuals will be reduced into mere animals.'[52]

Constructing or assigning transgender identity is no easy task. As Gayatri Reddy's extensive ethnographic study finds, hijra identities are shaped by a range of axes—such as kinship, religion, language, birthplace, and class—and cannot be reduced *simply* to sex/gender (although it remains an important one). She writes that 'viewing hijras solely within the framework of sex/gender difference—as the quintessential "third sex" or "neither man nor woman"—ultimately might be a disservice to the complexity of their lives'.[53] Justice Radhakrishnan cites Serena Nanda's work on hijras in India,[54] which, in Reddy's opinion 'inadvertently reinforces a division between Western dual gender systems and Indian accommodations of gender variation outside this binary framework

---

[50] This is not entirely clear. In the concluding directive, the judgment states: 'The petitioner has liberty to choose a different sexual/gender identity as a third gender in future based on the medical declaration, *if* there is any law put in place recognising FTMs as a third gender.'

[51] The High Court incorrectly categorizes the petitioner as a 'FtM' (female to male) transgender person.

[52] The judgment conflates transsexual persons, transgender persons, and the meaning of 'third gender'.

[53] Gayatri Reddy, *With Respect to Sex: Negotiating Hijra Identity in South India* (Chicago: University of Chicago Press, 2005), 4.

[54] Serena Nanda, *Neither Man nor Woman: The Hijras of India* (Belmont, CA: Wadsworth Publishing Company, 1990).

… hijras in Hyderabad did not always identify themselves as third-sex individuals in opposition to a binary framework'.[55] Instead of positing themselves a 'third' alternative, Reddy argues, hijras adopt cultural symbols of a feminine or masculine–feminine (combination) nature.[56] Quoting Margaret Trawick, Reddy contends that the hijra practices are akin to the 'intentional ambiguity of Indian life'. This liminality of identity is captured when Munira, a hijra, states in the book that 'we are neither men nor women, but at the same time we are both. Hijras are *adha-bic* [half-in-the-middle] people, and that is why we are both feared and respected'.[57]

Reddy also observed *fluid*, multiple identities. She observed 'constant movement and flux' within the *koti* spectrum (there even appeared to be infrequent crossing of the koti/*panti* divide): for instance, Srinivas, a hijra, was previously a zenana, and prior to that, a *siva-sati*.[58] Dual identities—as gay men and kotis—were not uncommon.[59] Thus, members of the transgender community need not have a *singular, stable* identity. Dutta and Roy, ethnographers working in Eastern India, adopt a similar argument, claiming that 'unruly and inconsistent' forms of identification in the koti (including hijra) community may be delegitimized by definitions which perpetuate a consistent model of identity.[60] In 'Decolonizing Transgender', they write:

> statist and developmentalist deployments of the transgender category may generalize linear narratives of transition and stable identification with the 'opposite' gender as defining features of trans identities, and even when they recognize possibilities beyond the gender binary such as

[55] Reddy, *With Respect to Sex,* 32.

[56] Reddy, *With Respect to Sex*, 224. In other words, their *frame* is in a *binary* context, only invoking 'thirdness' in specific contexts.

[57] Reddy, *With Respect to Sex*, 141.

[58] Reddy, *With Respect to Sex*, 208.

[59] The opinion of Justice Sikri in the NALSA case appears to be that gay and lesbian identity and transgender identity in India are separate. See *National Legal Services Authority*, 5 S.C.C. 438 at 501. This is confirmed in the clarification order, described later.

[60] Aniruddha Dutta and Raina Roy, 'Decolonizing Transgender in India: Some Reflections', *Transgender Studies Quarterly* 1, no. 3 (2014): 320–37. This has implications for the interaction of the community with the state and society, such as the difficulties of those with multiple identities facing difficulty with access to healthcare due to expectations of a single identity.

a 'third gender', they tend to delimit and define such categories through a model of stable, consistent, and authentic identification that seeks to clearly distinguish transgender from cisgender and homosexual identities. But South Asian discourses of gender/sexual variance may blur cis-trans or homo-trans distinctions, and community formations may be based also on class/caste position rather than just the singular axis of gender identity.

Derogatory Terminology

The judgment has also been criticized for liberal usage of stereotypical and offensive terms.[61] Semmalar states that definitions and word usages ignore the 'history of colonial, medicalized, oppression' of transpersons.[62] Offensive terms such as 'eunuch' are used, despite written submissions in the case clearly pointing out that it is considered derogatory.[63] Revathi writes in her memoir, 'we transgender activists have been spearheading a long battle to discontinue the use of these derogatory terms ... many of my trans women friends were hurt and distressed by this gross insensitivity'[64]. Semmalar's notes read, 'the judgment ... is problematic and uses transphobic language, pathologizing us, and is so confused and confusing it is difficult to say it represents inclusion or a clever exclusion of us from the mainstream'.[65]

There is no effort made to use gender-neutral pronouns: the binary 'his/her' is used multiple times immediately after an elaborate section on the psychological difficulties associated with growing up as a transgender person.[66]

Determination of Gender Identity

The judgment is unclear about self-determination of gender identity. As Dutta points out, the judgment does not mention the exact method

[61] Semmalar, 'Gender Outlawed'.

[62] Semmalar, 'Gender Outlawed'.

[63] Written submissions by Anand Grover, senior advocate, for the intervener, Laxmi Narayan Tripathi.

[64] Revathi, *A Life in Trans Activism,* loc. 2920 of 2985, Kindle.

[65] Gee Imaan Semmalar, 'Unpacking Solidarities of the Oppressed: Notes on Trans Struggles in India', *Women's Studies Quarterly* 42, no. 3/4 (2014): 286–91.

[66] *National Legal Services Authority*, 5 S.C.C. 438 at 500–1.

for gender determination.[67] Justice Radhakrishnan simply advises the application of the 'psychological test',[68] whereas Justice Sikri states that 'a person has a constitutional right to get the recognition as male or female *after* SRS, which was not only his/her gender characteristic but has become his/her physical form as well (sic)'[69]. While Justice Sikri's test is a downright biological essentialist one, Justice Radhakrishnan's 'psychological' test requires one to fit into rigid psychological notions and has the potential to lead to bureaucratic tangles. Transpersons will have to *prove* their identity, possibly before state-appointed boards. Surveys have revealed that this lack of clarity leads to practical problems, such as multiple, cumbersome procedures for changing identity.[70]

The judgment, by introducing gatekeepers for all purposes, ignores what Susan Stryker calls the 'social power of medicine'. Stryker points out that 'medical practitioners and institutions have the social power to determine what is considered sick or healthy, normal or pathological, sane or insane—and thus, often to transform potentially neutral forms of human difference into unjust and oppressive social hierarchy. This particular operation of medicine's social power has been particularly important in transgender history.'[71] When Justice Sikri writes that recognition as transmen or transwomen is permissible after SRS[72]—contingent on 'advancement in medical science' and permission 'by/in medical ethics'—he ignores this very aspect of the social power of medicine. Such medicalization restricts the freedom of choice and self-determination, leaving it to gatekeepers whose models of gender are usually outdated and based on binary, linear frameworks.[73]

[67] Dutta, 'Contradictory Tendencies.'

[68] Justice Radhakrishnan does cite the self-identification model of Argentina, but makes no further mention of it.

[69] *National Legal Services Authority*, 5 S.C.C. 438 at 501. It appears that this procedure applies, unless one is a member of the distinct Indian community of transgender persons that Justice Sikri refers to.

[70] International Commission of Jurists, '*Unnatural Offences*', 29–32.

[71] Susan Stryker, *Transgender History* (Berkeley: Seal Press, 2008), 42.

[72] Justice Sikri also takes an *ontological* view: to be recognized as a transwoman, in addition to SRS, the person must be of '*predominantly* female orientation'. Dutta and Roy in 'Decolonizing Transgender in India' argue against such an approach.

[73] Dutta, 'Contradictory Tendencies', 232. See also the discussion on the Nangai case above, where the petitioner with intersex variations was wrongly identified as a 'transgender' person.

The joint declaration towards the end only exacerbates the confusion: the second point (extracted earlier) states that the right to decide their 'self-identified' gender is upheld. On the other hand, the Expert Committee Report, which will be discussed subsequently, provides for a specified method of determination of gender identity.

Intersectionality

The judgment also fails to navigate difficult questions of intersectionality. In declaring that transgender persons are to be extended the benefit of reservations under Articles 15(4) and 16(4), the judgment makes no references to the caste of transgender persons, which forms the basis on which reservations are granted. Many transgender persons, who may presently have 'Scheduled Caste' (SC) and 'Scheduled Tribe' (ST) identities, may now be included in the 'Other Backward Class' (OBC) category. Moreover, under Articles 15(4) and 16(4) (read with Article 12), reservations or special provisions may be made by the 'State', and not the judiciary.[74] Ordinarily, the recommendation of the National Commission for Backward Classes, under the National Commission for Backward Classes Act, 1993 governs the fresh inclusion of classes into the list of socially and educationally backward classes. Thus, it is debatable whether the judiciary has the power to issue such directions.

The Clarification Petition

After the delivery of the judgment, the Union of India filed a clarification petition.[75] Although several questions were raised in the written submission, it appears from the Supreme Court order that the only question over which clarification was requested in the oral hearing was the scope of the term 'transgender'—and whether it includes members of the gay, lesbian and bisexual community. The Supreme Court stated that no clarification is needed since paragraphs 107 and 109 of the original judgment are sufficiently clear.[76] Paragraphs 107 and 109

[74] *Ashok Hurra v. Rupa Hurra*, (2002) 4 SCC 388, 399.

[75] 'Application for Clarification/Modification of Judgement and Order dated 15.04.2014 Passed By this Hon'ble Court and to Pass Appropriate Directions on Behalf of Union of India,' http://orinam.net/content/wp-content/uploads/2014/09/NALSA_UOI.pdf.

[76] I.A. No. 4 of 2014 in WP 400 of 2012. Order dated 30 June 2016. The order once again uses the term 'eunuch'.

state that the judgment only deals with distinct classes of transpersons like hijras.

Ministry of Social Justice and Empowerment Expert Committee Report

An Expert Committee was constituted by the Ministry of Social Justice and Empowerment (MSJE) 'to make an in-depth study of the problems being faced by the Transgender community' on 22 October 2013. The committee delivered its report on 27 January 2014.[77] The report defines transpersons as 'all persons whose own sense of gender does not match with the gender assigned to them at birth'. It recommends that transpersons should have 'the choice to declare himself/herself as either man, woman or transgender'. However, it stated that self-declaration would not be sufficient for change of gender assigned at birth. Instead, it recommends certification by a state authority, on the recommendation of a district-level screening committee comprising the district collector or magistrate (head), district social welfare officer, a psychologist, a psychiatrist, a social worker, two members of the transgender community, and such other persons deemed to be appropriate by the government.[78]

The Rights of Transgender Persons Bill, 2014

In December 2014, Tiruchi Siva, a member of Parliament (Rajya Sabha), introduced a Private Member's Bill[79] in the Rajya Sabha aimed towards undoing 'centuries of discrimination' that the transgender community has faced.[80] The bill adopts the definition of 'transgender person' provided by the MSJE committee report. With 'respect for inherent dignity', 'individual autonomy', 'non-discrimination', 'equality of

---

[77] This is the expert committee referred to by the Supreme Court in the NALSA case.

[78] Committee Report, 34, submitted on 27 January 2014, available at: http://socialjustice.nic.in/writereaddata/UploadFile/Binder2.pdf
'Report of the Expert Committee on the Issues relating to Transgender Persons'.. The criticisms presented in the discussion of the NALSA case applies here as well.

[79] Private Member's Bill is a bill introduced by a member of Parliament who is not a minister or a member of the Executive.

[80] The Statement of Objects and Reasons, Rights of Transgender Persons Bill, 2014, Rajya Sabha.

opportunity', 'accessibility', and inclusivity being 'guiding principles',[81] the bill imposes an obligation on the government to enforce constitutional and legal rights of transgender persons.[82]

It also provides for special provisions to protect transgender children.[83] Discrimination in employment is barred and governments are mandated to formulate schemes that facilitate vocational training and self-employment of transgender persons.[84] Chapter V directs the government to formulate social security schemes, healthcare facilities, rehabilitation programmes, and measures for cultural integration and participation of transgender persons. It is also mandated that state-aided educational institutions and government establishments reserve 2 per cent of the seats or posts (as applicable) for transgender persons. Under provisions of Chapter VI, the government is required to conduct and promote awareness and sensitization programmes. The bill also envisages the creation of national and state commissions for transgender persons[85] as well as transgender rights courts.[86]

Member of Parliament Rajeeve Gowda pointed out[87] that the bill does not specify the method or legal procedure by which transgender identity is determined. He also argued that references to transgender children lacks clarity, since children may not gain gender consciousness before a particular age.[88] This also affects provisions pertaining to reservation in primary educational institutions.

[81] The Statement of Objects and Reasons, Rights of Transgender Persons Bill, Section 3.

[82] The Statement of Objects and Reasons, Rights of Transgender Persons Bill, Chapters II and III.

[83] The Statement of Objects and Reasons, Rights of Transgender Persons Bill, Section 5, 11.

[84] The Statement of Objects and Reasons, Rights of Transgender Persons Bill, Chapter IV.

[85] The Statement of Objects and Reasons, Rights of Transgender Persons Bill, Chapter VII.

[86] The Statement of Objects and Reasons, Rights of Transgender Persons Bill, Chapter VIII.

[87] Rajya Sabha Debates, 13 March 2015, http://orinam.net/content/wp-content/uploads/2015/04/16.00pmTo17.00pm.pdf.

[88] See however, Kristina R. Olson, Aidan C. Key, and Nicholas R. Eaton, 'Gender Cognition in Transgender Children', *Psychological Science* 26, no. 4 (2015): 467–74 (study finding that children in the age group 5–12 years report a deep-seated and clear gender identity and are not 'confused'). See also Kristina

The bill was passed by the Rajya Sabha on 24 April 2015. It was the first private member's bill passed by the Rajya Sabha in over 45 years. However, the debates indicate that the bill was expected to be withdrawn after debate (as is the convention with private member's bills).[89] After Tiruchi Siva insisted that the bill be passed, the Leader of the House (Arun Jaitley) proposed that that either one could wait for a government bill to be introduced (as promised) or the private member's bill could be approved, albeit only to 'express a sentiment', like a resolution. Siva pressed for the latter option, and the bill was adopted.[90] It was widely hailed.[91]

The Rights of Transgender Persons Bill, 2015

The Ministry of Social Justice and Empowerment released a draft of the 'Rights of Transgender Persons Bill, 2015' on 3 December 2015, for public comments. The definition of 'transgender person' adopted by the bill is akin to the one adopted by the 2014 bill. It also clarifies that transgender persons must have the option to choose their preferred identity—man, woman, or transgender—independent of reference to surgery or hormones. Chapter II, dealing with transgender identity, reproduces the recommendations of the MSJE committee regarding the method of certifying identity.[92]

The rest of the bill reproduces most sections of the 2014 bill.[93] Notably, there are three major omissions: one, the provisions pertaining to *separate* (2 per cent) reservations;[94] two, the provisions pertaining to the institution of national and state-level commissions as well as the special courts; and three, the provisions relating to penalties for

R. Olson, 'Prepubescent Transgender Children: What We Do and Do Not Know', *J Am Acad. Child. Adolesc. Psychiatry* 55, no. 3 (March 2016): 155–6.

[89] Rajya Sabha Debates, 24 April 2015, http://164.100.47.5/newdebate/235/24042015/Fullday.pdf.

[90] The bill has been passed only in the Rajya Sabha, and not in the Lok Sabha.

[91] Meera Srinivasan, 'Turning Point in Transgender Rights', *Hindu,* 25 April 2015.

[92] A number of other provisions are (mostly out of context) verbatim reproductions of paragraphs from the Expert Committee report.

[93] Many criticisms delineated here are also applicable to the Tiruchi Siva Bill.

[94] It does however state that transgender persons *not* belonging to SC/ST class may be provided reservations under the OBC category (Section 23).

non-compliance with obligations. It is no surprise that many collectives and activists have opposed this exclusion.

Alongside these exclusions, the procedure for determination of identity has also been criticized. For *all* purposes, the bill mandates the procedure recommended by the MSJE committee report. There appears to be no reason why self-identification through notarized affidavits is insufficient for passports, licences, and the like, whilst *not* claiming any state benefits (such as reservations).[95] The bill also does not include intersex persons,[96] who face similar discrimination and stigma, but may not necessarily identify as transgender persons (that is, they may identify with the gender assigned at birth).[97]

Beyond the basic declaration of rights, the bill does not make changes or remedy the existing situation in civil and criminal laws.[98] Family laws, relating to marriage, adoption, inheritance, and so on, which are based

[95] See 'Response to MSJE's Rights of Transgender Persons Bill, 2015', Sampoorna Working Group, 5 January 2016, http://sampoornawg.wixsite.com/sampoorna/single-post/2016/1/4/SPWG-Response-to-MSJETG-Bill-2016.

[96] See UN High Commissioner for Human Rights: Intersex Factsheet 2015: 'Intersex people are born with sex characteristics (including genitals, gonads and chromosome patterns) that do not fit typical binary notions of male or female bodies... Because their bodies are seen as different, intersex children and adults are often stigmatized and subjected to multiple human rights violations'. The NALSA case and the subsequent legal developments are guilty of largely ignoring the concerns of intersex persons.

[97] See 'Telangana Hijra Intersex Transgender Samiti responds to MSJE Transgender Rights bill (2015)', 18 January 2016, http://orinam.net/telangana-samiti-response-msje-trans-rights-bill/.

[98] In the *Nangai case,* the existing situation is discussed: The Hindu Minority and Guardianship Act, 1956, while defining the terms 'natural guardian of a Hindu minor' states that in the case of a boy or an unmarried girl the father, and after him, the mother and in the case of an illegitimate boy or an illegitimate unmarried girl, the mother, and after her, the father and in the case of a married girl, the husband, is the natural guardian. Here also, the terms 'boy' and 'girl' have not been defined ... The Right of Children to Free and Compulsory Education Act, 2009 also defines a child to mean, a male or female child of the age of 6 to 14 years. This Act has also not defined as to who is a male or who is a female. [...] The Indian Penal Code 1860 deals with 'Gender' which states that the pronoun 'he' and its derivatives are used of any person, whether male and female (vide Section 8). Section 10 states the word 'man' denotes a male human being of any age and the word 'woman' denotes a female human being of any age. But, these terms 'male' or 'female' have not been defined in the Code.

only on binary notions of gender, are left untouched.[99] Provisions of criminal law, such as those pertaining to special protections to women, (for example, bar on arrest after sunset[100]) have not been extended to transgender persons. Well-reported problems such as that of police atrocities[101] have not been dealt with, except for an ambiguous clause that simply reads: 'Criminal and disciplinary action against delinquent police official in cases of violation of human rights of Transgender Persons'.

The bill also skips pressing questions of civil rights, such as bathroom access.[102] Associated questions of horizontal claims are omitted. Some obligations have been cast on (only) educational institutions—such as that of non-discrimination and reasonable accommodation—but with no mention of the consequences of non-compliance. Although the bill provides broad definitions of terms such as 'Public Building' ('a building, irrespective of ownership, which is used and accessed by the public at large'), the term is not used elsewhere. There is no mention of Section 377 of the Indian Penal Code (or limitation of application to non-consensual intercourse), or the misuse of laws such as the Immoral Traffic (Prevention) Act, 1956.[103]

[99] For illustrations, see *Nangai v. Superintendent of Police* 4 MLJ 12. For an overview, see Dipayan Chowdhury and Atmaja Tripathy, 'Recognizing the Right of the Third Gender to Marriage and Inheritance under Hindu Personal Law in India', *BRICS Law Journal* 3, no. 3 (2016): 43–60.

[100] Code of Criminal Procedure, 1973, Section 46(4).

[101] See *Human Rights Violations against Sexuality Minorities in India: A PUCL-K Fact-Finding Report about Bangalore,* February 2001, Karnataka: PUCL. ('In the testimonies we heard, oppression by the police turned out to be one of the major concerns of the gay, bisexual and transgender people.'), available at: http://www.pucl.org/Topics/Gender/2003/sexual-minorities.pdf. According to International Commission of Jurists, *'Unnatural Offences',* 3: 'the police, who should enforce the law in a non-arbitrary and non-discriminatory manner and protect the human rights of everyone, including queer persons, operate instead on the basis of stereotypes and prejudice, and often commit human rights violations against them.'

[102] Diana Elkind, 'The Constitutional Implications of Bathroom Access Based on Gender Identity: An Examination of Recent Developments Paving the Way for the Next Frontier of Equal Protection', *University of Pennsylvania Journal of Constitutional Law* 9 (2007): 895. See 'International Commission of Jurists',, *Unnatural Offences*, 8.

[103] Section 268 of the Indian Penal Code (public nuisance) is another provision used to target transgender persons.

The Transgender Persons (Protection of Rights Bill), 2016

After comments were solicited on the 2015 bill, the Cabinet reviewed it and introduced a fresh bill—the Transgender Persons (Protection of Rights Bill), 2016, in the Lok Sabha. The Statement of Objects and Reasons reads: 'Transgender community is one of the most marginalized communities in the country because *they do not fit into the general categories of gender of "male" or "female"*.... The Hon'ble Supreme Court [...] directed the Central Government and State Governments to take various steps for the welfare of transgender community and to *treat them as a third gender.*'[104] The statement clearly perpetuates misconceptions about gender identity. It ought to be no surprise that the text of the bill itself promotes stereotypical views.

The definition of the term 'transgender person' is most contentious. Section 2(i) defines transgender person as a person who is (a) neither wholly female nor wholly male; or (b) a combination of female or male; or (c) neither female nor male; *and* whose sense of gender does not match with the gender assigned to that person at the time of birth, and includes transmen and transwomen, persons with intersex variations, and gender-queers.'[105]

As Semmalar writes, the view of the Cabinet reflects 'the popular culture narrative of transpeople as phantasmagoric beings who are half man-half woman, or neither male/female.'[106] The definition appears to be a half-baked attempt to include intersex concerns in the transgender bill. It prima facie conveys a stereotypical and biological view of gender identity, with no option to identify as 'man' or 'woman' for transgender persons.

The bill provides for a 'district screening committee'—comprising the chief medical officer, district social welfare officer, a psychologist or psychiatrist, a representative of the transgender community, and an officer of the 'appropriate Government' to be nominated by that government—to consider applications for issuance of identity certificates.[107] Trans and intersex collectives have rightly questioned the need to medicalize the determination of identity by including a medical officer.[108]

[104] Emphasis mine.
[105] Emphasis mine.
[106] Gee Imaan Semmalar, 'Is this the Transgender Persons "Prohibition of Rights" Bill, 2016?' *Dalit Camera*, 4 August 2016.
[107] Transgender Persons (Protection of Rights Bill), Section 5, 6, and 7.
[108] 'Transgender Persons (Protection of Rights Bill), 2016: Responses from Trans and Intersex Communities', http://orinam.net/content/wp-content/

While obligations including that of non-discrimination have been cast on 'establishments' (whose definition extends to firms, agencies, institutions, and the like), only those establishments with a hundred or more workers are mandated to set up a grievance redressal mechanism.[109] This provision—like many labour laws—would therefore exclude vast swathes of the unorganized sector, denying many transpersons the benefit of this protection.

The 2016 bill removes the (albeit ambiguous) directions in the 2015 bill to criminalize police harassment and to amend the Penal Code to incorporate cases of sexual assault on transpersons. Provisions pertaining to reservations have also been excluded. There is no mention of gender-nonconforming children or transgender children either.

Many trans collectives have pointed out that the bill fails to understand the everyday realities of transpersons' lives.[110] For instance, the bill imposes a criminal punishment on those who 'force or entice' a transperson into begging or 'other similar forms of forced or bonded labour'. Such provisions effectively club begging with forced labour and criminalizes one among the few means of livelihood for transpersons.[111] Other statutes, such as the Bombay Prevention of Begging Act, 1959[112] (extended to Delhi) provide vague definitions of begging, such as 'having no visible means of subsistence and wandering, about or remaining in any public place in such condition or manner, as makes it likely that the

---

uploads/2016/08/Community-Response-to-TG-Bill-20161212pm_Monday_Aug81.pdf.

[109] Transgender Persons (Protection of Rights Bill), Section 12.

[110] 'LBT and ally groups write to Standing Committee on Trans Bill 2016', *Orinam* (blog), 12 November 2016.

[111] UNAIDS Consultation with Transgender Hijra Community and Experts, 'Charter of Demands: Revision on Transgender Bill 2016 introduced by Social Welfare Ministry India, 4 November 2016, New Delhi', available at: http://orinam.net/content/wp-content/uploads/2016/08/Charter-of-Demands-_UNAIDS_consult_TGBill_2016.pdf. See also Nanda, *Neither Man nor Woman,* 50 ('traditional and public occupation of hijras [is] that of asking for alms … begging can be a steady source of income'). Historical evidence suggests that the pre-colonial Indian states such as the Maratha State had granted hijras a *right* to beg, before it was discontinued by the colonial British government. Preston, 'A Right to Exist'.

[112] Other statutes such as the Karnataka Prevention of Beggary Act, 1975 provide similar definitions.

person doing so exist soliciting or receiving alms'.[113] Usha Ramanathan has rightly labelled this the criminalization of 'ostensible poverty'.[114]

The bill also states that one may be separated from one's natal family only by an order of the court, and that such persons outside the care of the natal family shall be 'placed' in a rehabilitation centre.[115] The natal family is often a site of violence, abuse, and patriarchy, where one is expected to conform to the gender assigned at birth.[116] Thus, many transgender children escape from home, to join hijra families, Jamaats, or dormitories, where 'the hijra elders [are] their adoptive parents, [and] the hijra community, their family and friends'.[117] Reddy even suggests that putting a *rit* (a ritual) in a hijra house and the *guru-cela*[118] (teacher–disciple) bond are among the *key* markers of hijra identity.[119] Analysing hijra families, Reddy adds that the hijra understanding of family is based on 'a notion of caring, indexed principally through a temporal and spatial) dimension of "being there" rather than biogenetic connections (through "blood" and marriage)'.[120] Indeed, consistent with their ascetic culture, one is expected to renounce ties with natal families.

While not recognizing such adoptive families, the bill instead chooses to 'place' transgender persons in rehabilitation centres (by order of a

---

[113]   Bombay Prevention of Begging Act, 1959, S. 2(1)(i).

[114]   Usha Ramanathan, 'Ostensible Poverty, Beggary and the Law', *Economic and Political Weekly* 43, no. 44 (2008): 33.

[115]   Transgender Persons (Protection of Rights Bill), Section 13.

[116]   Nanda, *Neither Man nor Woman,* 116–8 ('most hijras join the community in their youth … because of ill treatment by parents and peers for feminine behaviour [which] does not allow them to engage in cross-gender behaviour'). Nanda does however note that the decision to leave the natal home is marked by ambivalence.

[117]   'The Transgender Persons (Protection of Rights) Bill, 2016: Responses from the Trans & Intersex Communities', Round Table India, 8 August 2016. The issue of non-recognition of the system of family among hijras is not new. Preston's study finds that while grants of rent-free lands from the Maratha state was inherited by generations of hijras from master (guru) to disciple (*chela*), the British government refused to recognize this mode of succession. Thus, much of the granted land was escheated to the state upon the death of the immediate holder. Preston, 'A Right to Exist'.

[118]   A guru–chela bond is the 'primary axis of kinship and genealogical descent' in a hijra family. See Reddy, *With Respect to Sex,* 157.

[119]   Reddy, *With Respect to Sex,* 142–85.

[120]   Reddy, *With Respect to Sex,* 151.

court). The practice of sending the impoverished to such 'rehabilitation centres' in India has a notorious history. In Bangalore, for instance, in late 2014 'more than 200' transgender persons were 'arrested' by the police in a single day and sent to the 'beggars' colony', a rehabilitation centre under the Karnataka Prevention of Beggary Act, 1975.[121] The conditions at the beggars' colony is such that in 2010, more than a dozen 'inmates' died, and 200 fled from the colony.[122] This provision appears to be a manifestation of prejudice towards the transgender community and an attempt to exclude them and make them invisible.

Like the 2015 bill, the 2016 bill also does not revisit family laws and criminal laws. Provisions pertaining to reasonable accommodation have been removed. Non-discrimination obligations (without definitions) have been imposed on all persons, but with no mention of the consequences of non-compliance. A bureaucratic set-up in the form of the 'National Council for Transgender Persons' has been instituted, with only advisory functions.

***

In this chapter, I have surveyed major legal developments on transgender rights in India, beginning from the NALSA case to the 2016 bill.[123] My study has been limited in a sense that it does not extensively survey developments in states as well as in the private sector. For instance, despotic laws such as Section 36A of the Karnataka Police Act ('power

[121] Bangalore Mirror Bureau, 'Transgenders Sent to Beggars' Colony by Cops', *Bangalore Mirror*, 26 November 2014.

[122] 'Eight More Deaths in Beggars' Colony', *Deccan Herald*, 19 August 2010; Santosh Kumar R.B., 'Bangalore Beggar Deaths: Commotion at the Colony, 200 Inmates Flee', *Daily News and Analysis*, 20 August 2010.

[123] After a draft of this chapter was completed, the Standing Committee on Social Justice and Empowerment released its report on the 2016 bill (43rd report). The report repeatedly uses the term 'eunuch' and reaffirms the proposal to have gatekeepers (including medical officers) for the recognition of identity. It also appears to sanction a model where recognition as 'transgender' would not require any gender confirmation surgeries, but those who wish to identify within the binary (man/woman) would have to undergo such surgeries. The report has some notable recommendations, in that it seeks to revise the definition of the term 'transgender', expand the scope of the anti-discrimination clause to include state discrimination, and push for the recognition of civil rights of transgender persons.

to regulate eunuchs') continue to be on the statute books despite the NALSA case. However, Kerala has framed policy measures[124] to alleviate the historic stigma and discrimination against transgender persons and Orissa has introduced measures aimed at members of the transgender community.[125] There have been many firsts as well: the appointment of a transgender person as a police official (sub-inspector in Tamil Nadu),[126] and the opening of a transgender school (in Kerala)[127].

At the more central level—which has been the focus of this review—progress, one may conclude, has been a mixed bag. The incoherence of the NALSA judgment only foreshadowed future legal developments, which followed a similar pattern, of confusion and vacillation. First, there has been repeated failure to understand or recognize transgender identity. Attempts in the NALSA case and the subsequent bills are marked by issues such as imposition of the third gender and flawed definitions based in biological essentialist understandings. Second, there is a continued emphasis on gatekeepers for granting one's preferred identity. These prescribed gatekeepers also belong to the medical profession, ignoring the historical social power of medicine and the real possibility of medicalization of transgender issues. Third, legal action thus far has failed to appreciate the lived realities and experiences of the lives of transgender persons in India: for instance, traditional means of livelihood such as begging and the unique hijra system of family may be under threat if the 2016 bill is enacted. Similarly, a history of police brutality barely finds a mention. Fourth, civil and criminal laws based on binary notions of gender have not been corrected; and issues of fundamental rights such as non-discrimination, sexual autonomy, and right to health and education have not been pursued forcefully. Thus, while the delivery of judgment did appear to be a 'ray of hope', a closely scrutiny of the case and future development leads one to temper one's conclusions.

[124] State Policy for Transgenders in Kerala, 2015.

[125] 'Odisha becomes first state to give social welfare benefits to transgender community', *Economic Times*, 2 June 2016.

[126] *Pritika Yashini v. Chairman, Tamil Nadu Uniform Services Recruitment Board,* WP 15046 of 2015 (Madras High Court), judgment dated 3 November 2015.

[127] Kiran Gangadharan, 'India's first transgender school opens in Kerala', *Indian Express*, 30 December 2016.

12

Disability, Exclusions, and Resistance*

An Indian Context

Anita Ghai

The study of disability has been a major preoccupation of the last three decades of my life. I will make an attempt here to present disability as an epistemic category, which interrogates normalization, stigma, subjugated subjectivity, difference, deficit, and the disabled body. Disability, like questions of race, gender, caste, and class, is one of the most provocative topics among scholars who have an interest in marginality. Very few people accept the fact that disability is as much a social construct as other categories such as gender. In short, disability is conceived as a naturalized category. Society thus exhibits a structural amnesia about a particular category of people, who, because they do not fit into the hegemonic discourse of 'normality', are excluded, separated, and socially disempowered. This social and cultural apartheid is sustained by the existence of a built environment, which lacks amenities for the disabled and solely caters to the needs of the more complete and able-bodied 'Other'.

---

* Some sections of the present chapter has been drawn from my book *Rethinking Disability in India*. Routledge, 2015.

This social disregard coupled with experiences of social, economic, and political subjugation deny the disabled a voice, a space, and even power, to disrupt these deeply entrenched normative ideals that deprive them their social presence and any semblance of identity. Disabled people, especially women, are encouraged to be childlike and apologetic towards the able-bodied society, which judges them as the beings that would have been better dead than alive. To survive as a disabled person in such a blinkered social environment has meant coming to terms with unequal power relationships. This is reflected most clearly by an absence and invisibility in the most forward-looking social movements and dialogues in India, including the women's movement. Such disregard results in an ignoring of pertinent issues with regard to disability from the point of view of both active social struggle as well as contemporary academic discourse. Unfortunately, such incipient stigmatization against those who carry the insidious label of 'disability' results in an exclusion that creates both a sense of despair and distress, often leading to a suppression and non-recognition of the 'lack' that marks them initially as different.

As I grew up, I came to a painful and disillusioning realization that women in general occupy a multifarious and marginalized position in Indian society, based on their sociocultural identities that separate them into categories constructed according to such properties as caste, class, and residential position. Perhaps it is reflective of such socialization that, despite an attack of polio at the age of two, for over three decades, I refused to recognize my own limitations caused by my disability. With a body that was/is socially stigmatized as 'the Other' and labelled as disabled, my dilemma, like that of others like me, had been about whether to situate myself as a 'positive mind' or a 'negative body' in a largely unfriendly social environment. It was not till I was in my early thirties that a certain objectivity entered my world view and I began questioning my condition and that of others like me and the social responses to it. Exhibiting, I believe, a severe form of denial, I initially refused to acknowledge the processes which labelled me as disabled and sought to stamp me with a definite identity. Though conscious of the public eye and the confusion which would often result as I transgressed many of the limits that society imposed on my 'kind', I continued to be an active, independent, and mobile individual, unlike the expected social norm. However, neither my consciousness nor my self-proclaimed standing as a feminist gave me the courage to carry the basic assertion of the personal being political over to my disabled existence. However, women's movements, and feminist theory and practice in India continued to ignore the experiential realities of discrimination, ignorance, and neglect of women with disabilities. Consequently, the construction of disabled women remained outside the hegemony of patriarchy and normalcy.

Further, the rise of neoliberal states deepened the already severe oppression and exclusion on the basis of bodily ability and gender. However, women who can have plural identity markers find their daily experience perplexing and difficult. Despite the assumption of universal sisterhood, life is not easy for disabled women. Within India, the fact that the incidence of disability is intersected (or influenced) by gender has been realized in work by Das and Agnihotri,[1] Ghai,[2] and Hans and Patri.[3] The extrapolation of the available statistics have indicated that disabled women are marginalized much more than disabled men. Though the new bill was passed by the parliament in 2016 the image of women with disabilities is still problematic. While Indian cultural reality has never been favourable to the birth of daughters (as is clear by the consistent fall in the gender ratio), the onset of disability in a daughter is a fate worse than death. While women are fighting hard for equal rights in a patriarchal order, disabled women are rarely recognized as persons. The society that accepts the able-bodied norm subjects disabled girls and women to the most inhumane treatment possible. Thus, right from childhood, disability imposes a subordinate status on them, and increases the likelihood that their rights will be ignored. Women with disabilities also face discrimination at the hands of the feminist world which, as a frame to understand women's lives and position in society, has not benefited disabled women. The intermingling of disablement and gender marks the reality of a woman with disability in India. Opportunities for improving the quality of life of a disabled girl are virtually non-existent. Already living a life of subordination without education and employment, women can do without the burden of disability. As a mother lamented, 'Wasn't it enough that we have a hand-to-mouth existence? Why did God have to punish us further by giving a *Langri* (crippled) daughter?'[4] In a culture

---

[1] D. Das and S.B. Agnihotri, 'Physical Disability—Is There a Gender Dimension', *Economic and Political Weekly* 33, no. 52 (1998).

[2] Anita Ghai, *Rethinking Disability in India* (New Delhi: Routledge, 2015).

[3] Asha Hans and Annie Patri, eds., *Women, Disability and Identity* (New Delhi: SAGE, 2003).

[4] Anita Ghai, 'Marginalisation and Disability: Experiences from the Third World', in *Disability and the Life Course: Global perspectives*, ed. M. Priestley (Cambridge: Cambridge University Press, 2001), 31.

where being a daughter is considered a curse, being a disabled daughter is a fate worse than death for she has to contend with both her role as a daughter, when what was desired was a son, and with her disability. The desire for sons has to be understood in the context of the ritual value of sons as well as the social and economic burden in bringing up daughters.[5] The construction of daughter as a burden is rooted in the cultural milieu that looks at daughters as *parai* (Other). However, the implicit understanding in this practice is that whatever you are giving will be perfect. The prospective son-in-law, when offered a disabled girl, has to be compensated accordingly. If compensation is not possible, then compromises like being married to a widower have to be made. Disability in a son, on the other hand, though traumatic, will still be more acceptable as he does not have to be given away. Consequently, in a culture in which arranged marriages are the rule, disabled women are put in a difficult position. While there is a possibility of resistance (however difficult) to this cultural arrangement for the 'normal' women, for disabled girls, it is an uphill task. Some disabled girls in the rich or middle class might be able to negotiate the difficulties inherent in arranged marriages, albeit with a great deal of compromise. Disabled sons retain the possibility of marriage, as they are not gifts but the receivers of gifts. Disabled as well as non-disabled men seek 'normal' women as wives, and therefore participate in the devaluing of people because of disability. For instance, systems of inequality based on caste, race, ethnicity, and gender seem to rely on dichotomies, such as 'Us' versus 'Them', 'Self' versus 'Other'. All binaries in psychological parlance operate in the same way as splitting and projection. Thus, the centre expels its anxieties, ambiguities, and irrationalities onto the inferior term, filling it with the converse of its own identity. The other, in its very strangeness, simply mirrors and represents what is deeply familiar to the centre, but projected outside of itself. It is this process of marginality that produces resentment, enmity, and repugnance for the one who is sensed as the Other. Framing the argument in this form mandates a justification for inclusion of disability in the categorization discourse. However, disability provokes fears and anxieties about 'able body' mortality, and very easily renders itself as the 'Other'. This process of alterity needs to be understood to comprehend the experience of exclusion. 'Alterity' is a term that has been often used

[5] R. Johri, 'Cultural Conceptions of Maternal Attachment: The Case of the Girl Child' (unpublished PhD dissertation., Department of Psychology, University of Delhi, 1999), 78.

to signify 'Otherness'. The 'Other' in the work of Michel Foucault, for instance, consists of those who are excluded from positions of power, and who are often victimized within a predominantly liberal humanist view of the subject.[6] The Other is not simply a description of simple individual differences but refers to the regulated construction of classes of people. Alterity leads to the creation of prejudice and stigma. Initially, the attempt is to construct some group as Other and less than fully human. The next step involves projecting onto it those 'disabled' qualities we reject, fear, or disown in ourselves. It is not difficult to pinpoint ideologies that permit us to think of ourselves as 'normal', good, or worthy, and to think of others we perceive to be not like us in some way—physically, mentally, educationally—as disabled, and therefore not normal, not good, or not worthy. Then we assign qualities to variable human individuals based on their inclusion in this constructed alterity.

The preference for a son in the larger Hindu community in India, in keeping with its religious philosophy, has now been coupled with technology that can provide a test to screen and determine the gender of an unborn foetus. In a society where there is widespread female abortion, aborting imperfect children will not cause any stir or rancour. While there is an ongoing discussion of the ethical contradictions that prenatal gender testing poses for feminists, prenatal testing to identify and abort children at risk for disabilities does not get addressed.[7] Consequently, the much-needed political action has not been forthcoming. The resistance offered by disabled women has only led to a superficial acknowledgment of differences, with an implicit assumption that the core issue is gender. The perceived need is, therefore, to raise the gender issues presumably adequately enough to address all women's lives regardless of their backgrounds and differences. At least this recognition is responsible for the emergence of a discourse about difference; but I cannot ignore the reality that this discourse has not been able to effect much, if any, change—either in increasing acceptance of disabled women's concerns in social policy or in enhancing the quality of their lives. A great deal of thoughtful work by Indian feminists analyses the impact of the evaluative male gaze. However, the essential differences between being sexual objects and objects of the 'stare' have not been understood. If the male

---

[6] S. Stuart, *The Routledge Critical Dictionary of Postmodern Thought* (New York: Routledge, 1999).

[7] Anita Ghai, *(Dis)Embodied Form: Issues of Disabled Women* (2003; New Delhi: Shakti Books, 2006), 69.

gaze makes normal women feel like passive objects, the stare turns the disabled object into a grotesque sight. Disabled women contend not only with how men look at women but also with how an entire society stares at disabled people, stripping them of any semblance of resistance. This brings a throbbing pain in me when I realize that to remove stigma is next to impossible. When Hooks says, 'Ain't I a Woman?', I too want to say the same. Why is it that people do not understand the difference.' A few years back, I went to see the marble sculpture of Alison in Trafalgar Square. My first reaction was that it was a wonderful example from the life of the disabled artist Alison Lapper. Apparently, the sculptor Marc Quinn wanted to introduce some femininity into the square. The adjacent Nelson's Column seemed to be the epitome of a phallic monument. A significant statement, which was entitled, 'Alison Lapper Pregnant', could be appreciated. Nelson, who was 'crippled and blind', is thought of as a 'war hero'; his disability doesn't enclose him and pity is not aroused. A review told me that the able-bodied artist, Marc Quinn, said that 'the sculpture makes the ultimate statement about disability—that it can be as beautiful and valid a form of being as any other.' My contention is that indeed 'disability' as a social category is problematic, though beautiful but extremely complex. The statue not only personified courage and bravery, but it also signifies sexuality and maternity. I discovered that Alison Lapper is an artist in her own right, who has created an inspirational series of photographic self-portraits with her child. The statue in a way is a portrait of resistance. This sculpture seems to transgress normative ideals, yet it reminded me of the 'damaged' part. In a way, the representation of a disabled body is opposition to ideas of beauty. In society in India, any aberration from a normally accepted archetype is seen as a marked deviation; the impaired body becomes a symbol of imperfection. As Niranjana points out, 'focus on the body has been a symbolic one where the body is perceived as a sign or code important to the extent that it is speaking about a social reality other than itself.'[8] Suggestive as it may be to speak of the body as representing encoded social meanings, as an image of society, or even a metaphor for society, the question remains whether these perspectives can acknowledge the materiality of bodies, not merely as they are formed/represented in a culture, but how they constitute the lived reality of persons. Though

---

[8] Seemanthini Niranjana, 'Femininity, Space and the Female Body: Anthropological Perspective', in *Embodiment: Essays on Gender and Identity*, ed. M. Thapan (New Delhi: Oxford University Press, 1997).

this analysis takes up issues of cultural spaces and the female body, there is no mention of the disabled body. This omission reflects a historical practice that continues to render the disabled invisible in a manner very similar to the invisibility experienced by blacks in a white racist society. It is ironic that feminists engaged with the issue of difference, united in their attempts to empower the powerless and resolved to transform social inequalities, have not picked up on the issues concerning the meaning of impairment for disabled women. While the disability movement's failure to acknowledge disabled women can be fathomed as reflecting the patriarchal character of a society it accepts and aims to be included in, at least within India, its disregard by the feminist movement, which claims objectivity through its theoretical deconstruction of oppressive social suppositions, is less understandable. What is especially anguishing is that Indian feminist thought fails to recognize that the problematization of women's issues applies equally to disabled women's issues. I feel like a victim … such writings do not empower me. We have to find a way of making our experiences visible, sharing them with each other, and with non-disabled people, in a way that—while drawing attention to the difficulties in our lives—does not undermine our wish to assert our self-worth. The double disadvantage hypothesis therefore fails to produce concrete action as the outcome of the feminist discourse, and practice does not move beyond tokenism and rhetoric. This reflects what Harlan Hahn[9] (Thomson 1997, 25) calls 'asexual objectification', and also evidences the disregard of the dangers of sexual violation to which disabled girls are exposed. The assumption that sexuality and disability are mutually exclusive also denies that people with deviant bodies experience sexual desires and refuses them recognition as sexually typical despite their differences. Indian feminist scholarship has looked at embodiment along the axes of caste, class, and historical phases such as the impact of colonization; however, the impaired body has not been considered as having analytical consequence.

Here, I submit two examples. One matter that, though within the ambit of feminist thought, seems different from a disability perspective is the issue of caring for the mothers of disabled children in India. As I elaborate, 'although the stress of impairment impacts upon both the

[9] H. Hahn, 'Public Support for Rehabilitation Programmes: The Analysis of U.S. Disability Policy', *Disability, Handicap & Society* 1, no. 2: 121–37. Thomson, R.G. (1997). *Extraordinary Bodies: Figuring Physical disability in American Culture and Literature*. New York: Columbia University Press.

parents, it is usually the mother who bears the brunt of the child's disability'.[10] Instances abound where women have been divorced, abandoned, or tortured because they have given birth to a disabled child. Given the preference for sons, even here, the mother is blamed more severely in instances of a girl child. The fantasy of maternal omnipotence holds mothers responsible for providing the caring. Home care is usually the only option; there is often no question of choice. Indian feminists who have debated over the ethics of caring, and who are now in the process of initiating a debate over equality in caring,[11] have not taken note of the conditions in which disabled people, and especially girls, are placed. Within the traditional Indian system, the mother has been a source of succour for the children, especially for girls with disabilities.[12] In the absence of social and community support, disabled women have relied largely on the care provided by mothers, who undoubtedly have carried the extra burden. While it is perfectly justified to engage with their experiences of oppression in caring, the attempt to destabilize traditional notions in the absence of adequate alternative provisions might end up working against disabled women. Care is often demonized and represented as disabled women's experience of the simultaneity of sexism and disablism, which creates barriers to equal participation. I recall Julia Twigg's work on older people's experiences of being given a bath. What she says is illuminating: 'One person, strong and able, stands above and over another who is frail and physically vulnerable, forced to rely on their strength and goodwill. Being naked in the face of someone who is not, contains a powerful dynamic of domination and vulnerability, and it is often used in situations of interrogation and torture as a means of subjugating the individual.'[13] Thus, both the women who are caretakers of disabled daughters as well as disabled women need to be interrogated. In such a context, it will be worthwhile to engage with the cautionary note given by Anita Silvers that 'far from vanquishing the patriarchal

[10] Anita Ghai, 'Towards Understanding Disability', *Psychological Studies* 45 (2000): 47.

[11] Bhargavi Davar, 'From Mental Illness to Disability: Choices for Women Users/ Survivors of Psychiatry in Self and Identity Constructions', *Indian Journal of Gender Studies* 15, no. 2 (2008): 261–90.

[12] Ghai, 'Marginalisation and Disability', 21.

[13] Julia Twigg, *Bathing: The Body and Community Care* (London: Routledge, 2000), 21.

system, substituting the ethics of caring for ethics of equality threatens an even more oppressive paternalism.[14]

Sexuality

The portrayal of disability issues is exemplified in Reena22, a 24-year-old woman with mobility impairment, who could not have intercourse with her husband of five days. The husband was feeling frustrated with each passing day and was already lamenting as to why he had married a disabled girl. He forced her to go to the doctor and ask the gynaecologist as to why she was not able to give him satisfaction. The gynaecologist took one look at her. Without checking her internally, she made the following comment, 'Oh dear, polio does this to people. You should not have got married. Poor man! Anyway, I will write a lubricant for you. Let us pray that you are able to satisfy him, but do not hope too much.' The example is indicative of unsettling moments, as there is an interplay of disquieting assumptions that seem to be framing the young woman's experience. One such assumption is very easily discernible, since it is the wife who is in the medical room. Thus, there is a clear demonstration of patriarchy as the husband is pretty sure that the fault could not lie with him. The doctor, even though she is a woman, seems to participate in this view. Further she believes that a woman's role in sex is to provide satisfaction to the male partner. However, these observations have been made on innumerable occasions within the feminist discourse.

What is more significant for me is another source of fear, which is validated by the gynaecologist, that Reena's disability might have been responsible for her inability to participate in satisfying sexual relations. What is remarkable is that the doctor, even before suggesting a way out, is echoing and reflecting the society, which has always nurtured deep prejudices about the lives of disabled individuals. Another example is that of sexuality for disabled people in India. It has been a rather well-documented fact that, within the normative society, there has been a conspiracy of silence about the sexuality of disabled people, and it is not rated as being a high-priority issue even amongst those who are active advocates of the cause of disability. While the last two decades or so have been instrumental in bringing change in the form of equal opportunities

---

[14] Anita Silvers, 'Reconciling Equality to Difference: Caring (f)or Justice for People with Disabilities', *Hypatia* 10, no. 1 (1995): 30–5.

acts, the discourse still continues to be framed in medicalized and human rights terms. The reasons for this neglect could be a general invisibility of disabled people in environments that have structural amnesia and have innumerable communication barriers. The fact that the picture has not been very different in the west is evident from a volume dedicated to disability and sexuality in which Russell Shuttleworth, (2007, p. 2) comments that, historically, the disability rights movement has focused its energy on issues more amenable to social change, such as access to the built environment, education, and employment.[15] By virtually ignoring the sexual issues relevant to disabled people, the disability rights movement thus reinforced the individualized and medicalized view of disability and sexuality that held sway. The myth of the beautiful/athletic/perfect body defines the impaired body as unacceptable and undesirable. The roots of such thinking are found in Indian mythological instances, where Lakshmana, brother of Lord Rama, cuts off Shurpanakha's nose, when she is attracted to him. That this is the only way in which Lakshmana can respond to what he defines as non-acceptable behaviour—by disfiguring the ugly female monster—indicates how disfiguration and, by extrapolation, disability and de-sexing are equated in the Indian psyche. Consequently, the recognition that sexuality can and does play a significant role in forging personal and social identities is often overlooked. As Foucault says: 'In what way has sexuality come to be considered the confidential and loving place where our deepest "certainty" is read and expressed?'. Says Foucault, ' For that is the essential fact: an understanding of the self mandates an understanding that we exist only as fully embodied beings.' However, the cultural devaluation and the extent to which the juxtaposition of sexuality and disability is silenced makes it all the more difficult for disabled people to have a positive self-identity. The issue is not only that the disabled person must fight to be the author of her/his own sexuality but also must establish sexuality in the first place. What is wrong here is that the disabled person in this society has no sexuality at all.

Conversely, disabled girls in north India face no such prohibitions, as is evident from the personal narrative of Simi who shared the following experience. 'When I was young, I would be thrilled at being allowed to sleep in the same room as Vidin, who was my first cousin. However, as

---

[15] Russell Shuttleworth, 'Introduction to the Special Issue: Critical Research and Policy Debates in Disability and Sexuality Studies', *Sexuality Research and Social Policy*, 4(1): 1–14.

I grew up, I realized that this benevolent gesture of my family was to be understood as a complete desexualization of my body. Later, that same cousin once propositioned me and said that he was willing to satisfy my sexual desires, if I promised to keep quiet and not publicize the illicit liaison.' The assumption that sexuality and disability are mutually exclusive also denies that people with deviant bodies experience sexual desires and refuses them recognition as sexually typical, despite their differences.

My submission is that the split between the personal and political and, hence, the public and the private lives is a determining factor. It has led to the neglect of issues of sex and identity within disability discourse. It is quite paradoxical as it is evident that lives of disabled men and women have been dissected in public forums, and demands for access to public spaces and equal opportunities in education, employment, and other areas of life could not have been possible without evolving collective or group efforts. Thus, the introduction of private issues into public spheres should not have been difficult. However, the personal lives of disabled women and men continued to be excluded from discourse. It is significant though non-disabled too experience problems in the sphere of sexuality, but disabled need to establish authorship of being not only human but also a sexual being. Moreover, there is an internalised desire to prove and assert one's sexuality in face of the normative society As Alok a twenty year old with cerebral palsy says, Unlike my non-disabled peers, it is very hard for me to meet other young people who can be prospective partners. To make them understand that I too have sexual desires is an uphill task, as the non-disabled appear very close-minded to our sexuality.' One reason, according to Alok, is that non-disabled people 'do not grow up thinking of disabled people as sexual beings'. Alok's narrative reminds us that access to sexual relationships and sexual expression are often caught in barriers which bear a close resemblance to the ones faced by the disabled in their attempts to be included in the 'mainstream society'. All the same, though disabled people are socialized into a form of desexualized subjectivity, voices of disabled people put up resistance by recognizing their sexuality. Steven Seidman reminds us that 'there is one aspect of human life that has resisted disenchantment, [and that is] sexuality'.[16] For disabled people, it is really not the bodily difference which counts, but it also requires self-confidence that can

---

[16] Steven Seidman, ed., *Queer Theory/Sociology* (Cambridge: Blackwell Publishers, 1996).

resist the differences. Anupama, a 27-year-old visually impaired woman, says, 'More than being perfect, being sexual demands a confidence in yourself. How can I develop that confidence without good education and a job? At least, if I am earning well, someone might decide to marry me.' Material conditions thus curtail the full expression of sexuality. However, I am definitely not suggesting that, if advocacy efforts and policy development can provide universal access, expressions of sexuality would be ensured, as sexuality is further embedded in cultural and moral issues. The theoretical divide between what is categorized as a need and what is categorized as a desire is critical as it distinguishes between those claims or requirements that a society is committed to equity issues. My apprehension is that inclusion of sexual concerns of disabled people are not considered as "human" in the normative and patriarchal society .When the expression of sexuality is related to institutionalized set-ups such as marriage, the issue becomes more complicated.

Says Raksha, a 24-year-old young woman with visible mobility impairment,

> Society still thinks that if I am not married, I am not entitled to a sex life. This realization is very painful as I am also like everyone else with same bodily needs, like any other woman's inside. Consequently, I am forced to look for relationships which are undercover and while my desire does gets gratified to some extent, isolation of my life does not go away. Also, I am always scared as to what would happen to me if they were to discover that I have crossed my boundaries.

Resistance under such circumstances is fraught with turmoil. If someone wants to be celibate and single, it would be fine. However, in a scenario where sexuality is intimately tied to marriage, opportunities for sexual exploration among disabled people in India, particularly the women, are very limited. Marriage, which is considered a safe haven for women, is not an easy option for the disabled girls. Thus, for women, there is a reduction in life choices that also has an impact on sense of worth, which in turn affects sexuality. There is always a fear of being ostracized if discovered. What is more painful is that the 'tragedy' of disability for a woman has been perceived, not as the assumed effect on sexual activity, but on her ability to become a mother.

As Sneha puts it,

> Even if I am ready to break away from the codes that have been imposed on me, how do I go about searching for a partner? My dad's younger

brother once suggested that he might be able to 'help' me, but you think I can complain about him to my parents? I am doomed either way, as for them, the need to feel good about oneself cannot be associated with me. I feel that they have always devalued me so much, that I have no clue how to look for love and acceptance.

As Leonore Tiefer writes: 'Imagine how you would feel if playing gin rummy, and playing it well, was considered a major component of happiness and a major sign of maturity, but no one told you how to play, you never saw anybody else play, and everything you ever read implied that normal and healthy people just somehow "know" how to play and really enjoy playing the very first time they try!'[17]

I underscore the critical role that sex education can play in assisting disabled people assert their sexuality. Most disabled people grow up without receiving any form of sex education at school or home. This is assuming that they are not actively discouraged from the idea of sex altogether. It is difficult to place the onus on any one agency in particular, for excluding disabled people from in-depth sex education is difficult to know. Is it the government, is it schools themselves, mainstream or special, is it disability organizations and campaigners, or is it families and careers? The truth is that all parties bear responsibility. As Radha says, 'There is a general feeling that they don't have the education they need and have a right to,' adding that she has encountered students who do not know the basic facts about sex and are, hence, vulnerable to abuse. Seema, a hearing-impaired girl, says that the only sex education she ever received was from her peer group. While her grandmother had told her about menstruation, no one ever discussed the issue of womanhood. Consequently, there were no opportunities to talk about sexual issues. 'In any case, without any one consenting to marry me, what is the advantage of knowing about sex? Society still thinks that people like me are not entitled to a sex life. I find this very frustrating as my body is just like any other woman's inside.'

The fact that they can be vulnerable should indicate the need for teaching those with disabilities to have appropriate and safe sexual relationships. However, we often find that programmes on HIV as well as sexually transmitted diseases (STD) do not adequately cover the issues of disability. According to Shalini Khanna, director of the

---

[17] Leonore Tiefer, *Sex is Not a Natural Act* (Boulder: Westview Press, 1995), 21.

Centre for Blind Women, National Association for the Blind, 'Adult blind women have a burning issue of sexuality to be addressed as they feel hesitant in expressing their right to sexual freedom and pleasure. Sexual diseases/ ailments are another important area' (cited in Tarshi)[18]. Education about sexuality cannot become a reality unless the attitudes and perception of nondisabled people is worked upon'. We need to be unlocking the disabled body and creating avenues for a healthy sexuality, which is not constructed only within marriage. I have come across many examples of professionals, such as doctors, gynaecologists, and other service providers, who do not provide relevant information when requested and required. In general, they have a very unfriendly and negative approach towards sexuality and related queries. One has to be married to ask questions related to your sexual and reproductive health. The attitude with which you are given any information is always preceded with the question: Why do you need this information at all?

My contention is that precise information must be made available. Education is a key area as a lot of parents are anxious about their disabled child/adult being sexually active. The parents think that it's better for them not to know about it. However, many people still hold misconceptions about sexuality among developmentally disabled people, including the caregivers and parents of people with developmental disabilities. A closer analysis reveals that parents internalize the societal conceptualizations. In the case of the developmentally disabled, the image of them being 'eternal children' is very powerful. I think sex education needs to address the fact that there is enough research which proves that developmentally disabled people are learning all the time about many vital areas of life, which includes sexuality. They are fully capable of registering the difference between 'public' and 'private'. It is only by challenging prevailing sociocultural values and the binaries of normal and abnormal that disabled people can resist normative constructions of them as dependent, asexual, or deformed, and begin to forge new identities. We need to contest the notion that biology is a given destiny and identity is always fixed. Though the task may appear formidable, the recognition that our knowledge of the world is a matter of constructed meanings, and not irrefutable facts, will provide the catalyst for change. Media has a very important role to play in rethinking sexuality issues. As disabled

[18] TARSHI (2017) Sexuality and Disability in the Indian Context. Working Paper, Edition Two.

people, the invisibility of our lives becomes heightened by the fact that popular advertising implies the belief that the 'normal 'body is that which is desirable. The media emphasizes that there is an ideal weight, ideal size, and ideal colour time and again.

Once these messages become internalized, disabled people get trapped in subscribing to the non-disabled 'norms'. Consequently, comfort and health may be sacrificed, as there is always an attempt to be identified as 'normal'. Since disabled people exist in society as an excluded category, the struggle is onerous and often seditious. When Foucault says that bodies are a battlefield, he is pointing out that we are intimately involved in conventional social practices. If certain identities are to be permanently disabled, this means direct challenge by those who are willing to bear the costs of transgressing their own customary identities. Unless these activities are valorized as political action on the individual level, oppressive practices will go on. It is only when we are persistent in refusing to live with the images that society has of us that we fight the often insidious battle of expressing sexuality. It is in this context that not only women but also men with disabilities are prone to sexual assault and exploitation. Whereas Mohapatra and Mohanty note that 'women and girls with disabilities are particularly vulnerable to violence within their home situation, sexual abuse is quite common, especially among women with mental and/or hearing disabilities. Abuse by physicians and caregivers, for example, forced sterilization, is common.'[19] The research study covered 12 districts of Orissa and focused on 'domestic violence against disabled women'. Mohapatra and Mohanty concluded that there is no question that abuse of women with disabilities is a problem of epidemic proportions that is only beginning to attract the attention of researchers, service providers, and funding agencies. The gaps in the literature are enormous. For each disability type, different dynamics of abuse come into play ... certain commonalities exist across disability groups, such as economic dependence, social isolation, and the whittling away of self-esteem on the basis of disability as a precursor to abuse.[20] In contrast, Addlakha's research based on four case studies intensely depicts the 'deep sense of personal devaluation and foreboding' faced by the two

---

[19] S. Mohapatra and M. Mohanty, *Abuse and Activity Limitation: A Study On Domestic Violence Against Disabled Women In Orissa, India*, research report of a project funded by Oxfam (India) Trust (Bhubaneswar, Orissa: Swabhiman, 2004), 8.

[20] Mohapatra and Mohanty, *Abuse and Activity Limitation*, 35.

young men with visual and physical impairments.[21] The fact that the hegemony of the patriarchal and normative is very strong is indicated by the preference of these men for a non-disabled partner, so that they were able to compensate for their impairment by aligning themselves with 'a non-disabled spouse in a society which equates absence of vision with individual invalidation and social disfranchisement'. Addlakha asserts that 'both preferences show the importance of the "us–them" (disabled, non-disabled) distinction in the experiences of some persons with disabilities, be they in the area of education, employment or sexuality'.[22] My submission is that there is a complete absence of literature that addresses issues around the public participation of disabled people with respect to sexuality issues. Thus, intercourse sexuality should not is not be narrowly described as " the sexuality" Rather, the most important issue is that of intimacy and caring. However, the development of effective social policies that will address disabled people's sexual issues is a daunting challenge. The transgression of normative notions of embodiment and function—normative in the sense of being able to walk, talk verbally, perceive visually, hear audibly, cognize, or behave in a so-called rational way—affects not only how disabled people are viewed as persons in society but also how they are constructed as sexual subjects, which is often as asexual or hyper-sexual. The barriers to sexual expression, sexual well-being, and sexual relationships that many disabled people confront can often be traced to the symbolic meanings and values that are called up from the cultural imaginary by these transgressions of normative functions. To me, access is merely structural—the sociopolitical aspects of disablement. Finally, I would like to point out that gender differences intersect with the question of disability and sexuality. As a mother of a developmentally impaired girl commented, 'I am thankful that I have a disabled girl and not a boy. It would have been extremely difficult to curtail his sexuality.' Since, within the Indian scenario, men are expected to be active, dominant, and able to take the initiative, such a conclusion might not appear unwarranted. The assumption that loss of sexual function is of greater importance for a man is quite deep-seated in India. Though attitudes towards gendered behaviour are shifting, they

---

[21] R. Addlakha, 'Gender, Subjectivity and Sexual Identity: How Young People with Disabilities Conceptualise the Body, Sex and Marriage in Urban India' (Occasional paper series no. 46, Centre for Women's Development Studies, New Delhi, 2007), 119.

[22] Addlakha, 'Gender, Subjectivity and Sexual Identity', 121.

are limited. In any case, there is no serious reflection on the discourse surrounding disability and sexuality. Although the disability community itself has recognized that disabled men are far more capable of sexual feelings and activity than the stereotype allows, the presumed loss of self-directed independence has been seen as the most salient point. As Sudhir, a person with cerebral palsy, says, 'I think people do not rate sexuality as important because I am a wheelchair user; that is itself self-explanatory.' Thus, both disabled men and women get oppressed in an ableist society, which results in them living a single and isolated life against their will. It requires courage to challenge sexual normativities, particularly by those perceived as 'weak', but as David, who has a speech impairment, puts it: 'People on the fringe—and we are—need to position themselves, not in the secure mainstream, but they need to be on the edge and they need to take risks and gamble.'[23]

Notwithstanding the current situation, exclusion of disabled women within the Indian women's movement, I would argue that simply deciding to include them is insufficient. The problem cannot be resolved so easily by merely adding on disabled women as another category to the list of matters or kinds of issues requiring attention. Offering a feminist account of disabled girls is problematic because it requires including them in the discourse. However, writing a subject (for example, disabled women) into the ongoing discourse necessitates a certain exercise of power to construct that subject in some form, to give her shape, and to breathe life into her. This cannot be accomplished without knowing how she might construct herself. This process thus requires certain reflexivity. To explore the possibilities authentically and adequately requires that the process have a dialogical character. It is vital that both feminist discourse and practice engage in a concerted dialogue with the disabled women and the disability movement, so that a more inclusive theory as well as practice can emerge.

My own research and practice has led me to evolve and legitimize 'disability studies' as a discipline. Before I underscore the potential of disability studies, let me foreground some of the challenges that I believe have led to a development of disability studies. As a disabled woman, my own location in the field is complicated because it raises

[23] R. Shuttleworth, 'Defusing the Adverse Context of Disability and Desirability as a Practice of the Self or Men with Cerebral Palsy', in *Disability and postmodernity: Embodying disability theory*, eds, M. Corker and T. Shakespeare (London: Continuum, 2002), 112–26, 118.

perturbing yet important questions: What is my stance as an activist? With what authority can I speak about disability and disability studies? And why? Am I speaking with disabled people or about them? What language do I use to describe disability? Who has the power to name and label? How does understanding of disability studies exclude others from speaking out? Similarly, how will I negotiate with issues of diagnosis and certification?

Perhaps the simplest way to think of the emergence of the field is to identify disability studies as the academic side of the disability rights movement and the UN convention. The political theorist Michael Walzer has concisely characterized 'social criticism' as 'the educated cousin of the common complaint',[24] to make his argument that effective social theory must never move too far from the very real problems faced by everyday people. So, disability studies are an interdisciplinary study concerned with the representation of the concepts, cultures, and personal experiences of disability in all its variations. Disability studies in the west and some universities in India is already tackling the multiplicity of the goals of the field. One way to do this is to mark out the differences from other fields, for example, the term 'disability studies' cannot be a substitute for special education or rehabilitation sciences. The term also cannot be compatible with research into community support and inclusive education, though research in these areas is in accord with these issues. Though there is a movement from the medical to the social, framed in cultural contexts, an understanding of disability as legitimate knowledge is still missing. People-oriented movements have highlighted oppressive structures inherent in the marginalized communities; however, these voices do not include the knowledge base of disability. Both academia as well as activists work on the assumption that there are far more serious issues such as that of survival that need attention—as if disabled people should wait their turn until the issues of poverty and employment are fully sorted out. It may be noted that such objections are never raised while dealing with gender or racism or casteism. It is important to realize that the study of disability should question not only issues of medical cure or rehabilitation but also conceptualize disability as a social category on par with gender, class, caste, race, and sexual orientation. Disability studies has not been privileged within the academia. Perhaps the reason is that understanding of

---

[24] M. Walzer, *Interpretation and Social Criticism* (Cambridge, MA: Harvard University Press, 1987), 65.

disability is intimately connected to the study of ignorance, invisibility, and identity as academia has not evolved tools for understanding how and why various forms of knowing have 'not come to be, or disappeared, or have been delayed or long neglected, for better or for worse, at various points in history'. Absence of disability from the mainstream academia creates and maintains a status quo where the 'disabled' is incorporated within the existing social patterns as a 'problem'. Disability thus remains as an out-and-out state, both politically and academically—it is the source of its own oppression. Such an understanding suggests that more is at stake than a problematizing discourse of specific categories. By not exploring this relationship, higher education at large has delimited inquiry and pursuit of knowledge of disability. Possibly the reason is that schools, colleges, universities (overall community), remains a site where not only knowledge but also a middle-class orientation with its patriarchal, neoliberal, and normative values is produced and reproduced. An academic understanding of disability as a social, cultural, and political phenomenon is central to counter the notion of disability as an inherent, unchallengeable trait located in an individual. Such an approach rejects the view that disability is solely a medical problem or a personal tragedy. Disability studies thus places the responsibility for re-examining and repositioning the place of disability within society not on the individual, but on academia as well as society itself. Disability studies may be many things to many people, but if its full potential is to be realized, then it must avoid being seen as simply a new bottle for old wine. The purpose of making disability studies an academic discipline is to create a body of knowledge, which can provide challenges towards rethinking and reflecting upon aspects of our comprehension of disability and social marginalization. Disability studies exists at the uneven boundaries of the society, concurrently rebellious and celebratory in its insistence that disability is neither tragedy nor inspiration, but a satisfying and enjoyable way of 'being in the world' ... if only the (ableist) world would not get in the way! Just like the unforeseen possibilities of a new day, reflecting on the field of disability studies is also loaded with the unknown. For instance, knowledge of disability has to be engaged in 'the unlearning of traditional thinking's privilege'. So that, not only is one marginalized constituency in a position to listen to another, but also one learns to speak in such a way that disability studies academia can rewrite the relationship between the margin and the centre.

There are no easy answers to these never-ending questions of identity and inter-connections. There is no easy way of drawing boundaries between who should be in and who should be out; no easy inventory of the heterogeneity of innumerable disability communities. Both as an academician and advocate, I believe that disability studies 'make these questions relevant to everyone, whether they identify as disabled or not at any given time'. As an insider, I find that the ideas are wide-ranging with the most radical reimagining of possibilities. They produce few answers but rather embrace the practice of constantly troubling the questions. They make even the radical seem quite conservative. For instance, take any theory—humanism, psychology, Marxism, critical race theory, feminist theory, LGBT /queer theory, and so forth. You bring disability studies into its midst and pose questions such as: What are the conceptions of the normal? What is autonomy? When exactly is life not worth living? Why does rationality have to be the sole determinant of our humanity? How do we define limit? Issues such as euthanasia, institutionalization, trans-humanism, cochlear implants, and special schools /sheltered workshops are critical in disability studies discourse. It seems to me that identity is not an idle insertion into political discourse; rather it has critical implications for how the discipline of disability studies can expand and thrive within academia. Thus, disability studies embody unsettling ideas that refuse to disappear.

13

Processes of Shaming

The Limits of Disability Policy in India

Nandini Ghosh

Disability emerges from the social organization of society and the way the human body is stratified in relation to social practices and institutions that devalorize the capabilities of people with impairments.[1] Davis argues that the 'norm' reflects the cultural reproduction of ableism, by drawing boundaries around those bodies that transgress able-bodied whiteness.[2] Ableism is defined as 'a network of beliefs, processes and practices that produce a particular kind of self and body (the corporeal standard) that is projected as the perfect, as the species-typical,

---

[1] B. Gleeson, *Geographies of Disability* (London; New York: Routledge, 1999).

[2] L.J. Davis, 'Constructing Normalcy: The Bell Curve, the Novel, and the Introduction of the Disabled Body in the Nineteenth Century', in *The Disability Studies Reader*, ed. L.J. Davis, 2nd ed. (New York: Routledge, 2006), 3–16. Also, see L.J. Davis, *Enforcing Normalcy: Disability, Deafness and the Body* (London: Verso, 1995).

and, therefore, as essential and fully human'.[3] Ableism is entrenched in all societies and cultures, discernable through the behaviour and attitudes of both disabled and non-disabled people and reveals itself in the cultural inclination towards normalcy by way of correction, towards homogeneity by way of disparagement of difference.[4] Ableist ideologies operate at a macrostructural level as forms of social control[5] and at the micro level of evaluative judgements of everyday life.[6] The role of emotions, as normative evaluative judgements, helps in understanding social relationships within both macro and micro contexts. In the case of disability, such emotions make the exclusion of some bodies acceptable through a process of othering, which act as both moral and social agents by devaluing and debasing certain identity groups.[7] Disabled people identify emotions like pity, fear, shame, and disgust that mark out their bodies as different and thus devalued and excluded.[8] The role of affect has been to morally reframe structural disadvantage as a result of individual behaviour. Individualizing structural disadvantage is a necessary contingency to inscribing bodies as 'un/worthy' and thus 'un/deserving' of just rewards accordingly.[9]

[3] F. Campbell, 'Inciting Legal Fictions: Disability's Date with Ontology and the Ableist Body of the Law', *Griffith Law Review* 10, no. 1 (2001): 44.

[4] B. Hughes, 'Civilizing Modernity and the Ontological Invalidation of Disabled People', in *Disability and Social Theory: New Developments and Directions*, eds. D. Goodley, B. Hughes, and L.J. Davis (London: Palgrave Macmillan, 2012), 17–32.

[5] J.M. Barbalet, 'Moral Indignation, Class Inequality and Justice: An Exploration and Revision of Ranulf', *Theoretical Criminology* 6, no. 3 (2002): 279–97. See also J.M. Barbalet, *Emotion, Social Theory and Social Structure: A Macrosociological Approach* (Cambridge: Cambridge University Press, 1998).

[6] Andrew Sayer, *The Moral Significance of Class* (Cambridge, MA: Cambridge University Press, 2005).

[7] Martha C. Nussbaum, *Upheavals of Thought: The Intelligence of Emotions* (New York: Routledge, 2001). See also Martha C. Nussbaum, *Hiding from Humanity: Disgust, Shame, and the Law* (Princeton: Princeton University, 2004).

[8] R. Garland-Thomson, 'Integrating Disability, Transforming Feminist Theory', *NWSA Journal* 14, no. 3 (2002): 1–32. See also J.P. Shapiro, *No Pity: People with Disabilities Forging a New Civil Rights Movement* (New York: Times Books, 1993).

[9] Sayer, *The Moral Significance of Class*. See also B. Skeggs, *Class, Self, Culture* (London: Routledge, 2004).

Public policy discourses on disability frequently reference emotions such as shame or pity to describe the lived experience of disabled people. In India, laws and policies around disability have largely been influenced by the ableist sociocultural ideologies, drawing on cultural assumptions and dominant power equations. Till date, most of the policies, laws, and programmes for disabled people in India have been influenced by historical, economic, political, and social constraints that arise from legal, medical, political, and literary discourses of exclusion of people with real and perceived physical and mental deficits. After Independence, the state in India accepted social welfare as a state responsibility, seeking to promote the welfare of the weaker sections of society, which included, among others, disabled people.[10] The Constitution of India has guaranteed equality before the law and equal protection of law for all its citizens, and prohibited discrimination on the grounds of 'religion, race, caste, sex, place of birth'. The only article in the Constitution that mentions disabled people is Article 41 which stipulates, 'The state shall, within the limits of its economic capacity and development make effective provision for securing the right to work, to education and to public assistance in cases of unemployment, old age, sickness and disablement.'[11] Thus, there is an under-text that has always considered disabled people as incapable of productive work and thereby unable to achieve full citizenship. The religio-moral-medical model and associated socio-cultural assumptions prevalent in India, which looks at disabled people as objects of pity, lies at the root of the reluctance of the Indian state to formulate and implement a coherent disability policy.

In India, the paternalistic welfare state, building on the cultural attitudes of dependency, weakness, and incapability, has laid stress on normalization of the disabled person, through support for medical treatment, aids, and appliances; provision for special education; and welfare payouts like pensions. Assuming uniformity of disability experience, disability policies neglect the varied nature of the experience of disability, depending not only on the type and degree of disability but also on other socio-cultural factors that include regional, geographical, class, caste, religion, and gender identities. These expressions of power

[10] R.B. Billimoria, 'Educating the Mentally Retarded: A Study of Special Schools in Bombay' (unpublished PhD thesis, Tata Institute of Social Sciences, Mumbai, 1985).

[11] L. Advani, 'Rights by Law' (paper presented at the National Consultation Meet on Rights of Disabled Children, 1997).

differentials and unequal relationships further influence the experiences of disabled people, leading to different degrees of inclusion/exclusion within different social, cultural, economic, and religious contexts. Thus, disability policy has remained limited and inadequate as it is unable to envisage the lived realities and subjective embodied experiences of disabled people and impact of the social and cultural constructions that represent disability as deficiency. The implementation of disability policy by an administrative apparatus, impaired by the socio-religious and cultural ideas regarding disability prevalent in society, leads to the continued propagation of discriminatory attitudes and provisions at the grass-roots level.

In the light of social policies that have remained confined to providing basic entitlements in form of scholarships and rehabilitation support, the state has legitimized the disgust for unproductive bodies and undermined citizenship. The power of disgust is evident in its ability to compel those with impaired bodies to internalize the social judgements of devaluation. This chapter seeks to elaborate the processes whereby persons with impairments are socialized into accepting their own bodies as 'deviant/impaired' and consequently experience shame and stigma in society. This chapter uses qualitative case studies of men and women with different disabilities in India to reflect on how pity, disgust, and shame, influenced by sociocultural ideologies, operate within interpersonal interactions to ensure that disabled people remain othered in everyday life processes. The sociocultural ideologies around disability and impairments have been evinced through discussion by focus groups of mostly non-disabled people and in-depth interviews with key informants. The chapter will illustrate how disabled people experience internalized oppression, a phenomenon that has hitherto remained unaddressed by policy frameworks in India. The chapter will finally reflect on the ways in which disability policy in India has failed to address both the structural barriers and the socio-cultural attitudes that underpin the process of disablism.

Lived Experiences of Disabled People

Garland-Thomson stated that the cultural encoding of disabled bodies often operates through the social ideologies of able-bodiedness.[12]

[12] R. Garland-Thomson, *Extraordinary Bodies: Figuring Physical Disability in American Culture and Literature* (New York: Columbia University Press, 1997).

'Constructed as the embodiment of corporeal insufficiency and deviance, the physically disabled body becomes a repository for social anxieties about such troubling concerns as vulnerability, control, and identity.'[13] The ascription of economic, social, and cultural value to different bodies generates, cultivates, and sustains particular emotions, as normative evaluative judgements, about and on the impaired body. Thus,value judgments like 'disability','impairment', and 'limit' rely on the act of 'comparing individual bodies with unstated but determining norms'that dictate expectations for how human beings should look and act. The process of constructing the Other through an array of social and cultural processes reveals the ways in which social emotions make ethical judgements about bodies that transgress borders of the self in order to contain them. Disgust, propped up by the moral domain and learnt through socialization, operates within interpersonal relations to exclude and discredit certain groups of people as well as individuals.[14] In India, the process of othering, rooted in prevalent sociocultural ideologies, deeply influences the lived experiences of disabled people on an everyday basis. Like gender and caste, impairment becomes another crucial axis for the processes of othering to operate, by deeming which bodies are acceptable. These ideologies may vary spatially and by impairment category, but the experience of discrimination and oppression remains the same across regions and impairment groups. These micro-practices, although manifested differently in different contexts, feed into the larger global patterns or structures of discriminations against people who are othered.

Creating the Other: Public Processes of Shaming

Socio-cultural ideologies, attitudes, discourses, symbolic representations, practices, and activities within particular socio-material contexts influence and structure the social interactions that disabled people experience in their daily lives. Ideologies of ability and, thus, of inability operate as the greatest stimulator of disgust and shame, with both disabled and non-disabled people being socialized into such ideologies. Most disabled people learn disgust, shame, and pity through their interactions with people in the social world—within families and then in the larger public

---

[13] Garland-Thomson, *Extraordinary Bodies*, 6.
[14] Nussbaum, *Hiding from Humanity.*

domain. Parents of Anita and Agatha, two children born with 'grotesque' deformities, were castigated by community members about the supposed inabilities of their children. Anita's mother was subjected to comments like 'how did a woman who produced nine healthy children have a child like this?' and 'it is better to let her die than live with a deformed body like this'. Agatha's parents were informed by the doctors that 'the deformed baby will never be normal' and would have 'severe mental impairments'.

Community responses to impaired bodies and disabled people in India draw on pity in childhood and avoidance and negation in adulthood, both with the intention of restricting the social spaces that such people can inhabit. Disabled people are made to feel, from childhood itself through their various encounters in the world outside the home, that impaired bodies are not welcome in social spaces. Sujit recalls that in childhood, whenever his mother would carry him outside of the home, people would always cluck and commiserate loudly with his mother about her bad luck in having a disabled child. Chobi recounts that when she was a child, 'in the shops people would stare at me as they had never seen anyone like me ever before. People would ask my mother many questions about me. I remember that people would stare at me as if I was from another world, something to be looked and sneered at.' Parents and relatives usually choose to keep quiet and bear the rude behaviour as they also have inculcated the larger social ideologies that tend to look at disabled bodies as deficient and unfit for public spaces. Mam, a young girl with severe cerebral palsy, said, 'In the bus or trams, people were afraid to sit beside us. It seemed my arms and legs could cause them much hurt. Their expression when I started drooling was even worse. I started to feel that I should not be on the bus.' Such encounters in public spaces ensure that many disabled people, limited by their mobility and inaccessible spaces, are further circumscribed by the attitudes and behaviour of the people around them.

The feelings of shame intensify during adolescence, which becomes the most painful period in the lives of many disabled people, as they begin to realize the social implications of their impaired bodies. Asha, a woman with severe locomotor disability, started feeling ashamed of herself when she was 12 years old, when she would hear people pity her and make comments on her inability to walk. 'People would look at me and say, the poor girl. Why did God make her like this? When I listened to all these comments, I used to feel that I would never go out again.' Anita, a woman with dwarfism, recalls the ways in which she was publicly shamed, when people on the roads openly laughed at her or called her names. 'These names are so derogatory. I feel bad when I hear such things or see them laughing at me.' The sense of shame is inculcated from early childhood through stigmatizing encounters with the neighbourhood, community, and generalized public.

Many disabled people feel people in the community prefer to restrict their interactions with disabled bodies and thus exhibit emotions that compel disabled people to shun public spaces. 'When I used to go out, people would ask my companions, "Why does she crawl? Can you not carry her? What is the need to come to such crowded spaces?" Many people told me directly, why do you come with so much trouble?' Shame is further concretized through teasing and taunting to ensure that disabled people do not stray far out from their homes. In adolescence, Anita was more vulnerable to shame and never went out of home unless accompanied by someone. 'I would walk behind my sister-in-law and cover myself with her saree so that no one could see me. I used to feel ashamed, never spoke to anyone.' Thus, disabled people often live isolated lives within their communities. Asha recalls, 'I rarely go with my mother and sisters to our relatives' houses since the time I became too heavy to be carried. I did not like it at all because I had to crawl in front of everyone in order to go anywhere. People would stare and comment loudly. I feel it is better to stay at home.'

Social institutions reflect ableist ideologies and restrict entry and participation of disabled people. The message of being deficient is further concretized through the encounters within the school system, where both teachers and students reflect the larger socio-cultural ideologies that devalue impaired bodies. Schools look for excuses to reject disabled children based on the severity of the impairment, subjecting all children to ideologies that segregate and exclude. Sujata recalls, 'The village school refused to admit me saying that I was disabled. "How will she come to school? How will she manage in the class room?" They did not know me, but they did not want me. That really was distressing.' Once admitted, disabled children are subjected to processes of exclusion in terms of participation in school activities. Anowara recalls that, during sports and games, she was always told to sit in the classroom when the other children were playing. 'All of us were always told that I would not be able to play. I used to hide in the classroom.' On the other hand, teachers also pass on similar social attitudes by implying that disabled students need to work hard on their studies as other options could be closed to them. As Manju relates, 'Teachers would call me and tell me that I couldn't afford to be negligent about my studies. They said that my disability should compel me to study properly.' Urban schools can often be more intimidating for young disabled children with their show of disgust and lack of accommodation of different needs. Agatha recalls that the attitudes of the teachers and the school administration were oppressive in the first school where she was admitted. 'I had a urinary bladder problem and so I used to wear nappies and plastic panties but some of the children used to keep complaining, "She smells, we cannot sit with her." So the teachers moved my desk to just outside the classroom, beside the door. I was so ashamed and mortified. Then the principal called my parents and told them that I could come to school only for the exams. It was such a demeaning and embarrassing experience for me.'

Such feelings of disgust are often stimulated by the disability policies that represent disability as dependence and disabled people as recipients of dole. Public policies for the disabled in India offer concessions for travel to disabled people in state-sponsored transport systems. This rule is often interpreted by private transport operators as binding on them and thus they refuse to carry disabled passengers free of cost. Many disabled people report the abuse that they face while boarding, riding in, and alighting from buses and taxis. As Rita, a woman with moderate locomotor disability, recounted, 'Whenever I have travelled by buses, I have been made to feel unwanted by the angry behaviour of the drivers and conductors. They pass comments like, "now a disabled person is in the bus, the whole day will go bad".' Agatha also expressed similarly, 'Conductors are very cruel—they will say stop the bus, the disabled person wants to get in. When I hear such comments, I feel sad and hurt.' A recent incident posted in Facebook by a disabled person who used to be a university student and now teaches at the same university narrates how the conductor started talking derogatorily to him and his demeanour changed only when the disabled person insisted on paying his fare, and he came to know from other passengers that he was now a college professor. 'Other passengers sometimes also react in a similar manner making it clear through their expression and body language that they are disgusted by my being in the bus.' This happens more with persons with cerebral palsy where the uncontrolled movement and drooling attract more severe disgust.

The expression of disgust in public spaces however is balanced by expressions of private abuse, as the common experience of women with disabilities is to be physically and sexually abused by men in public spaces, on the assumption that the private shame of women along with the abjection of disability will never bring exposure. 'Men still manage to grope you if possible in the public buses. In this case, they do not care even if one is disabled.' As Agatha expressed, 'I have experienced bottom pinching especially on the roads and in public transport. The bus conductors and co-passengers also have a habit of pretending to help you and grabbing you from the front and enjoying a good feel. That's why I tell them I don't want any help; I will get on by myself.' Anita finds that people are crueller in their taunts outside of her village. 'People think because I am small, they can say anything to me. Their taunts are also sexually loaded, the teasing jokes, and things. In the bazaar, sometimes men joke with me, some say I will marry you, others say she is my wife. I feel bad listening to such comments.'

Public expressions of the ideologies of ableism and gender underscore the transgressions of a disabled body in public spaces, conveying and creating a feeling of shame, both in the disabled person and the people around. As Krishna relates, 'Once in the bus to work, two men sitting across me saw me struggle to sit down after unlocking my calliper and then continued to discuss about my legs, my disability, and the fact that despite being disabled, I was dressed so well. Such comments are very common in the public sphere—in buses, on roads, and markets. I feel if I conformed in dress code and did not wear jewellery or makeup, people would find it easier to accept my disability.' Disgust and shame are often countered through withdrawal from the social world and interacting only with one's closest circle, where one faces pity more than disgust. 'When I see someone is staring at me for a long time, I turn my face away, so that I don't have to see their faces. Strangers stare more openly and their voices are full of pity and mockery—all this makes me feel ashamed of myself and of my wish to go there to make a spectacle.'

Different strategies are used to express disgust and shame for a person with disability—from ignoring and turning away to loud whispers to stares and insensitive comments—all of which are influenced by the sociocultural ideologies of ableism and become ingrained in the minds of all people of a community, generating feelings of shame and disgust in both disabled and non-disabled people alike. The socialization into identities that are perceived as abject and disgusting and having bodies that are shameful is concretized in the public domain. Krishna pinpoints the social attitudes that reflect ableism. 'People find it difficult to accept my bodily flaws. I often used to wonder, what do I lack? Then I realized that I do not have a flawless body that is so valued by all in society.'

This internalized oppression becomes so strong by the time one reaches adolescence that disabled people recall that they also had fears of humiliation and rejection, sometimes even from their own friends. 'I feel that compared to other women, I am much less. Not being able to walk affects everything in my life. I feel less than other women and it must be true as all other people say so and I too feel it.'

Negating the Self: Families and Neighbourhoods

Within families, the expressions of disgust operate in subtle, unspoken ways. Often parents also mirror the disgust that is evident in the ableist ideologies, although sometimes it is tempered by love and protection. Dora, born with visible disabilities, feels deserted by her mother, who left her with her father when she was a few months old and never returned. 'Was she repelled by the sight of me? How can a mother reject her child like this?' speculates Dora, socialized into believing that mothers are the primary caregivers. Sumita's mother negates her work by continuously pointing out that she cannot walk. This is despite the fact that Sumita is the main breadwinner of the family, making puffed rice from 4 am to 3 pm. Asha's mother also repeats, 'Can she ever work like one of us?' These attitudes within the family are reflected in the behaviour of the larger family around. Relatives who come to visit also display similar pity and disgust through their often unspoken behaviour of avoidance. 'Our relatives always invite other family members to go and visit them when they are leaving. Once when they were leaving, I asked them why you are not asking me to visit your house. Then they said how will you come, you can't walk.' The assumption of both her limitations and her aspirations in terms of going out of the home further concretized the enculturation into ableist sociocultural ideologies.

Siblings, through the process of internalizing ableist ideologies, themselves treat the disabled child in ways that are exclusionary. Sumita recalls that her sister, in their early teens, refused to acknowledge her presence publicly. 'She never told her friends that she had a disabled sister, no one in her school knew about me though they knew about our brothers. She was ashamed of me and I too started feeling ashamed.' This behaviour of the siblings also depends on the nature of disability, as children with cerebral palsy remained lonely and without friends as they were not able to engage in the activities that the children of their own age were taking up. Swapna, a young woman with severe cerebral palsy, recalls that even her own brother and sister would not play with her. 'I used to sit on the verandah, while they went out to play.' Similarly, the presence of disabled siblings is seen as a barrier for their siblings' marriage, and so disabled people learn to disappear during marriage negotiations. 'When they come tomorrow to "see" my brother, I will not be around. Maybe my presence may pose a problem in my brother's marriage negotiations. No one really wants to marry into a family that has a disabled dependent person—I have a fear that the marriage may be broken off because of me.'

Within closed neighbourhoods, this process of othering is evidenced through avoidance behaviour and teasing and taunting the disabled child for their limitations. Most disabled people recall the stares and the hushed comments made by adults and other children to discuss their condition in the neighbourhood and community. The socialization of disgust operates by teaching both disabled and non-disabled children the valuation of certain bodies and thereby the negation, through ridicule, of all other bodies. As Mira, a woman with moderate locomotor disability recalls, 'Sometimes children of my own age in the village would tease loudly because one of my legs was thinner than the other and I walked with a limp.' Other disabled people report bullying by the children in the locality which leads to shame and self-disgust. Anowara, a woman with moderate disability, recalls, 'The children in the neighbourhood used to anger me by coining a derisive rhyme for me. I would cry all the time but still never quarrelled with them.' The feeling of reflected disgust is more in situations where disabled people are in the company of known people as it is easy to discount the opinion of people one does not know. 'I do not care what strangers feel about me, so if they pass comments, I can easily ignore it. But when they do so in front of my family or friends, then I feel self-conscious and am more shamed.'

This sense of being incomplete is reflected in the shying away from one's designated role in society, which involves participation in family rituals. Transgressing bodily normativity means also the inability to preserve the sanctity of the ritualistic performance which leads to self-disgust in many of the severely disabled women. Asha categorically stated that she does not do the puja at her home. 'I do not like doing puja because it is difficult for me to observe cleanliness—I move on my hands. How can they be clean enough for the puja? How will I take the lamp from room to room?' Here, Asha reflects the communal attitude towards the performance of the rituals and experiences self-disgust for not being able to perform them as per customary practice. On the other hand, Mamoni, a non-verbal cerebral palsy young adult, feels frustrated with her body that does not cooperate when she wants to indulge in her favourite pastime—her smart phone. 'I feel very disgusted that I cannot control my hands and legs. I love my smart phone, but when I become excited, I become so stiff that I cannot use it. I am disgusted with myself for my inabilities.'

The process of shaming within families continues in adulthood for disabled people, especially when elderly parents find it difficult to provide the care required and siblings and their spouses are not ready to take up the responsibility of providing active care. Gendered and ableist sociocultural ideologies severely affect women with disabilities who, as they remain single, become claimants to the natal property. Rita found that, if she did not accede to the demands of her elder brother and his wife of keeping silent on matters related to her home and family, she would not be allowed to stay on in her natal home. 'There was a lot of tension at home, with shouting and beatings happening on a regular basis. My parents were divided, with my mother supporting me and my father with my brother.' Her brother used the classic method to defame a woman by casting aspersions on her behaviour and relationships when she had been away for a period for work. 'They spread stories about my immorality and my character so that either I would be so ashamed that I would have to stay at home all the time or leave and not come back.'

The feeling of abjection in close and intimate relationships often causes more trauma than the shame evidenced in public encounters. Dora's romantic association with a disabled boy left her devastated, not only by the behaviour of the boy but also of his family members. They had known each other for 25 years and wanted to get married. However, they faced with intense opposition from the family of the young man who felt that she was trying to grab him for his money. 'His father is a doctor and he has his own computer business. His mother told him, "If you get married to her, she might take all your money and leave you." So he came and told me that his mother is not allowing us to marry.' Dora interprets the reaction of the man's family as disgust towards a marriage between two wheelchair users who are both dependent on others for their daily support needs. 'I don't think his parents want him to marry anyone. Maybe they don't want two wheelchair users in the same house. I think his mother feels that we both will be dependent on them, both for money and other support.'

The reflection of existing sociocultural ideologies becomes most evident when discussing issues around marriage and sexuality. Almost all disabled people have grown up to accept that they are asexual and unfit for married life. However, there is a distinct gender divide visible here—disabled men are more confident of finding wives who are non-disabled while disabled women cringe from the thought of marriage, citing the sociocultural ideologies that perpetuate shame and disgust towards them. Ravi, a polio-affected man, said he did not have any problems in finding a wife. 'I had some offers, but I chose my own life partner. She is non-disabled and hence we balance each other. I did not ever think of marrying a disabled girl.' On the other hand, the aspirations of marriage of women with disabilities are tempered by the notions of social acceptability which undergird the notions of shame and disgust. 'If I cannot fulfil the desires or wishes of the man I marry, if he is not happy, then what is the use of getting married?' Many of the women reflect the internalized gaze that constructs disabled women as deficient and focus on the way in which the public reacts to such people in relationships. 'A husband will expect me to go with him to social functions. How will he take me? Will he walk and I will crawl beside him? Will he carry me on his shoulders? Any husband will want his life partner to match his steps and walk with him. I can never do that so I refuse to even think of marriage.'

Disabled girls are, therefore, further vulnerable to being shamed by people in the community, especially if they decide to challenge prevalent sociocultural ideologies that deem them unfit for marriage. When a disabled girl gets married, she is confronted with a barrage of comments, all designed to convey to her, her unsuitability in the marital relationship. 'Many women say, look, he has married a disabled girl. "What did he see in her? What did he like?"' This causes a lot of self-disgust and shame in most women who also have been socialized into the same ideologies. This process of shaming is propagated within their new families by the affinal family members. When Aparna got married, her sister-in-law was opposed to her marriage. 'She kept saying my brother has brought the idol of God. "We will all work to feed her, while she sits immobile in one place." She kept saying I had snared her brother with the promise of sexual gratification. I used to cringe in shame from those comments.' The widespread desexualization of people and specially women with disabilities, which ensures that most disabled women remain unmarried, is used to highlight the alleged sexual aspirations of a disabled woman, which is unthinkable in the existing gender culture ideologies.

Processes of shaming are felt more severely in marital families. Since Anowara started saving money in a group, she has become vulnerable to comments from her in-laws. 'Sometimes my mother in-law taunts me by saying disabled people are now having bank passbooks. She taunts me that, because I am disabled, I will get special aid or jobs from the government.' Such taunts reveal that the process of shaming is couched in a belief that disabled people, being incapable, should remain dependent and submissive. Even Anowara's husband is not spared the comments as common perception believes that he will benefit from his wife's largesse. 'One neighbour came to visit and told my husband, "Now that you have a disabled wife, you are getting a lot of benefits. She can use her disability certificate for your advantage."' The processes of shaming are continued within families and communities and serves to control and circumscribe the behaviour of disabled people in public spaces. Asserting of selves seems to be a transgression of the parameters set by society for such groups of people. Anowara relates that when the self-help group that she belongs to had set up a food stall at a local fair, they attracted a lot of attention. 'Young and old men alike would sit at the teashops and discuss about us—"now it is better to be disabled, then you can go out every day and also get loans and don't have to work hard."'

Community patriarchal structures and practices deem disabled women as failing their family responsibility if there is any delay in the birth of children, leading to shaming in front of the community. Anowara had to hear comments like 'Is she barren?' regularly till the birth of her first child. The shame of barrenness, coupled with the audacity that the community perceives in a disabled woman daring to get married, manifests itself in more severe shaming. Yet when a disabled woman gets pregnant, there is further social speculation and censure to create feelings of fear and disgust within the disabled women themselves. Manju was heckled all throughout her pregnancy by the women in her neighbourhood about her capacity to bear and give birth to a non-disabled child. 'When I was pregnant, the local women taunted me, "Who knows if the lame girl will have the strength to push during labour?" They kept on saying the same thing over and over again also during my six-hour labour pain.' Anowara therefore requested her husband to take her to the local hospital for the birth of her second child.

Shame is often used as a strategy to negate the contributions of the disabled women within both natal and marital families, using the socio-cultural imaginary to downplay their productive work within homes and families. Most mothers and family members keep insisting that the disabled woman cannot work as any other person in the family. 'Can she do the work like a "good" person?' 'Can she ever manage all household work?' However, while the process of shaming in natal families depends on negating the capacities of the disabled person, in marital families this is compounded by the expectations from the daughter-in-law of the family. Aparna's husband degrades her by saying, 'A disabled girl like her cannot manage like other people.' He keeps denigrating her, 'She cannot do any heavy work and even light work that can be done in five minutes takes her one hour to complete.' Aparna's husband highlights the fact that he was a very 'good' man who has married a disabled girl, even though he was not compensated enough in the form of dowry. The shame and self-contempt experienced by Aparna is evident, when she repeats his words. 'I need more time to complete the cooking and cleaning of the house than other women. I also do the agricultural work to supplement the income. My husband taunts and says, "You used to do work at your parental home, why can't you do it here?"' The internalized oppression that disabled people face emerges time and again through the voices of disabled people themselves—the shamed echoing the justification for the shaming. Sujata echoes the sentiments of her family and community members when she says, 'Can I ever do what a "good" person can do? That saddens me—a "good" person can do so many things, everything that they want to do. What can I do? I can't do anything at all.'

***

Disability activists and academics point out that there is need for a nuanced understanding of disability and impairment as impairment also is created, defined, and understood within social contexts.[15] In India, the construction of disability has always been mediated by the socio-cultural and religious attitudes of society as well as of the policymakers. While the Constitution of India focused on the protection and care for persons with disabilities, in recent decades, western conceptualizations of disability have greatly influenced the evolution of the disability discourse in India, leading to slow processes of change in both laws for and social attitudes towards disabled people. As international disability policy upholds the principles of social justice, disability policy and programme in India advocate the idea of social justice and yet fall short of the same, both in intention and its implementation. This is because policy is framed and implemented by people who belong to the same sociocultural contexts in which disabled people live and exist and are discriminated against.

[15] T. Shakespeare, 'Social Models of Disability and Other Life Strategies', *Scandinavian Journal of Disability Research* 6, no. 1 (2004): 8–21.

Social valuations of bodies and their qualities, capabilities, and functionalities act as an agent of social, political, and economic control, operating through processes of shaming and segregating disabled bodies. Social imaginings of able-bodiedness, thus, relegates impaired bodies to outside of the accepted ideas around capabilities and functionalities which are based on the material practices of social production and reproduction. These processes of exclusion reflect the structural processes of disadvantage, inequality, and social hierarchy in India, which are dominated by traditional ideologies of pollution, avoidance, disgust, and fear of contamination like caste and gender. The widespread cultural acceptance of ideologies of pollution and avoidance that dominate social hierarchies in India has been used throughout history to exclude or marginalize groups of people. While ideologies of caste build the concept of pollution on the organization of work, gender and ableist ideologies rest on bodily differences that are then arranged hierarchically into 'normal/ acceptable' and 'aberrant/marginalized.'

Both able-bodiedness and disability are socially constructed and legitimized through ideologies that celebrate 'normality' and promote the display of disgust and shame towards bodies that are socially defined as impaired and deviant. Disability signifies violation of boundaries and accepted categories, and therefore is vulnerable to being subjected to emotions ranging from pity to stigma to shame and disgust, which result in avoidance and repulsion of disabled bodies. In India, the processes of shaming and abjection of disabled people are stronger than expressions of disgust. Such processes of disgust and shame rest on the visceral nature of impairments which means that the impairments, which signify variations of marked bodily characteristics and thus are plainly visible, evince more severe reactions. This also implies that impairments that signal less control over bodily movements and bodily fluids attract rejection and avoidance. Disabled people feel that the expressions of disgust are more prominent in adulthood, when bodies that exhibit lack of control are subjected to rejection and repulsion. These feelings are further intensified by the nature of contact—if a disabled person in seen in public spaces, they are tolerated, but if forced to come in close contact with such bodies, the disgust and repulsion are clearly visible. While disgust and shame are experienced through the daily interactions that disabled people have with others in families and communities, these are structured, concretized, and legitimized by legal provisions that are themselves representative of the dominant ideologies. Legal instruments promote certain ideologies but, unless backed up by the political structures, have little impact in terms of addressing stigma, shame, and disgust in the case of disability.

In India, there are few legislations that seek to establish a culture of rights for persons with disabilities—in some of these laws and few others that relate to all citizens, persons of 'unsound mind' have been deprived of many of their citizenship entitlements. Similarly, the Mental Health Act of 1987 focuses more on care and treatment rather than about upholding rights of persons with mental illness. The first rights-based law for disabled persons in India came in 1995, in response to nearly 10 years of intense lobbying by disabled people, activists, and international pressure, after which it was passed in a sitting of both houses of the Parliament—it was hailed for being passed without debate to grant rights to disabled people in this country. With the signing of the United Nations Convention on the Rights of People with Disabilities (UNCRPD), when it became mandatory to enact proactive legislation, the reluctant state constituted a committee in 2010 to draft the new law. This draft law was unique as disabled people across the country were involved in consultations to ensure representation of the issues, and yet the bill that was placed in Parliament in 2014 was a much mellowed version of the rights that disabled people had envisaged for themselves. The new law was passed finally in December 2016, once again without debate, nearly four years after it was first drafted and with many of the provisions and recommendations of disabled people themselves removed from the law. This delay in the passage of the bill and the removal or watering down of the provisions is a living example of the public disgust towards concerns of disabled people in India, coupled with the private shame of the disability sector, now tired of the struggle to ensure proper legislation and thus clamouring for any law to ensure rudimentary rights of disabled people in this country.

The Rights of Persons with Disabilities (RPD) Act 2016 has once again sought to medicalize disability, expanding the disability categories to 21. Although the term 'disability' is an inclusive umbrella term to signify a wide range and variety of conditions and impairments, the diversity that constitutes this category has ensured that different groups of people have emerged, each highlighting their own concerns and seeking redress on narrow/focused issues. The major challenge in the implementation of the RPD Act will be to ensure the uniform implementation of this law, even as different solutions are required for diverse categories of disabled people. The welfare orientation of the state coexists within the law with the rights perspective, thus locating the 'problem' within the individual, rather than addressing the systemic barriers as mandated by the UNCRPD. The new Act has also ignored the fact that each person has multiple identity markers and these markers may aggravate the situation of barriers and discrimination for persons with disability. For example, gender, caste, class, tribe, rural-urban locale, ethnicity, and so on, can all lead to the exacerbation of barriers and the extent of marginalization that a person with disability experiences. The RPD Act has stressed on the implementation of necessary programmes to safeguard and promote the rights of persons with disabilities for adequate standard of living, to enable them to live independently or in the community. While this is seen as a progressive step, the usage of terms like 'within the limit of their economic capacity and development' takes away the onus from the state, which can claim lack of funding for such a minority group. The Act also guarantees legal capacity to all persons with disabilities in all aspects of life, and yet is silent about the existing National Trust Act that mandates guardianship for persons with certain disabilities. The omission of punitive action has also diluted the effectiveness of the legislation and disabled rights activists are apprehensive that the present law is following a similar pattern.

Finally, political structures mobilize dominant sociocultural ideologies to garner support for their initiatives, deeming to speak for and on behalf of the disabled community. Very recently, the word *Divyang* has been incorporated into the official terminology to refer to disabled people in India, despite large-scale protests against such language. Although the word is a repository of disgust towards disabled people with its religious connotations of sin and punishment and relegating disabled people to the category of beggars, it is being repackaged as being closer to divinity. The larger connotation for policy remains the fact that if one is divine, one is above the law or does not require any legal provisions. On one hand, it denies agency to disabled people to decide how they want to be named; on the other hand, it reinforces emotions of disgust and shame towards disabled people by highlighting their sins and, by likening them to being part of God, discards social and political responsibility towards acknowledging disabled people as citizens deserving of respect and equal treatment as human beings.

14

What Is the Case against Muslims?

Aziz Z. Huq*

One might until quite recently have imagined that some species of tolerance of racial and religious minorities was a cornerstone of American and European liberal democracies. But from 2016 onwards, the news reports and Twitter feeds concerning Muslim citizens and migrants tell a quite different story. Some exemplary snapshots illustrate: In public schools in Maryland, a third of Muslim students experience insult or abuse from their peers on account of their religion. In August, an *imam* in Queens is shot and killed on account of his religion. In Dresden in September, a mosque is bombed with a homemade device. On a beach in the south of France a month earlier, armed police coercively disrobe a veiled woman. On both sides of the Atlantic, candidates and politicians call for or enact restrictive immigration and security policies that explicitly or covertly target Muslims.[1] In Slovakia, Prime Minister Robert Fico

---

* My thanks to Whittney Barth for editing help and comments on this chapter.

[1] Aziz Z. Huq, 'The Uses of Religious Identity, Practice, and Dogma in "Soft" and "Hard" Counterterrorism', in *Security and Human Rights*, eds, Liora Lazarus and Benjamin Goold (London: Hart, forthcoming).

declares that 'Islam has no place in Slovakia', while in Hungary, Prime Minister Viktor Orbán explains that 'Islam was never part of Europe'. And the newly elected US president's national security advisor calls Islam a 'cancer', and denies it is really a faith.

The public tolerance of Muslims, to say the least then, is no settled matter in liberal democracies today. To the contrary, in a global archipelago of putatively liberal democracies ranging from the United States through France and Hungary across to India, Muslims figure as at best liminal, and at worst inconceivable, vessels of citizenship, dignity, or rights. To live as a Muslim—or even to be perceived as a Muslim—in Europe or the United States today is to be forced towards an uneasy dual consciousness. It is to have one eye on the mundane business of day-to-day living, with its attendant strains and puzzlements. It is to have another eye constantly fixed on the possibility that the quotidian will be precipitously and unceremoniously overturned by hatred or violence, whether private or public. It is to be preternaturally attentive to any report of terrorist events in a Western city (at least if the perpetrator is a Muslim), and leery of the backlash to follow. It is necessarily to weigh carefully the strategies of daily self-presentation. It is, in other words, to sustain in one's peripheral vision a stinging awareness of how fragile, and how transient, the grudging tolerance of others may prove.

The existence of pervasive negative attitudes and behaviours that indiscriminately target a large and otherwise heterogeneous class of people such as Muslims calls out for explanation and response. What are the phenomenon's causes? How does anti-Muslim prejudice relate to other kinds of animus?[2] And what kind of claims or arguments might be marshalled in response? My central aim in this chapter is to bring to bear a large body of empirical work on the psychological and circumstantial predicates of anti-Muslim animus in the United States and Europe so as to better understand its relationship to other, somewhat more familiar strains of prejudice—in particular, racial and religious animus. Unlike other chapters in this volume, mine does not start from notions of bodily disgust. Although these are not absent from Western anti-Muslim views, I will point to other factors that play a larger role. The same analytic frame, however, may be inappropriate in other national contexts, such as the Indian one, where sexualized fear and revulsion at the 'other's' body may well loom larger.

[2] Elizabeth Young-Bruehl, *The Anatomy of Prejudices* (Cambridge, MA: Harvard University Press, 1996).

There exists already a larger body of scholarship theorizing anti-Muslim bias and prescribing responses. Working in a normative vein, this literature bifurcates between an approach that stresses freedom of conscience and a perspective that aligns anti-Muslim bias with racial discrimination. Much of that theoretical literature, however, develops its diagnoses without drawing upon the rich empirical study of popular anti-Muslim sentiment. By bringing the empirical and the theoretical into conversation, I hope to offer clarity about whether points of theoretical difference, in fact, lie. What seems like theoretical difference, I suggest, may well be better driven by distinct analytic focus on either individual, psychological dispositions or, instead, social and political formations. In contrast, real disputes emerge in asking how to remedy anti-Muslim bias, and, in particular, whether responsive legal measures are better organized around the idea of freedom of conscience or the freedom from racial discrimination.

The Logic of Anti-Muslim Prejudice

There are many different ways in which a diagnosis of anti-Muslim attitudes might proceed. One might begin by examining Islam's relation to Western liberalism from a historical perspective. Or one might start by trying to theorize contemporaneous flashpoints, including bitter controversies over the legality of veils or the construction of mosques and Muslim community spaces. I begin here instead with qualitative evidence from large-n surveys and experiments. These illuminate both psychological and ecological antecedents of anti-Muslim prejudice. They have the advantage of sharply framing, and then testing, specific causal hypotheses, thereby framing commonalities between other psychological and situational factors and anti-Muslim prejudice, as well as differences. This approach to the subject of anti-Muslim bias is useful, not least because it is potentially less subject to distortion due to my own potential interpretative idiosyncrasies. But at the same time, I recognize that large-n quantitative studies do not necessarily capture *dynamic* processes of cultural and social construction of identity, the effect of ideological formations (including conceptions of nationhood and rights) operating in the longue durée, or the catalytic role of specific political actors in mobilizing and channelling social differentiation. The net effect of this quantitative corpus is to provide a static image grab of the political psychology of bias, not a dynamic account of its development.

My threshold premise is that indiscriminate hostility towards Muslims and those perceived as Muslims as a class is, in fact, commonplace today amongst both Europeans and Americans. The available evidence supports this. In 2008, the German foundation Frederick-Ebert-Stiftung sampled populations in eight European countries to test the prevalence of various biases, including anti-Semitism, racism, anti-immigrant sentiment, and sexism.[3] Among these prejudices, it found that rates of anti-Muslim bias exceeded the prevalence of other biases—a finding later studies have corroborated.[4] Between one- and two-thirds of respondents in seven of eight nations perceived 'too many Muslims' in their country and more than half characterized Muslims to be 'too demanding'.[5] Precisely parallel statistics are not available from the United States, but there is reason to think the trend line there is not so different. In the United States, a 2013 Pew Charitable Trusts survey found Americans, especially self-identified Republicans, viewed Muslims more negatively than any other religious group.[6] Interestingly, a similar poll conducted in 2003 found widespread negative views of foreign Muslims, but much less negative sentiment respecting American Muslims.[7]

Attitudes produce actions, both legal and extra-legal. In the United States, anti-Muslim attitudes were 'more important' than even racial resentment in predicting opposition to President Obama at the ballot box.[8] Neither European nor American authorities collect comprehensive data about hate-crime rates; in the United States, the federal government solicits data from the states, but state-level record-keeping and reporting practices vary wildly. Private organizations have reported troubling rates of employment discrimination, bullying, and

---

[3] Andreas Zick, Beate Küpper, and Andreas Hövermann, *Intolerance, Prejudice and Discrimination: A European Report* (Berlin: Frederick-Ebert-Stiftung, 2011).

[4] Zan Strabac and Ola Listhaug, 'Anti-Muslim Prejudice in Europe: A Multilevel Analysis of Survey Data from 30 countries', *Social Science Research* 37, no. 1 (2008): 278.

[5] Zick, Küpper, and Hövermann, 'Intolerance, Prejudice and Discrimination', 61.

[6] Michael Lipka, 'The Political Divide on Views toward Muslims and Islam', Pew Charitable Trusts, 15 January 2015.

[7] 'Religion and Politics: Contention and Consensus' (poll, Pew Research Center, 24 July 2003).

[8] Michael Tesler, *Post-Racial or Most-Racial? Race and Politics in the Obama Era* (Chicago, IL: University of Chicago, 2016), 17.

overt violence.[9] By one measure, hate crimes against American Muslims were trending by late 2016 at five times pre-2001 levels. In 2015, hate crimes against Muslims that were reported to the Federal Bureau of Investigation (FBI) (as noted, an incomplete count) jumped 67 per cent from the 2014 statistic.[10]

But why hate Muslims? Perhaps the most obvious reason is the wave of terrorist atrocities beginning in 2001 in New York and Washington, echoing through London, Madrid, Toulouse, Orlando, Brussels, and San Bernardino. To be sure, terrorism by self-identified Muslim groups predates 2001, but it still seems plausible to think that moment was a watershed moment in terms of awareness and inclination to perceive Muslims in a hostile light.

And yet terrorism, while hardly inconsequential, is not the whole causal story. For one of the most important lessons of the empirical literature is the *contingent* role that terrorism events have played in generating anti-Muslim bias. To begin with, adverse judgments of Muslims were already deeply rooted and widely shared long before the cascade of terrorist attacks beginning in September 2001. In the American context, Muslims have figured as aversive figures in political debate since the 1780s. In the ratification debates, Anti-Federalists invoked the spectre of a Muslim president to demand religious tests in the 1787 Constitution.[11] In the contemporary context, quantitative studies of American news media coverage in the 1980s and 1990s find that Muslims were reliably depicted in negative terms.[12] In a European context, there is a long literary tradition, dating at least back to the twelfth-century *Chanson de Roland*, of treating Muslims as a 'civilizational' enemy. An equally long history of communal violence against (among others) Muslims striates the continent's history.[13] In the United Kingdom, strong anti-Muslim

[9] Aziz Z. Huq, 'Private Religious Discrimination, National Security, and the First Amendment', *Harvard Law & Policy Review* 5, no. 2 (2011): 350–2.

[10] Eric Lichtblau, 'Attacks on American Muslims Fuel Increase in Hate Crime, FBI Says', *New York Times*, 15 November 2016, A15.

[11] Denise Spellberg, 'Could a Muslim be President? An Eighteenth Century Constitutional Debate', *Eighteenth Century Studies* 39, no. 4 (2006): 492

[12] Christine Ogan, Lars Willnat, Rosemary Pennington, and Manaf Bashir, 'The Rise of Anti-Muslim Prejudice: Media and Islamophobia in Europe and the United States', *International Communication Gazette* 76, no. 1 (2014): 31.

[13] David Nirenberg, *Communities of Violence: Persecution of Minorities in the Middle Ages* (Princeton: Princeton University Press, 2015), 63–92.

sentiment was comparatively rare before the Indian mutiny of 1857, but quickly deepened subsequently. Event studies suggest that it is not solely terrorist violence that has stoked those sentiments. Modern controversies such as the 1989 contretemps over *The Satanic Verses*, for example, also conduced to spikes in negative sentiments towards Muslims.[14]

It is against this sturdy baseline of disdain and animus that each new terrorist atrocity of the new millennium has precipitated 'a spike [if not always] a plateau'[15] in anti-Muslim sentiment. For example, data collected by two Spanish scientists before and after the March 2004 bombing of Madrid's Atocha station (which unhappily punctuated their work) found a strong increase in anti-Muslim prejudice.[16] Another study exploited a Europe-wide survey that was ongoing when the October 2002 bombing of a nightclub, Paddy's Pub, in Kuta, Indonesia, killed 202 people, many Europeans among them. This study found sharp increases in anti-Muslim sentiment in several European countries after the attack.[17] More generally, a broad analysis of 2006 European and American data found that perceptions of a security threat from Islamist terrorist groups predicted negative views towards Muslims.[18] Such results suggest that the strategic logic of Islamist terrorism is, to an extent, doing its malign work: By fomenting animus against Muslims in Europe and America, organizations such as al Qaeda and the Islamic State lower their own recruitment costs. With the collaboration of nativists and national security hawks on the Western side, they shrink the available civil space for European and American Muslims—pressing them to flee, to renounce their faith, or to abandon their national loyalties.

Further reason for thinking that the effect of terrorism on anti-Muslim attitudes is contingent and indirect emerges from the aforementioned

[14]   Erik Bleich, 'Where do Muslims Stand on the Ethno-Racial Hierarchies in Britain and France?', *Patterns of Prejudice* 32, nos. 3–4 (2009): 388–9.

[15]   Klas Borell, 'When is the Time to Hate? A Research Review on the Impact of Dramatic Events in Islamophobia and Islamophobic Hate Crimes in Europe', *Islam and Christian-Muslim Relations* 26, no. 4 (2015): 411.

[16]   Agustin Echebarria-Echabe and Emilia Fernández-Guede, 'Effects of Terrorism on Attitudes and Ideological Orientation', *European Journal of Social Psychology* 36, no. 2 (2006): 259465.

[17]   Joscha Legewie, 'Terrorist Events and Attitudes toward Immigrants: A Natural Experiment', *American Journal of Sociology* 118, no. 5 (2013): 2018–19.

[18]   Richard Wike and Brian J. Grim, 'Western Views Toward Muslims: Evidence from a 2006 Cross-National Survey', *International Journal of Public Opinion Research* 22, no. 1 (2010): 4–5.

2006 cross-national survey. This study found that something more than a terrorist event is needed to activate anti-Muslim sentiment. Perceptions of security threat were not independent, but intertwined with perceptions of the *cultural* threat posed by Muslims—that is, the perception that the presence of Muslims in the polity undermined core cultural values (however defined). Complementing this finding, other cross-national studies have suggested that in contexts where security concerns have *not* been activated by local events, perceived cultural threats from Muslims had only limited and indirect effects on animus levels.[19] Perceptions of security and cultural threats, that is, may not alone engender animus. Rather, they operate in tandem to generate anti-Muslim animus. Such findings, necessarily tentative because of the absence of replication, suggest that anti-Muslim animus rests on a complex and entangled causal armature in which both external shocks and endogenous vulnerabilities play pivotal roles.

This is not the only evidence that the effect of terrorist events on anti-Muslim bias is not uniform or direct. Tellingly, European countries' average levels of anti-Muslim sentiment do not track their experiences of Islamist terrorism. Studies in 2006 and 2009, for example, found Germany and France to have much higher levels of such animus than the United States and United Kingdom.[20] Other studies have found the highest levels of anti-Muslim sentiment in the former Eastern bloc, where it has elicited political positions such as Fico's (Slovakia) and Orbán's (Hungary).[21] Anti-Muslim sentiment, that is, does not require a visible (or even non-negligible) Muslim population to sustain it.

At the same time, there is no evidence at all that terrorist attacks outside the Western hemisphere—where a majority of fatalities from Islamist violence occur—engender discernable shifts in American or European sentiment. Terrorist attacks outside the West receive markedly less media coverage in the West than occidental atrocities. The 2002 Bali attack, which targeted European tourists, provides a telling

[19] Borell, 'When is the time to hate?', 414.

[20] Michael Savelkoul, Peer Scheepers, William van der Veld, and Louk Hagendoorn, 'Comparing Levels of Anti-Muslim Attitudes across Western Countries', *Quality & Quantity* 46, no. 5 (2012): 1620 (2006 data); Zan Strabac, Toril Aalberg, and Marko Valenta, 'Attitudes toward Muslim Immigrants: Evidence from Survey experiments across Four Countries', *Journal of Ethnic and Ethnic and Migration Studies* 40, no. 1 (2014): 11 (2009 data).

[21] Strabac and Listhaug, 'Anti-Muslim Prejudice in Europe', 283.

exception. Faced with this evident disparity, the *New York Times*'s Anne Barnard wondered rhetorically whether 'in a supposedly globalized world, do nonwhites, non-Christians and non-Westerners count as fully human?'[22] As Barnard's comment suggests, responses to terrorism attacks are themselves inflected by a grammar of uneven and syncopated empathy. Rather than being a simple cause of anti-Muslim sentiments, therefore, news of terrorism is itself mediated by and strained through a persistent failure to take Muslim victims as persons of equal value to non-Muslim victims.

Consistent with this intuition, a different strand of empirical literature tries to dig down below the immediate experience of spectacular violence to seek deeper psychological roots of animus. This body of literature, which is known as 'terror management theory', or TMT, is focused on individual, psychological process, not shifts in mass sentiment. TMT suggests that anti-Muslim sentiment may be sharpened intermittently by toxic events in part because reminders of mortality tend to provoke antipathy to out-groups generally.[23] Inspired by Ernest Becker's integrative psychology of the early twentieth century, the theory postulates a basic proclivity to remain alive that is shared by humans and animals alike and a uniquely human awareness and fearful anticipation of death. Reminders of mortality, such as terrorist events, generate anxiety that is managed by a series of distal changes in preferences and normative judgments that reinforce self-esteem-generating world views.[24] Among those world views are hierarchical preferences for in-group members, and disdain and distance for out-groups. In the US post-9/11 context, this includes Muslims and Arabs.[25] In this fashion, TMT predicts that stochastic reminders of mortality and vulnerability translate into a durable animus against perceived out-groups.

[22] Anne Barnard, 'After Attacks on Muslims, Many Ask: Where is the Outpouring?', *New York Times*, 5 July 2016.

[23] Aziz Z. Huq, 'The Political Psychology of Counter-Terrorism', *Annual Review of Law and Social Science* 9 (2013): 78–9.

[24] M. Landau, S. Solomon, J. Greenberg, F. Cohen, and T. Pyszczynski, 'Deliver Us from Evil: The Effects of Mortality Salience and Reminders of 911 on Support for President George W. Bush', *Perspectives on Social Psychology Bulletin* 30, no. 9 (2004): 1136–50.

[25] D.R. Dupuis and S. Safdar, 'Terror Management and Acculturation: Do Thoughts of Death Affect the Acculturation Attitudes of Receiving Society Members?', *International Journal of Intercultural Relations* 34, no. 5 (2010): 436–51.

A related body of work seeks more enduring foundations of negative perceptions of out-groups beyond the immediate stimulus of a terror attack. In contemporary political psychology literature, tendencies towards intolerance, punitiveness towards dissidents, and animosity and aggression towards racial and ethnic out-groups are aggregated under the concept of 'authoritarianism'. The latter is defined to include a foundational predisposition to submit to authority and to prefer 'moral absolutism and conformity'.[26] Authoritarian predispositions are tightly linked to explicit racial resentment.[27] Studies deploying this analytic lens also pick out strong positive correlations between authoritarian predispositions and negative attitudes towards immigrants generally and Muslims specifically.[28] Different studies diverge, however, on whether negative attitudes towards Muslims only draw level with or outpace broader negative attitudes towards immigrants.[29]

Whether anti-immigrant or anti-Muslim sentiment is dominant, a substantially parallel dynamic appears to be at work in both contexts. Consistent with the cross-national studies discussed earlier, it appears that a key predicate of negative attitudes towards immigrants generally is the perception of cultural threat.[30] Similarly, experimental studies of anti-Muslim attitudes identify a specific fear that 'liberal and/or Enlightenment values' are imperilled.[31] Cultural insecurity, however, is not the only sort of perceived risk that might work as a psychological predicate for animus. A number of studies also point towards the importance of economic insecurity in predicting anti-Muslim sentiment. The

[26] Marc J. Hetherington and Jonathan D. Weiler, *Authorization & Polarization in American Politics* (New York: Cambridge University Press, 2009), 38–9.

[27] David C. Wilson and Darren W. Davis, 'Reexamining Racial Resentment',, *Annals of the American Academy*, no. 634 (2011): 126.

[28] See, for example, Kerem Ozan Kalkan, Geoffrey C. Layman, and Eric M. Uslaner, '"Band of Others"? Attitudes toward Muslims in Contemporary American Society', *Journal of Politics* 71, no. 3 (2009): 54.

[29] Compare Bram Spruyt and Mark Elchardus, 'Are Anti-Muslim Feelings More Widespread than Anti-Foreigner Sentiment? Evidence from Two Split-Sample Experiments', *Ethnicities* 12, no. 6 (2012): 808, with Strabac, Aalberg, and Valenta, 'Attitudes toward Muslim Immigrants'.

[30] Paul M. Sniderman, L. Hagendoorn, and M. Prior, 'Predisposing Factors and Situational Triggers: Exclusionary Reactions to Immigrant Minorities', *American Political Science Review* 98, no.1 (2004): 35–49.

[31] Spruyt and Elchardus, 'Are Anti-Muslim Feelings More Widespread', 86.

effect of the 2002 Bali bombing on rates of anti-Muslim animus, for example, seems to have been greatest in regions with a then-accelerating unemployment rate.[32] These findings provide further evidence that the effect of exogenous shocks on anti-Muslim sentiment is contingent rather than direct. Consistent with TMT studies and with earlier large-n studies, it would seem that a non-security sense of threat (whether cultural or economic) is an important element in the psychological pathway to anti-Muslim attitudes.

The basic takeaway from this empirical literature, in short, is that anti-Muslim animus can arise from an interaction between deeply held psychological beliefs (such as authoritarianism and mortality awareness), and immediate events (such as terrorist attacks, economic insecurity, or perceptions of cultural threat). At both stages, a plurality of social factors and psychological formations may be at work. Nevertheless, as might well be anticipated, it appears that highly salient terrorist violence— at least when targeting Europeans and Americans—triggers mortality salience and activates rooted authoritarian dispositions. In this regard, violent exogenous shocks are an accelerant rather than a necessary predi-cate of bias. Indeed, manifest violence is not the only, or even necessarily the most important, determinant of anti-Muslim attitudes or correlated behaviour. Even when a terrorist attack occurs, whether an uptick in animus follows depends in part upon whether Muslims are perceived to present a cultural threat and whether economic insecurity obtains at the moment of the shock—in addition to the extent to which authoritarian dispositions are widely held.

The resulting potential for causal complexity is nicely summarized by a recent study that analyses Americans' beliefs about Muslims in terms of their perceived correspondence to both positively and negatively viewed 'out-groups'. That study suggested that Americans can and do identify Muslims in divergent and inconsistent ways. Sometimes, the latter are styled as a religious/racial out-group, and sometimes as a cultural out-group characterized by different norms. Future attitudes to Muslim Americans, suggest the studies' authors, may well depend on whether they come to be viewed as a religious/racial group that can be accepted over time as 'part of the American melting pot', or instead as a cultural minority that can simply never be assimilated.[33] The degree to which Muslims are aligned to one or another of these poles likely depends on a

[32] Legewie, 'Terrorist Events and Attitudes', 1228.
[33] Kalkan, Layman, and Uslaner, 'Band of Others', 859—61.

range of exogenous and unpredictable events, including terrorist attacks, controversies that imply a cultural threat from Muslims, and economic shocks.

Theorizing Anti-Muslim Prejudice as Racial or Religious Discrimination

The legal and theoretical literature on anti-Muslim prejudice is characterized by a sharp internal dichotomy. Disagreement focuses on whether the central harm from anti-Muslim animus is captured by the idea of freedom of conscience, or whether such prejudice is better aligned with discrimination against racial minorities. These theoretical disagreements reflect divergent accounts of the causal aetiology of anti-Muslim attitudes, and disagreements over the appropriate normative and legal response to anti-Muslim attitudes. By starting with a better understanding of the causal aetiology of bias, it is possible to gain clarity on whether theorizing anti-Muslim sentiment as an instance of religious or racial discrimination tracks its known causal aetiology and provides useful direction in respect to remedies.

The two ways of theorizing anti-Muslim prejudice in the existing literature focus on either faith or race as guiding templates. I bracket for a moment the considerable difficulty of defining either of those concepts (although I do have something to say on that score in a moment). Rather than trying to work from the ground up in theoretical terms, I start with specific texts that have either described anti-Muslim bias as a form of religious or racial discrimination.

A leading exponent of the former is Martha Nussbaum. She has developed an account of the 'new religious intolerance' that places 'the conscience of the individual' at the heart of a principled response that 'avoid[s] confusion and panic'.[34] Intolerance of Muslims flows from the mismanagement of fear, which is displaced onto 'handy surrogate[s]'.[35] In response to this dynamic, which threatens equal dignity of all, Nussbaum proffers the concept of *liberty of conscience*. In this account, conscience is 'conceived as basically the essence of human dignity',[36]

---

[34] Martha C. Nussbaum, *The New Religious Intolerance*, (Cambridge: Harvard University Press, 2012), 59–97.

[35] Nussbaum, *The New Religious Intolerance*, 23.

[36] Nussbaum, *The New Religious Intolerance,* 65.

and is best supported by an 'accommodationist principle' capable of reaching even 'subtle' forms of discrimination.[37] One way (although not the only way[38]) such a principle has been operationalized in legal systems is in terms of *exceptions* from generally applicable laws that avail when a person tenders a claim that a faith practice has been burdened. A religious liberty framing in this fashion highlights the role of internal, psychological dynamics and beliefs.

The centrality of individuals' beliefs and the practices that flow from them to anti-Muslim bias can also be framed in cultural terms. Hence, Jocelyne Cesari cites evidence of cultural threat perceptions to argue that Europeans tend to believe that Islam and the beliefs of Muslims 'are incompatible with national and Western values', in particular, norms of gender equality and tolerance.[39] Cesari's focus on practice motivated by belief aligns her account with Nussbaum's. Both suggest that a focus on intolerance for divergent beliefs and practices is the crux of the phenomenon.

Nussbaum's account is largely psychological and individualistic in its focus. It does not train upon the institutional or political dimension of anti-Muslim bias as a form of religious discrimination, although some of her other work expressly addresses such dynamics elsewhere. Hence, it leaves open the question of how a religious identity evolves into a widely shared marker of exclusion and contempt. Other scholars, looking separately at the American and European contexts, do address the mechanisms whereby religious identity becomes politicized. Their work suggests that, even as whatever nominal consensus clings to anti-discrimination norms, exclusionary rhetoric around religious identity 'is a too-valuable political instrument and too-potent source of populist energy amidst the wreckage of the old political alignments to be completely put aside'[40]—albeit for different reasons in different national situations.

In the American context, historian Kambiz GhaneaBassiri frames anti-Muslim discrimination in the US context as one form of the

---

[37] Nussbaum, *The New Religious Intolerance,* 87.

[38] Martha C. Nussbaum, 'Perfectionist Liberalism and Political Liberalism', *Philosophy and Public Affairs* 39, no. 1 (2011): 42–5.

[39] Jocelyne Cesari, *Why the West Fears Islam* (New York, NY: Palgrave McMillan, 2013), 14–20.

[40] Paul Gilroy, '"My Britain Is Fuck All" Zombie Multiculturalism and the Race Politics of Citizenship', *Identities* 19, no. 4 (2012) 380–97.

'politicization of religion' that he believes to have reoccurred iteratively across American history at moments when 'confidence in America's democratic institutions are waning'.[41] Rather than grounding animus in the psychology of fear, as Nussbaum does, GhaneaBassiri explains the strategic political utility of religious identity as a shop-worn trope in American political discourse. Once deployed against Catholics and Mormons among others, it remains ready to be taken off the shelf and deployed by unscrupulous political actors. Today, a rich infrastructure of anti-Muslim interest groups and think-tanks stands ready and willing to accomplish that end.[42] In the European context, a similar story has been developed, although with distinct and different operative terms. In the Old World, opposition to Islam has become 'the main exclusionary project' among far-right political parties across a number of European countries.[43]

An alternative theoretical lens on anti-Muslim sentiments aligns the latter with racial prejudice. The characterization of anti-Muslim sentiment as a species of racism is propounded with most vigour by a range of British scholars. In a loosely related body of sociological and political theory work, Amir Saeed, Fred Halliday, Nasar Meer, and Tariq Modood have all argued for a notion of 'cultural racism', in which 'Muslim' functions as a 'quasi-ethnic' category.[44] In this view, the category 'Muslim' is not used to pick out a certain set of voluntary internal beliefs. Rather, it is used within a certain social context to refer (pejoratively, in the main) to a group that is defined by phenotype, national origin, and

[41] Kambiz GhaneaBassiri, 'Islamophobia and American History: Religious Stereotyping and Outgrouping of Muslims in the United States', in *Islamophobia in America: The Anatomy of Intolerance*, ed. Carl W. Ernst (New York: Palgrave, 2013), 55–7.

[42] Christopher A. Bail, *Terrified: How Anti-Muslim Organizations Became Mainstream* (Princeton, NJ: Princeton University Press, 2015).

[43] Farid Hafiz, 'Shifting Borders: Islamophobia as Common Ground for Building Pan-European Right-wing Unity', *Patterns of Prejudice* 48, no. 5 (2014): 481.

[44] Amir Saeed, 'The Representation of Islam and Muslims in the Media', *Sociological Compass* 10, no. 1 (2007): 3–4; Nasar Meer and Tariq Modood, 'Refutations of Racism in the "Muslim Question"', *Patterns of Prejudice* 43, no. 3–4 (2009): 339; Tariq Modood, *Multicultural Politics: Racism, Ethnicity and Muslims in Britain* (Edinburgh, UK: Edinburgh University Press, 2006); Fred Halliday, '"Islamophobia" reconsidered', *Ethnic and Racial Studies* 22, no. 5 (1999): 892–902.

culture—much as African Americans and Latinos have been picked out in the US context. Hence, in a European context, 'Islamic' culture is treated in a deterministic fashion just like race: It is a category impressed on individuals, and not chosen.[45] Demographic trends within European Muslim communities are framed in fearful, apocalyptic terms that assume a homogenous and biological basis to religious identity.[46]

Why would religious identity be conflated with markers of racial or ethnic identity? As a historical matter, this may arise because animus is shaped by the specific migratory history of European nations, which experienced a post-World War II influx of non-Caucasian immigrants who were predominantly Muslim. Under such circumstances, the distinction between ethnic and religious identity may have been distinctly secondary—at least from the perspective of the aggrieved native. Correlatively, under such demographic and social conditions, the role of conscience and the overt exercise of religious belief in triggering anti-Muslim animus may well play minor roles. Overt displays of Islamic identity—such as veiling or having a beard or speaking Arabic—are a sufficient cause for negative actions, but they may not be a necessary cause.

Even if one can trace two distinct theoretical formulations of anti-Muslim bias, the race/religion dichotomy described here is still neither totalizing nor without exception. There are many points of contact and overlap between the two accounts. In some instances, one theorization seems to collapse into the other. For example, even as Werbner insists on a racialized understanding of anti-Muslim bias, she argues that Islam involves heightened trepidation among Europeans because 'it invokes the spectre of puritanical Christianity'.[47] In effect, she suggests that historical categories of race and religion were not clearly disentangled: to talk of the Muslim Moor and the Christian Genovan was to indulge in oxymorons. Alternatively, racial animosity can emerge from a perception of cultural difference that is parasitic on a sense of religious division as a consequence of historical migration patterns. To try to tease apart race

---

[45] Hafiz, 'Shifting borders', 481.

[46] Nasar Meer, 'Racialization and Religion: Race, Culture and Difference in the Study of Antisemitism and Islamophobia', *Ethnic and Racial Studies* 36, no. 3 (2013): 394–5.

[47] Pnina Werbner, 'Folk Devils and Racist Imaginaries in a Global Prism: Islamophobia and Anti-Semitism in the Twenty-first Century', *Ethnic and Racial Studies* 36, no. 3 (2013): 455.

and religious discrimination under these historical and social circumstances, in short, is to parse angels on a pinhead.

Nevertheless, I think it is still useful to maintain a conceptual difference between anti-Muslim bias conceived as religious discrimination or instead as racial discrimination. A central difference between race and religion is the nature of the core category, notwithstanding the fact that both 'religion' and 'race' remain contested and unstable concepts. As Nussbaum's formulation suggests, the idea of a religious identity tends to begin from the internal perspective of one within the group, even if the resulting category is then misapplied to those who do not share the same set of beliefs. Religion is often associated with a set of beliefs, out of which flow attitudes and behaviours. In contrast, belief (or conscience) is rarely placed at the centre of *racial* categories. My belief that I am black or white is by no means irrelevant. But it is of distinctly less importance that others' judgments of my race. More so than religious identities, a racial identity is likely to be externally determined, and connoted by phenotypical or ancestral markers beyond the control of the individual. That is, there is a sense in which an understanding of race starts from an external perspective, whereas an understanding of religion must begin from the internal perspective of the believer.

Further, the decision whether to frame anti-Muslim bias as a matter of racial or religious discrimination may influence the choice of remedies. A decision to treat anti-Muslim bias as a form of religious discrimination leads to a regime of exceptions from generally applicable laws, in addition to bars on actions based on animus or irrational prejudices. The remedial implications of framing anti-Muslim bias as a form of racial discrimination are less clear, in part because the appropriate responses to race discrimination remain contested, especially in the United States. A central element in many anti-race-discrimination regimes, though, is the prohibitions on both disparate treatment and disparate impact. Although a disparate impact framework is similar in some ways to an exceptions-based mandate, it differs insofar as there is no need for a claimant to identify ex ante a religious practice as the predicate for legal relief: it is enough that a practice falls more heavily on certain religious groups, regardless of whether they are engaged in any exercise of their faith.

Racial and religious discrimination thus provide alternative ways of framing anti-Muslim bias. But which fits better the empirical evidence discussed in the first part?

Reconciling Theories of Anti-Muslim Prejudice

Let us consider first that the question is how to characterize the causal aetiology of anti-Muslim bias, whether as a matter of individual psychology or collective social action. The empirical record charted in the first section suggests that such prejudice is mutative, taking subtly different forms depending on the historical, demographic, and institutional contexts in which it arises. On this basis, it is a mistake to think that anti-Muslim bias can fit neatly within either one of those two conceptual boxes. Rather, its plural and protean nature as it oozes across different national contexts means that negative reactions can be triggered at different moments by the beliefs that are ascribed to Muslims, by the putative cultural differences that are tightly associated with religious identity, or by an implicit logic of racial stratification. For instance, in the United Kingdom, race and religion were once conflated because of historical patterns in South Asian immigration. As migrants settled in, the dynamic of cultural threat took on new importance due to specific events such as the Rushdie affair. Thereafter, as the spectre of Islamist terrorism loomed with lurid vivacity, Muslims came to be increasingly viewed in an unfavourable light even in comparison to other religious minorities because of the imputed security threat. Faith per se, in short, does not provide the pivotal axis of exclusionary differentiation.

Another reason to think that race- and religion-centred theorizations can be aligned is that theorists' disagreements might reflect not first-principles conflicts, but rather a focus on different macro- or meso-level dynamics. Nussbaum, for example, focuses on the tendency of *individual*-level fear based on a 'real problem' to be displaced onto a 'handy surrogate' of a religious minority.[48] The empirical literature on TMT and authoritarianism suggests that it is also possible for that 'surrogate' to be framed in racial terms. In contrast, GhaneaBassiri captures the strategic incentive of political entrepreneurs to leverage moments of widespread political anxiety and fear by identifying such a surrogate in *religious* terms. But again, it is available under the correct sociopolitical and historical conditions for political mobilization to be framed in racial terms. Hence, scholars such as Halliday and Modood focus on racial formations within the British context which are infused with that country's post-colonial legacy. At the individual level in that same context, however, it is quite possible that Nussbaum's approach would be

---

[48] Nussbaum, *The New Religious Intolerance*, 23.

illuminating, despite the macro-level importance of racial formations. The limited contribution of a specific terrorist threat in a given national context, and the significant effects of both economic threat and cultural threat further suggest that the actual behaviour of the group in question is not terribly determinative of prejudice's form. Depending on socio-political or historical circumstances, anti-Muslim bias can resemble ether racial or religious strains of prejudice.

From Theory to Practice in Responding to Anti-Muslim Prejudice

What of the optimal choice of responses to prejudices against Muslims? A threshold caveat must precede my answer: As I have stressed, anti-Muslim attitudes emerge from a complex mix of deeply held dispositions (for example, authoritarianism), trigger events (for example, economic, security, or cultural threat perceptions), and strategic political mobilizations. Their causal complexity and the variety of the ensuing observed forms of prejudice militate strongly against the possibility of a singular response. An effectual campaign to resist the stigmatizing, subordinating nature of Muslim identity requires tactical ingenuity about how to create social mobilizations, build political capital, maintain moral courage, and achieve legal successes. The resulting legal and political campaigns must vary with national circumstances. The contribution of theory, in contrast, seems to me a matter of second-order importance at best.

With this caveat in mind, I believe that a racial discrimination lens provides a better conceptual approach than one focused on religious liberty. This is to say that the focus on exceptions, while not unimportant in some instances, is less compelling as a framework for remediation than legal templates generated by past experiences with race discrimination. In particular, experience with racial subordination in the labour market and in policing contexts may prove more fruitful catalysts for experimentation in regard to legal and social responses than experiences with exceptions from generally applicable laws because it better promotes an ideal of non-subordination.

This is so for three broad reasons. *First*, the empirical evidence canvassed in the first part of this chapter suggests that anti-Muslim bias is in practice associated with, and operates in a similar way to, prejudices against immigrants and racial minorities. Indeed, 'Muslim' and 'migrant' are almost fungible categories in the rhetoric of the European (and increasingly American) far right. In the European context in particular, Muslims are also subject to systematic exclusion from the labour market in ways that align closely with readily cognizable forms of race discrimination, but seem quite distinct from historically dominant forms of religious discrimination.[49]

If anti-Muslim bias is structurally akin to racial discrimination, then exceptions will provide only a limited response. Racial discrimination in Europe and the United States takes the form of (among other things) pervasive social stratification across labour, housing, and other markets. None of these evils can be comprehensively addressed through a regime of exceptions. The latter sweep too narrowly, and demand too much of complaining parties, that is, that they make *religious* claims to trigger legal protection. Most importantly, they fail to address instances in which discrimination is triggered, not by an assertion of religious or racial identity, but simply by awareness that a person is a member of the protected class. They further fail to address the absence of alternative models of Muslims in popular discourse to compete with negative stereotypes. A parallel dearth in descriptive representation has been identified and addressed, by contrast, in the race discrimination context.

Second, the empirical evidence suggests that at least in part, anti-Muslim bias reflects an aversive generalization about a group based upon perceptions of security threat from a minority within the group. That perception might be amplified by concurrent cultural or economic threat perceptions. But such non-security-threat perceptions are still likely to strengthen the belief that Muslims are intrinsically dangerous. To me, the most apt historical analogy here is the persisting depiction of African American men as criminals and sources of violence. In both cases, the appropriate response to an aversive and unjustified generalization of a whole minority as violent 'by nature' is not the availability of an exception from a generally applicable law. To the contrary, the core of the problem resides in the exceptional nature of Muslims' treatment. Nor is it casuistic argument about the validity of the statistical discrimination. Even if it were true that more blacks are criminals or more Muslims are terrorists than some imagined comparator group, that still does not provide a reason to tar *all* African Americans or *all* Muslims with the same negative inference. The morally appropriate response in

[49] Claire Adida, David Laitin, and Marie-Anne Valfort, *Why Muslim Integration Fails in Christian-Heritage Societies* (Cambridge: Harvard University Press, 2016).

my view is instead categorical resistance to the negative generalization in the first instance. Animus against Muslims is, in other words, often best addressed by severing the conceptual link between group identity and violent behaviour, just as animus against African Americans must be addressed by resisting the association of skin colour and criminality.

In practice, this requires legal change. The federal Department of Justice's guidelines on racial profiling, for example, currently impose a categorical rule against inferences from racial or religious identity in the ordinary crime context. No such rule, however, applies to terrorism or national security investigations. But the available evidence of accurate risk assessment in the terrorism context—a science variously described as 'stagnant' and 'a futile enterprise' as currently pursued—provides scant evidence that religion provides an effectual proxy.[50] And this is setting aside the serious problem of the base-rate fallacy, which tends to inflate perceptions of the evidentiary value of categories such as race and religion. The sort of categorical ban I favour is desirable not only on normative, anti-discrimination grounds, but is also independently justified as a cost-efficient safeguard against reckless or lazy exercises of official discretion.

In contrast, it is not at all clear that the conceptual apparatus of religious conscience as protected by a regime of religious exceptions can respond well to aversive and violent stereotypes. One reason for this is the approach's general orientation. As already flagged, the focus of a conscience-centred approach is inward, addressing the beliefs and concerns of the affected group, rather than being directed outward at the prejudices and generalizations of the discriminator. A theoretical approach organized around the idea of conscience-triggered exceptions, moreover, seems to assume the existence of a regularized core of religious beliefs and associated practices. Insofar as it rests on a mechanism of generalization about the members of a protected class, a conscience or free exercise framing thus suppresses the needful tendency to view Muslims as each distinct and different in both belief and action—a matter of particular importance to the heterodox or apostate.

Third, the empirical evidence suggests that negative inferences are drawn against Muslims most commonly in the presence of cultural or economic threat. Although it may seem that these dynamics provide a

---

[50] John Monahan, 'The Individual Risk Assessment of Terrorism: Recent Developments', in *The Handbook of the Criminology of Terrorism*, eds, Gary LaFree and Joshua D. Frelich (London: John Wiley & Sons, 2016), 520–34.

reason to accommodate free religious exercise, it is, in fact, not at all clear that a theory focused on freedom of conscience provides the appropriate traction. Recall here the inconstant relationship between the number of Muslims in a jurisdiction and level of anti-Muslim sentiment. It does not seem to be direct exposure to Muslims' religious practices or free exercise that stimulates aversion. To the contrary, evidence from localities in which Muslims concentrate suggests that strategies for managing cooperation are abundant and reasonably successful.[51]

In my view, these advantages of anti-race-discrimination over religious exceptions obtain on both sides of the Atlantic. In Europe, anti-Muslim sentiments have precipitated into legal prohibitions on the veil in France, Belgium, the Netherlands and Bulgaria, and the construction of minarets in Switzerland. The logic of religious exceptions, to be sure, can usefully respond to some of these policies. That logic, however, does not address the structural exclusion of Muslims from the labour market, a background condition that preserves—to a far greater extent than a hijab ban—economic and cultural marginality. Paradoxically, market exclusion also conduces to stunted incentives for human capital acquisition, as social isolation furnishes a ready excuse for employers' failure to hire. Pan-European study of migrant assimilation suggests that, among second-generation migrants, only 'legally or socially disadvantaged groups' differ from 'mainstream values in any significant way'.[52] This sort of 'blocked acculturation' is best addressed by vigorous enforcement of employment discrimination laws (including bans on indirect discrimination) and large positive subsidies for housing and education of marginalized groups. Regretfully, it is precisely this sort of expenditures that a newly resurgent populist Right in Europe will most vigorously oppose.

By contrast, in the United States, Muslims do not generally occupy an economically subordinate niche. Nor are they geographically concentrated in dilapidated urban ghettos. Moreover, a widely accepted American norm of legal protection for religious exercise hinders (at last so far) open, formal discrimination of the sort manifested in European

---

[51] Anna C. Korteweg and Triadafilos Triadafilopoulos, 'Is Multiculturalism Dead? Groups, Governments and the "Real Work of Integration"', *Ethnic and Racial Studies* 38, no. 5 (2005): 663–80.

[52] Andreas Wimmer and Thomas Soehl, 'Blocked Acculturation: Cultural Heterodoxy among Europe's Immigrants', *American Journal of Sociology* 120, no. 1 (2014): 146–86.

anti-veil and anti-minaret laws. In the labour-market context, discrimination on the basis of religion is expressly barred in federal law. The most recent Supreme Court case to limn statutory employment discrimination even concerned a veiled, Muslim plaintiff-employee.[53] She won in a unanimous opinion.

But this is not to say, however, that religious discrimination is absent from American governmental policy. Instead of overt religious distinction, it is more common in the American context to see official discretion exercised in asymmetrical ways to the detriment of Muslims. Local resistance impedes or derails the construction of local mosques. Counterterrorism measures, from immigration sweeps after 11 September to extraterritorial detention programmes to recent 'counter-radicalization' programmes, de facto target Muslims alone, while excluding non-Muslim groups that resort to political violence. Religious exceptions, as I have explained, do not provide an effectual response to such dynamics in the way that a categorical ban on negative inferences from religious identity would.

Framings of anti-Muslim sentiments as a matter of racial discrimination or impingement on religious conscience, in sum, each highlight different elements of a complex set of psychological and social processes. As backward-looking *diagnoses*, they may well be complementary. As remedies, however, they diverge. Rather than looking to understandings of freedom of conscience, our historical experience with race discrimination provides a better starting point for thinking about effectual responses to anti-Muslim sentiment.

***

Contingent causal complexity means anti-Muslim sentiment translates into quite different institutional and legal forms on either side of the Atlantic. Hence, precisely calibrated legal and policy response to such bias should differ across national contexts. But in general, reformers' central thrust should not be conscience-based exceptions of the sort familiar from the religious liberty perspective, but rather dismantling racialized social, political, and intellectual structures that reproduce Muslims' socially and cultural subordinate status.

But all this is a bit Utopian. The tools I have advocated are politically out of reach today as the populist right racks up victories in both Europe

---

[53] *E.E.O.C. v. Abercrombie & Fitch Stores, Inc.*, 135 S. Ct. 2028 (2015).

and America. As I write this (at a time of increasingly militant and exclusionary populism), the idea of promoting equality and inclusion beyond baseline levels seems unreal. Instead, the burning question of the moment is not whether any of my inclusionary agenda will be pursued. It is whether the bare foundations of what toleration now obtains for Muslims will persist. To date, the notional reign of liberal tolerance has elected some homage for the semblance of even-handedness. That hegemony is cracking. As a result, we must ask today not only whether Muslims will be treated equitably, or integrated in a just fashion into currently exclusionary structures. We must wonder whether the veneer of civilized tolerance that allows Muslims to be part of ordinary, mundane life will persist, or instead be scorched away by the contemptuous heat of a white, white-hot populist rage.

15

Muslims and the Politics of Discrimination in India

Zoya Hasan

Discrimination has been a central category in understanding inequality and exclusion in most societies. The persistence of disparate educational, economic, financial, and health outcomes between social groups has been a long-standing concern for public policy in many countries across the world. But disparities vary in their scope and also in the specific socio-political and policy approaches that underpin them and the structures that underlie them. India has been, on the whole, more aware of social discrimination than other countries but this awareness is for the most part restricted to discrimination against historically disadvantaged caste groups by powerful upper-caste groups.[1] It does not extend to recognition of discrimination and exclusion of other groups, notably religious minorities. Religious identity, however, is an important axis of discrimination in India in the present day. Discrimination against Muslim communities is common but Indian governments have failed

[1] Vidhu Verma, ed., introduction to *Unequal Worlds: Discrimination and Social Inequality in Modern India* (New Delhi: Oxford University Press, 2015),1–38.

to acknowledge it adequately, with the result that the possible role of discrimination in explaining unequal outcomes for Muslims has not been fully explored or adequately understood.

Muslims, the largest minority in India, constitute a community of 180 million, amounting to roughly 14 per cent of the population. They are, after Indonesia, the second-largest Muslim community in the world. But they lag behind other groups in terms of most human development indicators. The roots of their deprivation run deep in India, nourished by long-held prejudices dating back to the Partition of India. Indian Muslims were blamed for the political events and compromises that resulted in the Partition and their consequent marginalization, while they themselves feel a sense of injustice and believe that institutionalized discrimination is responsible for it.

In India, social discrimination is an important issue for policymaking.[2] Indeed, much of social policy is framed to redress discrimination.[3] Yet, there are persistent differences in key outcomes between various social groups differentiated by caste as well as religion. These disparities are clearly heightened by institutional and policy preferences in favour of some groups and the persistent neglect and exclusion of others. In India, caste is the primary axis of social differentiation, and the bulk of policy intervention pertains to it, while other axes of social differentiation are overlooked for a variety of historical and political reasons. For the past seven decades, there has hardly been any affirmative action programme for minorities. Just about every government, regardless of ideology, has been reluctant to introduce it, leave alone implement it.[4] Courts too have rejected attempts by some central and state governments from time to time to introduce affirmative action for minorities.[5]

[2] Saugato Datta and Vikram Pathania, '"For Whom does the Phone (Not) Ring?": Discrimination in the rental housing market in Delhi, India' (working paper 2016/55, United Nations University, UNU-Wider, 2 May 2016).

[3] Sukhadeo Thorat and Katherine Newman, eds,, *Blocked by Caste: Economic Discrimination and Social Exclusion in Modern India* (New Delhi: Oxford University Press, 2010).

[4] Ashwini Deshpande, 'Caste at Birth? Redefining Disparity in India', *Review of Development Economics* 5, no. 1 (2001): 130–44. See also Ashwini Deshpande, *The Grammar of Caste: Economic Discrimination in Contemporary India* (New Delhi: Oxford University Press, 2011); Thorat and Newman, *Blocked by Caste*; Zahra Siddique, 'Evidence on Caste Based Discrimination', *Labour Economics* 18, no. 1 (2011): 146–59.

[5] For example, the Andhra Pradesh government granted 4 per cent reservations to Muslims on the basis of social and economic backwardness. The Andhra

This chapter seeks to understand discrimination with reference to Muslims in the light of growing socio-economic inequality in India. Disparities between the rich and poor exist along with various forms of group discrimination that exacerbate disparities. There is evidence of discrimination against Muslims in employment, education, and housing, but this article does not deal with discrimination in these spheres.[6] While acknowledging the existence of such discrimination, it focuses squarely on the problem of policy discrimination and institutional bias that disadvantage individuals due to their membership of a particular social group. Both types of discrimination have an exclusionary impact on marginalized groups, especially minorities who are seeking public education and public employment in larger numbers than before. Given the high levels of inequality in Indian society, the need for a common starting point imposes higher obligations on state institutions than on the private ones.[7] The article draws attention to the structure and role of public policy and public institutions. This is also in keeping with the conclusions of recent academic studies and findings of government-appointed committees which highlight institutional and structural reasons for the exclusion of Muslims.[8] Exploring this dimension is especially crucial for understanding Muslim discrimination in the context of the heightened majority–minority conflict in India today, which has taken a turn for the worse since the formation of the Bharatiya Janata Party (BJP) government at the centre in 2014 on a majoritarian platform. The consolidation of Hindu majoritarianism poses a central challenge to the sustenance of an inclusive democracy based on the principles of non-discrimination and justice.

Taking off from this broader concern, the chapter examines two cases of institutional discrimination: the persistent denial of the claims for Scheduled Caste status of Dalit Muslims (and Christians) by successive central governments and the curious decision of the National Human

---

Pradesh high court struck it down but the Supreme Court upheld its constitutional validity.

[6] Sukhadeo Thorat, Anuradha Banerjee, Vinod K. Mishra, and Firdaus Rizvi, 'Urban Rental Housing Market Caste and Religion Matters in Access',, *Economic and Political Weekly* 50, nos. 26–27 (2015).

[7] Verma, introduction to *Unequal Worlds*, 7.

[8] Laurent Gayer and Christophe Jaffrelot, eds, *Muslims in Indian Cities: Trajectories of Marginalization* (London: Hurst, 2012). See also Rakesh Basant and Abusaleh Shariff, eds,, *Handbook of Muslims in India: Empirical and Policy Perspectives* (New Delhi: Oxford University Press, 2010).

Rights Commission (NHRC) to investigate the complaints of Hindu exodus from a town in the north Indian state of Uttar Pradesh. Although quite different in their origin and implications, both cases are signposts of institutional bias that minorities must confront. The exclusion of minorities from the discourse of development and policymaking and the institutional bias reflected in the working of public institutions is deeply problematic in the light of the growing significance of majoritarian politics and the wider social and political context in which religion and religious politics has come to dominate public discourse in India with little scope of redressal of minority grievances at the institutional level. Yet, political parties of various ideological hues and governments they control proscribe any policy that could ameliorate the deprivation of religious minorities on the specious ground that the Constitution does not allow it. By addressing this complex of issues, we hope to question extant frameworks of thinking about discrimination and promote the need for new policies of non-discrimination in India which can go beyond caste.

Social Discrimination

In India, there is no anti-discrimination law, but Articles 14, 15, and 16 of the Constitution prohibit the state from discriminating against any individual or group on grounds of religion. The various provisions of the Constitution explicated in the chapters on Fundamental Rights (justiciable) and on Directive Principles of State Policies (non-justiciable) delineate the state's obligation to provide equal opportunities to all its citizens in social, political, and economic spheres. Yet, the ubiquitous presence of stark inequalities continues to pose a challenge to the construction of an inclusive society visualized by the makers of the Constitution.

Discrimination as an ideology has two distinct aspects—as a principle for organizing social relationships and as a set of political practices and policies effected through formal and informal institutions in the realm of the state, market, and civil society.[9] The ideology of discrimination and the institutions through which it is operationalized constitute,

---

[9] Barbara Harriss-White and Aseem Prakash, 'Social Discrimination in India: A Case for Economic Citizenship', www.southasia.ox.ac.uk/.../Oxford%20University%20CSASP%20-%20Work%20in%, accessed on 6 December 2016, 1.

as Barbara Harriss-White and Aseem Prakash point out, a 'regime of social discrimination'.[10] This chapter is concerned with the regime of discrimination in this sense of the term.

Social discrimination that originates in religious identity was never given serious consideration in policy processes in India. As far as issues of development were concerned, differences of religion were considered irrelevant. All characteristics of identity, except for caste and gender, were subsumed under universal categories derived from political citizenship—hence, there are universalist programmes for drought-prone areas, backward areas grant, small and marginal farmers, pregnant and lactating women and their children, famine-affected regions, 'emergencies', and so on. But this universalism did not rule out important and specific schemes and funds earmarked exclusively for deprived social groups such as Scheduled Castes and Scheduled Tribes.

Social discrimination was accepted as a fact with regard to these groups in the scheme of constitutional development and this was reflected in the affirmative action policies in the case of Scheduled Castes and Scheduled Tribes, as they were seen as groups facing specific kinds of difficulties on account of their historical experience of social exclusion and discrimination. The policies of reservations were initially limited to education and the provision of public-sector jobs to only these two groups. This was later extended to development schemes and budgetary allocations. Certain proportions of seats were also reserved for Scheduled Castes and Scheduled Tribes in Parliament and state legislative assemblies. Reservations in jobs and educational institutions were extended to Other Backward Classes (OBCs) in the 1990s. But through this expansion, the constitutional bar on reservation on the basis of religion remained intact and thus ruled out reservations for minorities.

In the absence of reservations for minorities, how has the Indian state fared in addressing the socio-economic concerns of minorities? Has it managed to mitigate long-standing deprivations and disadvantage suffered by them? To answer these questions, it is important to note some basic facts, before we explain the role of the state in sustaining social discrimination.

For several decades, the policy failure with regard to the economic development of minorities was obscured by the lack of evidence. But in the past decade, this lacuna has been rectified to a great extent.

[10] Harriss-White and Prakash, 'Social Discrimination in India: A Case for Economic Citizenship', 1.

Considerable data have been collected to delineate the contours of the development deficit with regard to the social progress of Muslims. In 2005, the Government of India constituted a 'high level committee' to prepare a report on the social, economic, and educational status of the Muslim community of India. The report, known as the Sachar Committee Report of 2006, laid to rest the political fiction about the Muslim condition and demonstrated that, on most socio-economic indicators, they were standing on the margins of structures of political, economic, and social relevance and their average condition was comparable to or even worse than the country's acknowledged historically most backward communities, the Scheduled Castes and Scheduled Tribes.[11] It specified the development deficits of the majority of Muslims in relation to education, livelihood, and access to public services and the employment market across the states.[12]

Among the many issues it highlighted was the huge mismatch between the proportion of Muslims in the population and in all categories of jobs in all departments of the central government as well as state governments, central and state government public-sector undertakings, and banks and financial institutions. It revealed that Muslims exist almost entirely outside India's mainstream economy (both the organized private and public sector), since most of the organized sector or even the unorganized businesses rarely hire Muslims, perpetuating economic exclusion regardless of however highly qualified they are. The evidence for formal sector employment shows that in no state does the representation of Muslims match their population share. Direct and indirect discrimination is a key reason for this. More than ten years after the Sachar Committee submitted its report, there has been

[11] The prime minister constituted a 'High-Level Committee on the Social, Economic and Educational Status of the Muslim Community of India', charged with investigating the socio-economic status of Muslims in 2005. *Social, Economic and Educational Status of the Muslim Community of India, Prime Minister's High Level Committee*, Cabinet Secretariat, Government of India, November 2006. The committee chaired by Rajinder Sachar, former chief justice of the Delhi High Court, submitted its report to the prime minister in November 2006.

[12] For an assessment of the implementation of the Sachar Committee recommendations, see Zoya Hasan and Mushirul Hasan, 'Assessing UPA Government's Response to Muslim Deprivation', in *India Social Development Report 2012*, eds, Zoya Hasan and Mushirul Hasan (New Delhi: Oxford University Press, 2014).

no major change in the conditions of India's Muslims.[13] More recently, the Congress-led United Progressive Alliance (UPA) government commissioned yet another committee, known as the Kundu Committee, to evaluate the implementation of decisions taken pursuant to Sachar Committee recommendations. The Kundu Committee Report concluded that though 'a start has been made, yet serious bottlenecks remain'.[14]

Policy Discrimination

How then is discrimination perpetuated through state and policy institutions? State policies that exclude people from the process of development and affirmative action on account of their identities have the most severe impact on minorities because their exclusion is reinforced by institutionalized discrimination. It is important to understand the state's approach at the macro policy level and note its implications for exclusionary and discriminatory tendencies at the micro level.

At the macro level, the most conspicuous instance of policy discrimination is the denial of Scheduled Caste status to Muslim and Christian Dalits.[15] The significance of the exclusion of these two groups from the protections accorded to disadvantaged groups is most acute in this case because they suffer from multiple forms of discrimination. They are discriminated against on the basis of both their religious identity and their ethnic identity as members of Dalit communities. Dalit Christians and Muslims have for several years been demanding inclusion in the Scheduled Caste category. These groups claim that they

[13] The most telling figures are in the Indian Administrative Service (IAS) and Indian Police Service (IPS), the country's top officialdom. The Sachar Committee recorded the percentage of Muslims in the IAS and IPS as 3 per cent and 4 per cent, respectively. These numbers were 3.32 per cent and 3.19 per cent, respectively, on 1 January 2016, Home Ministry data show. Zeeshan Shaikh, 'Ten Years After Sachar Report', *Indian Express*, 26 December 2016.

[14] Post-Sachar Evaluation Committee, Chairperson Amitabh Kundu, Government of India, Ministry of Minority Affairs, New Delhi, 2014.

[15] Three writ petitions have been filed by Christians in the Supreme Court and seven writ petitions filed by Muslims in the High Courts. All these petitions challenge the Constitution (SC) Order, 1950 as discriminatory and violative of Fundamental Rights guaranteed under Articles 14, 15(4), and 16(4) of the Constitution.

occupy a position comparable to those officially designated as Scheduled Castes.[16] Despite a long campaign, they have so far not received official recognition as Scheduled Caste.[17] Denying Scheduled Caste status to them is a glaring example of policy discrimination. Receiving official Scheduled Caste status is not simply about gaining access to reserved government jobs. It brings various other benefits, which are now denied to them simply because of their religion. These include special development programmes, scholarships and hostels for students, reserved seats in educational institutions, special laws against atrocities on Dalits, and so on, all of which do not apply to them.

Evidence of the reality of economic and social backwardness of a group/caste should entitle it to be categorized as a Scheduled Caste. Justice, as a matter of fact, requires that similarly placed groups are treated equally and evenly without religion being brought into play to deny some among them equal treatment under the law. But in India, the boundaries and definition of backwardness remain contested; the process of identification and how they are identified by the government is a matter of political expediency, disputation, and litigation. It has led to controversies regarding the nature of social disabilities and the framework of special treatment arising out of it. It raises important questions with regard to the relationship between caste and religion and the neutrality of reservation policies.[18] It also raises issues pertaining to the relative importance of ritual aspects of social disabilities in the definition of Scheduled Castes. Another problem relates to the position of various groups in this conflict. Dalit Hindus are apparently opposed to the inclusion of these two non-Hindu groups because they fear that their benefits and entitlements would be diluted and decreased with an increase in the

[16] A study was commissioned by the National Commission for Minorities (NCM) on the status of Dalits in the Muslim and Christian communities. For this, see *Dalits in the Muslim and Christian Communities: A Status Report on Current Social Scientific Knowledge* (New Delhi: National Commission for Minorities, Lok Nayak Bhawan, 2008), http://www.ncm.nic.in/pdf/report%20 dalit%20%20reservation.pdf, accessed on (hereafter NCM Report Dalits in the Muslim and Christian Communities 2008).

[17] The section on the claims of Dalit Muslims and Christians for Scheduled Caste status is based on chapter 7 of my book: Zoya Hasan, *Politics of Inclusion: Castes, Minorities and Affirmative Action* (Oxford: Oxford University Press, 2009).

[18] Padmanabh Samarendra, 'Religion and Scheduled Caste status', *Economic and Political Weekly* 51, no. 31 (2016):13–16.

number of claimants. Sections of Christians and Muslims themselves are opposed to recognizing caste within their religions because they believe their faiths are egalitarian, while the Dalits among them insist that caste inequalities are rampant in these theoretically egalitarian religions.[19]

Exclusion is justified by the state on the grounds that Hindu religion sanctioned untouchability, while more egalitarian faiths like Christianity and Islam do not.[20] Also, it is argued that the Muslim and Christian equivalents of the Scheduled Caste can be included in the OBC list. This resistance is mainly on the grounds that religion-based reservations are unconstitutional. However, the Muslim Dalit demand does not fall in the category of religious reservations since the Muslim community as a whole will not be automatically entitled to it. But excluding them means that the existing Scheduled Caste category is for all practical purposes a Hindu category because other religions are excluded from it on the basis of religion. This issue is at the heart of the debate on social discrimination. The debate here is as much normative as empirical.

The fact is that all Scheduled Castes are assumed to be Hindus, and any individuals converting to Islam or Christianity are no longer entitled to the benefits that accrue from being a Scheduled Caste. As early as 1950, Christian leaders questioned both the prime minister and the president on the exclusion of Christian Dalits from the Scheduled Caste group and, by implication, the discrepancy that this represents between the secular nature of the Constitution and the religious bias of the Presidential Order. But the matter has never been resolved. Since then, the criterion for inclusion of any community in the Scheduled Caste category is that the community 'should suffer from extreme social, educational and economic backwardness arising out of traditional practices of untouchability'.[21]

Courts have by and large deferred to the executive and upheld the exclusion of non-Hindus and the established criteria of low social and ritual standing for the designation of Scheduled Castes. Converts to Islam or Christianity are hence not included in the Scheduled Caste list. Courts have sustained this exclusion on the grounds that 'acceptance of

[19] Mohammed Aftab Alam, 'Discrimination and Exclusion: A Case of Dalit Muslims in India', in *Unequal Worlds: Discrimination and Social Inequality in Modern India*, ed. Vidhu Verma (New Delhi: Oxford University, 2015), 371–95.

[20] Hasan, *Politics of Inclusion*, Chapter 7.

[21] Civil Writ Petition No. 180 of 2004. *Centre for Public Interest Litigation v. Union of India*.

a non-Hindu religion operates as a loss of caste'. The basic issue pertains to caste disability and how it is to be established. Basically, the claimant groups need to establish that they are worse off than their co-religionists, that this is due to their caste status, and that this status is comparable in status to the Hindu, Sikh, and Buddhist Dalits. In other words, it is not enough to say that Dalit Christians and Muslims share the same economic and social status as their counterparts in the Hindu Dalit community, it is necessary to show that the similarity is due to their caste identity rather than other possible causes. The question is complicated by the need to establish a causal link between caste inequalities and social backwardness.

The belief that caste disabilities of Dalit Muslims and Christians after conversion must resemble those of Hindus to entitle them to special treatment is somewhat misplaced. Moreover, the point is that these benefits have been extended to converts from Hinduism to Sikhism and Buddhism, even though both religions do not recognize the caste system. If non-acceptance of the caste system in Islam and Christianity is the basis for disallowing reservation benefits to those members of these two groups, then the same benefits should not be extended to Sikh and Buddhists. If the justification is based on the reasoning that Christianity and Islam are egalitarian faiths and their adherents therefore have no caste, then this principle must also apply to Sikhs and Buddhists, who belong to faith as egalitarian as Christianity and Islam. These two religions emerged as protest movements against the evils of the institution of caste in Hinduism. The reason for extending the benefits to them seems to be political and is clearly supported by the assumption that they are of indigenous origin, while Muslims and Christians are external to this fold as their religions originated outside India.

As it is, rejection of Scheduled Caste status has created new arenas of conflict and competition with regard to the fairness of these policies and the justifications for the exclusion of non-Hindu groups. At a basic level, the controversies are fuelled by the belief that official classifications and reservations are not based on just criteria but on the assertion of power and clout and driven by prejudice.[22]

It is no surprise that the most vocal opposition to the inclusion of converts from Islam and Christianity in the Scheduled Caste list has come from the proponents of Hindu nationalism spearheaded by the

---

[22] For an analysis of the campaign for Scheduled Caste status for Christians, see Laura D. Jenkins, *Identity and Identification in India: Defining the Disadvantaged* (London: Routledge Curzon, 2003), 119–26..

Rashtriya Swayamsevak Sangh (RSS)/ BJP. An important aspect of their opposition stems from the conflation of 'Hindu' and 'Indian'. They are keen to include Dalits of religions they consider 'Indian', within the Scheduled Caste category, but are opposed to 'foreign' religions, that is, Christianity and Islam. In other words, when a Hindu Dalit converts to a new faith, which professes to possess a casteless character, the stigma of being a Dalit disappears. So, Hindu Dalits can be given the advantage of reservations because reservations were principally reparations for those who were the victims of discrimination and injustice in the Hindu caste system.[23] Recognition of Dalit Christians and Muslims as Scheduled Caste would violate a Supreme Court judgment that 'caste discrimination and oppression was a feature unique to Hindu society, not applicable to Muslims or Christians'.[24]

For the Sangh Parivar, the very concept of Dalit or Scheduled Caste is Hinduism-specific. By highlighting Hindu Dalit oppression and contrasting it with that of Muslims or Christians, Hindu nationalists seek to deflect charges that their opposition was essentially communal. The emphasis on oppression and victimization of Hindu Dalits in this context (when it is usually denied in most other situations) was actually a strategic use of discrimination to divert attention from the issue of communal prejudice underlying the opposition. One effect is to demonstrate that Hindu Dalits will be hurt by such policies and the other is to draw boundaries between groups in order to safeguard them from encroachment by others. Such an ideological move allows communal prejudice to be subdued, while an agenda based on anti-discrimination, which supposedly subsumes disadvantaged groups, is promoted. Hence, the BJP warned the Congress-led UPA government that it would have 'to reckon with a nationwide crisis' if it went ahead with their inclusion in the Scheduled Castes. This move has to be seen alongside a determined effort to appropriate the legacy of B.R. Ambedkar, the leading icon of the Dalit movement, in order to integrate Dalits within the Hindu fold.

Another reason for the opposition to reservations for Dalit Muslims and Christians is the fear of conversions.[25] Claiming that extending reservation in government jobs to Dalits of minority communities

---

[23] Jenkins, *Identity and Identification in India,* 119–26.

[24] Judgment cited in Hasan, *Politics of Inclusion*, 206.

[25] On conversions, see Rowena Robinson and S. Clarke, *Religious Conversions in India: Modes, Motivations and Meaning* (New Delhi: Oxford University Press, 2003).

would encourage conversions,[26] Union Minister for Social Justice and Empowerment in the Modi government, Thawar Chand Gehlot (2014–), said the centre has told the Supreme Court that it was 'not agreeable to' granting them such rights.[27] The minister also said any such step would 'weaken the Hindu religion'.[28] Far from encouraging conversion, courts are actually encouraging *ghar wapsi* (reconversion to Hinduism).[29] This judgment puts a judicial seal on the concept of reconversion and also seems to incentivize reconversion with the inducement of Scheduled Caste reservations.[30]

There is, therefore, good reason to believe that 'Scheduled Caste reservations are in effect a system of reservation for Hindus'.[31] In other words, the affirmative action programme has been built explicitly on religious identity lines, even as it is presented as an opposition to religion-based reservation when, in fact, it reflects a deep-seated opposition to the extension of the same to Muslims and Christians because the Constitution supposedly bars it. The above-mentioned judgment illustrates the glaring inconsistencies in the state's approach to Scheduled Caste reservations.[32] It exposes the majoritarian logic: simultaneously

[26] There are eight anti-conversion legislations: Orissa Freedom of Religion Act, 1967; Madhya Pradesh Dharma Swatantrya Adhinimyam, 1968; Chattisgarh Freedom of Religion Act, 1968; Arunachal Pradesh Freedom of Religion Act, 1978; Tamil Nadu Prohibition of Forcible Conversions of Religion Act, 2002, Gujarat Freedom of Religion Act, 2003; Rajasthan Dharma Swatantraya (Freedom of Religion) Bill, 2006; and Himachal Pradesh Freedom of Religion Bill, 2006.

[27] 'SC Status to Dalit Muslims and Christians Will Encourage Conversion, Says Minister', *DNA* (Daily News and Analysis, Mumbai), 15 February 2016.

[28] 'SC Status to Dalit Muslims and Christians will Encourage Conversion, Says Minister', *DNA*.

[29] 'Once such a person ceases to be a Hindu and becomes a Christian, *the social and economic disabilities arising because of Hindu religion cease* and hence it is no longer necessary to give him protection and for this reason he is deemed not to belong to a scheduled caste,' says the ruling, in an attempt to explains why Christian Dalits are ineligible for reservations. Shoaib Daniyal, 'How the Supreme Court Ruling on Reservation Benefits Has Given a Boost to Ghar Wapsi', *Scroll*, 28 February 2015.

[30] Daniyal, 'How the Supreme Court Ruling on Reservation Benefits Has Given a Boost to Ghar Wapsi.'

[31] Mukul Kesavan, 'Keeping them in the Fold', *The Telegraph*, 13 January 2007.

[32] Kesavan, 'Keeping them in the Fold'.

uphold the position that caste discrimination goes away with conversion to Christianity, but it does not go away when the same person reconverts to Hinduism.

Opposition to affirmative action for minorities is particularly problematic after the implementation of the Mandal Commission Report which extended 27 per cent reservations to the OBCs in central government jobs and central higher education system. One consequence of the expansion of reservations beyond Dalits was to render invisible the specific category of discrimination based on historical wrongs. It raised the basic question of whether these programmes can continue to exclude minorities and, if so, whether alternative programmes are required for them. In the fragile post-Mandal equilibrium, the reservation coalition, as Vinay Sitapati has pointed out, has transitioned from a discourse of social justice to a discourse of majoritarian politics.[33] 'Reservations were no longer seen as arising out of a specific ethical imperative; they now came to be understood merely as an assertion of political power for jobs and opportunities.'[34] We cannot avoid the conclusion that the social justice component of secularism applies only to cultural groups that remain within the Hindu fold and discriminates against non-Hindu minorities.

Prejudice and Fear

If discrimination is acted upon through the state policies, actions of political parties, and in market exchange, it is nurtured and acquires deeper roots in the realm of political and civil society.[35] It is here that the ideas sustaining and supporting the values of discrimination are disseminated. What is the nature of prejudice which gives birth to and sustains discrimination?

Prejudice against Muslims is not new to Indian society, but this phenomenon has been on the rise in the past few years. Unlike other South Asian states that chose to define themselves in terms of their dominant faiths, in India, political virtue was synonymous with pluralism and

[33] Vinay Sitapati, 'Reservations', in *The Oxford Handbook of the Indian Constitution*, eds, Sujit Chowdhary, Madhav Khosla, and Pratap Bhanu Mehta (New Delhi: Oxford University Press, 2016).

[34] Sitapati, 'Reservations'.

[35] Phillipa Williams, 'India's Muslims, Lived Secularism and Realising Citizenship', *Citizenship Studies* 16, no. 8: 979-995, DOI: 10.1080/13621025.2012.735023.

celebrating diversity, despite its huge Hindu majority.[36] India's rich history of religious pluralism is under increasing stress from a rising tide of Hindu nationalism. Any separation of religion and the state always weak is now even weaker; consequently, new religio-political discourses have gained ground. This has produced a false sense of majority victimhood and a strong mistrust of minorities as categories of people who are unlike the majority and therefore need to be shown their place. This discourse, which is explicitly majoritarian, is dominated by ideas of ethnic nationalism that want to remake India into a Hindu nation. One consequence of this is the hardening of the Hindu–Muslim divide. This shift had started in the aftermath of the Babri Masjid demolition of 1992, followed by the riots and serial blasts of 1993. The demonization of Muslims gained ground following the New York terrorist attacks of September 2001 and the 26/11 attacks in Mumbai in 2008 and this has further fuelled prejudice against them. Like never before, the Muslim was viewed not just as the other but as the root cause of the nation's problems.

Subordination and subjugation of minorities is clearly one aspect of the change; the other is the new deference to Hindu sensibilities in the public sphere and the state system.[37] This interlinked change relates to the growing influence of Hindutva as a political ideology that aims to establish a Hindu State. Muslims and Christians do not fit into this scheme, because according to the RSS, though India is their place of birth and place of work, it is not their land of origin and their holy land. Therefore, they are outsiders. Since its inception in 1925, the RSS has never deviated from this fundamental ideological premise. This explains the aggressive and antagonistic attitude towards Muslims. Another reason for hostility is that they are blamed for the Partition of the country; it is assumed that they are loyal to Pakistan even though the majority of India's Muslims opted to stay in India at the time of partition; their population is said to be growing faster because they are polygamous, which is a completely fallacious argument; and finally, they are beef-eaters who do not venerate the cow worshipped by sections of upper-caste Hindus.

The Hindu right has played on the inflated fears of the Hindu majority that the Muslim minority was trying to increase its numbers by converting Hindus to their faith to alter the demographics of the country. There is no evidence of large-scale conversions to Islam since the mass

[36] Mukul Kesavan, 'The Republic's Commonsense', *The Telegraph*, 21 September 2015.
[37] Kesavan, 'The Republic's Commonsense'.

conversion of a few thousand Dalits to Islam in Meenakshipuram in Tamil Nadu in 1981. Even in the absence of conversions, it remains a significant issue in the Hindu imagination. Moreover, the belief that Muslims will somehow outnumber the Hindu population ignores the fact that growth in Muslim population is actually falling faster than the Hindu population growth rate.[38] But the fear of small numbers is a major preoccupation of the Hindu right from the turn of the twentieth century and has given rise to divisive politics on issues such as 'love jihad' (romances between Muslim men and Hindu women), or 'ghar wapsi' (the reconversion of Muslims and Christians to Hinduism) in the early decades of the twenty-first century.[39] It has become a regular feature of political mobilization to push forward the agenda of Hindu nationalism. The RSS/ Vishwa Hindu Parishad (VHP) is particularly incensed by 'love jihad', a phrase it has used to describe a Muslim strategy to convert young Hindu women by luring them into romance and marriage under false pretenses. According to the RSS, these Hindu–Muslim unions will end up with Hindu women giving birth to Muslim children, thereby increasing the Muslim population and contributing to a change in the country's demography. 'Love jihad' is often cited as a justification to bring these women back into the Hindu fold and, in the process, broaden the propaganda against Muslims to secure the support of the Hindu community against this mischief. This is propagated as a conspiracy to distort the population ratio with Muslim men projected as lustful and Hindu women and girls being unsafe from prying eyes of Muslim men. This is predicated on references to the aggressive and libidinal energies of the Muslim male, creating 'an exclusivist grammar of "difference" in the intimate regimes of love and marriage'.

This sense of alarm is further escalated by the lack of reform in Muslim personal laws and the fear that a man marrying multiple women, made possible by instant, arbitrary, and unilateral divorce, would again result in a rise in the Muslim population.[40] The much-hyped political campaign against triple talaq or instant divorce by the ruling party and the prime minister on behalf of his 'Muslim sisters', as Modi put it in his speech to the National Executive Committee of the BJP, signals an

[38] Abusaleh Shariff, 'Myth of Muslim Growth', *Indian Express*, 2 September 2015.

[39] On this, see Arjun Appadorai, *The Fear of Small Numbers: An Essay on the Geography of Anger* (Durham, North Carolina: Duke University Press, 2006).

[40] Abdul Shaban, 'A New normal in UP', *Indian Express*, 17 March 2017.

understanding that Muslim women who are trapped by the patriarchy of Muslim personal laws need to be liberated from the clutches of Muslim men. The growing pressure to ban triple talaq is not because of a concern for Muslim women's rights, but because of worries of Muslims outstripping the Hindu population due to multiple marriages.[41] In the Sangh's imagination, Muslim men, because they have the option of multiple wives, are out-producing Hindu men and producing more children. They enjoy the unfair advantage of unreformed gender-insensitive laws while Hindu personal laws were reformed.[42]

Institutional Bias

Discrimination in the realm of civil and political society has frequently extended to the institutional sphere under the rising influence of Hindu nationalism. The decision of the NHRC, the premier human rights body in India, to depute a team to investigate the BJP's claims of Hindu exodus from western Uttar Pradesh towns at the hands of Muslim criminals is a pointer to the penetration of the Hindu nationalist discourse inside public institutions, which then act to protect the interests of the majority community, often at the expense of the minority community.[43] In June 2016, the BJP's Lok Sabha Member of Parliament (MP) Hukum Singh released a list of 346 members of Hindu families that had allegedly fled Kairana town in Shamli district of western Uttar Pradesh due to persecution and pressure, fearing atrocities at the hands of Muslim criminals and extortionists.

[41] Indu Agnihotri, 'Is the BJP's Sudden Interest in Abolishing Triple Talaq Really About Empowering Muslim Women?', *Wire*, 24 April 2017, https://thewire.in/127767/triple-talaq-muslim-women-bjp/, accessed on 11 May 2017. The BJP government introduced a law in December 2017 to ban instant triple talaq or Talaq-e-Biddat. According to the proposed Muslim Woman Protection of Rights on Marriage bill, a husband who resorts to instant triple talaq can be jailed for up to three years and be fined.

[42] Ajaz Ashraf, 'Love in the Time of Triple Talaq: BJP's New Love for Muslim Women is Based on an Unrealistic Fantasy', 22 April 2017, *Scroll*, https://scroll.in/article/835097/love-in-the-time-of-triple-talaq-the-bjps-newfound-affection-for-muslim-women-is-that-of-a-stalker, accessed on 9 May 2017.

[43] Analysis of the Kairana exodus. See Zoya Hasan, 'Politics of Exclusion: Kairana Exodus', *Hindu*, 20 October 2016.

The forced exodus claim was denied by the state government and the district administration. Several investigative reports by the media also exposed these claims.[44] They found them to be exaggerated and false as many of the people had migrated for various reasons and some had done so in search of better opportunities. After Hukum Singh's allegations, the NHRC got into action and issued a notice to the Uttar Pradesh government which was ruled by the Samajwadi Party for its report on the alleged exodus, while the Uttar Pradesh government itself ordered a probe into the issue. The commission constituted a team from its investigation division to look into the complaints of exodus of Hindu families. There was really no justification for this investigation into what seemed to be a minor issue. The BJP took full advantage of the NHRC investigation as a vindication of its claims.

The findings of the NHRC report point to a breakdown of law and order and some people leaving due to fear of criminals.[45] It does not confirm the exodus theory as Singh claimed. The report did find that several Hindu families have migrated because of the worsening law-and-order situation after victims of the Muzaffarnagar riots settled there. It stated that:

[44] See, for example, Omar Rashid, 'Kairana: BJP Hardens Line even as Officials Nail "Exodus" Lies', *Hindu*, 18 October 2016, http://www.the-hindu.com/news/national/Kairana-BJP-hardens-line-even-as-officials-nail-%E2%80%98exodus%E2%80%99-lies/article14427985.ece, accessed on 15 October 2016; Aditi Vatsa, 'Kairana Exodus: BJP List of "Hindus" Forced Out includes Those Who Died, Migrated for Better Job', *Indian Express*,16 June 2016, http://indianexpress.com/article/india/india-news-india/kairana-mass-exodus-shamli-hindu exodus-akhilesh-yadav-up-elections-bjp-hukum-singh-2851411/, accessed on 15 October 2016; Aman Sethi, 'NHRC Report on Kairana's Hindu "Exodus" Wrecks Its Credibility', *Quint*, 7 October 2016, https://www.thequint.com/news/politics/nhrc-report-on-kairanas-hindu-exo-dus-wrecks-its-credibility-bjp-hukum-singh, accessed on 15 October 2016; Rohan Venkataramakrishnan, 'BJP Refuses to Let Facts Get in the Way of the "Hindu Exodus" Story in Kairana', *Scroll*, 16 June 2016, https://scroll.in/arti-cle/810101/the-daily-fix-bjp-refuses-to-let-facts-get-in-the-way-of-the-hindu-exodus-story-in-kairana, accessed on 15 October 2016.

[45] Amit Bhardwaj and Kshiti Malhotra, 'The Problems with NHRC's Report on Kairana', *Newslaundry*, 24 September 2016, https://www.newslaun-dry.com/2016/09/24/the-problems-with-nhrcs-report-on-kairana, accessed on 30 March 2017.

In 2013, the post-rehabilitation scenario resulting in resettlement of about 25/30 thousand members of Muslim community in Kairana town from district Muzaffarnagar, Uttar Pradesh, the demography of Kairana town has changed in favour of the Muslim Community becoming the more dominating and majority community. Most of the witnesses examined and victims feel that the rehabilitation in 2013 has permanently changed the social situation in Kairana town and has led to further deterioration of law and order situation.[46]

The NHRC report came to this conclusion on the basis of verification of six victims/persons and telephonic verification of members of four displaced families in three randomly selected residential localities, which makes it a total of 10 out of the 346 cases of migration from Kairana for reasons of insecurity. It provides no details of the total number of families who migrated from Kairana, the specific time frame for when these families left, and the exact reasons behind their decision to do so.[47] The five-page report comprises brief statements on the criminal incidents given by select witnesses. But there is no evidence that these crimes were committed by displaced people who had settled in Kairana, even though the report asserts that the presence of Muzaffarnagar riot victims has changed the demography of the town and this has led to a further deterioration of law and order in the town. However, there is no corroboration to back the figure of 25,000–30,000 Muslim victims having settled in the town. The attempt to paint a largely criminal phenomenon with a broad communal brush without citing any independent and credible evidence is surprising from an institution mandated to investigate human rights violations of citizens. The report blames the Muzaffarnagar riots victims without citing any evidence.

The 2013 communal violence had initially displaced over 75,000 people. A 2016 report, *Living Apart: Communal Violence and Forced Displacement in Muzaffarnagar and Shamli*, based on detailed ground-level research done by the non-governmental organizations Aman Biradari and Afkar India, found 50,000 people still scattered all over Muzaffarnagar, Shamli, and other districts, of whom nearly 30,000 victims were in 65

[46] National Human Rights Commission Report, 'NHRC calls for action taken report from the Government of Uttar Pradesh over the findings and recommendations of its investigation team about exodus of families from Kairana area', NHRC Press Release, 21 September 2016.

[47] Bhardwaj and Malhotra, 'The Problems with NHRC's Report on Kairana'.

internally displaced people colonies.[48] According to this report, 270 families (approximately 2,000 people) had settled in Kairana. It found that, even after three years, riot victims are living in ghetto-like resettlement colonies with little support from the state administration. It further notes that the Uttar Pradesh government not only failed to rehabilitate riot victims displaced from their homes and villages, it also actively encouraged Muslim refugees, who used to live in Hindu-majority villages, to resettle in Muslim-majority colonies, thus escalating the social divide.

The large-scale displacement caused by communal violence in 2013 was not investigated by the NHRC. Even though communal mobilization and internal displacement is a process that still continues in many parts of western Uttar Pradesh, it finds no mention in the NHRC report. It is mentioned only in relation to the displacement from Kairana for which the NHRC blames those who are themselves displaced by communal violence. This displays complete lack of sympathy for people who have been affected and displaced by violence. Rather than supporting them, what the report has in effect done is to double their victimization by tagging them as people whose presence 'has led to further deterioration of law and order situation'.[49]

A team of the National Commission for Minorities (NCM) which looked into the issue did not find much evidence to back the NHRC claim. 'For instance, the (NHRC) report claims that the rise in crime in Kairana was linked to the resettlement of refugees. There is no paperwork that can verify this. It also said that the riot-displaced persons changed the demographics of the town since about 30,000 people came and settled here. However, local NGOs said the figure in Kairana is not more than 200 people.'[50]

This particular investigation undertaken by the NHRC at the behest of the BJP does not take away from the critical role this institution has played in investigating violations of human rights in the country.[51] 'In

[48] Harsh Mander, Akram Akhtar Chaudhury, Zafar Eqbal, Rajanya Bose, *Living Apart: Communal Violence and Forced Displacement in Muzaffarnagar and Shamli* (Delhi: Yoda Press, 2016).

[49] NHRC Report quoted in Zoya Hasan, 'Politics of Exclusion: Kairana Exodus', *Hindu*, 20 October 2016.

50 'Minorities Panel Challenges NHRC Report on Kairana', *Hindu*, 1 December 2016.

[51] Harsh Mander, 'Not NHRC's Finest Hour', *Indian Express*, 5 October 2016.

2002, the Commission, under former Chief Justice J.S. Verma, was the first public body to visit Gujarat after the riots, and it subsequently moved the Supreme Court to transfer cases outside the State to secure a fair trial.' This legacy creates unparalleled social expectations but it also invites civil society scrutiny from national and international actors for any potentially detrimental action by the apex body. Its neutrality is important because that is what gives its reports and decisions credibility as a record of ground reality, without serving any person or party's interest. This was compromised by the decision to investigate an exodus list supplied by a political party with a clear stake in upping the communal ante before the crucial Assembly elections which were due in March 2017 and in which the exodus issue figured prominently.[52] The report vindicated the ruling party's claims but it compromised its own autonomy and non-aligned status. This is an inevitable consequence of interpreting broader societal trends like migration and security through a communal prism, which sets a dangerous precedent of giving an ethnic colour to law-and-order problems.

As an icon of independence, the legitimacy and credibility of the NHRC or of any human rights body rest on its ability to address the problems relating to human rights in a society generally, and not those of a particular community. The public needs to have the confidence that the commission will investigate cases of rights violation without fear or favour. Hence, the effectiveness of human rights commissions depends on how a particular commission locates itself in a society and is able to confront the issues before it. It is the responsibility of the rights watchdog institution to prevent majoritarian tendencies from dominating institutions. For democracy to thrive, an institution such as the NHRC has to play a counter-majoritarian role.

***

The consistent opposition of the Indian state to the claims of reservations for Dalit Muslims and the promptness with which the NHRC decided to investigate the Hindu exodus illustrate the institutional discrimination inherent in the majoritarian approach to questions of equity and justice. The issue is that there is no level playing field: the state 'dangles carrots for conversions to Hinduism and brandishes a

---

[52] Mander, 'Not NHRC's Finest Hour'.

stick for conversions out of Hinduism'.[53] The NHRC report, on the other hand, shows double standards for citizens, undermining the very idea of citizenship: the large-scale displacement because of communal violence of over 75,000 people from the villages of their birth because of the communal attacks in Muzaffarnagar in 2013 did not result in any investigation or actions by the NHRC, whereas the exodus of less than 350 Hindus not only resulted in an investigation but also a recommendation to constitute a high-level committee to meet displaced families to facilitate their return to Kairana.

The active promotion of Hindu nationalism and the perseverance of policy and institutional bias underscore the great need for anti-discrimination laws. In fact, there has probably never been a time when an anti-discrimination legislation was more needed in India than at present. The Anti-Discrimination and Equality Bill 2016, introduced by Congress party MP Shashi Tharoor, in the Lok Sabha in March 2017, seeks to correct these anomalies by creating a comprehensive framework to address various injustices, and has not come a day too soon.[54] In an atmosphere of rampant intolerance and bigotry the law can only do so much, but it is nonetheless very important that such legislation is available for victims who then at least have recourse to institutionalized redress.

---

[53] Daniyal, 'How the Supreme Court Ruling on Reservation Benefits Has Given a Boost to Ghar Wapsi'.

[54] Tarunabh Khaitan, 'Protection Whose Time has Come', *Indian Express*, 25 March 2017; also see Tarunabh Khaitan, 'The Architecture of Discrimination law', in *Unequal Worlds: Discrimination and Social Inequality in Modern India*, ed. Vidhu Verma (New Delhi: Oxford University Press, 2015), 119–63.

16

Class and Classification

The Role of Disgust in Regulating Social Status

Laura Weinrib

Disgust plays a curious role in structuring class distinctions. On the one hand, to loathe the unsanitary living conditions and disease-spreading drug use and sexual practices that purportedly suffuse poor communities appears compatible with liberal assumptions about the preconditions for nurturing human potential. Depictions of the poor as dirty, disease-ridden, violent, and sexually promiscuous rarely provoke public outcry, even (or especially) among the educated elites who condemn other forms of prejudice. To be sure, many balk at accounts that ascribe such social pathologies to personal failings, as opposed to inadequate education and healthcare. Appropriately couched, however, the tendency to recoil from poverty is ordinarily considered to be natural, innocuous, or even salutary. Indeed, to the extent poverty overlaps with membership in other low-status categories, it is thought to explain or excuse more recognizably pernicious forms of discrimination.

On the other hand, policies that marginalize or segregate the poor are rarely framed as responses to physical revulsion. As with the other areas of exclusion examined in this volume, disgust has been an often unarticulated impetus for laws that denigrate and quarantine the poor, ranging historically from vagrancy and 'unsightly beggar' laws to compulsory sterilization. Yet, in most cases, the regulation of wealth and social status undeniably serves additional ends. The multitude of laws that operate to safeguard property rights or confer benefits on the wealthy are conventionally understood, depending on one's perspective, either to promote innovation and productivity or to entrench existing privileges, but not to avoid contagion.

These two features, taken together, present a quandary for law: namely, whether repudiating disgust is likely to facilitate or impede efforts to mitigate economic inequality in a period when America's wealth gap is expanding and parental income is largely determinative of future earnings.[1] If the visceral force of disgust helps to naturalize social hierarchy, then exposing its effects as illegitimate might serve to spur structural reform. At the same time, the power of disgust to unsettle middle-class complacency might, appropriately directed, function as an impetus for change. This chapter evaluates whether the existing legal framework adequately shields the poor from efforts to segregate and contain them. It asks whether and how law might be used to dismantle the status-based stratification that exacerbates and legitimates disgust. Finally, and more tentatively, it considers whether, under some circumstances, disgust might be redeployed to spur legal and social change.

Defining Class-Based Disgust

Despite its long history, class prejudice in the American context remains comparatively undertheorized. For reasons of policy and doctrine, discrimination on such bases as race, religion, national origin, and disability emerged during the mid- to late twentieth century as discrete concerns, stripped of their class entanglements. Social class declined as an object of academic inquiry just as scholarship on disgust made important strides in integrating psychological research with philosophical inquiry and literary and social theory.[2] Still, there is a substantial body of recent work

---

[1] See, for example, Pablo Mitnik, Erin Cumberworth, and David Grusky, 'Social Mobility in a High Inequality Regime', *Annals of the American Academy of Political and Social Sciences* 663, no. 1 (2016): 140–83.

[2] See Paul Rozin and April E. Fallon, 'A Perspective on Disgust', *Psychological Review* 94, no. 1 (1987): 23–41.

that helps to illuminate the role of disgust in defining and maintaining class boundaries.

'Disgust,' to use William Ian Miller's formulation, 'evaluates (negatively) what it touches, proclaim[ing] the meanness and inferiority of its object.'[3] Those who come in contact with the source of disgust are themselves sullied, and they feel compelled to avoid the disgusting object lest it defile them. Disgust thus demarcates social boundaries, and it is ordinarily directed downwards, towards disfavoured groups. In the class context, its object is the working class or (to use a term that is steeped in social hierarchy) the underclass. Although those at the bottom may feel disdain or even disgust for the effete habits of the rich, 'a war of disgusts is one that those less socially privileged are unlikely to win'.[4]

Depictions of poverty are laden with the language of disgust. In Martha Nussbaum's influential account, disgust in its primary form is associated with 'human animality and mortality'; 'projective disgust' functions as a mechanism for buffering the 'dominant group more securely from its own feared animality' by manufacturing a class of 'quasi humans' who embody those traits.[5] One need look no further than Henry Mayhew's formative research on London's 'metropolitan poor', which strongly influenced nineteenth-century writers and reformers, for a catalogue of projective disgust. Mayhew regarded London's 'street children' as an 'ample field ... alike for wonder, disgust, pity, hope, and regret'—though it is the disgust that comes across most clearly, insofar as he considered 'the most remarkable characteristic of these wretched children [to be] their extraordinary licentiousness', an 'extreme animal fondness for the opposite sex' that is saturated in 'filthiness and ... uncleanliness'.[6] Subsequent observers emphasized crime and illness, as well. The confinement of poverty to overcrowded and undesirable neighbourhoods—or, more aptly, the 'herd[ing] together' of the poor

---

[3] William Ian Miller, *The Anatomy of Disgust* (Cambridge: Harvard University Press, 1997), 9.

[4] Kathryn Abrams, 'Fighting Fire with Fire: Rethinking the Role of Disgust in Hate Crimes', *California Law Review* 90, no. 5 (2002): 1423–64.

[5] Martha C. Nussbaum, *From Disgust to Humanity: Sexual Orientation and Constitutional Law* (New York: Oxford University Press, 2010), 13–15; see also Martha C. Nussbaum, *Hiding from Humanity: Disgust, Shame, and the Law* (Princeton: Princeton University Press, 2004), 87–98.

[6] Henry Mayhew, *London Labor and the London Poor* (London: Griffin, Bohn, and Co., 1861), 477.

with 'alien[s]' and criminals—served to focus and amplify stigma. Those higher up in the social hierarchy coalesced around a shared aversion to those 'veritable hotbeds of disease', the 'filthy and oftentimes unutterably disgusting slums'.[7]

Notwithstanding the myth of a classless America, such descriptions were equally prevalent across the Atlantic. As Nancy Isenberg documents in her recent history of class in the United States, 'seeing the indigent as wastrels, as the dregs of society', was core to American society from its inception.[8] The colonists dispatched to the New World were the 'offals of our people', and the colonies functioned as 'emunctories', filtering Britain's waste.[9] Such images abounded at every stage of American history. Thomas Jefferson used the term 'rubbish',[10] but the station of America's 'waste people' was captured most pithily in the middle of the nineteenth century, with the emergence of the label 'white trash'.[11] The poor, moreover, were routinely classified by their breeding potential, in explicit comparison with animal husbandry.[12]

Depictions of this kind are more than historical artefacts. British scholars have characterized the recent emergence of the 'chav' figure, the representational object of 'intense class-based abhorrence',[13] as an exercise in differentiating the middle and upper classes from the poor in a period when traditional status markers have become less probative.[14] In the face of a conspicuously rising wealth gap,[15] journalistic accounts of

[7] Arthur Whetnall, 'Sermon at Rose Mount Church', *Journal of the Royal Institute of Public Health* 15 (1907): 618–23, 621.

[8] Nancy Isenberg, *White Trash: The 400-Year Untold History of Class in America* (New York: Viking, 2016), 21.

[9] Isenberg, *White Trash*, 22 (quoting contemporary descriptions). As Isenberg observes, Cicero described the poor in similar terms.

[10] Isenberg, *White Trash*, 91.

[11] Isenberg, *White Trash*, 135–7.

[12] Isenberg, *White Trash*, 141.

[13] Keith Haywood and Majid Yar, 'The "Chav" Phenomenon: Consumption, Media and the Construction of a New Underclass', *Crime, Media, Culture* 2, no. 1 (2006): 9–28, 16.

[14] Imogen Tyler, 'Chav Mum Chav Scum', *Feminist Media Studies* 8, no. 1 (2008): 17–34, 18.

[15] See, for example, Daniel Dorling et al., *Poverty, Wealth and Place in Britain, 1968 to 2005* (Bristol: Policy Press for the Joseph Rowntree Foundation, 2007).

the chav as 'disgusting, selfish, [and] violent'[16] have operated to 'produce a disgust which is not simply reactive but is constitutive of social class'.[17] Meanwhile, in the United States, disgust towards 'welfare queens' and 'white trash' continues apace.[18] The latter is captured colourfully by critical responses to the reality television show 'Here Comes Honey Boo Boo', featuring (*Forbes* complained) 'a horde of lice-picking, lard-eating, nose-thumbing hooligans south of the Mason–Dixon line';[19] although the *Hollywood Reporter* decried its 'dehumanization and incremental tearing down of the social fabric', the show attracted millions of viewers.[20]

The stigmatization of the poor appears to be deeply ingrained. Neuroimaging studies have revealed that homeless people are perceived as 'less than human' and 'elicit the worst kind of prejudice—disgust and contempt'.[21] Often, dehumanization of this kind occurs unconsciously: 'Participants realize rationally that homeless people are literally human, but they respond to them as if they are not.'[22] Many people, however, are unabashed about their disgust, as is evident in the massive circulation of *Bumfights*, a video compilation of impoverished men paid to perform humiliating acts and to batter one another on camera.[23] Displays of this sort are self-reinforcing. By portraying the poor as utterly lacking

[16] James Delingpole, 'A Conspiracy against Chavs? Count Me In', *Times*, 13 April 2006, 25.

[17] Tyler, 'Chav Mum Chav Scum', 19.

[18] See Ange-Marie Hancock, *The Politics of Disgust: The Public Identity of the Welfare Queen* (New York: New York University Press, 2004), 9.

[19] Julia Bricklin, 'TLC's "Here Comes Honey Boo Boo" Isn't All That Bad', *Forbes*, 12 August 2012.

[20] Tim Goodman, '"Honey Boo Boo": That Joke Isn't Funny Anymore', *Hollywood Reporter*, 22 August 2012; see Julia Leyda, 'Class, Cuteness, and Disgust in Here Comes Honey Boo Boo', https://workingclassstudies.wordpress.com/2015/10/19/class-cuteness-and-disgust-in-here-comes-honey-boo-boo/.

[21] Lasana T. Harris and Susan T. Fiske, 'Dehumanizing the Lowest of the Low: Neuroimaging Responses to Extreme Out-Groups', *Psychological Science* 17, no. 1 (2006): 847–53, 848.

[22] Lasana T. Harris and Susan T. Fiske, 'Perceiving Humanity or Not: A Social Neuroscience Approach to Dehumanized Perception', in *Social Neuroscience: Toward Understanding the Underpinnings of the Social Mind*, eds, Alexander Todorov, Susan T. Fiske, and Deborah A. Prentice (Oxford: Oxford University Press 2011), 123–34, 128.

[23] Rick Lyman, 'Judge Dismisses "Bumfights" Felony Charges', *New York Times*, 17 January 2003.

in self-worth and radically dissimilar in their values and choices, they render reform apparently impossible and continued poverty inevitable. According to the National Coalition for the Homeless, humiliation and stigma affect 'practically every homeless individual'.[24]

Of course, identifying disgust as an independent and illegitimate source of class hierarchy and social inequality requires extricating class-based disgust from prejudice directed towards other identity traits for which poverty often serves as a proxy. Historically, the disgust associated with poverty was closely associated with the stigmatization of disabilities that rendered individuals unable to work.[25] Similarly, transgressions of gender norms by impoverished women have provoked disgust towards their bodies.[26] And it is impossible to study the salience of class in America without exploring its intersection with race.[27] Consider, for example, the term 'white trash', which requires a modifier only because abject poverty is modally non-white.[28]

The notion that class, apart from or even more intensely than race, might serve as a source of prejudice and disgust has encountered hostility from competing quarters. Many scholars and activists worry that shifting attention from racial to economic justice will hamper efforts to redress racial inequality. In the affirmative action context, for instance, class-based proposals have proven more palatable than their race-conscious alternatives, with potentially deleterious consequences for the latter.[29] At the same time, some reformers who are committed to

[24] National Coalition for the Homeless (NCH), 'Discrimination and Economic Profiling among the Homeless of Washington, DC' (policy briefing paper, National Coalition for the Homeless (NCH), April 2014), 3.

[25] See Susan M. Schweik, *The Ugly Laws: Disability in Public* (New York: New York University Press, 2009); Beverley Skeggs, *Class, Self, Culture* (New York: Routledge, 2004).

[26] See, for example, Hancock, *Politics of Disgust*.

[27] On intersectionality, see Kimberlé W. Crenshaw, 'Mapping the Margins: Intersectionality, Identity Politics and Violence Against Women of Color', *Stanford Law Review* 43 (1991): 1241–79; John A. Powell, 'The Race and Class Nexus: An Intersectional Perspective,' *Law and Inequality* 25, no. 2 (2007): 355–428.

[28] British 'chavs' are likewise white, but theirs is a 'contaminated' whiteness, either insufficiently white or excessively so. Tyler, 'Chav Mum Chav Scum', 25.

[29] On the inadequacy of class-based affirmative action, see, for example, Deborah C. Malamud, 'Class Based Affirmative Action: Lessons and Caveats', *Texas Law Review* 74 (1996): 1847–1900.

equality for people of colour and other marginalized groups themselves harbour prejudice against the poor. Barbara Ehrenreich complained more than 25 years ago that '"enlightened" people, who might flinch at a racial slur, have no trouble listing the character defects of an ill-defined "underclass", defects which routinely include ignorance, promiscuity, and sloth'.[30] Such assessments resonate with broad social acceptance of the apologist rationalization 'it's not about race, it's about class' to excuse elite prejudice against impoverished minority communities.[31] It is class, many Americans now argue, that is responsible for the perceived cultural chasm between elite whites and communities of colour.

Notably, critics of this sentiment typically reject it not because it legitimizes class prejudice, but rather because it minimizes persistent racism.[32] The apparent upshot is that if poverty alone, stripped of its racial overlay, were truly the source of the prejudice, few would object. Certainly many policymakers and social theorists regard economic inequality as a social pathology. But however much they regret the stigmatization that follows from poverty and deprivation, they rarely argue that it is unfounded or irrational, as is typical in the context of race. Race may be a social construct, but poverty, while certainly sustained by social practices, is a material reality.

This is not, of course, to suggest that all of the attributes associated with poverty are disgusting in some neutral or primary sense. On the contrary, the projection of disease and uncleanliness onto the poor is a crucial component of maintaining class hierarchy. Such is the thrust of George Orwell's iconic investigation of the British working class, *The Road to Wigan Pier*, which ascribes the intractability of class prejudice in the West to a belief among the upper classes that '*the lower classes smell*'.[33] For

---

[30] Barbara Ehrenreich, *Fear of Falling: The Inner Life of the Middle Class* (New York: Pantheon, 1989), 7.

[31] See, for example, Adolph Reed, 'The Real Divide', *Progressive*, November 2005, 27–32. William Julius Wilson famously argued that 'class has become more important than race in determining black life-chances in the modern industrial period'. William Julius Wilson, *The Declining Significance of Race: Blacks and Changing American Institutions* (Chicago: University of Chicago Press, 1978), 150.

[32] See Mario L. Barnes and Erwin Chemerinsky, 'The Disparate Treatment of Race and Class in Constitutional Jurisprudence', *Law and Contemporary Problems* 72, no. 4 (2009): 109–130, 124.

[33] George Orwell, *The Road to Wigan Pier* (London: V. Gollancz Ltd., 1937), 159 (italics in original).

Orwell, it is this '*physical* feeling', instilled in the middle class in child-hood, that prevents a 'European of bourgeois upbringing, even when he calls himself a Communist', from relating to a 'working man as his equal'. Whether the lower classes smelled in fact was beside the point; 'the essential thing is that middle-class people *believe* that the working class are dirty … and, what is worse, that they are somehow *inherently* dirty.'[34]

Put simply, as with race, the disgust directed towards the lower classes (even if 'as a whole, they are dirtier than the upper classes') is often imagined.[35] Orwell believed this visceral reaction prevented meaningful mingling of the classes and impeded efforts at reform. Contemporary opponents of economic redistribution evidently share Orwell's insight. Reflecting on a documentary film about the Occupy movement that he directed, Stephen Bannon asserted that 'when you finish watching [it], you want to take a hot shower … You want to go home and shower because you've just spent an hour and fifteen minutes with the greasiest, dirtiest people you will ever see'.[36] In Bannon's insistence that the Occupy movement—with its trenchant attack on American income inequality—was defined by 'raping, pillaging, [and] pooping'[37] as opposed to political ideals, one finds a chilling affirmation of Orwell's understanding that the best way to disarm class agitators is to disdain or dehumanize them. 'Race-hatred, religious hatred, differences of education, of temperament, of intellect, even differences of moral code, can be got over,' Orwell explained, 'but physical repulsion can-not.'[38]

Legal Manifestations of Class-Based Disgust

Just as it is challenging to disentangle class-based disgust from other forms of prejudice, it is difficult to isolate the influence of disgust, as distinct from other motivations, in framing the legal regulation of poverty. Many laws that classify or exclude on economic grounds serve purposes

[34] Orwell, *The Road to Wigan Pier*, 159–60, 162; see also Miller, *Anatomy of Disgust*, 247.

[35] Orwell, *The Road to Wigan Pier*, p. 162.

[36] Connor Friedersdorf, 'The Radical Anti-Conservatism of Stephen Bannon', *Atlantic*, 25 August 2016.

[37] Adam Wren, 'What I Learned Binge-Watching Steve Bannon's Documentaries', *Politico Magazine*, 2 December 2016.

[38] Orwell, *The Road to Wigan Pier*, 160.

that do not obviously implicate disgust. For example, governments eager to conserve public resources or to preserve public safety routinely condition access to public facilities on ability to pay, as with rental and permitting fees. State universities effectively exclude many students by charging tuition. Governments regularly restrict access to professional employment based on such class-linked criteria as educational attainment or solvency, as in the case of accreditation and licensing laws. In short, pricing of goods and services in a market economy necessarily disadvantages the poor, regardless of whether private or government actors are the providers. Presumably, prejudice is rarely the principal motivation for requiring payment, even if the consequence is to stigmatize low-status groups and even to hold them in poverty.

Comparatively few laws have distinguished among citizens on the basis of their class *status*, as opposed to ability to pay. Nonetheless, some such laws existed and, indeed, structured the very emergence of western democracy. Laws conditioning the right to vote or hold office on property ownership were meant to block redistributive policies, but they also conveyed beliefs about the inferior capabilities of the lower classes. The United States Constitution itself was carefully crafted to insulate against the unruly masses.[39] Again, such policies probably were intended more to ensure national solvency (or, more cynically, to preserve the founders' financial interests) than to perpetuate hierarchy per se. Still, the hardening of class stratification has been an undoubted effect of legislative enactments and constitutional design.[40]

Setting such laws to one side, it is possible to identify a number of cases in which stigma and disgust have played formative, if not exclusive, roles in shaping law. The force of disgust is most obvious in laws obscuring poverty from view, examples of which abound. For many purposes, pricing has served as a reasonably effective stand-in for a Jim Crow-style network of anti-poor laws: housing costs have typically segregated working-class families in low-rent areas. Yet pricing alone does little to deter those in extreme poverty, who cannot afford housing of any kind and

---

[39] See Charles A. Beard, *An Economic Interpretation of the Constitution of the United States* (New York: Macmillan, 1913); Michael J. Klarman, *The Framers' Coup: The Making of the United States Constitution* (New York: Oxford University Press, 2016).

[40] See, for example, Beverly Moran and Stephanie Wildman, 'Race and Wealth Disparity: The Role of Law and the Legal System', *Fordham Urban Law Journal* 34, no. 4 (2006): 1219–38.

might be inclined to beg and sleep in the streets and parks of wealthy neighbourhoods. Many communities responded with vagrancy laws, which had originated in medieval England and 'were built for hierarchy and social order'.[41] Together with sumptuary laws requiring individuals to wear clothing appropriate to their rank and the 'poor laws' that regulated the neediest individuals, they reflected and reinforced social stratification and confined the poor to designated spaces. Vagrancy laws thrived in America from the colonial period onward, in part because they ensured a ready workforce. With the emergence of wage labour and the expansion of American industry, Amy Dru Stanley has explained, individuals who elected to beg rather than work 'hovered outside the bounds of commodity exchange', and criminal law intervened to quiet 'the almsgiver's moral dilemma'.[42] Convicted vagrants were fined, jailed, or set to hard labour.

Still, disgust was a core component of the vagrancy project; the laws, which were explicitly status-based, included 'rogues and vagabonds, or dissolute persons who go about begging' among the kinds of people it rendered criminal.[43] Historian Risa Goluboff's observation that vagrancy laws targeted 'people out of place' implicitly echoes Mary Douglas's seminal insight that boundary violations often trigger concerns about contagion.[44] Disgust reactions to poverty and law's policing of class boundaries are mutually constitutive. Fear of contamination leads to enforced spatial separation, which in turn fosters marginalization and disgust.

In the late nineteenth century, a new strain of local ordinances developed alongside vagrancy laws and channelled disgust even more explicitly. The so-called 'unsightly beggar' or 'ugly' laws, which emerged in the wake of the Civil War, are best known for excluding people

---

[41] Risa Goluboff, *Vagrant Nation: Police Power, Constitutional Change, and the Making of the 1960s* (New York: Oxford University Press, 2016), 2.

[42] Amy Dru Stanley, *From Bondage to Contract: Wage Labor, Marriage, and the Market in the Age of Slave Emancipation* (Cambridge: Cambridge University Press, 1998), 100.

[43] *Papachristou v. City of Jacksonville*, 405 U.S. 156, 1972, at 156 n. 1. See also Caleb Foote, 'Vagrancy-Type Law and Its Administration', *University of Pennsylvania Law Review* 104, no. 5 (1956): 603–50, 631 (documenting vagrancy arrests on the basis that 'the appearance of the victims was not attractive').

[44] Mary Douglas, *Purity and Danger: An Analysis of Concepts of Pollution and Taboo* (London: Routledge & K. Paul, 1966) (describing 'matter out place').

with disabilities from public places.[45] But they also encompassed the indigent, whose begging in streets and parks marred the landscape and induced physical discomfort. Thus, Chicago's 1881 City Code imposed a fine against the exposure to 'public view' of 'any person who is diseased, maimed, mutilated, or in any way deformed, so as to be an unsightly or disgusting object', but also of any 'improper person', which included the able-bodied poor.[46] The resolution promoting the ordinance cited the intrusion on Chicago's streets and sidewalks of 'numerous beggars, mendicants, organ-grinders and other unsightly and unseemly objects', which were 'disagreeable' to residents of the city, disruptive of local businesses, and sometimes dangerous.[47] As Susan Marie Schweik makes clear in her comprehensive study of the regulations, 'it is always perfectly possible to attribute disfigurement to the poor as a group, and the pressing destitution in the body politic is capable of embodying the unsightly in and of itself.'[48]

The legacy of these laws persisted well into the twentieth century, and indeed, endures today. Although the Supreme Court invalidated some species of vagrancy laws as unconstitutionally vague in the 1970s,[49] states and localities retained authority to prohibit the act of begging, and a new wave of criminalization has followed the economic downturn. Local governments have pursued a broad range of regulations to displace poverty from public view, including enforcement of general disorderly conduct laws, specific prohibitions on solicitation, and even restrictions on sharing food.[50]

The purification of public spaces has taken many other forms. Governments have experimented with a bevy of policies to erase urban blight, including zoning, slum clearance, eminent domain, and subsidies for private redevelopment. The California legislature recently catalogued the 'long history of discriminatory laws and ordinances that

---

[45] See generally Schweik, *Ugly Laws*. The term 'ugly laws' originated in Marcia Pearce Burgdorf and Robert Burgdorf Jr, 'A History of Unequal Treatment: The Qualifications of Handicapped Persons as "Suspect Class" under the Equal Protection Clause', *Santa Clara Lawyer* 15, no. 4 (1975): 855–910.

[46] The ordinance is reproduced in Schweik, *Ugly Laws*, 293.

[47] Schweik, *Ugly Laws*, 293.

[48] Schweik, *Ugly Laws*, 32.

[49] *Papachristou*, 405 U.S. 156.

[50] Reports on recent laws targeting homelessness are available at http://homelessnesslaw.org and http://nationalhomeless.org.

have disproportionately affected people with low incomes and who are without homes'. In addition to unsightly beggar and vagrancy laws, it included state-sanctioned segregation; Depression-era prohibitions against facilitating entry into the state of impoverished 'Okies'; sundown town ordinances, which prevented 'minorities, homeless persons, and other persons considered to be socially undesirable from remaining within city limits after sunset'; and 'quality of life ordinances', which effectively confined the poor to 'crowded, unsanitary, substandard and unhealthful accommodations'.[51]

Disgust has also fuelled measures to manage people more directly. Poor-relief and welfare programmes have long been designed and administered to stigmatize recipients of public aid as lazy and incapable.[52] Notwithstanding the Statue of Liberty's bold invitation to the 'poor', the 'homeless', and the 'huddled masses yearning to breathe free'—or, more to the point, to the world's 'wretched refuse'[53]—Congress elected to exclude from admission to the United States 'aliens who are paupers, professional beggars, or vagrants', or 'are likely at any time to become public charges'.[54] Those who managed to slip through were subject to deportation.[55]

Sometimes, government actors have sought to eradicate the indigent rather than exclude or relocate them. In the early twentieth century, the very social workers and charity leaders who advocated aid for society's most desperate individuals occasionally succumbed to disgust. For some, who embraced eugenics, the preferred solution to destitution was forcible sterilization.[56] Poverty had evolved from a moral failing to a genetic

---

[51] 'California AB-5, Homelessness, 2013-2014', http://leginfo.legislature. ca.gov/faces/billNavClient.xhtml?bill_id=201320140AB5.

[52] See, for example, Michael B. Katz, *In the Shadow of the Poorhouse: A Social History of Welfare in America* (New York: Basic Books, 1986), 155. For an argument that New Deal-era federal public assistance sought to move instead to a rights-based model, see Karen M. Tani, *States of Dependency: Welfare, Rights, and American Governance, 1935-1972* (New York: Cambridge University Press, 2016), 59.

[53] Emma Lazarus, 'The New Colossus', 1883, available at https://www.nps. gov/stli/learn/historyculture/colossus.htm.

[54] *Graham v. Richardson*, 403 U.S. 365, 1971, at 377; 8 U.S.C. §§ 1182(a) (8), (a)(15) (1982). In the colonial period, towns accomplished the same task by 'warning out' those without means of supporting themselves.

[55] 8 U.S.C. § 1251(a)(8) (current version at 8 U.S.C. § 1227)).

[56] See Schweik, *Ugly Laws*, 50–2.

defect—the affliction of an inferior breeding stock that threatened to infect the human race.

Combating Class-Based Disgust

Assuming that disgust has served as an illegitimate impetus for laws that regulate access to public spaces and allocate scarce resources to people in need, what can be done to counter its pernicious effects? Can law ameliorate the damage disgust has wrought?

In the United States, opponents of discriminatory laws have often turned to the Constitution as a foundation for rights claims, and legal scholars have advanced a variety of arguments supporting constitutional protection for the poor.[57] Looking forward, however, the Constitution appears an unlikely tool for dismantling social hierarchy, at least at the federal level.[58] Although the United States Supreme Court has interpreted the Equal Protection Clause of the Fourteenth Amendment to reach discrimination on the basis of gender and religion in addition to race, it has afforded government actors tremendous latitude to disfavour the poor.

For a short period during the late 1960s and the early 1970s, it seemed as if the court might adopt a different approach. In a series of cases involving the exercise of rights that the court deemed fundamental, such as the rights to vote, run for office, and marry, as well as the procedural rights of criminal defendants, it required states to except the indigent from payment of fees.[59] Although these cases only indirectly

---

[57] This wide-ranging literature includes Archibald Cox, 'Foreword: Constitutional Adjudication and the Promotion of Human Rights', *Harvard Law Review* 80 (1966): 91–122; Frank Michelman, 'Foreword: On Protecting the Poor Through the Fourteenth Amendment', *Harvard Law Review* 83 (1969): 7–59; Peter B. Edelman, 'The Next Century of Our Constitution: Rethinking Our Duty to the Poor', *Hastings Law Journal* 39 (1987): 1–61; William E. Forbath, 'Caste, Class and Equal Citizenship,' *Michigan Law Review* 98 (1999): 1–91.

[58] On state constitutional alternatives, see Emily J. Zackin, *Looking for Rights in All the Wrong Places: Why State Constitutions Contain America's Positive Rights* (Princeton: Princeton University Press, 2013).

[59] For example, *Griffin v. Illinois*, 351 U.S. 12, 1956 (access to trial transcripts); *Douglas v. California*, 372 U.S. 353, 1963 (right of indigent to counsel on direct appeal); *Harper v. Virginia Board of Elections*, 383 U.S. 663, 1966 (voting fee); *Boddie v. Connecticut*, 401 U.S. 371, 1971 (divorce); *Bullock v. Carter*,

implicated social class, they gave some hope to poverty law advocates. In striking down Virginia's poll tax, for example, the court explained that 'lines drawn on the basis of wealth or property, like those of race are traditionally disfavored'.[60] Several justices indicated in concurring opinions that they were prepared to recognize wealth as a 'suspect classification' for equal protection purposes.[61]

Soon, however, a majority of the Supreme Court signalled its intention to hold its modest line. 'In the area of economics and social welfare', it explained in 1970, 'a State does not violate the Equal Protection Clause merely because the classifications made by its laws are imperfect'—even when its policies 'involve[d] the most basic economic needs of impoverished human beings'.[62] Advocates raised the issue of poverty as a suspect classification squarely in *Rodriguez v. San Antonio Independent School District*, which challenged gross inequalities in the financing of public education. A lower court accepted the plaintiffs' argument, but the Supreme Court reversed it.[63] Although it did not (yet) conclusively rule out the possibility that wealth-based classifications might trigger special scrutiny, a majority of justices assumed that 'the class of disadvantaged "poor" cannot be identified or defined in customary equal protection terms'.[64] In so doing, they implicitly rejected the lawyers' argument that 'the poor, like racial and ethnic minorities, have been unable to secure basic rights through the legislative process' and were therefore 'among the "discrete and insular minorities" for whom the court exercises special solicitude.'[65]

In the years after *Rodriguez*, the Supreme Court made clear that 'poverty, standing alone, is not a suspect classification'.[66] Even as it extended constitutional protection to expenditures to influence the electoral process,[67] the court rejected the notion that the poor are inadequately

---

405 U.S. 134, 1972 (filing fee for participation in primary); *Zablocki v. Redhail*, 434 U.S. 374, 1978 (marriage).

[60] *Harper*, 383 U.S. 663, at 668.

[61] *Boddie* 401 U.S. 371 (Justices Brennan and Douglas, concurring); see also *James v. Valtierra*, 402 U.S. 137, 1971 (Justice Marshall, dissenting).

[62] *Dandridge v. Williams*, 397 U.S. 471, 1970, at 485.

[63] *Rodriguez v. San Antonio Independent School District*, 337 F. Supp 280, W.D. Tex., 1971.

[64] *Rodriguez* 411 U.S. 1, at 19.

[65] Brief for appellees, No. 71-1332, *Rodriguez* 411 U.S. 1, 1973, at 39.

[66] *Harris v. McRae*, 448 U.S. 297, 1980, at 323.

[67] *Buckley v. Valeo*, 424 U.S. 1, 1976.

represented in ordinary politics.[68] Other avenues of constitutional protection have proven to be dead ends, as well. The court has declined to expand the list of Equal Protection 'fundamental rights'. Although it invoked the Privileges or Immunities clause to prohibit California from conditioning assistance payments on length of residency in the state, it framed its analysis narrowly around the right to travel.[69] It has interpreted the Due Process Clause of the Fourteenth Amendment to require states to provide evidentiary hearings before terminating welfare payments once it has initiated them, but it has preserved plenty of leeway for states in setting the terms of support.[70] And while the court has accepted that a law premised on prejudice and stigma might run afoul of the Constitution, even in the absence of a suspect classification or fundamental right, its reasoning offers little hope in the vast majority of cases affecting the poor, which are seldom motivated by a 'bare ... desire to harm a politically unpopular group'.[71]

Might highlighting the role of disgust have strengthened the case for constitutional protection? Perhaps. It might have buttressed the argument that 'classification of the "poor" as such, ... like classification of racial minorities as such, [is] popularly understood as a badge of inferiority': that poverty, like other protected classes, carries a stigma.[72] The Supreme Court has drawn on a variety of metrics (some more consistently and persuasively than others) to assess the vulnerability of particular groups, including evidence of past persecution and the 'immutability' of the disfavoured trait.[73] Confronting the court with the depth of class prejudice and the breadth of its legal scaffolding might have moved it to recognize that the indigent, in certain relevant respects, resemble other vulnerable groups. And although poverty is often assumed to be a temporary state, statistics on class mobility reflect that social class is

[68] See, for example, Stephen Loffredo, 'Poverty, Democracy and Constitutional Law', *University of Pennsylvania Law Review* 141 (1993): 1277–389, 1281–2.

[69] *Sáenz v. Roe*, 526 U.S. 489, 1999.

[70] *Goldberg v. Kelly*, 397 U.S. 254, 1970; *Dandridge* 397 U.S. 471.

[71] *Romer v. Evans*, 517 U.S. 620, 1996, at 634.

[72] Michelman, 'Foreword'; 21; see also Barnes and Chemerinsky, 'Disparate Treatment of Race and Class', 119; Inez Smith Reid, 'Law, Politics and the Homeless', *West Virginia Law Review* 89 (1986): 115–47.

[73] *Lockhart v. McCree*, 476 U.S. 162, 1986, at 175; *Regents of the University of California v. Bakke*, 438 U.S. 265, 1978, at 360–1.

barely more mutable than other identity markers, such as religion, that enjoy constitutional protection. To be sure, redistributive policies could intervene to erode class distinctions. But the elected branches have often acted to exacerbate, rather than mitigate, wealth disparities, and the courts have not stood in the way. Ironically, the theoretical capacity of law to reduce economic inequality has marked social class as a permeable category that is considered undeserving of heightened constitutional scrutiny, even while the denial of constitutional protection has hardened class boundaries on the ground.

Of course, even if laws targeting the poor had garnered heightened scrutiny, the reach of constitutional protection would be limited. Wealth classifications can generally be justified as measures to conserve public resources or incentivize productive behaviour. In a doctrinal framework that requires evidence of discriminatory intent, not just disparate impact, they would almost always pass constitutional muster. Moreover, the Equal Protection Clause applies only to state action. It cannot touch the domain of private employment and housing, where prejudice against the poor most palpably reinforces the cycle of poverty. Certainly there are symbolic reasons to seek constitutional recognition, just as prohibiting race discrimination may be crucial to constitutional legitimacy, notwithstanding the persistence of dramatic inequality.[74] Asserting as a constitutional matter that government may not single out the poor for disfavoured treatment on the basis of stigma or prejudice might have dignitary value, regardless of its practical effect. Still, given the reality of the current constitutional landscape, activists in recent years have turned primarily to legislative channels to secure protections for the poor.

On the whole, legislatures too have been inhospitable forums. The widespread conviction that poverty is the consequence of sloth, ineptitude, or culture rather than foreclosed opportunities has made it considerably more difficult for the poor to advance their cause in the political branches.[75] For centuries, observers differentiated between the 'deserving' and 'undeserving' poor, that is, 'those who are incapable of

---

[74] Conversely, constitutional protection might function as window dressing, legitimating inequality.

[75] See, for example, Alice O'Connor, *Poverty Knowledge: Social Science, Social Policy, and the Poor in Twentieth-Century U.S. History* (Princeton: Princeton University Press, 2001); Loic Wacquant, 'Scrutinizing the Street: Poverty, Morality, and the Pitfalls of Urban Ethnography', *American Journal of Sociology* 107, no. 6 (2002): 1468–532.

working', and 'such as are able, but unwilling'.[76] The latter class was presumed vastly to outnumber the former, and 'whatever [was] given to these miscreants [was] considered as applied to the rising fund of vice and immorality'.[77] Because poverty was attributed to individual rather than social failings, the preferred remedies were oriented towards personal improvement. 'There is no doubt that the great cure of unsanitary conditions is the elevation of the individual,' a typical commentator advised in the early twentieth century.[78] Legislative solutions were consequently futile: 'You cannot make people moral by act of Parliament.'[79] In the era of modern social science, this trope of personal and cultural deficiency evolved into a behavioural critique of the underclass. As much as or more than the structural conditions of poverty, scholars identified the tendency of 'ghettoization' to exacerbate the cultural insularity of the poor,[80] and policymakers foregrounded assimilation rather than material assistance as a solution.[81]

It is no surprise, then, that social class is rarely included among the many identity categories safeguarded from discrimination in federal and state legislation. Title VII of the 1964 Civil Rights Act encompasses 'race, color, religion, sex and national origin'. The Fair Housing Act adds disability and familial status. Many state statutes and local ordinances extend to sexual orientation and gender identity. Some include such factors as age, immigration status, or genetic information. A few even ensure that no employer 'discriminate against an individual … because the individual is a smoker or nonsmoker'.[82] Yet barely any include poverty among the forbidden grounds of discrimination.[83]

[76] A.F.M. Willich, *The Domestic Encyclopaedia*, vol. 1 (1802) (London: Printed for Murray and Highly [et al.]), 245 (entry on 'beggars').

[77] Willich, *The Domestic Encyclopaedia*, 245.

[78] Whetnall, 'Sermon', 622.

[79] Whetnall, 'Sermon', 622.

[80] For example, Douglas S. Massey and Nancy A. Denton, *American Apartheid: Segregation and the Making of the Underclass* (Cambridge: Harvard University Press, 1993).

[81] See Elijah Anderson, *Code of the Street: Decency, Violence, and the Moral Life of the Inner City* (New York: Norton, 2000).

[82] KRS 344.040 (Kentucky).

[83] Some such laws have existed for decades, though homeless individuals report ineffective enforcement. See National Coalition for the Homeless (NCH), *Discrimination and Economic Profiling among the Homeless of Washington, DC* (Washington, DC: NCH, 2014).

In the past several years, however, a few states have begun to enact new laws prohibiting discrimination against the poor.[84] In 2012, through the efforts of the Rhode Island Coalition for the Homeless and Occupy Providence, among other groups, Rhode Island became the first state to enact a 'Homeless Bill of Rights'. The statute, which provides for remedies including injunctive relief and monetary damages (as well as attorneys' fees), gives homeless people the right to use public spaces freely, guarantees equal treatment from state and municipal agencies, confers privacy protections for personal property, and prohibits employment discrimination based on lack of a permanent address.[85] Other states have followed suit.[86] Advocacy groups have also advanced legislation to include homeless status in national hate crimes legislation.[87]

New legislation of this kind seeks first to check abuses of government power. Advocates contend that laws that prohibit sleeping in public spaces or sitting down on sidewalks are 'cruel, inhuman, and degrading', and they violate 'constitutional rights'. But they also make clear that 'criminalization measures', while the 'most egregious … civil rights violations', are merely one part of a comprehensive programme of discrimination. Thus, advocates also agitate for 'equal treatment by state and municipal authorities'. They ask the state to extend protection to society's most vulnerable people by making it possible, for example, for homeless people to access public services despite lacking an address. And they impose costs on non-state actors, including employers and landlords. Among other goals, such efforts are explicitly intended to 'combat stigma': to 'confront the foundation of prejudice upon which

[84] Some protections predated the Rhode Island bill, including the McKinney-Vento Homeless Assistance Act, reauthorized as Title XI, Part C of the No Child Left Behind Act, which requires equal access for homeless children to public school and preschool programmes.

[85] Puerto Rico had already enacted similar legislation. See Sara K. Rankin, 'A Homeless Bill of Rights (Revolution),' *Seton Hall Law Review* 45 (2015): 384–433.

[86] 'Discrimination and Economic Profiling among the Homeless of Washington, DC' (policy briefing paper, National Coalition for the Homeless, Washington, DC, April 2014) (Connecticut and Illinois).

[87] See National Coalition for the Homeless (NCH), *No Safe Street: A Survey of Hate Crimes and Violence Committed Against Homeless People in 2014 & 2015* (Washington, DC: NCH, 2015), advocating hate crimes legislation in response to 1,650 violent crimes against homeless individuals between 1999 and 2015, including murders, rapes, and mutilations.

discrimination against homeless people is based', and to 'underscore the importance of protecting the civil and human rights of *every* American'.[88]

Laws like these target prejudice against the poor. Most do not purport to combat poverty itself, except insofar as stigma and discrimination impede opportunities for escaping its pull. There are, of course, a great many reasons to structure a legal system in a manner that ensures the basic needs of all citizens are met; the extent to which the government is obligated to equalize opportunity and outcomes is among the most important and intractable inquiries of modern times, and introducing disgust as an ingredient of class relations will hardly resolve the debate. Indeed, as poverty law advocates presumably understood when they framed their constitutional challenges capaciously, legal reform directed merely towards disgust would clearly be inadequate. Economic inequality provokes protest even in the absence of unattractive and unsanitary conditions—a reality impressed by the residents of the well-manicured model town of Pullman, Illinois in 1894 when they initiated their ill-fated strike. As President Barack Obama emphasized in his 2013 inaugural address, social mobility is crucial to democratic legitimacy: it is fundamental to the American 'creed [that] a little girl born into the bleakest poverty knows that she has the same chance to succeed as anybody else'.[89]

Still, understanding the ways in which disgust naturalizes wealth disparities and discourages empathy with the poor has the capacity to advance the discussion. As one advocate explained: 'Once police are no longer given the power to remove homeless people from visibility we may be able to make more progress in the larger national conversation around ... social justice, and equality.'[90]

The Uncertain Upside of Disgust

Perhaps the thorniest question about the relationship between law, disgust, and social class is neither whether disgust infuses legal regulation

---

[88] National Law Center on Homelessness and Poverty, *From Wrongs to Rights: The Case for Homeless Bill of Rights Legislation* (Washington D.C., n.d.), 6–7, https://www.nlchp.org/documents/Wrongs_to_Rights_HBOR.

[89] Inaugural Address by President Barack Obama, 21 January 2013, https://obamawhitehouse.archives.gov/the-press-office/2013/01/21/inaugural-address-president-barack-obama.

[90] Paul Boden, 'Didn't Work Then, Won't Work Now', *Huffington Post*, 31 January 2013.

nor whether law can mitigate disgust, but rather whether disgust can ever be made an engine of legal progress. It is a puzzle that has long plagued reformers. In 1935, the poet Edwin Muir mused that 'if one hates the slums one may do something about them; but if one is filled with disgust of them there is nothing to do but to turn away'.[91] There is much to Muir's insight. History is replete with examples of social workers, legislators, and social scientists who opted to hide people living in poverty more than they helped them.

At the turn of the nineteenth century, a prominent encyclopaedia summarized the conventional wisdom aptly when it presumed, in its entry on 'beggars', that the poor who were 'incapable of working ... may be considered as real objects of charity; but they ought not be suffered to infest the streets, and expose their distorted limbs, or disgusting sores'.[92] One century later, the 'slum spots in our great cities' were considered 'the danger and disgrace of our modern civilization'; the only allowable conclusion was that 'the slums should be swept away'.[93] Although the rhetoric has changed, similar sentiments are surprisingly common today. 'The destitute ... are not supposed to soil public space with their urine, their feces, or their exhausted bodies', Barbara Ehrenreich poignantly complained, lest their odours or appearances 'spoil the landscape'.[94] As experiments in broken window policing have made clear, efforts to eliminate the aesthetic blight of poverty tend to stigmatize the poor without improving underlying conditions.[95] The homeless communities targeted by the recent wave of regulations limiting access to public spaces perceive the laws as 'knock[ing them] to the side like ... a piece of meat or a piece of paper', rather than trying 'to get to the root of the problem'.[96]

One response to this deeply troubling legacy of disgust is to reject disgust altogether as a basis for social policy. Thus, Martha Nussbaum

[91] Edwin Muir, *Scottish Journey* (London: W. Heinenmann, 1935), 117.

[92] Willich, *Domestic Encyclopaedia*, 245.

[93] Whetnall, 'Sermon', 621.

[94] Barbara Ehrenreich, 'Why Homelessness Is Becoming an Occupy Wall Street Issue', *Mother Jones*, 24 October 2011.

[95] Robert J. Sampson and Stephen W. Raudenbush, 'Seeing Disorder: Neighborhood Stigma and the Social Construction of "Broken Windows"', *Social Psychology Quarterly* 67, no. 4 (2004): 319–42.

[96] Alan Blinder, 'South Carolina City Takes Steps to Evict Homeless from Downtown', *New York Times*, 25 August 2013.

has written that disgust is a 'particular and highly questionable historical formation, one that has the social function of maintaining injurious hierarchies', and the 'really democratic act would be to criticize and to undo that social formation'.[97] To be sure, disgust is often lurking in laws that are independently desirable. In such cases, however, Nussbaum regards it as preferable to 'search for rationally defensible' justifications that are compatible with a 'political tradition based on equal respect'.[98] Disgust, for Nussbaum, is too normatively irrational and too entangled with stigma and hierarchy to serve as a productive basis for legal regulation.

In the domain of purely projective disgust—the troubling social stratification built on race, gender, sexual orientation, and disability, for example—there is much to recommend this view. But it is worth asking whether there is something distinctive about class-based disgust that might be turned to constructive ends. That is, might disgust towards destitution ever function as an appropriate and even catalysing human response?

One possible avenue for retooling disgust in the service of legal reform would be, following Dan Kahan, to 'reform its objects so that we come to value what is *genuinely* high, to despise what is *genuinely* low'.[99] Kahan argues that certain forms of rankings are inconsistent with liberalism, including 'those based on race, gender, and class', but that the proper response is to repurpose disgust to 'advance liberal ends':[100] to relegate intolerance and discrimination to the bottom of the hierarchy, as the appropriate objects of liberal disgust. Extrapolating from Kahan's analysis of 'pedophiles and sadists', one might properly evince disgust towards those who harass and dehumanize the poor: the producers of *Bumfights*, for example, or the perpetrators of hate crimes against the homeless. Rather than repudiate disgust, Kahan urges the law to recognize its inevitability and even to embrace it.

But it may be possible to steer a third course between these two poles. Liberal commitments to equality and human dignity render disgust towards members of most low-status groups an illegitimate basis for law. At least until the political upheaval of the past few years, it was a matter

---

[97] Martha Nussbaum, 'Foul Play', *New Republic*, 17 November 1997, 32–7, 36.

[98] Nussbaum, *Disgust to Humanity*, 20.

[99] Dan M. Kahan, 'The Anatomy of Disgust in Criminal Law', *Michigan Law Review* 96 (1998): 1621–57, 1653.

[100] Kahan, 'The Anatomy of Disgust in Criminal Law', 1652.

of broad consensus among American thinkers that a certain (concededly contested) set of identity markers should never serve as sources of disgust, and that even if disgust persisted, it should never motivate policy choices. In debates over affirmative action, for example, there is a shared disavowal of animus-based discrimination; disagreement at least ostensibly turns on whether preferential treatment of women and people of colour serves to reinforce their inferior social status or rather to help remediate it. In the class context, however, all but the most radical thinkers assume that continued inequality is an inevitable, even desirable, condition. In a capitalist economy, class stratification is definitional.

It does not follow, of course, that disgust towards the poor is equivalently unavoidable. A healthy dose of pluralism is important, and it would be all too easy to war against difference in the name of social progress. Still, the powerful role of law in structuring economic transactions and sustaining class hierarchy counsels a certain sensitivity to the consequences of poverty. Transposing the lessons of liberal pluralism and egalitarianism onto the problem of class, it is tempting to cast the consequences of poverty as alternative lifestyle choices, the dignified outputs of cultural difference. But doing so threatens to legitimate deprivation. Respecting a class culture that rejects deodorants or table manners does not necessitate celebrating the halitosis of dental decay or the untreated ulcers of chronic disease. In romanticizing working-class disdain for polite society, we come dangerously close to normalizing poverty and deprivation.

George Orwell has rightly been criticized for centring his classic account of class difference on a family with uncharacteristically unsavoury habits, such as storing a 'full chamber-pot under the breakfast table'.[101] But it is noteworthy that Orwell considered it 'a pity that those who idealise the working class so often think it necessary to praise every working-class characteristic and therefore to pretend that dirtiness is somehow meritorious in itself'.[102] In seeking to undermine disgust, Orwell argued, socialists were 'merely giving colour to the notion that working-class people are dirty from choice and not from necessity'. 'Actually', Orwell quipped, 'people who have access to a bath will generally use it'.[103] Building from Orwell's insight, it is one thing to loathe

---

[101] Orwell, *Wigan Pier*, 17.

[102] Orwell, *Wigan Pier*, 162.

[103] Orwell, *Wigan Pier*, 162. In the same vein, one homeless man remarked that he would rather sleep outside than in a shelter, adjacent to someone with 'hepatitis, tuberculosis, or what have you'. National Coalition for the Homeless,

the poor, and another to feel disgusted with particular circumstances, such as ill health or poor hygiene, that disproportionately afflict low-income populations. In fact, disgust towards conditions that are unsafe and unsanitary, and that we are complicit in producing, may be a necessary brake on expanding inequality. Surely there is a stark distinction between soup slurping and open sewage.

Of course, relying on disgust is not without its dangers. A war on poverty fuelled by disgust alone would leave deep inequality intact; indeed, slums that were made aesthetically pleasing might serve to mask and thereby legitimate class stratification. Similarly, it is all too easy for proposals premised on disgust to prescribe assimilation to middle-class culture and conformance to conservative ideals. Beautification policies imposed from without tend to reinforce the notion that the poor are incapable of self-improvement. The nineteenth-century muckrakers who sought to alleviate poverty by confronting the upper classes with evocative images of slums achieved some notable successes,[104] but they also traded in cultural stereotypes.[105] More baldly, a mid-twentieth century proponent of subsidized housing construction in Canada declared in the House of Commons that it was 'hardly sufficient' to regret, lament, or cry over the 'thousands of Canadians live[ing] in disgusting slums'; the appropriate reaction was to build affordable housing, because a 'subversive idea never gets past the threshold of young home owners'.[106]

Moreover, as a tool of social awareness, disgust has often misfired. Upton Sinclair famously sought in the *Jungle* to provoke public outcry over the exploitation of Progressive Era meatpackers and managed instead to elicit disgust at the unsavoury state of American meat.[107] In keeping with the typical workings of disgust, middle-class consumers

---

Swept Away: Reporting on the Encampment Closure Crisis (Washington, DC; NCH, 2016), 5.

[104] For example, Jacob A. Riis, *How the Other Half Lives: Studies among the Tenements of New York* (New York: C. Scribner's Sons, 1890).

[105] See, for example, Eileen Boris, *Home to Work: Motherhood and the Politics of Industrial Homework in the United States* (New York: Cambridge University Press, 1994). Abortion protestors' displays of images of aborted foetuses reflect a similar intuition about motivation for change; viewers are meant to channel their disgust towards abortion providers, not towards the foetuses themselves.

[106] Lionel Bertrand (Terrebonne), Canada House of Commons Debates, Official Report, vol. 3, 2803.

[107] Upton Sinclair, *The Jungle* (New York: Doubleday, Page, & Co., 1906).

fretted that their food was tainted both literally and figuratively by its proximity to poverty and disease. As Sinclair tellingly reflected, 'I aimed at the public's heart, and by accident I hit it in the stomach.'[108]

Above all, it will always be tempting to thrust the disgusting from view, to displace rather than remediate squalor, as the history of vagrancy, zoning, and slum clearance makes painfully clear. But it would be a mistake to conflate these remedies for disgust with the underlying emotional response. It may be that what was pernicious about these policies was the policing of boundaries and preservation of privilege rather than the disgust that motivated them.

Indeed, if disgust is a repudiation of our animal natures, perhaps it is uniquely suited to affirm our common humanity. It is chilling to imagine an individual who, confronting the poorest among us, felt no queasiness or unease about the indignities that squalor imposes. The potential for empathy is even stronger in times of acute economic uncertainty, when poverty as a category becomes more permeable and its contingency more acute. The precariousness that renders the poor something other than a 'discrete and insular minority' for equal protection purposes may lead those on the margins to preserve hierarchy all the more fiercely, but it might also be made the basis for shared concern.

Generations of reformers have believed in the power of disgust to provoke social change. What these reformers recognized was that disgust does not always or only impel us to avert our gaze. On the contrary, we often find ourselves peculiarly unable to look away. And this compulsion to regard the object of disgust might hold our focus for long enough to encourage rational reflection. Upon consideration, it might turn out that what disgusts us is not a human being, but rather the needless erosion of what makes us human.

[108] Upton Sinclair, 'What Life Means to Me,' *Cosmopolitan*, vol. 41, no. 6 (October 1906), 591–5, 594.

17

The Point of Discrimination Law

Securing the Freedom to Flourish

*Tarunabh Khaitan**

The Good Life: A Value-Pluralist Account

The point of discrimination law is to promote (an aspect of) personal well-being. Well-being is a measure of how successful one's life is. A successful life is one spent pursuing (through valuable means) valuable—moral, worthwhile—personal goals, nurturing valuable relationships, making valuable choices, and living virtuously. For a life to be successful, the pursuit of at least some personal goals should have a positive result. While a modest degree of failure in our pursuit of valuable goals may not affect our well-being, consistent failure at most of our pursuits will. Thus, the success of one's life depends not only on the availability of certain goods and on personal effort, but—at least to some measure—on luck. In requiring that our pursuits be 'valuable', what is

* This chapter is an excerpt from Chapters 4 and 5 of Tarunabh Khaitan, *A Theory of Discrimination Law* (New Delhi: Oxford University Press, 2015). I am grateful to Marlena Valles for invaluable assistance in finalizing the same.

being presented is a 'perfectionist' understanding of human flourishing, one that is based on an objective account of the human good. It differs from anti-perfectionist accounts which seek a connection between well-being and the subjective satisfaction of one's preferences and desires, or the pleasure one may derive from such satisfaction. It insists that our well-being is not served by the pursuit of valueless goals: well-being has a decidedly moral character. Despite the label, a perfectionist account need not require a life to be 'perfect' in order to be successful. At least the version being endorsed here only insists that whether a life has been successful can only be determined objectively.

The perfectionism of this account of well-being is tempered by several assumptions. First, this account assumes the truth of value pluralism— the idea that 'there are various forms and styles of life which exemplify different virtues and which are incompatible'.[1] There are innumerable and mutually incompatible ways of living a successful life, but no one life can, even in theory, achieve total perfection. Second, an unrestrained perfectionist may argue that even though there are innumerable ways of living a good life, for a particular person—given their particular talents and tastes—there is one, or only a few, best ways of living. So, for example, a person with a particular facility for music should, one may say, become a musician of some sort to fully realize her potential. But, in my account, even if she does not become a musician, her life may yet be successful. A successful life need not be one that is fully self-realized in this sense. As long as the life is characterized by value, it is sufficiently successful. Third, as Aristotle puts it, we must examine 'a complete life. For one swallow does not make a summer, nor does one day; and so too one day, or a short time does not make a man blessed and happy.'[2] A life's overall success is to be judged across its entire span, and not in relation to a particular moment in time or in the context of any particular event(s). Fourth, the success of a life is to be judged holistically from the point of view of the person whose life it is, in light of the resources and opportunities available to her.[3] The life of a poor woman who, against

---

[1] Joseph Raz, *The Morality of Freedom* (Oxford: Clarendon Press, 1986), 395.

[2] Aristotle, *The Nicomachean Ethics,* trans. David Ross (Oxford: Oxford University Press, 2009), I.7, 1098a18–19. See also Gerald Dworkin, *The Theory and Practice of Autonomy* (Cambridge: Cambridge University Press, 1998), 16

[3] Joseph Raz, *The Morality of Freedom* (Oxford: Clarendon Press, 1986), 299.

great odds, ensured that her children were well fed and educated is not necessarily less successful than that of a rich philanthropist whose charity has helped hundreds of other lives. Having said that, without at least a minimum access to the basic goods we are about to consider, a successful life does become impossible. Finally, the goals, relationships, choices, and so on that contribute to the success of our lives are themselves to be evaluated holistically.

These caveats remind us that one should be slow to evaluate people's lives and pursuits, and do so with due caution, mindful of the context and in light of the resources, opportunities, and possibilities. But they retain the original insistence that our well-being is not served merely through the satisfaction of our desires and preferences. The moral value of our pursuits is relevant to the success of our lives, and therefore to our well-being. In order to live a good life, we need secured access to at least four basic goods necessary for freedom: (a) a set of goods which will adequately satisfy one's biological needs; (b) negative freedom, that is, freedom from unjustified interference by others in one's person, projects, possessions, relationships, and affairs; (c) an adequate range of valuable opportunities to choose from; and (d) an appropriate level of self-respect. These goods are deeply interconnected. The emphasis here is on *sufficiency* and *security* of access—it is not enough to have access to the goods here and now. One must also be free from reasonable fear of losing this access.

This chapter supports the growing philosophical opinion that it is freedom rather than equality which provides a better foundation for discrimination law.[4] What these other freedom-based theories of discrimination lack (or, at least, fail to make sufficiently explicit) is the insight that the freedom we are entitled to also depends on the freedom that others enjoy. In other words, our liberty-interest is relative, because three of the four basic goods that constitute this interest have an essential connection with what others enjoy. Secured negative freedom cannot be enjoyed if there are particularly striking power

---

[4] See John Gardner, 'On the Ground of Her Sex(uality)', *Oxford Journal of Legal Studies* 18, no. 1 (1998): 167–87; Hugh Collins, 'Discrimination, Equality and Social Inclusion', *The Modern Law Review* 66, no. 1 (2003): 16–43; Sophia Moreau, 'What is Discrimination?', *Philosophy and Public Affairs* 38, no. 2 (2010): 143–79. Collins combines the fraternal ideal of solidarity with a liberal one (autonomy) to justify discrimination law. Gardner and Moreau use 'personal autonomy' and 'deliberative freedom', respectively.

imbalances between different societal groups. The range of opportunities that is adequate for us to have a flourishing life depends on the range of opportunities it is possible to have, which in turn depends on how much access the better-off people have. Even our self-respect has a relative dimension, inasmuch as it depends on how much respect others show to us, and how successful we believe our lives to be in relation to the success of the lives of others.

Goal of Discrimination Law

The question at hand is: What is it that discrimination law seeks to do?[5] This is one of the first questions legislators ask themselves before designing any legislation: What is the mischief that the law should seek to correct? It is also a question that a judge, when interpreting or making new law in the course of adjudication, may need to furnish some answer for. But it is, essentially, a legislative rather than an adjudicative question. It does not concern, at least not at any level of detail, the specific rights or obligations of particular persons involved in a given dispute. One may think that simply framing the question as a functional one is question-begging, inasmuch as it might be taken to have been assumed that every area of law has some teleological function.[6] This is not so. One could ask this question, at least in a thin sense, for all areas of law. Criminal law punishes persons for certain types of conduct. Contract law enforces certain types of agreement. Tort law compensates for certain types of injuries. It is only in this thin sense that I ask the functional question with respect to discrimination law: What does it do? It should be obvious that our responses are likely to turn on the most salient features of a given area of law: its subject matter, mode of operation, or the remedies it provides. Unlike other areas of law, however, it is not immediately obvious what the function of discrimination law is. This difficulty clearly relates to the diversity of tools that this area of law uses, the numerous contexts in which it applies, and the various enforcement mechanisms that are used to effect its implementation. So, in order to discover what it is that

---

[5] Notice that the question is framed not as what discrimination law actually *does*, but what it seeks to do. Even the best laid plans go awry. One cannot discover what discrimination law actually does from general conceptual analysis—that would require contextualized empirical investigation.

[6] See John Gardner, 'What is Tort Law For? Part 1: The Place of Corrective Justice', *Law and Philosophy* 30, no. 1 (2011): 1–2.

discrimination law seeks to do, we need to turn to its essence: there are four conditions that all anti-discrimination norms must satisfy:[7]

- The Personal Grounds Condition: The duty-imposing norm in question must require some connection between the act or omission prohibited or mandated by the norm on the one hand and certain attributes or characteristics that persons have, called 'grounds', on the other.
- The Cognate Groups Condition: A protected ground must be capable of classifying persons into more than one class of persons, loosely called 'groups'.
- The Relative Disadvantage Condition: Of all groups defined by a given universal order ground, members of at least one group must be significantly more likely to suffer abiding, pervasive, and substantial disadvantage than the members of at least one other cognate group.
- The Eccentric Distribution Condition: The duty-imposing norm must be designed such that it is likely to distribute the non-remote tangible benefits in question to some, but not all, members of the intended beneficiary group.

Before we pursue what we can discern from these conditions regarding the functions that discrimination law seeks to perform, we must define certain terms. *Protected grounds* are personal characteristics that satisfy the first three conditions above. They are characteristics with which norms of discrimination law require the acts they regulate to have some connection, and which divide persons into groups such that at least one of those groups is relatively disadvantaged. *Protected groups* are those groups whose members are significantly more likely to suffer abiding, pervasive, and substantial disadvantage than the members of at least one other cognate group. Women, for example, are a protected group. *Cognate groups* are the relatively privileged groups that share a protected ground with protected groups. So, men are cognates of women, because they share the ground 'gender'. When we speak of 'disadvantage' here, we are referring to systemic disadvantage suffered by protected groups, removal of which (I will argue) is the purpose of discrimination law. It does not refer to the injury or harm that may be caused by particular acts or omissions, which we may characterize as 'discriminatory'. To put

---

[7] For details on how these four conditions are derived, see Khaitan, *A Theory of Discrimination Law*, Chapter 2.

it differently, past acts of discrimination need not be the reason why a relatively disadvantaged group is protected.

Let us now return to the functional question at hand: What is it that discrimination law does? It should not be controversial that discrimination law is protective in nature—all its duties seek to protect or benefit certain persons under specified circumstances.[8] A superficially attractive, if tautological, claim that can be made is that:

> *Discrimination law seeks to protect persons from discrimination based on protected grounds.* (P1)

P1 not only explains discrimination law in terms of discrimination, it is also too simplistic an account of what discrimination law does to aid understanding. First, it fails to account for the salience of groups in discrimination law. This salience is suggested not just by the cognate groups and relative disadvantage conditions, but also by the eccentric distribution condition: discrimination law's curious non-universal distribution pattern makes sense only if one can see that the intended beneficiaries are groups rather than individuals. This is entirely compatible with a claim that the primary objects of moral concern are individual persons, not groups: one can be concerned with group disadvantage mainly (even solely) because of the impact it has on individuals. Second, discrimination law does more than prohibit discrimination *based on* protected grounds. P1 readily captures only the prohibitions on direct discrimination and harassment. Some linguistic juggling is required to show that indirect discrimination is *based on* a protected ground, whereas affirmative action can only be understood as compensating for past acts of discrimination under this formula. We should therefore refine our claim thus:

> *Discrimination law seeks to benefit some members of protected and cognate groups.* (P2)

P2, no doubt controversially, recognizes the centrality of groups in discrimination law (and also, indirectly, of grounds—which are essential to the definition of cognate groups). The clarification that only *some* members benefit accommodates the eccentric distribution condition. It still does not go far enough. Relative group disadvantage is not simply a qualifying hurdle that a personal ground needs to jump over in order to

---

[8] For brevity, I will use the term 'protection' to include 'benefit'.

be protected (as required in the relative disadvantage condition). Even after a ground becomes eligible for protection, the protection of discrimination law is largely (or, sometimes, completely) asymmetric—members of relatively disadvantaged groups tend to receive exclusive or stronger protection. In other words, it is not simply the case that 'gender' is a protected ground only because there is a substantial and abiding advantage gap between men and women. It is also the case that discrimination law tends to benefit women more than men. This is not just because women are more likely to bring a successful case of discrimination in practice, but also because legal doctrine itself tends to permit affirmative action to favour women, but not men. If gender was like eye colour, men would get as much benefit from discrimination law as blue-eyed people: which is none at all. It is hard to escape the conclusion that the ultimate purpose of discrimination law is to make gender as (in)significant as eye colour. Of the conditions that relate to grounds (that is, the first three conditions), only the relative disadvantage condition differentiates gender and eye colour. For the purposes of discrimination law, gender will become as (in)significant as eye colour only when women are no longer significantly more likely to suffer abiding, pervasive, and substantial disadvantage than men. Thus:

Discrimination law seeks to reduce (and ultimately remove) any significant advantage gap between a protected group and its cognate groups. (P3)

With the caveat that 'significant' here elliptically refers to 'substantial, abiding, and pervasive' advantage gaps, we now have a reasonably accurate statement of what it is that discrimination law does. This is the big-picture, systemic, concern of discrimination law. There may be considerable opacity between precise rules of anti-discrimination and this overall purpose. But the practice of discrimination law, *on the whole*, is geared towards achieving this goal. We must now turn our attention to whether this goal is morally justified.

Justification of the Goal

Given that discrimination law seeks to reduce (and ultimately remove) any significant advantage gap between a protected group and its cognate groups, we now need to know whether this is something worth pursuing. Broadly, the question we need to confront is whether reducing substantial, abiding, and pervasive disadvantage suffered by a group in comparison with other cognate groups (hereinafter, 'relative group disadvantage') is of moral concern. As a preliminary objection, one may ask why we ought to be concerned with relative group disadvantage only between groups defined by the same ground. It is possible that groups that are not so defined can also have a significant advantage gap between them. All that is logically required is that the membership of the two groups is (more or less) mutually exclusive (for example, whites and Muslims in the United Kingdom—respectively defined by race and religion). If they are not mutually exclusive, we cannot sensibly talk of relative disadvantage between groups. By definition, these groups will (more or less) be mutually exclusive only if most whites in the United Kingdom are not Muslims, and vice versa. Thus, the two groups can be understood to be based on the same ground (whites and Muslim non-whites based on race, or Muslims and white non-Muslims based on religion). Remember that we are using the term 'group' loosely— it is not necessary that the members of the group attach any salience to their affiliation.[9] The fact that there is some overlap between these groups should not bother anyone. People can and do belong to multiple groups—a person with a Jewish mother and a Sikh father may well consider herself Jewish as well as Sikh.[10] All that is required for relative group disadvantage is that the membership of the two groups is *more or less* mutually exclusive. Whenever this is the case, groups are likely to be cognates of each other. The preliminary objection must therefore be rejected. Our focus on relative disadvantage between only protected groups and their cognates is justified.

Relative group disadvantage is of moral concern because it disrupts secured access to the basic goods and therefore adversely affects the ability of the members of the disadvantaged group to be free. Members of protected groups do not have secured or adequate access to these goods. This tends to be true of all members of such groups, even those who may seem to be materially well-off. Since every person has an interest in his or her own well-being, members of protected groups have an interest in

---

[9] However, as we will see shortly, salience of group membership may indeed be relevant to a person's ability to have self-respect. All I am suggesting here is that it is not *necessary*.

[10] Kimberlé Crenshaw, 'Demarginalising the Intersection of Race and Sex: A Black Feminist Critique of Antidiscrimination Doctrine, Feminist Theory and Antiracist Politics', *The University of Chicago Legal Forum*, no. 1 (1989): 139–67.

changing this state of affairs so that they come to have secured access to these basic goods. Moreover, given the fundamental importance of these goods to human flourishing, this interest is particularly weighty. If human freedom is of moral concern, as I will assume it is, protecting the liberty interest of members of relatively disadvantaged groups is also a legitimate—nay pressing—moral concern.

Members of protected groups are, by definition, significantly more likely to suffer abiding, pervasive, and substantial disadvantage compared to members of their cognate groups. Here, disadvantage is understood holistically, to include political, socio-cultural, and material disadvantage. Protected groups tend to be disadvantaged in at least two of these three facets. Religious and sexual minorities, for example, tend to be disadvantaged at least politically and socio-culturally. Even if the group as a whole is not materially disadvantaged, its poorer members tend to suffer material disadvantage acutely. Women face greater socio-cultural and material disadvantage (and, despite their share in the electorate, even political disadvantage). Dalits, Roma, and disabled persons are disadvantaged materially, politically, and socio-culturally.

A multifaceted understanding of disadvantage can relatively easily be restated in terms of a lack of access to basic goods. Sociocultural and material disadvantage includes being the object of hostility and violence, which results in a breach of negative freedom. All tangible forms of disadvantage can be reframed as a lack of access to valuable opportunities. And sociocultural disadvantage has crucial links with the ability to have self-respect. These connections between the basic goods and various forms of disadvantage are obvious when we think of disadvantage in an *absolute* and *individual* sense, that is, the disadvantage of an individual judged against some non-relative standard of the sort of advantage one ought to have. Our predicament is to determine if there are any links between *relative group* disadvantage and the basic goods. To this task I shall now turn my attention.

Negative Freedom

Let us first consider the impact that relative group disadvantage has on one's negative freedom. Power is a function of what you are able to will and achieve; interference is the subjection of the will of another to your own will. Relative group disadvantage makes interference with members of one group by those of another easier—the greater the advantage gap between the groups, the more power the dominant group has over the disadvantaged one. This is because power, in the sense that is relevant to negative freedom, is a relative concept—you have power *over* or *against* someone else. In this sense, it is different from a mere ability to do something. It is easier for the more powerful group to interfere with and even dominate the less powerful. Given how power operates in human societies, it is reasonable to think that a relatively disadvantaged group will remain in danger of being dominated by the more powerful group, in the sense that the will of its members would frequently be subjected to the will of the members of the powerful group. Often, such subjection will be unjustifiable, resulting in the loss of negative freedom. This is particularly likely to be the case when a group suffers sociocultural disadvantage, in the form of widespread hostility and prejudice. This hostility will often translate into indirect interference (through acts of exclusion or boycott) and sometimes direct interference (crimes, torts). Material and political disadvantage will underline its inability to defend itself against interference and domination. Political indifference could also lead to poor security and policing services in minority neighbourhoods, and therefore to a situation where members of weaker groups are more likely to be victims even of crimes not perpetrated by members of dominant groups.

The supposition that relative group disadvantage is likely to lead to domination of weaker groups, of course, needs corroboration with actual evidence to show that its members are indeed disproportionately more likely to be victims of criminal, tortious, and discriminatory acts. All such acts, when unjustified, result in an unacceptable loss of one's negative freedom. Although my project is theoretical rather than empirical, there appears to be significant evidence from diverse contexts that women, religious minorities, racial minorities, gays and lesbians, transpersons, and disabled persons are indeed disproportionately more likely to have their negative freedom interfered with than members of cognate groups.[11]

It may be that this claim is not always true for all groups in all societies. Even when it is true, not every member of the protected group will necessarily have their negative freedom interfered with. Even so, the

---

[11] See, for example, Sylvia Walby, Jo Armstrong, and Les Humphreys, *Review of Equality Statistics (UK Equality and Human Rights Commission)* (Manchester: Equality and Human Rights Commission, 2008), 65, 84, 88–9; US Census Bureau, *Statistical Abstract of the United States* (United States: US Census Bureau, 2011), 200.

power imbalance between groups that necessarily results from relative group disadvantage will make the enjoyment of negative freedom by all members of the weaker groups insecure. The existence of relative group disadvantage generates a pull towards domination. The extent to which a society can resist actual domination while groups continue to have significant advantage gaps between them is fortuitous and inherently unstable. If anything, power is self-sustaining and self-entrenching. For members of disadvantage groups to enjoy secure negative freedom, there is no alternative but to break the nexus between group membership and disadvantage. It is quite right, therefore, for discrimination law to seek to protect relatively disadvantaged groups.

Adequate Range of Valuable Opportunities

Like the absence of secured negative freedom, lacking secured access to an adequate range of valuable opportunities constitutes disadvantage. But we now know that the focus of discrimination law is not to deal with absolute disadvantage faced by individuals. That is a function of welfare law or socio-economic rights. The main purpose of discrimination law is to ameliorate and eradicate any significant relative group disadvantage. How does this impact a person's access to an adequate range of valuable opportunities?

The adequacy threshold that every individual needs access to in order to live a good life is not fixed, but changes across time and space. In particular, it is pegged to the type of life opportunities it is possible for one to have. This in turn is determined by the lifestyle of the members of the dominant group and the opportunities they enjoy. This insight suggests that relative disadvantage and absolute disadvantage are not divided by a bright line. Significant relative disadvantage is very likely to translate into absolute disadvantage too. It follows, then, that many members of a protected group are likely to lack access to an adequate range of valuable opportunities.

But the variability of the adequacy threshold only explains why we should care about *relative* disadvantage. It does not, in itself, justify our concern with *group* disadvantage. It probably is the case that many members of relatively disadvantaged groups also suffer absolute disadvantage in the sense of lacking access to an adequate range of valuable options. We still do not know if *most* members lack such access. This is an empirical judgement beyond the scope of this argument. But the notion of security once again helps us properly appreciate what it is like to belong to such a group. One's access to an adequate range of valuable opportunities must be secure. Even when they have adequate access at any given point in time, most, if not all, members of protected groups are unlikely to have confidence in the sustainability and security of such access.

This is the case for several reasons. Although discrimination law does not insist on proof of any particular cause, human agency is often responsible for relative group disadvantage. Given the serious and high-threshold terms in which we have defined it, it is unlikely to be caused by random factors, although it is possible that some non-human factors may bring it about in exceptional cases. The most obvious of these human factors is the frequent interference with the negative liberty of members of weaker groups. When criminal, tortious, or discriminatory acts against members of a group become endemic, it is not surprising that the access of its members to an adequate range of valuable opportunities is also progressively compromised. The basic goods are interlinked, and denial of any one has implications for access to others. Infrequent violations of one's negative liberty can have devastating effects on one's own life. But when frequent violations are visited upon many members of a group who are relatively powerless to defend themselves, disadvantage acquires a group dimension. When these interferences relate to key opportunities such as one's education, employment, domicile, relationships, and personal safety, they have a ripple effect on all other opportunities one is able to access. Furthermore, if the group suffers relative political disadvantage too, it will find it hard to use the political muscle of the state to provide opportunities to its members. So, even if a rich black man living in the United States enjoys access to an adequate range of valuable opportunities, it may often be the case that he is not secure in his continued access to these opportunities.

Once disadvantage acquires a group dimension, it becomes self-perpetuating and intensifies over time. This is because members of the dominant group acquire an interest in maintaining the status quo which gives them access to greater power and opportunities. This very access also makes them more capable of maintaining this status quo. It is this inertia in favour of relative group disadvantage which makes the institution of discrimination law in most societies such a remarkable political feat—made achievable by a combination of its protection of a multiplicity of grounds which builds a broad coalition of many different vulnerable groups, its incremental and gradual approach to dealing with relative group disadvantage, and the extension of at least some of its protections to dominant groups as well so that everyone has some stake in its success. Without external intervention, the strong connection between existing disadvantage and future disadvantage of a group will result in a vicious cycle of intensifying disadvantage over generations. It is no surprise that members of relatively disadvantaged groups lack secured access to an adequate range of valuable opportunities. For that very reason, discrimination law is justified in treating them as protected groups.

Self-Respect

Finally, relative group disadvantage also inhibits one's ability to have self-respect, if one is a member of a weak and vulnerable group. Of the basic goods we are concerned with, self-respect is the most starkly relative in character. One's ability to have self-respect is a function of the respect shown by others as well as one's standing in relation to others. Relative disadvantage, in particular relative sociocultural disadvantage, can make it difficult for a person to keep self-respect. This is so because sociocultural disadvantage often manifests itself in either the dominant group's indifference towards the need to accommodate the cultural practices of the minority group in the mainstream public sphere, or, what is worse, in hostility, prejudice, and stereotyping of the members of the protected groups. This is especially the case when the group becomes more than a mere collection of individuals—with an understanding of its own existence as a group with a history, a rank, a culture, and a particular relationship with other groups based on the same ground. As Weber explained, 'the power of political structures has a specific internal dynamic. On the basis of this power, the members may pretend to a special "prestige", and their pretensions may influence the external conduct of the power structures.'[12] Relative group disadvantage, which is but a reflection of the enormous power of the dominant group, often results in the coming about of such group consciousness. When group identities get entangled with relative group disadvantage in this way, the sociocultural disadvantage that the minority group suffers usually becomes acute.[13]

---

[12] Max Weber, *From Max Weber: Essays in Sociology* (London: Routledge & Kegan Paul, 1970), 159.

[13] Hellman presents a variation on this theme in terms of 'humiliation' and 'demeaning' treatment suffered by the victims of discrimination: Deborah Hellman, *When is Discrimination Wrong?* (Cambridge: Harvard University Press, 2008).

Normally, intense socio-cultural disadvantage makes it difficult for members of the group burdened by it to have self-respect. However, this very same disadvantage may also catalyse a sense of pride in the membership of the group, to counter the prejudicial claims of the dominant group about the worth of its members. The emergence of queer pride and Dalit politics of recognition in the late twentieth century epitomize this phenomenon.[14] Even so, the struggle that many gay people and Dalits continue to have with internalized homophobia and casteism shows that so long as deep-rooted sociocultural disadvantages remain, one's ability to be secure in the knowledge that one's life is valuable and worthwhile remains compromised. Gay pride and ubiquitous public statues of Dr Ambedkar (the foremost author of India's Constitution and a Dalit) may give a person self-respect, but only the eradication of widespread homophobia and casteism can make it secure.

It is true that, under certain circumstances, relative political and material disadvantage is compatible with self-respect. This is especially true in feudal societies, where it is easier to have self-respect and dignity in one's rank-determined low station in life. The near impossibility of social mobility brings with it the solace of the knowledge that one's life could not have been much better than it is. If success in one's life must be measured against what is possible, a person is more likely to retain self-respect if another life is beyond the pale of the possible. Not so in modern industrial democratic states, where the discourse of equality and spectacular, if rare, rags-to-riches narratives serve as constant reminders that any continuing political, socio-cultural, or material disadvantage—even if only relative—must be down to our own choices. The tragedy is that we have come to believe we are free to make of our lives what we will, when, in fact, our ability to do so remains seriously constrained. Under these circumstances, self-respect becomes the first casualty. The solution must lie in a more realistic assessment of the human condition (without, obviously, turning our back on the idea that all persons deserve recognition and respect simply because they are persons) and the fetters that continue to bind us, alongside attempts to break free of at least some of the most egregious constraints. Abiding, pervasive, and substantial

---

[14] Robin Brontsema, 'A Queer Revolution: Reconceptualizing the Debate over Linguistic Reclamation', *Colorado Research in Linguistics* 17, no. 1 (2004): 1–17; Sonia Sikka, 'Untouchable Cultures: Memory, Power and the Construction of *Dalit* Selfhood', *Identities: Global Studies in Culture and Power* 19, no. 1 (2012): 43–60; Bhimrao Ambedkar, *Annihilation of Caste* (London: Verso, 2014).

relative group disadvantage, which also turns out to be self-perpetuating and ever-intensifying, is one such constraint. In seeking to deal with relative group disadvantage, discrimination law contributes to our ability to have self-respect. In addition, and more directly, discrimination law itself has come to acquire particular expressive salience in our societies. The mere declaration by discrimination law that a relatively disadvantaged group will be treated as a protected group is of direct expressive significance for the ability of its members to have self-respect, quite apart from the impact its success may have in breaking the group membership and individual disadvantage nexus.[15] Thus, the need to facilitate our having self-respect also justifies the law's protection of these groups.

Discrimination Law and the Basic Goods

Although relative group disadvantage has an impact on each of the basic goods, given their interrelationship, even an impact on only one of them will affect others. Imagine that a group only faced relative sociocultural disadvantage and consequently its members struggled to maintain their self-respect. Assume further that they were frequently discriminated against and harassed by the dominant group. As social power translates into economic and political power, it is likely that these vulnerabilities will, over time, impede their access to valuable opportunities. It is the nature of these basic goods that we can securely enjoy any of them only if we have secure access to all of them. In this respect, they are somewhat different from the first basic good—if we do not have secure means to satisfy our basic biological needs, no doubt we will also fail to access the other goods. But the reverse is not true. It is possible for us to have our bodily needs of food, clothing, shelter, and such like fulfilled while the remaining three goods continue to elude us. It is no surprise then that different tools (welfare guarantees and socio-economic rights) are needed to provide access to the first basic good.[16]

---

[15] Samuel Bagenstos, '"Rational Discrimination", Accommodation, and the Politics of (Disability) Civil Rights', *Virginia Law Review* 89 (2003): 844: Discrimination law 'serves an important expressive purpose by offering to previously excluded groups a tangible invitation of admission as full members of society'.

[16] It is true, of course, that not all socio-economic rights relate to the first basic good. The right to education, for example, primarily enhances our access to a range of valuable opportunities.

At any rate, we should now be able to see the connection between relative group disadvantage and certain forms of denial of access to the basic goods. There is one other aspect of this connection which requires some elaboration. Relative group disadvantage affects all members of protected groups, but it does so in varying degrees. Those who are most disadvantaged also tend to be most vulnerable to the exercise of social, political, and economic power by the dominant groups. A rich white woman in the United Kingdom, although vulnerable, is likely to be less so than a rich black woman. Both of them are likely to be less vulnerable than a poor black woman, and so on. Given the eccentric distribution condition, discrimination law allocates benefits to members of protected groups without specific reference to their individual level of disadvantage. No obvious prioritarian instinct of benefitting the worst-off first can be discerned in the actual distributive pattern of its benefits.

However, at the general level, we can show that discrimination law is compatible with prioritarian impulses. Breaking the group membership and individual disadvantage nexus is likely to benefit the worst off the most (simply because they suffer the most). It so happens that dealing with relative group disadvantage does not easily lend itself to a regime which self-consciously eradicates its effects on those worst-affected first. When the nexus is broken, it will be broken for everyone—it simply cannot be broken for some and yet survive for other members of the group. A temporal priority is difficult to build into the overall purpose of discrimination law, although its overall purpose is sensitive to the greater need of the worst off within a protected group.

I do not intend to suggest that nothing more can be done or ought to be done to make discrimination law more prioritarian. Continuing debates on intersectional and multiple-group discrimination or on how affirmative action policies should be framed tell us that there is indeed scope for improvement. However, these reforms are primarily addressed to the distributive worries in discrimination law. We can surmise that discrimination law seeks to reduce and remove relative group disadvantage, which denies to individuals optimal access to the basic goods, and that this denial is the most acute for those who are most disadvantaged.

Since these goods are basic (that is, fundamental to human flourishing), reducing and eliminating significant relative group disadvantage is of pressing moral concern. P3 stands vindicated. It should also be clear by now that our concern with relative group disadvantage is based on a concern for individuals. Groups are salient to discrimination law because group membership has a significant impact on the life-chances of a person. On this understanding, it will be a mistake to romanticize groups for their own sake, especially given their capacity to oppress their own members. Group membership is valuable only when, and to the extent that, it adds value to a person's life.[17]

Perfectionism in Discrimination Law

The account of discrimination law presented in this essay is at variance not only with egalitarian accounts but also with other approaches. In focusing on group disadvantage rather than ground irrelevance, my account distances itself from relevance-based accounts. These descriptive relevance-based accounts make the rationalist claim that the purpose of discrimination law is to prohibit discrimination on grounds which are irrelevant to the legitimate objectives of the employer, landlord, or other discriminator. For example, race discrimination is prohibited in employment because race does not usually have any bearing on a person's ability to perform a job.[18] Even assuming that a general legal duty to act rationally can be justified (which will be difficult, if not impossible, alongside a commitment to liberalism), these relevance-based accounts are utterly inadequate to explain the general justifying aim of discrimination law. We know well that the law prohibits discrimination even in contexts where the ground in question is indeed descriptively relevant to the performance of a job (think pregnancy, certain types of disabilities, and sometimes even race—say, the race of a bartender in a pub whose patrons are largely racist). These relevance-based accounts also show no sensitivity to relative group disadvantage, which we have seen is a key obsession in discrimination law. Without this reference to disadvantage, they struggle to explain why the liberty of the victims of discrimination trumps that of the duty-bearers to go about their business without legal interference. As I have shown, the dimension of disadvantage is key to focus our minds on the most egregious denials of liberty in the form of basic goods.

[17] We have largely focused on congruence between the interests of the group as a whole and its individual members. When individual and group interests are in conflict, it may help to remember that groups are valuable for the sake of their members. See generally, Leslie Green, 'Rights of Exit', *Legal Theory* 4, no. 2 (1998): 165–85.

[18] Donal Nolan, 'A Right to Meritorious Treatment,' in *Understanding Human Rights*, eds, Conor Gearty and Adam Tomkins (Pinter: London, 1996).

For all their faults, these relevance-based accounts (unlike most egalitarian ones) correctly appreciate that grounds are important to discrimination law. Where they go wrong is in their understanding of the reason why grounds are so important. In this chapter so far, we have understood the significance of grounds only derivatively—as definitional markers for salient groups. But the role of grounds is important in another respect, independent of relative group disadvantage: they are *normatively* irrelevant. They embody the perfectionist element in discrimination law, and are the reason why anti-perfectionist liberal accounts will also be unsuccessful. Perfectionist liberals are willing to allow the state to make certain (severely constrained) normative judgements about what a good life is, whereas anti-perfectionists refuse to do so. A good life is lived in pursuit of value, and our understanding of value has been significantly qualified so that it is pluralistic, not too demanding, agent-centred, contextual, and holistic. The account I have given of well-being is perfectionist, yet liberal.

I have argued that discrimination law facilitates the pursuit of a good life by seeking to reduce and remove significant relative group disadvantage which impedes such pursuit by limiting our access to certain basic goods. But only when the membership of a group is valuable (more accurately, not immoral) will it contribute to a good life. Discrimination law assesses the value of such membership by examining the moral significance of the ground in question. Let us see how.

A ground's division of persons into more and less advantaged groups is only one of two preconditions that make it eligible for protection. The other condition is that the ground must either be immutable or it must constitute a valuable fundamental choice.[19] We should start by revising P3 to make explicit the qualification inherent in the notion of a 'protected group':

Discrimination law seeks to reduce (and ultimately remove) any significant advantage gap between a protected group (defined by an immutable or valuable ground) and its cognate groups. (P4)

[19] Notice that a morally thin (anti-perfectionist) account will mainly be able to account for relative disadvantage. It will struggle to explain the additional requirement that the ground must be not-immoral. For the defense of an anti-perfectionist approach to discrimination law, see Deborah Hellman, 'Equality and Unconstitutional Discrimination,' in *Philosophical Foundations of Discrimination Law*, eds, Deborah Hellman and Sophia Moreau (Oxford: Oxford University Press, 2013).

We can rephrase this by saying that discrimination law's central purpose is to ensure that members of groups based on immutable or valuable grounds do not suffer abiding, pervasive, and substantial relative disadvantage. Immutability is to be understood expansively to include not just an inability to change the relevant characteristic, but also a lack of control over its acquisition. Furthermore, *effective* immutability will suffice—it is enough to show that changing the characteristic will impose significant personal costs. A mutable ground is also protected so long as it constitutes a valuable fundamental choice. These are but two different ways of determining whether the candidate ground is compatible with the pursuit of a good life.[20] This will always be the case if the ground is immutable. When it constitutes a fundamental choice, discrimination law cares not just about group disadvantage, but also about whether the group in question is valuable (not-immoral) for its members. It is for this reason that discrimination against terrorist groups is not prohibited by discrimination law, whatever their advantage status—becoming a terrorist is simply not a valuable choice.[21]

The concept of a ground can be said to exist in two orders. In the higher *universal* order, a ground applies to all individuals. In the *particular* order, different instances of a universal ground attach to different people. So, gender is a universal order ground, while maleness is a particular instance of gender. Usually, if one particular instance (say, whiteness) of a given universal order characteristic (race) is compatible with a good (valuable) life, all other particular instances (in this case, blackness, Asian-ness, and so on) of that universal order characteristic are also likely to be so. But such results are coincidental, arrived at after considering each particular order characteristic. Let us imagine a hypothetical religious sect, the Stravinskyites, who perform the *Rite of Spring* involving human sacrifice.[22] If performing the *Rite of Spring* is an essential part of being a Stravinskyite, then life as a Stravinskyite is

---

[20] Moreau refers to these grounds as 'normatively extraneous': Moreau, 'What is Discrimination?'.

[21] This is not true of former terrorists, those who have now renounced violence. Our low-threshold judgement of value may not automatically deny them the protections of discrimination law, provided that other conditions are satisfied

[22] Igor Stravinsky's ballet *The Rite of Spring*, from which the reference has been borrowed, has human sacrifice as its central theme.

not valuable. Stravinskyism will not qualify as a valuable fundamental choice, even though it might be a 'religion'.

This discussion shows that a decision to protect any particular order ground has little to do with how we have assessed *other* particular order grounds that are subsets of the same universal order ground. A person's pregnancy, Christianity, or atheism are all morally valuable characteristics, while her homosexuality, heterosexuality, disability, or blackness are at least morally irrelevant (but potentially morally valuable too, especially if they entail the membership of a nurturing community). What becomes clear is that the fundamental unit of protection qua grounds exists in its particular order (femaleness) rather than in the universal order (gender).

We are now in a position to appreciate the role that (particular order) grounds play in discrimination law. First, they provide the organizational basis for groups. Second, they demand that membership of the group serves perfectionist freedom by being conducive to the pursuit of a flourishing good life. Egalitarian accounts tend to ignore the perfectionist role of grounds and focus primarily on disadvantage. Rationalist accounts focus solely on the relevance of the ground in question to the legitimate objectives of a discriminator. Anti-perfectionist accounts cannot distinguish between value-compatible and valueless grounds. All of them miss the point to different degrees. The real relevance that discrimination law seeks is between the particular order ground and a good life. This objective moral assessment of protected grounds is an essential part of discrimination law, as is its relationship to relative group disadvantage.

This insight has important implications for the debate on multiple-ground discrimination. Consider the case of Mackie, a woman of Indian origin who claimed to have been unfairly dismissed.[23] Her womanhood and her Indian-ness are independently either morally irrelevant or morally valuable traits. In Mackie's case, the respondent company's Indian directors disapproved of Asian women working there, but did not have any problems with men (including Asian men) or non-Asian women. The tribunal found that Mackie 'was not treated less favourably because she was a woman nor simply because she was Indian, but

---

[23] *Mackie v. G & N Car Sales Ltd t/a Britannia Motor Co* [2004] ET/1806128/03, as summarized in Nicholas Bamforth, Colm O'Cinneide, and Maleiha Malik, *Discrimination Law: Theory and Context* (London: Sweet & Maxwell, 2008), 526.

because she was an Indian woman'.[24] In this instance, she belonged to a unique intersectional category, which could not have been captured by her womanhood or her race. Our insight that it is the particular order characteristic of individuals that matters tells us that, at least at the normative level, the relevant questions to ask are only these: (a) Is Indian womanhood a normatively irrelevant or valuable characteristic? (b) Does it define a relatively disadvantaged group (Indian women)? If it did not, we would have asked further if it defined a relatively advantaged group that we have reasons to nonetheless protect.

***

I have shown that membership of certain relatively disadvantaged groups has a serious impact on a person's secured access to three primary goods, and therefore to the person's well-being. We know that protected grounds define the contours of the protectorate of discrimination law, while protected groups add texture to its protection. Although we have somewhat elliptically been referring to protected grounds and groups, the law on discrimination is ultimately about the protection of *persons*. My claim is the general justifying aim of discrimination law is to further the well-being of persons by securing access to the basic goods to those who lack such access because of their affiliation to protected groups. These groups are in turn defined by particular order grounds whose possession is compatible with a good life.

---

[24] *Mackie* ET/1806128/03.

18

Economic Theories of Discrimination

The Positive and the Normative

*Richard H. McAdams**

Do different forms of prejudice and discrimination have a common core? The social sciences discuss whether there is or could be a unified *positive* theory of discrimination. For example, are the psychological or social processes that cause race discrimination the same as those that cause religious or disability discrimination? The legal and philosophical literature discusses whether there is or could be a unified *normative* theory of anti-discrimination law. For example, is the wrong or harm of race discrimination that justifies its prohibition the same as the wrong or harm of gender or sexual orientation discrimination? Often, it is assumed without inquiry that the analogy between these different forms of discrimination is sound and that whatever justifies one legal intervention justifies the other.

* I thank Jessica Clarke, Dhammika Dharmapala, Margareth Etienne, Martha Nussbaum, Laura Weinrib, and Heather Whitney for insightful comments on an earlier draft, as well as the participants at a faculty workshop at the University of Illinois College of Law and the Delhi conference on 'Prejudice, Stigma, Discrimination: Combatting Exclusions Through Policy and Law'.

Yet when we examine the details of anti-discrimination law, we see that it does not always treat one form of discrimination like another. In the United States, for example, most law has a reciprocal structure as where the prohibition of job discrimination along racial lines (or some dimension *X*) prohibits employers of any race (any *X*) from discriminating against employees of any race (any *X*) on the basis of race (*X*). By contrast, American federal law prohibits age discrimination in employment only against those over 40 years, and discrimination against those who are disabled, so the old and the young are legally free to discriminate against those under 40, and the abled and disabled are free to discriminate against the abled. A unified normative theory would explain structural choices like this one, between reciprocal and non-reciprocal prohibitions.[1]

In this short contribution, I do not seek to resolve whether a unified positive or normative theory is possible, or to develop one, which would require exploring the entire architecture of anti-discrimination law. Instead, I aim only to illustrate the inquiry and to push it in a novel direction, paying particular attention to the implications of positive theory on the normative. Most normative theorizing of the law is deontological, an undertaking to explain the moral wrong of discrimination. In this chapter, I take a different path, examining the possible consequentialist justifications based directly on the social harm of discrimination. The concern for consequences takes me into the social science, specifically positive economic theories, of discrimination, supplemented by a dose of psychology. Economics is reductionist; it seeks to explain the most with the least. That will prove useful in identifying possible similarities between different forms of discrimination.

For a consequentialist normative theory, the starting point is a positive inquiry into what discrimination is and what its causes are. Part of what I hope to demonstrate is that different descriptions of discrimination predict different kinds of social harm with different normative implications. The 'is' and the 'ought' are distinct, but the 'is' has strong implications for the 'ought'. The competing economic theories posit that discrimination (a) arises from the effort to satisfy a 'taste' for avoiding association; (b) results from rational statistical generalizations; and (c) is the product of group-based status competition. In addition, I borrow

[1] Naomi Schoenbaum, 'The Case for Symmetry in Antidiscrimination Law', *Wisconsin Law Review* 2017 (2017): 69–146; Bradley A. Areheart, 'The Symmetry Principle', *Boston College Law Review* 58 (2017): 1085–135.

from psychology to explore different forms of irrational stereotyping (which I fold into category (b) as both focus on beliefs).

The first part begins with a single aspect of the problem, just race discrimination and primarily as it occurs in employment. The next part expands this view to include other types of discrimination. The third part concludes.

Economic Theories of Race Discrimination

Economics attempts to explain human behaviour with a relationship between means and ends. The ends are individual desires, what economists call 'preferences' or 'tastes'. The means are strategic actions based on beliefs formed with imperfect information. It is not surprising, therefore, that economics has two dominant theories for explaining discrimination that track the desire/belief distinction: that race is an effort to satisfy a 'taste' for avoiding association with people of a different race,[2] and that it is the product of rational statistical inferences about racial groups.[3] According to a third approach, the 'status production' theory, individuals discriminate to produce status for their racial group.[4] In this part, I present these theories, supplemented with ideas from psychology, and consider their normative implications.

A Taste for Avoiding Association

Positive Theory

The original economic description of race discrimination was Nobelist Gary Becker's model of individuals satisfying a 'taste' for avoiding

[2] Gary Becker, *The Economics of Discrimination*, 2nd ed. (Chicago: University of Chicago, 1971).

[3] Early contributions are Edmund S. Phelps, 'The Statistical Theory of Racism and Sexism', *American Economic Review* 62, no. 4 (1972): 659; and Kenneth J. Arrow, 'The Theory of Discrimination', in *Discrimination in Labor Markets*, eds. Orley Ashenfelter and Albert Rees (Princeton: Princeton University Press, 1973), 3–33. For a review, see Hanming Fang and Andrea Moro, 'Theories of Statistical Discrimination and Affirmative Action: A Survey', in *Handbook of Social Economics*, vol. 1A, eds. J. Benhabib, A. Bisin, and M. Jackson (The Netherlands: North Holland, 2011), 133–200, Chapter 5.

[4] See Richard H. McAdams, 'Cooperation and Conflict: The Economics of Group Status Production and Race Discrimination', *Harvard Law Review* 108 (1995): 1003–84.

'association' with members of another race. Whites who harbour a racial animus against African Americans are said to incur a cost when they associate with them, as by employing or working alongside them. Of the many positive implications of this description, the most important may be that a person with discriminatory preferences is worse off for having them because their satisfaction requires forgoing otherwise desirable transactions. Becker therefore analogizes discriminatory preferences to transportation costs: both raise the cost of transactions between certain parties. A producer located closer to customers will incur lower transportation costs and be able to sell at a cheaper price. An employer without discriminatory preferences will benefit from being able to hire the most productive workers regardless of race.

Normative Implications

Some economists, most prominently the Nobelist Milton Friedman, used Becker's model of race discrimination in employment to make two arguments against the adoption of Title VII of the 1964 Civil Rights Act, the American federal law banning employment discrimination (for race and other grounds).[5] The first argument was that the law was unnecessary because market competition would, over time, limit the effect of employer discrimination. The idea is that black workers only need to find a single employer who does not discriminate and the market will reward those who can employ the most productive workers without regard to race. The shorthand is that markets drive out discrimination.

Yet, decades later, although discrimination has greatly declined, there remains evidence of race discrimination in employment and other markets, despite competition.[6] One reason is that Becker ignored search costs. Later economic models show that if employees bear costs finding a job, which they obviously do, then the presence of discriminatory

[5] Milton Friedman, *Capitalism and Freedom* (Chicago: University of Chicago, 1962), 108–18.

[6] See, for example, D. Pager, 'The Mark of a Criminal Record', *American Journal of Sociology* 108 (2003): 937–75; M. Bertrand and S. Mullainathan, 'Are Emily and Greg More Employable than Lakisha and Jamal? A Field Experiment on Labor Market Discrimination', *American Economic Review* 94 (2004): 991–1011; W.A. Darity and P.L. Mason, 'Evidence on Discrimination in Employment: Codes of Color, Codes of Gender', *Journal of Economic Perspectives* 12, no. 2 (1998): 63–90.

employers can cause black workers to earn lower wages even though these workers eventually find non-discriminating employers.[7] Second, Becker's model implied that competition would drive out *employer* discrimination, but Becker also discussed *co-worker* and *customer* discrimination, and here the prediction is that markets would meet demand. If discriminatory customers will pay more for goods or services created and provided by white workers, then even employers with no discriminatory preferences would discriminate against black workers.[8]

Yet Friedman had a second, more essential argument against Title VII. As a general matter, welfare economics treats preferences alike, so the satisfaction of preferences for non-association would count as a normative good, just like the satisfaction of any other preference. To justify a ban, one must argue that there is something about the non-association preference that distinguishes it from other preferences. A common argument for distinguishing discriminatory preferences is the immutability and irrelevance of the physical characteristics associated with race. But the same can be said of many preferences we take for granted, for example, a desire for a singing voice of a certain tone or 'quality', which may depend in part on the immutable characteristics of the singer's vocal apparatus. These characteristics also seem morally irrelevant, but we generally allow people to engage in voluntary transactions to indulge their preferences for such arbitrary characteristics. As Richard Epstein later put the point: 'The taste for discrimination is just another preference.'[9]

A deontologist can easily imagine an argument against satisfying discriminatory preferences. Surprising perhaps, a similar move is possible within welfare economics. Though controversial, some welfare theorists would 'launder' preferences to exclude utility from satisfying negatively interdependent preferences, such as spite or hatred or sadism, where one gains directly from the loss inflicted on others.[10] As John Harsanyi puts it:

---

[7] See D.A. Black, 'Discrimination in an Equilibrium Search Model', *Journal of Labor Economics* 13, no. 2 (1995): 309–34.

[8] See John J. Donohue, 'Antidiscrimination Law', in *Handbook of Law and Economics, Volume 2*, eds, A.M. Polinsky and Steven Shavell (Oxford: Elsevier, 2007), 1407–9, 1387.

[9] Richard Epstein, *Forbidden Grounds: The Case against Employment Discrimination Laws* (Cambridge, MA: Harvard University Press, 1995), 42, 43. Friedman used the singing example in *Capitalism and Freedom*, at 110.

[10] See, for example, Matthew D. Adler and Eric A. Posner, *New Foundations of Cost-Benefit Analysis* (Cambridge, MA: Harvard University Press, 2006),

Some preferences … must be altogether excluded from our social-utility function. In particular, we must exclude all clearly antisocial preferences, such as sadism, envy, resentment, and malice.

According to utilitarian theory, the fundamental basis of all our moral commitments to other people is a general goodwill and human sympathy. But no amount of goodwill to individual X can impose the moral obligation on me to help him in hurting a third person, individual Y, out of sheer sadism, ill will, or malice…. That part of his personality that harbours these hostile antisocial feelings must be excluded from membership, and has no claim for a hearing when it comes to defining our concept of social utility.[11]

Following Harsanyi, we can see a consequentialist argument for banning race discrimination, which begins by classifying racial preferences as antisocial. At least to the extent that the taste for non-association reflects racial animus, it is a form of hatred or malice. If so, then the harm of discrimination (that victims lose a valued interaction and suffer the stigma of exclusion) is not balanced by the satisfaction of discriminatory preferences, because such satisfaction is not counted in the social welfare function. The discrimination against singers with an undesired vocal tone harms the excluded singer, but the preference for a vocal tone is not antisocial, not something like malice, hatred, or sadism. By contrast, when we do not count the welfare created by satisfying racist preferences, the harm to the discrimination victim is not offset by a socially cognizable gain. Race discrimination then causes a net loss to social welfare. We therefore may enhance overall welfare by blocking satisfaction of such preferences.

Now we come to the interesting part. If this were the normative theory of discrimination, it would have surprising implications. In this theory, discrimination is objectionable only when its motivation is antisocial, the satisfaction of malice or hatred. The theory supplies no reason to prohibit discrimination that does not satisfy such preferences. Consider selective altruism. Feeling a certain kinship with a group does not have to involve malice or hatred of other groups. A person might favour his

150–3; Robert E. Goodin, *Utilitarianism as a Public Philosophy* (Cambridge, UK: Cambridge University Press, 1995), 132–48.

[11] See John C. Harsanyi, 'Morality and the Theory of Rational Behaviour', in *Utilitarianism and Beyond*, eds, Amartya Sen and Bernard Williams (Cambridge, UK: Cambridge University Press, 1982), 39, 56.

group out of a sense of selflessness, but treat others with purely rational selfishness. Or a person might treat everyone with a modicum of altruism, but treat his or her own group with a stronger version of it. Either person gains no utility from excluding other races, just an extra warm glow of altruism when dealing with others like oneself. Harsanyi's argument gives no reason to reject counting this utility in the social welfare function. (We can say the same thing about discrimination that arises from biased beliefs that are not themselves the result of antisocial preferences; the preferences satisfied count even if beliefs are wrong.)

The prescriptive implication is that the law should prohibit discrimination only when a person discriminated *because* he or she gains from the victim's suffering. This is a far narrower prohibition than current law, which prohibits disparate treatment even if the discriminator acts without malice and certainly when based on stereotype. One might imagine here an argument based on administrative costs: that the malicious preferences rationale is what justifies a ban on race discrimination, but that we make the law broader because of the difficulty of determining what the discriminator's motivation was. Yet this argument seems untenable for several reasons: (a) we might think that discrimination that is non-malicious is so prevalent that the level of error in ignoring the distinction is enormous; (b) we could reverse the burden of proof and let the discriminator prove that his or her motive was *not* the satisfaction of a malicious preference; (c) current law is also administratively complex, sometimes requiring a counterfactual inquiry into whether the defendant would have acted differently had the plaintiff been of a different race; thus, narrowing the law in the manner described would save administrative costs.

Thus, if we begin with the positive theory of the preference for non-association, we reach normative implications for law that point far away from the existing anti-discrimination regime.

Rational and Irrational Statistical Discrimination

Positive Theory

In a second economic approach, beliefs, rather than preferences, cause discrimination. The original theory posits that the beliefs arise from rational statistical inference.[12] Because information about individuals is

---

[12] Becker, *The Economics of Discrimination*. See also Glen C. Loury, *The Anatomy of Racial Inequality* (Cambridge, MA: Harvard University Press, 2003).

costly, people economize by judging an individual member of a group by the statistical average or reputation of that group. Race becomes a proxy for some other relevant trait. Consider an employer who discovers that members of their high school marching band tend to be good employees because they understand precise teamwork or, conversely, tend to be bad employees because they are overly rigid. Given the costs of observing these traits directly, it is rational for the employer to treat marching band experience as some evidence that the applicant will have the average characteristics of band players, even though this generalization will be false in many individual cases. One could avoid making false inferences by investigating each individual more thoroughly, but the rationality of the generalization (like all generalizations) is that the costs of acquiring more specific information exceed the benefits.

Race discrimination can result from this kind of inference. As Richard Epstein explains: 'If white workers on average have higher levels of productivity (say, because they have had a better education), then the employer is better off engaging in statistical discrimination....'[13] If education were fully observable, there would be no reason to rely on the proxy of race, but if the quality of, say, a particular public high school were unknown, but white workers tend to attend higher-quality high schools, then race might correlate with the quality of education. Of course, public high school quality may itself be the result of discrimination. But the point is that an employer who harboured no discriminatory preferences might engage in race discrimination based on these kinds of accurate generalizations.

Economics emphasizes the rationality of generalization, but other social sciences (and even a little economics) have also proffered theories of *irrational* belief formation to explain race discrimination. Most famously, perhaps, there is a large psychological literature on implicit bias, which means generalizations that are not fully conscious and therefore not fully subject to rational control.[14] Of course, one may want a theory to explain why the biases take the form they do and here we might link irrational belief formation back to taste for racial discrimination.

---

[13] Epstein, *Forbidden Grounds*, 33.

[14] Anthony G. Greenwald and Linda Hamilton Krieger, 'Implicit Bias: Scientific Foundations', *California Law Review* 94 (2006): 945, 951, 961; Kirstin A. Lane, Jerry Kang, and Mahzarin Banaji, 'Implicit Social Cognition and Law', *Annual Review of Law and Social Science* 3, no. 1 (2007): 427, 433.

We know that beliefs are influenced by motivations; to some degree, people believe what they find pleasant to believe. The desire to avoid or harm a racial group may then inspire or sustain beliefs in their inferiority or disgusting traits. One might experience cognitive dissonance from refusing to deal with productive and attractive members of other races and resolve the dissonance by believing them to be unproductive and repellent.

The psychological literature on the belief in a just world suggests another irrational possibility.[15] That literature suggests that people tend to believe that outcomes are more merited (earned, deserved, and so on) than is rationally warranted. They tend to give the successful more credit and victims more blame than the evidence rationally warrants, as if seeking to preserve a belief in the basic justness of the world, or to minimize its perceived unjustness. Thus, when past discrimination causes racial minorities to fail economically, observers who are biased towards believing the world is just *under*-attribute their failure to discrimination, and over-attribute it to the shortcomings of the minority race members. The result is a 'vicious circle' of discrimination because the inference that the minority group is at fault for its current failures justifies another level of future discrimination.[16]

In sum, discrimination may be the result of a rational or irrational process of belief formation.

Normative Implications

Outside of economics, theorists criticize stereotypical generalizations, but economics views statistical inferences as an efficient way of making the most out of the imperfect information one has. Yet statistical discrimination plausibly causes a market failure, the main example being that it causes those who expect discrimination to underinvest

[15] For reviews, see Carolyn L. Hafer and Robbie Sutton, 'Belief in a Just World', in *Handbook of Social Justice Theory and Research*, eds, C. Sabbagh and M. Schmitt (New York: Springer-Verlag, 2016), 145-60; Claudia Dalbert, 'Belief in a just world,' *Handbook of Individual Differences in Social Behavior,* eds, M.R. Leary and R.H. Hoyle (New York: Guilford Publications, 2009), 288–97.

[16] Gunnar Myrdal, *An American Dilemma* (New York: Harper, 1944), 75–6. 207–8. See also Dhammika Dharmapala, Nuno Garoupa and Richard H. McAdams, 'Belief in a Just World, Blaming the Victim, and Hate Crime Statutes' 5 *Review of Law and Economics* 5 (2009): 311.

in developing human capital (the skills, knowledge, and experience that make them productive employees).[17] If one expects to be judged negatively by one's membership in a racial group, then the pecuniary returns from a level of unobservable education or skills-training may be lower. With statistical discrimination, even though a dollar of education improves one's expected productivity by more than a dollar (discounted to present value), one may not make the investment because one expects to be judged more negatively than one's true productivity. Underinvestment in human capital may, in turn, preserve the value of the statistical generalization that group membership predicts lower productivity. The negative generalization becomes self-fulfilling.

Suppose this is true. What are the normative implications? Here the theory again provides a poor fit with existing law. If rational generalizations about a particular race have the negative externality of deterring members of that race from investing in human capital, then the solution is to push against that generalization. Government may wish to prohibit discrimination based on the generalization, but whatever the form of legal intervention, the human capital theory gives no reason for prohibiting discrimination against the statistically *favoured* racial group. The theory predicts discrimination that is one-way, only against the members of the race(s) for which employers treat race as a proxy of low-quality education (or something else). But the quality is low only in comparison to some other race—the one the generalization favours. The positive theory does not predict that the favoured race will underinvest in its human capital (it may overinvest). The human capital theory therefore justifies a one-way and not a reciprocal ban on race discrimination. In the United States, for example, the ban on discrimination against whites is, in this view, entirely unjustified.

Irrational beliefs, such as implicit bias, might cause the same underinvestment in human capital. But even if that is not the case, irrationally biased beliefs might justify a prohibition on race discrimination. The idea might be that the discriminators would come to see the benefit of

---

[17] Shelly Lundberg and Richard Startz, 'Private Discrimination and Social Intervention in Competitive Markets', *American Economic Review* 73 (1983): 340; Stewart Schwab, 'Is Statistical Discrimination Efficient?', *American Economic Review* 76 (1986): 228; Lisa R. Anderson, Roland G. Fryer Jr, and Charles A. Holt, 'Discrimination: Experimental Evidence from Psychology and Economics', in *Handbook on Economics of Discrimination*, ed. W. Rogers (Cheltenham, UK: Edward Elgar, 2006).

the decisions they made under the constraints of the law. They would hire someone they otherwise would refuse on grounds of race and then discover that the new worker was the best person for the job. Yet here too, if implicit bias is the positive theory, the normative implication is one-sided, not reciprocal intervention. On average, American racial minorities—African American, Hispanic, and Asian—exhibit a slight implicit bias in the same direction as do whites, a bias *for* whites and against their own group, though with considerable variation.[18] Thus, if implicit anti-minority bias is the normative basis of anti-discrimination law, it justifies only the ban on discriminating against disadvantaged racial groups, not a reciprocal ban.

Status Competition

Positive Theory

In previous work, I explored a third economic possibility, that race discrimination is a pathological form of status competition.[19] The theory begins with the observation that, as social animals, humans care what others think of them not only as a means, but also as an end. Individuals have a preference for *esteem*.[20] And individuals bestow esteem on others—think well of them—for reasons that are not entirely voluntary. A person who values accomplishments in art, sport, or child-rearing will reflexively esteem someone who demonstrates the right kind of mastery. We may think of an individual's social *status* as a kind of aggregation of the esteem judgments others in society have about that individual.

Given this premise, note three points. First, an individual may seek esteem or status by distinguishing himself positively, which may be done directly, by observable positive achievements, or indirectly, by making others look comparatively worse. Overtly denigrating others may be risky if the audience disapproves of such behaviour, but it sometimes works.

---

[18] The variation includes many African Americans exhibiting a pro-black bias, though the average favours whites. See Brian A. Nosek, Mahzarin Banaji, and Anthony G. Greenwald, 'Harvesting Implicit Group Attitudes and Beliefs from a Demonstration Web Site', *Group Dynamics* 6 (2002):101, 105.

[19] McAdams, 'Cooperation and Conflict'.

[20] Geoffrey Brennan and Philip Pettit, *The Economy of Esteem* (Oxford, UK: Oxford University Press, 2004); Richard H. McAdams, 'The Origin, Development, and Regulation of Norms', *Michigan Law Review* 96 (1997): 338.

Second, an individual may seek esteem individually or as part of a group. A group has status by virtue of the status of its members. One gains 'reflected glow' by belonging to high-status groups, which, for most people, is the only way to gain esteem from strangers. Where membership is voluntary, one seeks to join high-status groups and exit low-status groups. Where membership is not voluntary, however, as where it is based on traits like those associated with race, one can only invest in directly or indirectly changing the status of the trait-based group.

Third, competition for status may be positive sum or zero sum. Status competitions increase welfare when humans compete on different dimensions and care most about the dimensions of status along which they excel (for example, the body builder not caring much about his lack of chess prowess and the chess player not caring much about his physique). But sometimes status competition is zero sum. When people compete for status on the same observable dimension, one person's gain is another's loss. For example, when people compete for relative income, they may face an 'arms race' problem, where the resources invested in earning 'more than others' are wasted when the others ratchet up their own efforts at earning more.[21]

Now I can state the status production theory of race discrimination: individuals in racial groups compete for status by trying to raise the relative rank of their group. Discrimination is an indirect means of raising one's group status by lowering the status of other groups. The point is not to avoid association with members of other races, as Becker described it, but to avoid hierarchical associations in which one holds what others perceive as a lower (or equal) rank and to *seek out* hierarchical associations in which one holds what is perceived as a higher rank. Employment discrimination for higher status jobs is particularly effective. First, exclusion is demeaning. Second, exclusion inflicts an economic loss in a culture that respects wealth.

The American South of the Jim Crow era is useful for illustrating the point because there was no attempt to conceal the nature of the racism. Southern whites sought segregation where an association would imply equal status—such as being a co-worker or co-congregant or sitting at the same lunch counter—but whites *favoured* employing black workers

---

[21] Richard H. McAdams, 'Relative Preferences', *Yale Law Journal* 102 (1992): 1.

in service roles. Having a black maid or nanny was traditional;[22] black men were freely employed to do yard work and 'handyman' work. The irony is that the employment of black domestic servants involved a more intense and intimate *association* between blacks and whites than the associations that were shunned (for example, working at the same job in the same textile mill or sitting in the same section of a movie theatre). Black servants worked in the home, where they prepared food, washed linens and undergarments, bathed children, and learnt family secrets. This is not consistent with a taste for avoiding something as general as 'association'. It reflects a motive to avoid only the wrong kind of hierarchical associations, which the status production theory explains.

One could add to this list the asymmetric nature of the ban on interracial sexual relations. Formally, the Jim Crow era ban applied equally regardless of whether the couple was a black woman and a white man or a black man and a white woman. But the social reality was that white men frequently lost their virginity to black prostitutes and wealthy white men could socially survive the disrepute of maintaining a long-term relationship with a black mistress as long as they were not too overt about it.[23] Yet the ban on relationships between black men and white women was a strict and unforgiving obsession at the core of Jim Crow. White men used the possibility of such relationships as the rationalization for pervasive and brutal violence against black men.

This sexual asymmetry would be puzzling for Becker's theory or one of statistical discrimination, but makes perfect sense for a status theory as soon as one acknowledges the strong sexual double standard by which non-marital sex was understood to debase women but not men. Under prevailing mores, non-marital sex between white men and black women debased the black participant, confirming the racial hierarchy, but such sex between white women and black men debased the white participant, inverting the hierarchy. Confirming this interpretation is the fact that the interracial *marriage* ban was symmetric. Unlike non-marital sex, marriage between members of two families implied an equal status of those families, not debasement of one by the other, a consequence that could not be tolerated for white men marrying outside their race any more than for white women.

---

[22] Myrdal, 'American Dilemma', 650, 1435; McAdams, 'Cooperation and Conflict', 1037nn125–7.

[23] McAdams, 'Cooperation and Conflict', 1037nn128–9.

There is one more component of the status production theory. The theory requires individuals of the dominant race to engage in costly cooperation with other individuals of that race. The cooperative behaviour—discrimination—is costly because it means the discriminator shuns an otherwise productive relationship or exchange with members of other races in order to contribute to the status enjoyed by the entire dominant race. Why wouldn't white individuals instead selfishly choose to 'free-ride,' that is, to enjoy the status produced when other whites discriminate against non-whites, but to gain the personal benefits of relationships and exchanges with members of other races?

The potential for free-riding turns out to be an important insight of the theory because it explains the strong Jim Crow norms constraining whites as well as blacks. Consider the norm that required black citizens to show respect for white citizens by using honorific titles (for example, Mr, Mrs) and last names, even though white citizens would never use such titles when referring to black citizens, addressing even elder leaders (for example, the local minister) by his or her first name or by 'boy' or 'girl' (or worse). There was also a norm that required black citizens to use the back door when approaching and entering homes or businesses owned by whites, even though whites used the front door when visiting homes or businesses owned by blacks.[24] A crucial feature of these norms is that they also compelled customary behaviour *by whites*. White southerners would informally sanction other white southerners for failing to honour these and other racist norms, by gossip, verbal confrontation, ostracism, and violence.[25]

Becker's theory of the preference for avoiding association cannot explain this behaviour. Nor can a theory of statistical discrimination. But the behaviour makes perfect sense if discrimination is about status production and sanctioning is needed to prevent free-riding, that is, to ensure that everyone cooperates in the costly discriminatory behaviour that preserves and enhances white status. Capturing this dynamic is the potent and offensive term 'n****r-lover', by which whites called out other whites for their lack of racial solidarity, and implicitly threatened them with the same victimization as they inflicted on black citizens.

Moving beyond Jim Crow, the associational taste model suffers from empirically dubious implications about contemporary discrimination. First, with associational preference, discriminatory white police officers

[24] McAdams, 'Cooperation and Conflict',1041nn146–7.
[25] McAdams, 'Cooperation and Conflict', 1040–1nn142–5.

would prefer to stop *white* drivers for speeding; they would prefer to avoid even the short interaction required to give a ticket to an African American driver. Once they made a stop, discriminatory white officers would prefer to end the encounter more expeditiously when the driver was African American. Yet the available evidence suggests the opposite.[26] Ian Ayres notes a similar point in his study finding race discrimination in the sale of automobiles.[27] Sales personnel giving worse deals to African Americans spent *more* time in close negotiations with them. The associational preference model predicts the opposite: that discriminatory white salespersons would seek to spend as little time negotiating with black buyers as possible, thereby giving such buyers a bargaining edge. Again, status production fits the evidence. Discriminatory white police officers and car-sales personnel gain from interactions that lower the status of African-Americans. Forcing black drivers to incur the costs of a traffic stop or to pay more for their car produces the status gain.[28]

Normative Theory

Indirect status competition is a zero-sum game. One group gains by another group's loss. It is a purely distributional struggle in which investments in lowering the status of other groups—discriminatory acts—move status around without producing any more of it (or of any other form of social wealth). The investments are costly—discrimination gives up the benefits of a valuable exchange with the other race. When status gains are matched by status losses, then the investments are wasted; they constitute a 'deadweight loss' and the competition is inefficient.

An analogy is theft. Economics justifies the ban on theft not because the owner is morally entitled to the property he owns, but because of

---

[26] See, for example, Matthew R. Durose, Erica L. Schmitt, and Patrick A. Langan, *Contacts Between the Police and the Public: Findings from the 2002 National Survey* (Table 9, U.S. Department of Justice, Bureau of Justice Statistics 8, 2005), https://www.bjs.gov/content/pub/pdf/cpp02.pdf; Stephanie Seguino and Nancy Brooks, 'Driving While Black and Brown in Vermont', 9 January 2017, http://www.uvm.edu/giee/pdfs/SeguinoBrooks_PoliceRace_2017.pdf.

[27] Ian Ayres, *Pervasive Prejudice? Unconventional Evidence of Race and Gender Discrimination* (Chicago: University of Chicago Press, 2001), 19–124.

[28] Jacob Gersen, 'Markets and Discrimination', *NYU Law Review* 82 (2007): 689, 732 (finding mixed support for the status production model of race discrimination though an analysis of discrimination complaints across different industries).

the transactional sterility just described: the investments by thieves in robbing owners and the investments by owners in protecting their property against theft do not create wealth, but move it around in a zero-sum way. The normative implication of the positive theory is that, just as we prohibit theft to minimize the investments made in theft and theft-prevention, we should prohibit race discrimination to minimize the investments made in status appropriation and the resistance to status appropriation.

The ban on theft is reciprocal—once we define property rights, we do not prohibit a particular group from stealing from another (say, the rich from the poor) but anyone stealing from anyone. The same reasoning suggests at least a presumption that the ban on race discrimination should be reciprocal, to prohibit an individual of any race from discriminating against an individual of any race. Most obviously, we need to prohibit the dominant race or any other from discriminating against a dominated race, which is the primary wasteful investment. But we may also want to prohibit discrimination against the dominant race (likely a response to the status competition that damages them) because it is also inefficient, forgoing beneficial trades to move status around in a zero-sum manner. Thus, status production allows a normative argument in favour of the basic reciprocal structure of most anti-discrimination law.

We should consider, however, the complication of affirmative action—a preference in favour of the historically disadvantaged races. First, note that affirmative action, in the United States, does not undo the essentially reciprocal structure of the ban on race discrimination because it is limited to diversifying a workplace or remedying past discrimination. Outside of those purposes a business cannot discriminate against white applicants or employees. A business with predominantly black employees, for example, cannot legally prefer to hire black employees, to the detriment of white applicants. The basic structure of the ban on race discrimination is reciprocal despite some exceptions for affirmative action.

Second, the status production supplies one reason for affirmative action. Affirmative action increases the incidence of racial integration, which in turn diminishes the productivity of competing for status by race. This effect is not the standard claim that racial *contact* increases tolerance. Instead, racial integration works to link the status of people of different races in the integrated group. If one's workplace, neighbourhood, and social club are all racially homogeneous, then race discrimination works only to increase the discriminator's status. But if one's workplace, neighbourhood, and social club are racially diverse, then subordinating people on the basis of race inevitably works, to some extent, to lower the status of the discriminator's own integrated groups. Affirmative action offers to speed up integration and the status linkages between races that, in turn, undermines the productivity of race-based status competition.

Yet the long-standing debate on affirmative action identifies possible offsetting effects, such as stigma for the benefited group and reifying the construct of race. I do not offer to evaluate these claims, much less to balance them against the advantages. I just note that the normative implications of the status-production model are that the basic ban on race discrimination should be reciprocal, without requiring or forbidding a limited exception for affirmative action.

Applying the Theories to Other Forms of Discrimination

This part considers the application of the three theories to discrimination on bases other than race. In this first section, I examine how each positive theory applies to discrimination based on factors such as gender, sexual orientation, and religion. In the second section, I return to the normative implications of each positive theory.

Positive Theory

Start with Becker's *preference theory*. One might easily imagine the same explanation—a taste for avoiding association—works for discrimination against those of another ethnicity, religion, sexual orientation, and perhaps also against the elderly and the disabled. The abstract nature of the theory might seem to be an advantage in extending across these various domains. Yet, staying with positive theory, it has always struck me as a decisive weakness to Becker's approach that it does not plausibly explain gender discrimination. Heterosexual men do not generally seek to avoid association with women. Although heterosexual men sometimes join male-only clubs, it seems unlikely that the reason is a general aversion to women. Thus, the error I identified above regarding race discrimination—that discriminators seek to avoid only certain *types* of association, rather than any association—is immediately evident for gender discrimination. I claim subsequently that the status production theory will do a better job at explaining the differences in the associations men do and do not seek with women.

Statistical discrimination, by contrast, can explain gender discrimination. If women are given fewer fair opportunities than men at acquiring human capital (not only less education, but also fewer school or work tasks requiring leadership/management and fewer chances at competitive activities such as sports or chess), then the average woman may be less prepared for a job than the average man. Gender may be a rational proxy for the kind of abilities that employers seek.

False beliefs can be an equilibrium when discrimination prevents the discovery of evidence that would demonstrate the falsity of the beliefs causing the discrimination. For example, in the United States a few decades ago, women were mostly excluded from many sports. When no women competed in running the marathon, it was possible to maintain the common view that women were, somehow, physiologically incapable of running the distance without causing themselves serious harm. When no women were accepted as astronauts, it was possible to maintain the view (supported by John Glen in 1962) that women lacked the ability to serve. Given a prior belief that women are incapable of some task, it is 'rational' not to update the belief, because (given the discriminatory conditions) contradictory evidence is absent.

As with race, however, irrational beliefs may also support gender discrimination. This would obviously be true of implicit bias, and the other instances of bounded rationality discussed above. Indeed, when we think of the action of 'blaming the victim', perhaps the first instance that comes to mind is blaming women for their own sexual assault. The psychological literature on the belief in a just world offers an explanation, but whatever the irrational processes that allow blame in such an extreme situation can also produce blame for the victims of economic gender discrimination when they suffer economic failures.

One can apply these various mechanisms of rational and irrational beliefs to explain other forms of discrimination, on the basis of ethnicity, religion, sexual orientation, or disability. Sexual orientation discrimination offers a particularly strong example where the effect of discrimination was—for a long time—to block the evidence refuting the basis for discrimination. When the fear of discrimination, especially violence, kept people 'in the closet' about their sexual orientation, the cultural mainstream could maintain extreme beliefs about them. People could believe that they had never encountered a gay person before, when they had (as Justice Lewis Powell once famously claimed, not knowing one of his employees was gay). This ignorance allowed people to hold bizarre stereotypes that even the slightest exposure to reality would have exploded.

What about status production? As I criticized Becker's theory because of its inapplicability to gender discrimination, I should begin there. Status competition between the sexes is greatly complicated by the fact that the family connections between the sexes—by blood, marriage, and co-habitation—ensure that an individual's status usually depends in part on the status of individuals of the opposite gender. This fact does not rule out the status competition theory. Here I merely sketch an explanation, venturing briefly into territory long explored by feminist theory.

The basic idea for gender-based status competition is similar to race, where status production causes the dominant race to seek associations that reinforce the desired hierarchy but avoid associations that imply equality or an inferior position in the hierarchy. Men can generally pursue the same strategy as by creating and maintaining male-only clubs; excluding women from high-status jobs in business and government; denigrating the status of jobs held predominantly by women; lowering the status of women in their own workplace, as by sexual harassment; and generally endorsing and perpetuating demeaning stereotypical views of women.

Yet men face a trade-off with the women who are their mothers, sisters, wives, and daughters. If these women are of low status, that lowers the status of the men connected to them. To some extent, men try to have it both ways, competing for status by seeking to preserve the status of their female family members but, at the same time, lower the status of other men's female family members. But this competition between men is potentially destructive to the larger project of men to cooperate in preserving the status of maleness. So there is a trade-off: given family connections, raising the status of maleness lowers the status of the women to whom men are related, which lowers their status.

Men competing for status can navigate the trade-off in two ways. First, and most obviously, the traditional family is structured with men as the head. As long as that primacy is generally acknowledged, the positive status women in the family achieve in the society is no threat to the status of the father or husband to whom they are subordinate. Being the accepted head of a family with high-status women raises the man's status.

Second, traditional gender roles give women a tightly constrained channel of achieving status as women, a channel that reaffirms the greater status of men, because the traditional gender role accepts ultimate male authority. That men honour women who conform to the construct of 'a good woman' (and the components 'good daughter', 'good wife', and 'good mother') is a kind of limited truce in the male competition for status, as if the men had agreed to limit their competition by declaring 'good women' as non-combatants. Part of any such truce is the norm that men compel women in their family to conform to gender roles. The goodness of a daughter, wife, or mother depends on achieving stereotypical traits of femininity—being nurturing, emotionally intuitive, domestically adept, and sexually chaste. The good wife and mother is granted a limited domestic domain of authority, but, remains ultimately subordinate to certain male relatives. That the gender roles for women are idealized and nearly impossible to achieve serves the status interests of men because the general failure of women to achieve the nearly unobtainable ideal is part of what raises the status of men. Thus, women who fail to conform are fair game for status denigration and women who do conform embrace a role ultimately subservient to men.

This idea of a constrained gender-based status competition may help to explain a curious moment in American politics. After the revelation that then-presidential candidate Donald Trump had once bragged on video about behaviour towards women that would constitute sexual assault, a number of male politicians of his political party condemned him while calling attention to the fact that they were husbands of wives and fathers of daughters. The same locution occurred when male Hollywood celebrities condemned Harvey Weinstein after numerous women came forward to accuse him of sexual harassment and assault. In this context, the emphasis on the particular women in one's family seems misplaced when one could easily condemn Trump and Weinstein out of a generalized concern for female (or male) victims of sexual degradation.

The emphasis on their female relatives makes sense, however, under a theory of status competition. With race, I said that whites in the Jim Crow South enforced hierarchical norms to which other whites were obligated to contribute. For gender, men assert their claim to status through the masculine gender role, an assertion of strength and dominance, but this role is not merely an opportunity but also an obligation. Some male politicians and celebrities criticizing Trump or Weinstein therefore feel more comfortable or credible expressing this criticism of a man for degrading women by noting it is not a betrayal of male status and solidarity—not a general call for ending status competition nor a refusal to contribute to it—but a part of the limited status 'truce' that forswears such degrading behaviour against 'good' women. These men justify and qualify their criticism by reminding other men that male status is generally vulnerable to the status of female family members and by identifying their personal stakes in the truce, the number of women in their close-knit family, on whom their status depends.

Another example of men enforcing masculinity obligations against each other is their discrimination against gay men: the fear that some such men are occupying a feminine role and transgressing the norms of male status production. If status competition can explain race and gender discrimination, and some part of sexual orientation discrimination, then I believe it is straightforward to use it to explain discrimination on the basis of some other factors, such as ethnicity, national origin, or religion.

I foreswear the most reductionist ambitions of the theory by noting how status production may work in tandem with another cause of discrimination—irrationally biased beliefs. The solidarity that a group achieves in producing status for itself may motivate beliefs in its natural superiority and other groups' inferiority. A standard option for lowering the status of an individual or group is to insult them effectively and the insulter may come to believe in their libellous message. This is all the more likely if people are inclined to believe in a just world, and want to believe that a group fails because of its own defects rather than as a result of discrimination. The status production effort may be the engine of the most extreme stereotypes, the sort that help to produce the emotion of disgust.

Normative Theory

Becker's preference theory has the same implications for every other form of discrimination that it has for race discrimination. Becker's theory could count against anti-discrimination law, as Friedman contended, or, if we include the Harsanyi point, it could justify anti-discrimination law, but with the unexpected implications noted above. First, if the purpose is to prohibit harmful behaviour only when the preference being satisfied is antisocial, then the law should only prohibit discrimination when the motive is hate or malice, and not when people discriminate solely out of altruistic favouritism towards those who share their ethnicity, national origin, gender, sexual orientation, and so on. Thus, the theory implies a law far narrower than what we observe.

The information theory also has the same normative implications as it did for race. The fact that women, for example, expect employers to discriminate against them will diminish their return from higher education, which rationally diminishes their investments in acquiring human capital. There is an equilibrium in which the discrimination causes harm that, in turn, causes individual employers to continue the discrimination. Indeed, parents and educators might reason in a way that further perpetuates the discriminatory equilibrium: Why devote scarce resources to educate a person who will gain less from the education—the girls who will be subject to employer discrimination—when you can use those resources to educate a person who will gain more—the boys who will benefit from discrimination against the girls. The normative implication is that one can enhance social welfare by breaking this cycle of discrimination, making it possible for more girls to develop their human capital and enter the labour force, thus terminating the value of gender as a proxy for ability.

To the extent there are rational or irrational negative beliefs about a gender, religion, or sexual orientation, the law may advance social welfare by prohibiting actions based on these beliefs. This is particularly likely to be true if the beliefs will be refuted by the results of non-discrimination. For example, when gay people come out of the closet and women succeed at traditionally male occupations, then the beliefs underlying discrimination are naturally displaced. And yet, the implication is that law need only intervene to protect those who suffer from negative stereotypes. On this account, there is no need in the United States to prohibit discrimination against white, straight, Christian, men, unhindered by disability. There is no need for the structure of anti-discrimination law to be reciprocal.

Finally, status production supports a ban on the forms of discrimination it explains, for reasons given above. When individuals of one group discriminate against members of other groups, they sacrifice productive interactions to produce status for their own group by damaging the status of the other. These sacrifices are wasted on a zero-sum competition that merely shifts status around without producing anything of social value. As I said, one might view status production as an engine of motivated beliefs in false stereotypes of other groups, in which case the harms caused by these false beliefs are part of the inefficient investment in status competition. Where the positive theory applies, it justifies the reciprocal prohibition on discrimination that we commonly observe.

***

Legal theorists debate whether there is a unified normative theory justifying anti-discrimination law, one that spans the different targets of discrimination, such as race, gender, caste, sexual orientation, religion, age, or disability. One way to normatively evaluate acts of discrimination is to ask what harm they cause. Using that approach, it turns out that the harm of discrimination depends in part on what causes discrimination. In economic theory, individuals might discriminate because they have a taste for avoiding association, engage in rational statistical generalization, or compete in groups for status. Psychology expands the possibilities to include different irrational forms of stereotypical belief formation. The choice among these theories is important because they have different normative implications. Among other things, belief-based theories imply that anti-discrimination law should not have a reciprocal structure, but should merely prohibit discrimination against the traditional targets of discrimination. By contrast, the status production theory implies the need for a reciprocal prohibition of discrimination, by or against the traditional perpetrators as well as the traditional targets of discrimination. The ultimate answer is probably that some pluralistic combination of theory provides the best overall explanation for the anti-discrimination law that exists in the world.

Editors and Contributors

Dipesh Chakrabarty is the Lawrence A. Klimpton Distinguished Service Professor of History and South Asian Languages and Literature at the University of Chicago; affiliated faculty of English; resource faculty of Cinema and Media Studies and Comparative Literature; courtesy appointment in the Law School; and faculty fellow of the Chicago Center for Contemporary Theory. He is a founding member of the editorial collective of *Subaltern Studies*, a consulting editor of *Critical Inquiry*, and a founding editor of the journal *Postcolonial Studies*. Chakrabarty received the 2014 Toynbee Foundation Prize for his contributions to global history. He was awarded an honorary DLitt by the University of London (conferred at Goldsmiths) in 2010 and an honorary doctorate by the University of Antwerp in 2011. He was awarded the Distinguished Alumnus Award by the Indian Institute of Management, Kolkata (conferred on the occasion of the 50th anniversary of the institute in 2011). He was elected an honorary fellow of the Australian Academy of the Humanities in 2006 and a fellow of the American Academy of Arts and Sciences in 2004. In 2015, he delivered the Tanner Lectures in Human Values at Yale University. In 2016, Chakrabarty presented the Munich History Lecture at Ludwig Maximilian University, Munich. His most recent book is *The Calling of History: Sir Jadunath Sarkar and His Empire of Truth* (2015). He is currently working on two books, provisionally titled *The Climate of History* and *The Time of the Present*.

Emilio Comay del Junco is a doctoral student in the joint programme in philosophy and social thought at the University of Chicago, USA. He is writing a thesis on Aristotle's natural philosophy and has equally serious interests in political and philosophical issues of race and social justice.

Ashwini Deshpande is professor of economics at the Delhi School of Economics, New Delhi, India. Her primary fields are international economics and the economics of discrimination. She is the author of *Grammar of Caste: Economic Discrimination in Contemporary India* (2011) and *Affirmative Action in India* (2013). She is the editor of *Boundaries of Clan and Color: Transnational Studies of Inter-Group Disparity* (2003); *Globalization and Development: A Handbook of New Perspectives* (2007), *Capital Without Borders: Challenges to Development* (2010), and *Global Economic Crisis and the Developing World* (2012). She received the 2007 VKRV Rao Award for Indian economists under 45.

Justin Driver is Harry N. Wyatt Professor of Law at the University of Chicago Law School, USA. He joined the faculty in 2014, after teaching at the University of Texas, USA, since 2009. His primary interests include constitutional law and the intersection of race with legal institutions. His important article 'Recognizing Race', *Columbia Law Review* 2012 has been a touchstone for discussion of the way race is treated by US courts. He is currently completing a book about the constitutional rights of students. His article on the complex relationship between Richard Wright's character Bigger Thomas and Justice Thomas (who says in his autobiography that he deeply identifies with Bigger!) appeared in *Fatal Fictions: Crime and Investigation in Law and Literature*, edited by Alison LaCroix, Richard McAdams, and Martha C. Nussbaum (2017).

Emily Dupree is a doctoral student in philosophy at the University of Chicago and a third-year law student at the University of Chicago Law School, USA. Her research focuses on ethics and political philosophy, feminist social epistemology, and the metaphysics of gender.

Anita Ghai is associate professor in the Department of Psychology at Jesus and Mary College, New Delhi, India. She has published extensively on disability and the relationship between gender and disability. She also edits widely, including *Disability Studies Quarterly*, *Scandinavian Journal of Disability*, and *Disability and Society*.

Nandini Ghosh is assistant professor at the Institute for Development Studies Kolkata (IDSK), India. Her PhD in social sciences is from the Tata Institute of Social Sciences, Mumbai, India. She has published numerous articles on disability policy, disability, and gender, the methodology of disability studies, and the cultural construction of disability.

Zoya Hasan is professor emerita, Centre for Political Studies, Jawaharlal Nehru University (JNU), former Dean, School of Social Sciences, JNU, and currently distinguished professor, Council for Social Development, New Delhi. She is a former member of the National Commission for Minorities, National Integration Council, Central Advisory Board of Education (CABE), and the National Book Trust. She is currently a Trustee of the Jawaharlal Nehru Memorial Fund (New Delhi), a member of the *Hindu Centre for Politics and Public Policy* (Chennai), and a member of the Boards of the Centre for Equity Studies and the Centre for Multilevel Federalism (New Delhi). She is also a member of the Editorial Boards of the *International Political Science Review, Secular Studies* (Brill), *Journal of Human Development in India and Antyajaa: India Journal of Women and Social Change*. Her recent books include *Congress After Indira: Policy, Power and Political Change 1984-2009* (2012) *Equalizing Access: Affirmative Action in Higher Education in India, the United States, and South Africa* (co-edited, 2012), *India Social Development Report 2012*, Council for Social Development (co-edited, 2013), *Democracy and the Crisis of Inequality: Collection of Essays* (2014), and *Agitation to Legislation· Negotiating Equity and Justice in India* (2018).

Aziz Z. Huq is Frank and Bernice J. Greenberg Professor of Law at the University of Chicago Law School, USA. His teaching and research interests include criminal procedure, constitutional law, and constitutional design. As a senior consultant analyst for the International Crisis Group, he researched the implementation of constitutional norms in Sri Lanka, Nepal, Pakistan, and Afghanistan. He has also directed the Liberty and National Security Project of the Brennan Center for Justice at NYU Law School, and has clerked for Justice Ruth Bader Ginsburg. With Tom Ginsburg, he is co-editor of the 2017 volume *Implementing Constitutional Design*. He also co-edited a volume on the UN's response to Al Qaeda. His numerous articles include a focus on the rights of terrorism suspects and on the influence of security issues on discrimination against minorities. He won the Law School's Teaching award in 2015. Born in London to a Bengali family from India, Huq has a deep interest in India, and especially issues of religion-based discrimination.

Tarunabh Khaitan is a leading younger scholar of Indian law and of legal theory generally, Khaitan is associate professor of law in the law faculty of Oxford University and the Hackney Fellow in Law at Wadham College, UK. Educated in India, he received his law degree from the National Law School in Bangalore, then came to Oxford on a Rhodes Scholarship and completed his MPhil and DPhil there. He is the author of *A Theory of Discrimination Law* (2014).

Saul Levmore is William B. Graham Distinguished Service Professor of Law at the University of Chicago Law School. He was dean of the Law School from 2001 to 2009. One of the leading thinkers in the field of law and economics, Levmore has also written about intellectual property and about the relationship between law and literature. With Nussbaum, he co-edited the volume *American Guy: Masculinity in American Law and Literature* (2012), and is co-editor with Alison LaCroix and Nussbaum of the collection *Power, Prose, and Purse: Law, Literature, and Economic Transformations*, forthcoming. He and Nussbaum co-authored *Aging Thoughtfully: Conversations about Retirement, Romance, Redistribution, Wrinkles, and Regret* (2017).

Richard H. McAdams is Deputy Dean and Bernard D. Meltzer Professor of Law at the University of Chicago Law School, USA. He is a leading expert on criminal law and criminal procedure, and also writes extensively on law and social norms, the expressive function of law, and law and inequality. He has served as a member of the National Science Foundation panel for law and social sciences. His book, *The Expressive Powers of Law: Theories and Limits*, was published in 2015, and he has also published *Fairness in Law and Economics*, co-edited with Lee Anne Fennell (2013). He was the key organizer and editor of the volume *Fatal Fictions: Crime and Investigation in Law and Literature*, edited by Alison LaCroix, Richard McAdams, and Martha Nussbaum (2017). He is also an accomplished actor, excelling in roles ranging from Angelo in *The Merchant of Venice* to Andrew Undershaft in Shaw's *Major Barbara*.

Martha C. Nussbaum is Ernst Freund Distinguished Service Professor of Law and Ethics, appointed in the Law School and the Philosophy Department, University of Chicago, USA. She holds associate appointments in classics, divinity, and political science, and is a member of the Committee on Southern Asian Studies and a Board Member of the Human Rights Program. Her most recent book is *Anger and Forgiveness:*

Resentment, Generosity, Justice (2016). Her long-standing connection with India can be seen in the books *Women and Human Development: The Capabilities Approach* (2000), *The Clash Within: Democracy, Religious Violence, and India's Future* (2007), *India: Implementing Pluralism and Democracy* (co-edited with Wendy Doniger, 2015), and in many articles. She has worked with UNDP-Delhi and with the Lawyers Collective. In 2008, she and Zoya Hasan held a comparative conference in Delhi on affirmative action in higher education, co-sponsored by the University of Chicago Law School and Jawaharlal Nehru University, New Delhi, which became the book *Equalizing Access: Affirmative Action in Higher Education in India, the U. S., and South Africa* (2012). Her most recent awards are the Kyoto Prize in Arts and Philosophy (2016) and the Philip Quinn Prize of the American Philosophical Association for service to the profession (2016). She was the 2017 Jefferson Lecturer for the National Endowment for the Humanities, delivering the lecture 'Powerlessness and the Politics of Blame'. Like McAdams, she is a keen performer in law school theatricals, appearing as Clytemnestra in *Oresteia*, Mrs Peachum in *Threepenny Opera*, and Lady Britomart Undershaft in *Major Barbara*.

H.R. **Vasujith Ram** is a 2017 graduate of the West Bengal National University of Juridical Sciences, Kolkata, India, where he was a lead editor of the *Journal of Indian Law and Society*. He is pursuing an LLM degree at Harvard Law School, USA.

Jeffrey A. Redding is New Generation Network, Australia India Institute and senior research fellow, Melbourne Law School. He was previously an associate professor of law at Saint Louis University Law School. He received his JD in 2000 from the University of Chicago Law School, USA, where he headed the LGBT group OutLaw. He has held Fulbright and other grants to work in Pakistan with feminist activist Asma Jahangir and in India with Lawyers Collective. He has taught law at Lahore University of Management Sciences (LUMS), Pakistan, and at the American University in Cairo. He is a widely published expert on gender and sexuality law and family law in South Asia. Currently he is writing on the transgender community in Pakistan, and also on non-state Muslim courts in India.

Vidhu Verma is professor in the centre for Political Studies, JNU, New Delhi. Her areas of research include Comparative Political Theory, feminist politics, affirmative action and social justice. She has recently edited and contributed to a volume on *Unequal Worlds*. She is author of three books *Non-discrimination and Equality in India: Contesting boundaries of Social Justice*, *Malaysia: State and Civil Society in Transition*, and *Justice, Equality and Community* and besides articles in several journals. She is currently a principal investigator, in a project on 'Changing Conceptions of Legal Justice in India'.

Laura Weinrib is professor of law at the University of Chicago Law School and an associate member of the University of Chicago Department of History, USA. A legal historian, her scholarship explores the intersection of constitutional law and labour law in the United States. She is the author of *The Taming of Free Speech: America's Civil Liberties Compromise* (2016), which traces the emergence during the first half of the twentieth century of a constitutional and court-centered concept of civil liberties as a defining feature of American democracy.

Index

Ableism, 263–4, 271; *see also*
Disability *and* Discrimination on
the Basis of Ability
Affirmative Action: and merit,
22, 38; and stigma, 27–8, 31,
32–5, 37; and uptake, 27–31; as
reparations, 353–4; on the basis
of caste, 21–40, 126, 307, 309,
313–15; on the basis of class, 329;
on the basis of gender identity,
192; on the basis of minority
status, 304; on the basis of race,
63, 345, 384–5
African Americans, xv–xvi, xx, 42–60,
65, 70–1, 74, 78, 150, 152, 157,
169, 170, 209–210, 294, 298–9,
372, 379, 381–3
Age: xvii, xxii, 109, 117, 121; and
friendship, 142, 147, 159–62; and
productivity, 129, 131–3, 137;
and retirement, *see* Retirement;
as a neutral proxy, 132–3; hiding
one's, 128, *see also* Cosmetic
Surgery; the positive value of,
127, 154; discrimination, *see*
Discrimination on the Basis of
Age
Ageing, xvi–vii, xxi–ii, 128, 134,
137–40, 146–8, 152–163
Ahmed, Sara, xxiii, 212, 218

Akrasia: racial, 65–6, 75–8, 80–1
Alterity, 246–7
Ambedkar, B.R., xii–xiii, xvi, xxvi,
13, 27, 167–8, 186–8, 313, 361
American Association for Retired
Persons, 158–60, 163
Americans with Disabilities Act, 153,
162
Animality, xii, xv, xxii, 3, 67, 97,
149–50, 155, 169, 172, 208, 214,
216, 326, 347
Animals: xv, 3, 15–19, 149, 168; and
death,13, 15, 20, 173, 288; and
interactions with humans, 19
Animus, xvii, xxiv, 68, 166, 171,
185, 188, 190, 282, 286–91,
293–5, 299, 345, 372, 374
Anthropocene, 13–18
Anthropocentrism, 4, 15, 19–20
Appadurai, Arjun, 215, 317
Assimilation, 23, 33–9, 290, 300,
340, 346
Authoritarianism, 289–90, 296–7
Autonomy: individual, 85, 93,
108, 126, 128, 163, 222, 233,
242, 262, 350; organizational,
117–118, 322

Beauvoir, Simone de, 96, 147
Becker, Gary, xxvi, 81, 371